VOICES FROM THE NORTH

6000569343

WITHDRAWN

Voices from the North

New Trends in Nordic Human Geography

Edited by
JAN ÖHMAN
KIRSTEN SIMONSEN

ASHGATE

© Jan Öhman and Kirsten Simonsen 2003

All rights reserved. No part of this publication may be reproduced, stored in a retrieval system, or transmitted in any form or by any means, electronic, mechanical, photocopying, recording, or otherwise without the prior permission of the Publisher.

The editors have asserted their moral rights to be identified as the authors of this work in accordance with the Copyright, Designs and Patents Act, 1988.

Published by
Ashgate Publishing Company
Gower House
Croft Road
Aldershot
Hants GU11 3HR
England

Ashgate Publishing Company
Suite 420
101 Cherry Street
Burlington, VT 05401-4405
USA

Ashgate website: http://www.ashgate.com

British Library Cataloguing in Publication Data
Voices from the north : new trends in Nordic human
   geography
   1.Human geography - Scandinavia
   I.Simonsen, Kirsten II.Öhman, Jan
   304.2'0948

Library of Congress Cataloging-in-Publication Data
Voices from the north : new trends in Nordic human geography / edited by Jan Ohman and Kirsten Simonsen
       p. cm.
   Includes bibliographical references.
   ISBN 0-7546-3425-6 (pbk. : alk. paper)
      1. Human geography--Scandinavia. 2. Scandinavia--Economic conditions. 3. Scandinavia--Social conditions. I. Öhman, Jan. II. Simonsen, Kirsten, 1946-

   GF611 .V65 2003
   306'.0948--dc21
                                                                    2002028127
ISBN 0 7546 3425 6

Printed and bound in Great Britain by MPG Books Ltd., Bodmin, Cornwall.

Contents

Part II   Welfare State, Planning and Human Geography

List of contributors

Hans Thor Andersen, Ph.D, Department of Geography, University of Copenhagen, Denmark.

Roger Andersson, Professor, Institute for Housing and Urban Research, Uppsala University, Sweden.

Ann-Cathrine Åquist, Ph.D, Department of Social Sciences, Örebro University, Sweden.

Bjørn T. Asheim, Professor, Department of Social and Economic Geography, University of Lund, Sweden, and Centre for technology, innovation and culture, University of Oslo, Norway.

Jørgen Ole Bærenholdt, Associate Professor, Department of Geography and International Development Studies, Roskilde University, Denmark.

Nina Gunnerud Berg, Associate Professor, Department of Geography, NTNU, Trondheim, Norway.

Eric Clark, Professor, Department of Social and Economic Geography, University of Lund, Sweden.

Gunnel Forsberg, Professor, Department of Human Geography, Stockholm University, Sweden.

Jouni Häkli, Professor, Department of Regional Studies and Environmental Policy, University of Tampere, Finland.

Michael Haldrup, Ph.D, Department of Geography and International Development Studies, Roskilde University, Denmark.

Frank Hansen, Associate Professor, Department of Geography, University of Copenhagen, Denmark.

Hille Koskela, Ph.D, Department of Geography, University of Helsinki, Finland.

Ari Aukusti Lehtinen, Professor, Department of Geography, University of Joensuu, Finland.

Anders Löfgren, Associate Professor, Department of Geography, NTNU, Trondheim, Norway.

Anders Malmberg, Professor, Department of Social and Economic Geography, Uppsala University, Sweden.

Peter Maskell, Professor, Department of Industrial Economics and Strategy, Copenhagen Business School, Denmark.

Irene Molina, Ph.D, Department of Social and Economic Geography, Uppsala University, Sweden.

Jan Öhman, Associate Professor, Department of Social and Economic Geography, Uppsala University, Sweden.

Gunnar Olsson, Professor, Department of Social and Economic Geography, Uppsala University, Sweden.

Kenneth R. Olwig, Professor, Department of Landscape Planning, Swedish University of Agricultural Sciences, Alnarp, Sweden.

Anssi Paasi, Professor, Department of Geography, University of Oulu, Finland.

Kirsten Simonsen, Professor, Department of Geography and International Development Studies, Roskilde University, Denmark.

Introduction:
Is there a 'Nordic' human geography?

Kirsten Simonsen and Jan Öhman

One widespread acknowledgement within contemporary human geography is about the contingent and contextual character of knowledge/s. As expressed in notions such as Haraway's '*situated knowledges*' (1991) or Said's situated and travelling theory (1984), knowledge/s has to be grasped in the place and time out of which it emerges. Even though situated knowledges is not necessarily local knowledges, each author – also the ones contributing to this collection – is situated in many different ways, the social and cultural context of the production of knowledge do matter. This is not a claim on social theory and knowledge to be inescapably context-bound, but rather an acknowledgement of the way in which it always carries some particularity and some inherent assumptions from its place of origin. More than any other line of thought, postcolonial discourse has informed this acknowledgement, and it has provoked many authors to position themselves and reflect on their own situatedness. Given the concern of this bulk of work, it has primarily given rise to discussions on representations and power-knowledge relationships between 'the West' and the rest of the world. From our point of view, however, it is important to acknowledge that 'the West' is not homogeneous either; it is permeated by a multiplicity of axes of distinction, by difference in languages, traditions and cultural and political histories. In the current production of knowledge within human geography these differences are often blurred in hegemonic 'Western' discourses in which British/North American particularities achieve the status of universals. Any interest in destabilising such power-knowledge systems calls upon interventions from 'other voices'. It is against this background the aims of this book shall be seen. We want to reflect on the 'Nordicness' of contemporary 'Nordic' human geography, to fill in gaps in its Anglophonic circulation and to present (but not claim to represent) new trends in this discourse/s. In that connection, we want to explore the way in which these voices at the same time intervene in 'international' debates and produce their own specificity/ies. That is, to pose and seek to answer the question: Is there a 'Nordic' human geography?

Now, a designation like 'Nordic' should of course be used with caution. When a historical scholar such as Benedict Andersson ends up defining a nation as an '*imagined community*' (Haraway 1991), doubt must necessarily be cast upon calling anything inherently Nordic. National as well as 'Nordic' identities are phenomena of discourse, constructed at distinctive junctures in time, and for specific purposes. The invention of 'the Nordic' can, in fact, be traced back to nationalist-Romantic movements of the nineteenth century. Alongside the spread of a nationalist discourse within the individual Nordic countries, a transnational ideology extolling a Scandinavian or Nordic spirit of communality arose. Interest in the uniquely Nordic past (e.g. the Vikings) was part of national as well as Nordic imaginations.

Acknowledging 'the Nordic' as a construction – an imagined community – does however not mean that this construction doesn't work in a material sense, or that particular connections and collaborations do not exist. Indeed, Nordic cooperation has a long tradition, especially when it comes to cultural collaboration rooted in the civil society. Alongside the more formalised organisations such as The Nordic Associations, the Nordic Council and the Nordic Council of Ministers, cooperation has developed between movements – e.g. the folk high school movement, labour movements and feminist movements – and between professions, scientists, painters and writers who have maintained close ties through Nordic conferences and inter-Nordic journals. Human geography is no exception to that. The rather informal 'Nordic Symposia in Critical Human Geography', that have been conducted (almost) yearly since 1979, and the associated journal *'Nordisk Samhällsgeografisk Tidskrift'* are but one example. Also, even though the Nordic countries are not as different from other European countries as ideology would sometimes have us believe, certain distinctions do prevail. It is difficult to talk about a 'Nordic model' per se, but throughout the twentieth century the Nordic countries have probably undergone a smoother modernisation than most other countries in Europe, and the welfare state has stood its ground. The background to that might be traced in the tradition of the labour movement as well as other popular movements and their relative success in being accepted as negotiating partners in the development of the welfare regimes.

This social and cultural context also constitutes part of the background from which much contemporary Nordic human geography takes off, generally and amongst the contributions to this collection. Some authors directly address the welfare state, including its current contested and uncertain situation, for others welfare issues are more or less conscious assumptions that permeate their theoretical and/or empirical formulations. This connection is a double-edged one, the risk of importing into academia the kind of welfare state 'nationalism' or 'Nordism', which has grown in popular discourse concurrently with challenges from immigration and European integration, is not negligible. At the same time, however, the prevalence of the welfare state ideology has carried a persistent clinging to egalitarian values such as social justice, social equality and politics of redistribution. And, in particular in Sweden, the marriage between human geography and the welfare state has resulted in a strong orientation towards planning and applied research. Even though this connection is less prevalent in the other Nordic countries, the orientation towards welfare and equality has resulted in a focus on issues such as regional development, labour markets, planning, social reproduction and the organisation of everyday life while, for instance, research into identity formation, representations and imaginations (with a few exceptions) has been less prominently featured, only to be embarked upon in more recent years. Both these trends will of course be represented in this book.

Theoretically, Nordic human geography (like other social sciences in the Nordic countries) has been marked by a specific situatedness at the interstices of Anglo-Saxon and continental intellectual movements. Both as regards geographical thinking and more general social theory affiliations have to a different degree existed to, for instance, German, French and Anglo-American circles. While these influences have to a certain degree articulated with local features, different currents have also characterised the different Nordic countries. These differences are historically based and due to academic traditions and merits (of pioneers), the institutional settings and organisational structures of the universities, and economic and political-ideological conditions in the countries (see e.g. Asheim 1987, Öhman 1994). In short, in all countries the history of the subject has been marked by ideas of utility, in relation to either training of teachers or forming a basis for planning. In the cases of Denmark, Finland and Norway training of teachers remained the dominant function of geography until the 1970s. That is probably why discourses on 'landscape' as a notion connecting physical and social circumstances of regions maintained a strong position in geography in these countries, and the subject repeatedly faced discussions on the synthesis between human and physical geography. Swedish human geography, on the contrary, can both when it comes to institutional organisation and subject matter be described as a social science since the 1930s. But it has been a particular kind of social science – an applied one based on a close connection between human geography and regional and local planning. This marriage opened up great opportunities for the Swedish human geographers when it comes to a practical and methodological development of the subject, but it has also caused problems as regards the addressing of more philosophical and theoretical questions. Another distinction comes from the way in which Denmark, probably due to a stronger affiliation to political movements in other parts of Europe, in the 1970s/80s experienced a strong radical human geography inspired by continental (German and French) cross-disciplinary neo-Marxism. Through joint critical human geography conferences this trend also diffused into the other Nordic countries, but it never gained an equal strength in these places. Other distinct, but not as dominant, traits have been a relative early concern with humanistic questions in Finland and a certain affiliation to a socially hegemonic 'local community' discourse in Norway. The point we want to make by in this way touching on the history/ies of Nordic human geography is that despite the relative similarities between these countries, specific academic developments have occurred, and they also influence the contemporary geographical discourse/s. Having said that, however, there is no doubt that the formation of networks across the Nordic countries, in particular between critically orientated geographers, as well as an increasing participation in 'international' discussions have levelled some of these differences and created cross-national 'language games'. This subsequently also giving occasion to joint projects of different kinds.

What can be drawn from the above then is the – not very surprising – conclusion that there is no *one* Nordic human geography, no unitary focus or sole mainstream in the Nordic countries' geographical discourse. Differences in philosophical and methodological approaches are overlaid by the described differences in 'national' discourses in the making of a web of different interests and ideas. Our own acknowledgement of these differences comes from experiences of Nordic 'networking' and participation in the critical human geography conferences, and the selection of contributions to this book derives from these circles as well, including writers joining them at different junctures of theoretical debate. If we, very cautiously, should try to identify some common traits from the contemporary discussions, it would be a search for different possibilities of combining social constructionism and the critique of essentialism with some kind of ontological realism. This also involves a widespread refusal to draw a clear-cut distinction between constructivism and materialism, or between politics of identity and politics of redistribution.

In an earlier book written in Scandinavian languages – '*Traditioner i Nordisk Kulturgeografi*' (Öhman 1994) – a cross-Nordic composed group of authors explored the different traditions of human geography and discussed them from a philosophical and epistemological perspective. This exploratory review was closed by a discussion of radical and humanist approaches as they were conducted in the 1970s and early 1980s. The present book should in some sense be seen as a sequel of the former one. It aims at illustrating some of the contemporary trends and developments in Nordic human geography; the non-positivist, 'post-Marxist' and 'poststructuralist' (in a broad sense) contributions as they are performed in different fields of the subject. However, because of the variety of approaches represented in the current research, we desist from making any kind of philosophical/theoretical categorisations, instead asking the authors themselves to reflect their situatedness and positions in traditions and current debates. This of course leaves us with the question of how to organise the book and present the different debates. One option that as mentioned we resisted was to try to identify different theoretical/methodological approaches. Another possibility was to follow more traditional lines of division and in succession present sections on 'economic geography', 'social geography' and so on. Such a strategy however would reproduce a kind of division that in contemporary discussions is more often transgressed in productive ways. Instead, therefore, our strategy has been to try to identify themes and issues that in some sense are able to represent contemporary debates in Nordic human geography. Such an endeavour is of course a risky business. So, on the one hand we would not claim greater legitimacy to the result than having found a useful order of presentation for our current purpose, on the other we do believe that this choice offers an entry into contemporary 'Nordic' human geography grasping the two-ways relationship between its 'international' affiliations and its 'Nordic' situatedness. The five themes in which the contributions are grouped are: (1) Production, social institutions and local development, (2) Welfare state, planning and human geography, (3) Spatiality, identity and social practice, (4) Nature, landscape and environment, and (5) Difference, distinction and power.

Even though some shift in emphasis in human geography – also in the Nordic countries – has occurred during the latest decades, issues about regional development still have an important position in the discourse. But their treatment has as other parts of the subject undergone a profound transformation. In this way our first theme – 'Production, social institutions and local development' – is one that obtains attention from both economic and social/cultural orientated geographers. The selected contributions, which in their exploration of the theme in different ways address issues such as knowledge, learning and innovation and their spatial connections, should demonstrate that. First, *Anders Malmberg* and *Peter Maskell* discuss industrial competitiveness in the increasingly globally integrated world economy, in particular in relation to small, open, industrialised economies as the Nordic ones. They identify two processes of ubiquitification, the process of globalisation of factor and commodity markets and the process of codification of knowledge, and argue that knowledge creation and the development of *localised capabilities* that promote learning processes are key features for competitiveness in this situation. *Bjørn Asheim* picks up this thread. He in his contribution discusses how and why regional clusters can support innovation and competitiveness in 'post-Fordist learning economies'. He connects his argument to a 'bottom-up' innovation model, seeing innovation as a culturally and institutionally contextualised, interactive learning process, but also emphasises the need, analytically as well as politically, to distinguish between different types of regional innovation networks and systems. This insight is used to discuss the potentials of regional innovation systems within a framework of globalisation and an emerging 'new economy' and subsequently to argue for a multi-level approach to innovation systems, connecting different forms of knowledge and learning to different geographical scales. The last paper in this section, by *Jørgen Ole Bærenholdt* and *Michael Haldrup*, focuses on the 'economy-culture nexus'. They argue that the way both economic and socio-cultural issues have been dealt with in Nordic human geography open to a development of this discussion, even though the possibilities haven't been satisfactorily explored. As an attempt to remedy this gap, they develop a model in which the notions of *social capital* and *reflexivity* are used to connect innovation, institutional regulation, networking and formation of identity. The model is put into work on North Atlantic and East Central European case localities. So, even though critical tensions do exist between these contributions, they are also connected through joint efforts. That is, to conceptualise the way in which local development and localised learning depend on institutional regulation, including local governance, social institutions and cultural identity.

Perhaps the most conspicuous challenges to the Nordic countries in these years concern the development of the welfare state. The second group of articles reflects that, as well as the general importance of the welfare state to Nordic human geography. All authors relate to one or another level of the welfare state. *Frank Hansen* is interested in the relationship between welfare state regimes and social polarisation. He criticises mainstream social geography for not paying enough attention to the role of the welfare states, and contemporary discussions of welfare state regimes for having a reduced conception of social differentiation/polarisation. From this starting point the article aims at developing a framework grasping different regulation complexes' significance for social polarisation. The model outlined, besides welfare regulation, includes families and family ideology, regulation of work-life, and regulation of civil rights and equality. All these institutions, it is argued, produce axes of polarisation that work together in complex socio-spatial articulations. The second paper, written by the Danish-Swedish constellation *Hans Thor Andersen* and *Eric Clark*, continues the discussion of welfare regimes and social polarisation. In their title they provocatively ask: *Does welfare matter?* Under this heading they critically discuss how Scandinavian cities since the early 1980s have experienced an increasing social polarisation and segregation. They relate this development to globalisation processes and to welfare state policy, and drawing on different empirical studies they explore the paradox that the very pride of Scandinavian housing policy more recently has become part and parcel of processes of 'ghettoisation'. The next two papers reflect the connection between planning and Swedish human geography. *Jan Öhman* explores the way in which this particular link has influenced the development of the subject since the 1930s. He emphasises the influence gained by the human geographers as 'experts' in planning and spatial development, but also the retroaction on the subject in the form of a long preponderance of empirical and quantitative research. From that, the author turns to an analysis of the current development of Swedish municipal planning, implying that its change towards more decentralised and flexible forms sets new standards for planning-oriented research. In the last paper in this section *Ann-Cathrine Åquist* argues for a perspective of everyday life as being conclusive to urban planning. She discusses different theories of everyday life with particular emphasis on Nordic approaches and argues for time geography to be an appropriate method connecting everyday life and planning. Throughout the article, the connection between everyday life and planning is addressed and developed with feminist questions in mind.

In the third group we, under the heading of 'Spatiality, identity and social practice', have brought together four articles that in different ways discuss socio-spatial practices and spatial imaginations. What connects these contributions is their insistence on weaving together geographical imaginations and material embodiment – on combining a non-essentialist thinking that recognises the fact of construction with an acknowledgement of the contextuality and materiality of social practices. The first paper, written by *Anssi Paasi* and *Jouni Häkli*, locates itself in the heart of the theme with a discussion of the social construction of identity as related to social spatiality. They start by deconstructing the concept of identity and discussing the social construction of places, regions and nations as centres for territorial identity. While doing so, they argue for an anti-essentialist understanding of spatial identities and relate their construction to ideology and social power. The approach is illustrated by describing the historical process of regional administrative reform in Finland. This paper is followed by a contribution from *Kirsten Simonsen*. She opens by arguing for an approach to human/social/cultural geography starting from social *practice*. The meaningful, intersubjective and not least embodied character of practice is emphasised. This subsequently initiates two interconnected discussions; on the gendered character of bodies/practices and on the spatiality of the body as constitutive to an understanding of social spatiality. The finishing part of the paper on this basis outlines a tentative entry into 'the embodied city' – into the relationship between spatial/moving bodies and the construction of cities. From cities then we move on to rural areas. Drawing on their own work on urban-rural migration in Norway and Sweden respectively, *Nina Gunnerud Berg* and *Gunnel Forsberg* discuss discourses on rurality and gender in Britain and Scandinavia. Their concern is with travelling theory in the light of the influence of British rural geography in other parts of Europe. Starting from the concept of '*rural idyll*' and adding one of '*gender idyll*' they demonstrate how such spatial imaginations are quite different in Scandinavia and Britain, due to differences in the material basis of their construction. The last paper in this section is one by *Anders Löfgren* on socio-spatial life projects of young people. He discusses the concept of youth from the perspective of socio-spatial consequences of modernity. In continuation of that, a more specific discussion is conducted in which the relationship between youth and place are expanded through the notions of 'home' and 'venturing'. These two discussions are used to develop a conceptual 'toolbox' to put into work in empirical studies.

In the next section of the book we move from space and place to nature and landscape. The two authors writing in this section can be seen as representatives of 'new' social and cultural approaches to nature, but both of them would probably argue that it is not so new after all. Likewise, they both seek to track specific 'Nordic' formulations and to evolve their own ideas from them. The tracks that are followed are however different. *Kenneth Olwig* is conducting an 'archaeological' search of a Nordic landscape. He argues that it is possible to trace a 'Nordic' way of thinking about landscape that is different from both a 'British' pictorial scene scenic approach and a 'German' layered, blood from soil, one. This 'reflexive' approach is characterised by a concern with history, custom/law and language and culture in the formation in landscape and landscape polities. Olwig traces the historical construction of this conception as it has taken place in tension with outside influences, and he ends the article discussing contemporary examples. *Ari Lehtinen's* emphasis is on the politicisation of nature. He positions his interpretation of nature and environment in a 'Nordic' critical geography tradition and as such links environmental inequalities to class, gender and regional ones. His '(post)constructionist' approach develops from the two concepts of 'bio-politics' and 'environmental justice' – a framework that is put into work in relation to contemporary restructurings of the Nordic forest industry. The main argument is that during the current local-global transformation Nordic forest communities meet challenges, which in turn influences our understanding of socio-ecological governance, sustainability and sense of justice. Ari Lehtinen ends his article by drawing consequences to the subject that challenges Nordic (and international) discourses as regards scientific delimitations, power relations and theory-praxis relationships.

'Difference' is one of the keywords in the current 'international' discourses of human geography and has of course also prevailed in the 'Nordic' debate. So, questions on difference, othering and power are issues connecting the contributions in the last section of this presentation – even though the way to approach them and the concepts of power at work are different. It has been claimed that in their emphasis on equality, the Nordic welfare states have been less inclined to deal with difference. It is probably a more ambiguous matter than such a simple statement can tell, for instance are the Nordic countries relatively well-off when it comes to questions on gender and sexuality? But it is a matter in need of serious concern from critical human geographers, and it is beyond doubt that the ideology of the welfare states builds on presuppositions of a homogeneous population; such as the first authors in this section – *Roger Andersson and Irene Molina* – claim. Like the above presented one by Hans Thor Andersen and Eric Clark, their article deals with urban segregation – more precisely ethnic residential segregation. They argue for what they call a 'holistic' approach to ethnic segregation in order to grasp the complexity at stake in this process. As an attempt to fulfil this purpose they suggest two complementary and cooperating models of explanation: First, a '*racialization model*' including dominant discourses, political practices and 'othering' processes that make race an issue on the housing market; and secondly a '*migration model*' focusing on the mobility of individuals and groups in the city and thus on the dynamics in the generation of segregated urban patterns. The development of the models is infused with material from the authors' empirical work on Swedish cities. We stay in the urban realm in the contribution from *Hille Koskela*. She starts her enquiry from a 'geography of fear' and the issue of safety in American and Nordic cities respectively. This forms the background for the main discussion, which also includes the author's empirical work from Finland. It is on the ambiguous visibility involved in video surveillance of public space. The 'panopticon'-like power relations and the gendered character of the surveillance are revealed, and the paper ends up discussing the production of space performed through emotions and the 'micropolitics' of everyday life. The last voice given the floor in this collection is the one of *Gunnar Olsson* who has probably been the most persistent challenger of any claims of certainty in Nordic (and other) human geography/ies. Emotions and power, as well as many other notions appearing in this book, are included in his 'landscape of landscapes'. Gunnar Olsson explores a set of dichotomies – 'Stonescape'/'Mindscape', reification/deification, fetishism/alienation, perspectiva naturalis/perspectiva artificialis – and the limits of translation between them. As a 'cartographer of power', he maps the power of categorising and naming, ultimately seeing power as 'a game of ontological transformation'.

These are the contributions that we hope together will be able to diminish the lack of a collected representation of 'Nordic voices' in contemporary human geography. We would like to thank all the contributors to this volume for participating in the project and receiving all our comments with friendliness. We also thank 'Nordisk Kulturfond' and the 'Joint Committee of the Nordic Social Science Research Councils' for rendering possible this project through their financial support.

References

Asheim, B.T. (1987) 'A critical evaluation of postwar developments in human geography in Scandinavia', *Progress in Human Geography* 11:3, 333–354.

Haraway, D. (1991) *Simians, cyborgs and women: The reinvention of nature*, London: Routledge.

Öhman, J. (ed.) (1994) *Traditioner i Nordisk kulturgeografi*, Uppsala: Nordisk Samhälls-geografisk Tidskrift.

Said, E. (1984) *The world, the text and the critic*, London: Faber and Faber.

PART I
PRODUCTION, SOCIAL INSTITUTIONS AND LOCAL DEVELOPMENT

Chapter 1

Localised capabilities and industrial competitiveness

Anders Malmberg and Peter Maskell

Since the early 1970s, it has become increasingly recognised that the geographical location of economic activity cannot be properly understood in isolation from its wider socio-economic and technological context, and thus that we cannot understand spatial economic change without linking it to the overall processes of transformation of capitalist production systems, institutions and markets (Massey 1979, Maskell 1986).

Within this broader contextualisation of economic geography, the practice of the sub-discipline has changed substantially over the last few decades, in the Nordic countries and beyond. While the late 1970s and most of the 1980s saw economic geographers being preoccupied with problems related to deindustrialisation and restructuring of traditional industrial core regions, the 1990s has seen a marked turn towards the study of the role of knowledge in creating and sustaining industrial competitiveness, and the role of location in the process of learning.

The advantages of being in the right type of local milieu in general and the benefits of spatial proximity between actors involved in business interaction have been held to explain differences in the innovative performance of firms and industries (Asheim 1992, Feldman and Florida 1994, Saxenian 1994, Morgan 1997, Cooke 1995, Maskell et al. 1998), the existence of industry agglomeration (Lung et al. 1996) as well as the durability of patterns of regional specialisation (Malmberg and Maskell 1997).

In this paper we focus on the impact of geographical location on the ability of firms to create and sustain competitiveness in an era of increased economic globalisation. The paper addresses a series of questions related to industrial competitiveness on the one hand, and the development of regional and national economies on the other. Thus, the discussion will revolve around three inter-related questions:

- What is competition about in today's economy, and how is the performance of firms and industries related to space and place?
- Why do geographical areas (local milieus, cities, regions, and countries) specialise in particular types of economic activity, and why are patterns of specialisation once in place, so durable?
- How can firms in high-cost regions sustain competitiveness and prosperity in an increasingly globally integrated world economy?

In short, the view of the (economic) world that has come to underpin recent analyses of these issues may be summarised in six points (cf. Malmberg 2000):

- Ability to learn and innovate is more important than cost advantage
- Innovation is not just high-tech
- Innovations emerge through interaction within systems of interrelated economic activity
- Spatial proximity matters in such interactions
- Industrial systems are locally embedded
- Local knowledge is more important than natural resources.

In this paper, we will elaborate on some of these issues. In doing so, we will take our point of departure in a competence-based view of the firm, before addressing how *localised capabilities* play a role in the process by which firms, and systems of firms, develop and retain knowledge, innovation and competitiveness.

The Nordic context

The development of the discipline of economic geography in the Nordic countries can in part be understood as a result of some specific characteristics of the Nordic setting: the small size, general openness, industry structure and relatively high levels of prosperity of the economies of Denmark, Finland, Iceland, Norway and Sweden. At the outset of the paper, therefore, we will briefly discuss some distinguishing features of small, industrialised countries in general, and the Nordic countries in particular.

Small economies differ from larger economies in several ways (Grossman and Helpman 1991). It is to be expected that the size of the regional or national economy exerts some influence on its degree of openness. A country encompassing the globe would be fully self-sufficient in all meaningful aspects of the word. And the reverse is equally true: the smaller the country, the more it will have to depend on the others. Thus, small economies are, as a rule, *open economies*.

It is therefore not surprising that most small developed countries long ago started actively to advocate the adoption of a non-tariff, non-barrier world trade system (Balassa 1965, OECD 1995). Initially their main motive was presumably to acquire the needed inputs and to secure market access for their products. Subsequently the opening of the economy was found also to be a prerequisite for obtaining economies of scale in the production of goods and intangibles such as knowledge (Archibugi and Michie 1995); for curbing domestic monopolies; for enabling additional product differentiation and for ensuring the continuous international exposure to enhance the overall industrial competitiveness. Furthermore, the small countries' lack of political or military power to imitate or impede any US-style 'voluntary import restraints', when emerging competitors threaten domestic producers (Brander and Spencer 1983), does point towards the same conclusion. Protectionism is simply not a viable option for small, industrialised countries.

In his influential analysis Katzenstein (1985) links the small size of the national economy to a certain inclination towards a policy of free trade and openness, and a strong affinity towards corporatism resulting from a general perception of common fate and the spread of common fears. Additionally, he detects in the small countries a penchant for neutrality; a weakness of the political right (see also Amin and Thomas 1996); a dependence on foreign capital to supplement internal savings, and a tenor of domestic political stability induced by the need to secure access to export markets. As a response to their position in the international economy small countries have developed specific institutions – e.g. for rapid exchange-rate adjustments, etc. – to maintain competitiveness in key industries and mechanisms to compensate domestic losers when readjustment becomes necessary by imported disruptions, etc. (Korkman 1992, Maskell 1997).

The degree of openness of the economy of differently sized countries – size here refers simply to the magnitude of the national economy, measured e.g. as gross domestic product – can easily be demonstrated empirically (see Maskell et al. 1998 for data). Thus, foreign trade is more than twice as important for the group of medium-size countries (like Germany, France, Italy, the UK) than for the large ones (the US, Japan) in relation to their total manufacturing output. And foreign trade is on average more than four times as important for the economically small countries (like the Nordic ones, Austria, Belgium, the Netherlands, Canada, and Australia). This economic openness forces the governments of small countries to devote special efforts to secure their balance of trade, just as big capital investments tend to be undertaken with an eye on foreign rather than domestic trade. Any disruption and cyclical turn in the international economy is immediately reflected internally, favouring the development of indigenous institutions to compensate losers and to flatten the amplitude of the imported disturbance (Katzenstein 1985).

Firms in smaller countries are, moreover, significantly more exposed to foreign competition, than are firms in larger countries. The possibly advantageous long-term effects of a constant high degree of exposure to international competition are sometimes even seen as a triggering factor in the economic development of small countries (Menzel and Senghaas 1980). Others have taken such an exposure as a point of departure when explaining how small countries can become and remain competitive by specialising in a limited number of industries (Porter 1990).

In a sense, small countries are in this respect similar to more narrowly defined regions. It can be argued that the difference between countries and regions is increasingly in degree, rather than in kind (Maskell et al. 1998). This is particularly so for small countries. Their general degree of openness and exposure to international competition makes them in important respects similar to regions, seen as parts of broader economic and political entities.

Small size is also likely to mean that, within each industry, the number of actors is limited. Therefore, it is probable that, in the Nordic context, size is a factor explaining why scholars in economic geography and related disciplines have been particularly interested in the analysis of how networked relations across firms in various industrial systems help create stable specialisation patterns, and how innovation and competitiveness emerge from interactive process with a markedly localised component.

Firms and localised capabilities

Firms are core actors of the industrial world. According to the emerging *competence-* or *resource-based view of the firm* (see Penrose 1959, Wernerfelt 1984, Rumelt 1984, Prahalad and Hamel 1990, Foss 1996), competitiveness is built on heterogeneous resources or competencies: on the firm's access to and control over something wanted by others, or ability to do something, which the competitors cannot do as well, as rapidly or as cheaply. Such heterogeneity is often a result of the way firms manage to combine initially homogeneous resources in new and unique ways (Dierickx and Cool 1989: 1507).

No firm is self-contained in the sense that it can operate regardless of all factors in its environment. Some complementary assets are needed and firms engage with each other to obtain these. Firms acquire resources on factor markets at a local, regional, national or sometimes even global level. But as long as not all factors are acquired on global markets, the competitiveness of firms will diverge because of difference in geographical location. The specific combination of localised factors that influence the distribution of economic activity, between and within each country or region, constitute the area's *localised capabilities*. Thus, firms might differentiate themselves by their location and – as a consequence – by being able to utilise dissimilar territorially specific resources and localised capabilities.

In order to enhance the competitiveness of firms, the specific localised capabilities of the area of location must represent a combination of assets of significant value and rareness. As the locational demand of firms changes over time, the localised capabilities must adapt and transform in order to remain valuable. Hence, capabilities are not just a passive reflection of what has happened in the region or country throughout history. They are also modified or reconstructed by the deliberate and purposeful action of individuals or groups within or outside the area.

Firms interact on markets that are social constructions, embedded in territorially specific institutions, which define and secure property rights and enable economic transactions (North 1994: 360). Well functioning and organised markets for products and production factors can be seen as a specific (non-tradable) localised capability. Localised capabilities thus link the concepts of regions and countries to the concept of the firm.

Firms of a certain kind find some localised capabilities more valuable than other. The originally chosen location of an industry might have been basically accidental. But once in place, the specialised demands from the firms will influence the future development of the localised capabilities, making it advantageous for the industry to remain in the area, and for outlying firms to relocate there (Enright 1994). The market selection mechanisms ensure that firms located in areas where the localised capabilities are specially suited to their needs will have a better chance of survival and growth than will similar firms located elsewhere. Gradual modifications in the built structures, the skills and competencies of the work-force, or the institutional endowment of the area will all tend to make the localised capabilities even more valuable for the firms located there. Consequently their competitiveness vis-à-vis competitors located elsewhere is further augmented.

The process of territorial economic development will, for the same reason, tend to be path-dependent. A well developed local supply base represents, for instance, a set of constraints and opportunities which in practice can be directional for the possible choices a firm might make, just as some distinctive feature of the demand structure in the region or country might further enhance an already exceptional pattern of specialisation. The differences in capabilities between regions or countries will (by definition) be revealed in discrepancies in the competitiveness of firms located there, with consequences for their long-term survival rate. Once in place, localised capabilities will continuously be retained and reinforced by positive feedback loops, as long as they are considered valuable.

Globalisation, ubiquitification and the erosion of localised capabilities

In the following we discuss how formerly valuable localised capabilities might be converted into 'ubiquities'. We argue that the process of globalisation does in fact threaten to erode the localised capabilities of the high-cost areas of the world, thus undermining the competitiveness of firms located there.

Globalisation is a process in which, among other things, the production and exchange of commodities gradually expand beyond the territory of the nation state to include still larger parts of the globe (Dicken 1998). The driving forces behind this process of globalisation are the economies of scale and scope resulting from a deepened territorial division of labour. The process of globalisation is fuelled by increasing efficiency of international exchange of goods and services, resulting from e.g.: improvements in the systems of transport, communication and capital transfer; governmental agreements on the reduction of economic and non-economic barriers (Sykes 1995); expansion in the number, in scale and scope of cross-border inter-firm collaboration and of internationally operating firms (Dunning 1958); and the escalating efficiency in down-stream mass distribution and sales (Kline 1991). In traditional location theory (Weber 1909), a distinction was made between two types of production input. On the one hand, there are factors of economic importance for the operation of a firm for which the costs differ significantly between locations, so called *localised inputs*. On the other hand, there are materials and other production inputs that in practice are available everywhere at more or less the same cost, which are called *ubiquities*. Weber used the distinction between localised materials and ubiquities to determine the degree of market-pull on the location of industries: the larger the element of ubiquities in the final product, the more strongly would the potential savings in transportation cost pull the industry away from the sources of raw material towards a location near the customers.

The Weberian distinction still holds, even though changes have occurred over time in the list of critically important location factors. But when the significance of one location factor decreases, the relative importance of some other factor will be rising. Historical illustrations of this point include shifts from waterpower to coal to electricity, or from channels to railroads to motorways.

Traditionally two processes have determined the shifts in the relative importance of location factors. Either there has been a cease in demand for a formerly important factor. This may be caused by some innovation in the production process, leading to the use of other inputs than before or a change in the magnitude of various inputs already being used. Alternatively the supply of a localised input has been changing:

natural deposits become exhausted while new sources are discovered elsewhere; labour is becoming scarce where it used to be abundant; suppliers relocate; the geographical concentrations of demand are shifting, etc.

As a repercussion of the ongoing globalisation, a third process has recently emerged, which *actively converts formerly localised inputs into ubiquities*. In another context, we have introduced the term ubiquitification process to capture this. A large domestic market is less of an advantage when transport costs are negligible and when trade barriers are eroded. Domestic suppliers of the most efficient production machinery become less important when identical equipment is available worldwide, and at essentially the same cost. Hence, the relevance of the Weberian distinction has not disappeared, as globalisation has progressed and transportation costs have diminished in relation to production costs. On the contrary, the distinction between localised and ubiquitous factors provides the link between location theory and modern competence- or resource-based theory of the firm.

No firm can build competitiveness on ubiquities alone, and little economic progress would be made anywhere, if everyone were able to do exactly the same in all places at once. In order to enhance the competitiveness of firms, a localised capability must thus be valuable, and in order to be valuable it has to be rare. If, however, a formerly important and rare localised capability somehow is turned into a ubiquity – making the localised capability equally available at the same cost to all firms more or less regardless of location – the capability loses its importance. Firms whose competitiveness was depending on it will be penalised in the market just as, at an aggregate level, the established patterns of regional or national specialisation will be jeopardised. In other words: as ubiquities are created, localised capabilities are destroyed.

When the globalisation process gradually converts previously important location factors into ubiquities, the competitiveness of firms exposed to international competition will increasingly be associated with one of the remaining localised factors, upgraded by the process of globalisation: labour costs. The intertwined process of globalisation and ubiquitification thus presents genuinely new opportunities for domestic or foreign firms in low-cost countries and regions.

In the same process, firms in the world's high-cost areas run the risk of being eliminated. Their benefit from an expansion in global demand can be more than offset by their loss of competitiveness as previous regional or national capabilities are turned into ubiquities. Firms in high-cost countries cope with such challenges in various ways. Some raise their capital/labour ratio through massive investments, while others out-source or relocate parts of or all their activities to low-cost areas. 'Automate, emigrate or evaporate' as the saying goes. Or 'innovate', as we will argue in the following.

Knowledge creation as a response to ubiquitification

Many firms do, however, meet the challenges of globalisation not by seeking competitiveness through cost-reduction, but by generating entrepreneurial (Schumpeterian) quasi-rents through enhanced knowledge creation (Spender 1994). This phenomenon as such is not new, but the extent to which knowledge creation influences and shapes the economy – and the extent to which this phenomenon is being acknowledged in economic research is certainly increasing. Gradually a knowledge-based economy is materialising, where the competitive edge of many firms has shifted from static price competition towards dynamic improvement, favouring those who can create knowledge faster than their competitors (Porter 1990, Chandler 1992).

There is a spatial aspect to this transmutation. Some regional or national settings are more predisposed than others to support and advance the knowledge creation process in the industry of today (Mjøset 1992, Saxenian 1994, Gertler 1997). This adds a new entry to the list of currently important location factors influencing the geographical pattern of industry: the knowledge assets and learning abilities of local, regional or national milieus.

In the following, we will expand on this line of thinking. In doing so, we regard knowledge and knowledge creation in the broadest possible sense. Knowledge creation thus includes activities such as investment in R&D and the development and adoption of leading-edge technology. Equally important, however, is the 'low-tech' learning and innovation, that takes place when also firms in fairly traditional industries are (more or less) innovative in the way they handle and develop resource management, logistics, production organisation, marketing, sales, distribution, industrial relations, etc. Based on an analysis of some general characteristics of knowledge and knowledge creation and a discussion of the distinction between tacit and codified knowledge, we put forward the argument that codification of tacit knowledge is a process very similar to the process of ubiquitification discussed above. We then go on to discuss how firms can go about protecting their knowledge assets from losing value by codification and its close follower: ubiquitification.

Knowledge creation in the firm

Knowledge distinguishes itself from all other input in the production process by its durability: the use of knowledge does not reduce the stock. Actually, the use of knowledge often creates new knowledge as an integral part of the performance of all kinds of activities carried out within and between firms (Prahalad and Hamel 1990). Firms get more knowledgeable of their products, their production process, their customers and suppliers, etc. as time goes on.

Learning from experience (Arrow 1962, Lucas 1988) gives rise to incremental improvements in firms and on markets. These improvements accumulate over time, and gradually result in new and better ways of doing things (Boldrin and Scheinkman 1988). New knowledge can be created intentionally, as a resource-consuming effort, e.g. through public or firm-based R&D activities. Still, deliberate knowledge creation is an activity where the necessary relevant information to facilitate rational decision-making is absent (Dosi and Orsengio 1988). Knowledge is, furthermore, in itself always associated with some ambiguity as to what it is really about and what use can be made of it (Reed and DeFillippi 1990, Alvesson 1993).

Firms seem to handle this basic uncertainty by developing internal procedures and routines when searching for possible solutions. Such procedures and routines that a firm develops will determine the distribution of its specific actions within the range of possibilities that are open to it at any given time (Dosi 1990, Nelson and

Winter 1982). Intentional knowledge creation is thus strongly path-dependent (Arthur 1994), representing 'the transmission in time of our accumulated stock of knowledge' (Hayek 1960: 27). Firms, regions or countries that already have a large stock of R&D and experience-based know-how, a specialised labour-force or infrastructure and so on, are often in a better position to make further break-throughs, to add to their existing stock of knowledge, than those that have only a limited initial endowment of such factors. Both major, path-breaking innovations and insignificant incremental improvements accumulate in the organisational structure and routines of the firm and will gradually result in new and better ways of doing things.

The same process, however, also tends to create internal bonds and firm-specific commitments that can make routines more durable than needed: they are retained and sometimes even aggressively defended long after changes in the external conditions of the firm have made them redundant (Demsetz 1988). It is difficult to unlearn successful habits of the past, also in cases where it is obvious to everyone concerned that they hinder future success (Imai et al. 1986, Hedberg 1981). Lack of unlearning often goes hand in hand with an increasing resistance towards new ideas, a growing bureaucratic inertia and a general organisational degeneration, especially when the firm is operating in generous markets (Eliasson 1996).

Occasionally also regions and countries get caught in specific, initially successful, ways of doing things, which later events have converted into shackles hindering further progress (Elbaum and Lazonick 1986). Entire industries can find themselves in such situations for quite a while, until someone breaks the deadlock by introducing new ways of doing things. The accumulation of useful knowledge in an economy is thus dependent not only on the knowledge creation that takes place in each firm, region or country, but also on the speed in which path-dependent lock-in situations are broken and knowledge creating activities are restored by the activities of undogmatic entrepreneurs (Schienstock 1997).

Knowledge creation through interaction in industrial systems

Firms rarely learn or innovate in isolation. On the contrary, rather robust research results indicate that most innovation results from interactions and collaborations between two or more firms and organisations. Firms interacting with each other can be said to form industrial systems. The idea that firms are parts of industrial systems has gained currency in recent years, in research as well as industrial policy circles. There exist, in the literature, a multitude of 'systems concepts' which partly complement and partly compete with each other. Inter-firm relations keeping systems together can be of different types, such as transaction links between customers and suppliers; competition between firms operating in the same product of factor market, technological collaboration between firms taking part in joint R&D projects or strategic alliances, and various knowledge spill-overs, linking firms between which knowledge flows form one to the other, with or without intention of the parties involved.

Adopting a systems approach brings the advantage that it helps in getting around the division of the economy into a series basically artificial dichotomies, which so often tend to characterise – and weaken – academic discourse and analysis as well as policy initiatives in the field. Such 'false dichotomies' typically include divisions between, for example, small and large firms; manufacturing and service industries; or high-tech and low-tech activities. When notions of industrial systems are brought to the fore, such distinctions become less significant. Any single industrial system will typically display inter-linkages and dependencies between very dissimilar types of activities.

The system approach includes analyses based on 'production systems' (Hirschman 1958, de Bernis 1966, Stewart 1977), 'business systems' (Whitley 1994a, 1994b, 1996), or 'innovation systems' (Lundvall 1992, Nelson 1993, Lundvall and Maskell 2000). Other 'systemic concepts' advanced in recent years in research on industrial transformation include industries, commodity chains (Gereffi 1994), networks (Håkansson 1989, Axelsson and Easton 1992), industry clusters (Porter 1990), development blocs (Dahmén 1950, 1988), technological systems (Carlsson 1997), competence blocs (Eliasson 1998). A common characteristic of all these concepts is that they draw our attention to the fact that the analysis of industrial growth and transformation should focus, not simply on the individual firm as such, but rather on the dynamics of the broader systems of which individual firms are constituent parts (Walker 1988).

When faced with the richness and variety of systemic notions, one can make two observations (Dicken and Malmberg 2001). The first is that existing concepts, or models, differ in the way they incorporate the spatial, or territorial dimension, in the definition of the system and the analysis of its working. The approaches/concepts listed above are functionally defined. This means that the system is defined in terms of various types of manifest relations between the actors/firms that are seen to make up the system. Within this overall category of relational/functional systems, individual approaches vary in the degree to which they emphasise the spatial dimension of these relations.

The second observation is that some of the approaches primarily focus on the complexity of production organisation while others are preoccupied with the logic of learning and innovation, respectively. The first type aim at coming to grips with what Schumpeter referred to as the 'the circular flow of economic life' as it runs 'on in the same channels years after year' (Schumpeter 1934). They focus on how the division of labour between firms differs across industries, how production chains are organised, and how relations between trading partners are managed.

Systems notions explicitly focusing on innovation and learning, on the other hand, are rather different in the sense that they take only marginal, if any, interest in the actual organisation of production but focus mainly or exclusively on the way varied skills and competencies are combined through various interactions to result in new knowledge and innovation. Innovations is then defined in broad Schumpeterian terms to include not only the introduction of new goods or production methods, but also the opening of new markets, the conquest of new sources of supply or the creation of new organisational systems.

In a *competence bloc*, as defined by Eliasson (1998), innovations are seen to occur when various competencies are brought together within the framework of a system comprising of five different types of actors/competencies: (a) competent *customers* demanding new and sophisticated solutions; (b) *innovators* who create such solutions, (c) entrepreneurs who identify innovations and create businesses based on them; (d) *venture capitalists* who supply finance to innovators and entrepreneurs; and (e) *industrialists* who produce and market the new product/ service/method on a large scale.

For Porter (1990), innovations occur within the framework of *industry clusters*. These consist of producers of primary goods, suppliers (of specialty inputs, machinery and associated services), customers and related industries. The mechanisms creating dynamism and innovation in such a cluster are captured in the much quoted diamond model and are partly overlapping with those identified by Eliasson.

Thus, the presence of sophisticated customers plays a key role in Porter's model as well. Other important factors include competent suppliers, appropriate factors conditions (including the interesting and novel concept of selective factor disadvantage) and rivalry between the core firms of the cluster.

Tacit knowledge, codified knowledge and ubiquitification

Initially most pieces of knowledge probably appear in a form, which is exclusively tacit (Polanyi 1958, 1966). Such purely tacit knowledge is at first accessible to the individual only, and much new knowledge will remain that way (Eliasson 1996). Over time, many pieces of knowledge gradually get more codified. Codified knowledge can be communicated by symbols and language, and thus has the necessary features to be tradable (Dosi 1988), if and when the sufficient market conditions occur. Codification can take place in different ways, some of which are mainly unpremeditated consequences of tacit knowledge being used.

Besides the mainly unintended or even unanticipated ways of knowledge creation and codification, also quite deliberate efforts might be made (Antonelli 1995). Owners of some piece of knowledge, which they envisage will be valuable to others, can feel a strong incentive to engage in a codification process in order to reach these potential customers. Codification is usually needed, e.g. to embody the knowledge in software or in the hardware of a machine. The more a firm is able to codify its tasks, the less time and money is needed for instruction, guidance, training and supervision of the employees. Some degree of codification is indispensable in order to obtain economies of scale and scope. One would, perhaps, expect that the accumulated effect of this effort would be a steady increase in the codified knowledge base, and a corresponding decrease in the volume of seasoned tacit knowledge, still uncodified. This, however, does not seem to be the case.

First, not all pieces of knowledge are in fact potentially codifiable. Certain things, which can be fairly easy to learn, can be very difficult and costly to describe or codify (von Hippel 1994). Even knowledge shared by large groups of people – for instance the knowledge of how to use a language as a means of communication – cannot be codified at all easily. Such knowledge might remain for ages in a more or less tacit form within one or more countries, while linguists struggle to identify and disentangle its intricacies (Polanyi 1958, 1966).

Furthermore, it appears that some tacit knowledge is almost always required in order to use new codified knowledge (Dreyfus and Dreyfus 1986, Pavitt 1987, Rosenberg 1990, David 1992, Foray 1992, Gertler 1995). It is difficult for people to learn certain things without at least some small but significant prior (tacit) knowledge, gained by hands-on experiments and training. The requirement of possessing tacit knowledge before being able to utilise any codified knowledge must, if universally true, necessarily lead to a cumulative growth in the tacit knowledge corresponding to the growth in the codified knowledge base.

When Grossman and Helpman (1991) demonstrate how global access to knowledge leads to increasing convergence in real income growth-rates, one might add that any attempt to obtain above-average growth rates will thus to some degree depend on the ability to utilise some spatially confined tacit knowledge (Zander 1992, Baumol et al. 1994). The size and composition of the tacit knowledge-base of a region or country does perhaps constitute fundamental ingredients in its ability to perceive and absorb any valuable innovation generated outside its borders.

The rent-seeking possessor of any piece of knowledge will have a strong economic incentive to protect as much as possible from becoming generally available. But even if or when the process of dissemination is slowed down by such action, neither firms nor individuals can hope to preserve the new codified knowledge forever. Any codification of a piece of knowledge will eventually lead to its diffusion, thereby undermining the present possessor's possibility to use as an ingredient in sustaining competitiveness (Allen 1983). When formerly tacit knowledge is converted into a fully codified form, a process is initiated which will sooner or later – usually sooner – turn it into a ubiquity by making it accessible on the global market.

The linkage between codification and ubiquitification has severe consequences for the firms in high-cost areas of the world, such as in the Nordic countries. The more or less immediate effect of codification is the same as for all other former assets, which have been turned into ubiquities: the knowledge loses its potential to contribute to the competitiveness of the firm. No firm exposed to international competition and located in a high-cost area can therefore depend solely on already fully codified knowledge.

Two distinct processes of ubiquitification are thus simultaneously at work in devaluing previously precious regional or national capabilities: the process of globalisation of factor and commodity markets, and the process of codification of knowledge. But if all factors of production, all organisational blueprints, all market-information, and all production technologies became readily available in all parts of the world at (more or less) the same price, few possibilities would exist for producing in a high-cost environment (Nelson and Winter 1977, Loasby 1990).

In high-cost as well as low-cost environments the process of ubiquitification thus erodes some of the potential fields in which a firm can distinguish itself on the market. What is not eroded, however, is the non-tradable/non-codified result of knowledge creation – the embedded tacit knowledge – that at a given time can only be produced and reproduced in practice.

The fundamental exchange inability of tacit knowledge increases its importance as the globalisation of business markets proceeds. It is a logical and interesting – though usually overlooked – consequence of the present development towards a knowledge-based economy that the more easily codified (tradable) knowledge is accessed by everyone, the more crucial tacit knowledge becomes in sustaining or enhancing the competitive position of the firm.

Hence, the process of ubiquitification will contribute to cripple the competitiveness of firms in high-cost regions and countries of the world if not countervailed and compensated for in some way. In the current knowledge-based economy this means that firms in the high-cost areas must either shield some valuable pieces of knowledge from becoming globally accessible, or be able to create, acquire, accumulate and utilise codifiable tacit knowledge a little faster than their cost-wise more favourably located competitors.

The relations between firms within a local or regional milieu differ extensively: from rapprochement to detachment and indifference or uncompromising rivalry. A relatively close business environment does not necessarily lend itself to cooperation and interaction. Especially small firms often envision the fellow producer down the street as their main competitor and often try hard to outsmart him or her without damaging the firm's own reputation. Local rivalry of this kind stimulates the entrepreneurial spirit and reinforces the productivity in the milieu. But even though examples of non-collaborative attitudes are copious, the conduct of firms in these environments is usually constrained by the knowledge of the unattractive consequences of misbehaving. Opportunistic behaviour will immediately be noticed. The information of such misbehaviour will be passed on to everyone, who in the future will tend to take their business elsewhere. Worse still, by becoming a local outcast the firm is deprived of the flow of knowledge, including its tacit parts, which can prove very difficult to substitute. So even if the business environment in regions and small countries does not force firms to cooperate, if they are not inclined to do so, its intrinsic mechanism for penalising opportunism encourages trustful cooperation and ensure low barriers to the exchange of knowledge, whether codified or tacit. This is one of the main arguments behind the strong claim – advanced in much recent research in economic geography and related fields – that industrial systems in important respects can gain competitiveness from agglomerating in specific local milieus.

Conclusions

In the introduction we raised three broad questions that have been directing our line of argument throughout the paper. The first question was related to what competition is about in today's economy, and how the performance of firms and industries is related to space and place. The second was concerned with why geographical areas tend to specialise in particular types of economic activity and why patterns of specialisation are so durable. The third question, finally, directed our interest to the question of competitiveness: how can high-cost regions sustain competitiveness and prosperity in an increasingly integrated world economy? The latter question is of particular importance in small, internationally exposed economies like those in the Nordic countries.

In a way, we have provided the same answer to all three questions: it has to do with knowledge creation and with the development of localised capabilities that promote learning processes. This answer is of course neither entirely original, nor fully exhaustive. Lots of questions remain to be answered. What is actually learnt in the interaction between organisations? The product innovation literature has firmly established that firms learn from each other when interacting (see for instance Freeman 1982, 1991, Håkansson 1989, Kline and Rosenberg 1986, Hagedoorn and

Schakenraad 1992, OECD 1992). But do we see 'sticky knowledge' (von Hippel 1994) in a rather absolute sense where the division of labour and the combination of different capabilities is the main aspect of the interaction? Or, do we also see interactive learning (Lundvall 1992) where the agents develop the competencies and skills as a major outcome of the interaction? In order to answer such questions there is a need to develop a theoretical basis for analysing learning and knowledge creation that must go beyond the existing insights (Nonaka 1991, Lundvall and Johnson 1994, Gibbons et al. 1994, Foray and Lundvall 1994, Lazaric and Lorenz 1998). We also need to address the more fundamental question of why and how knowledge was dispersed in the first place, thereby necessitating subsequent inter-firm interaction to reassemble knowledge into new useful forms.

The present analysis makes us suspect that inter-firm learning is subject to both thresholds, before the knowledge-bases of firms divided have grown sufficiently apart for interacting to imply learning, and ceilings, after which the cognitive distance become too great for firms to bridge, and where learning, consequentially, will cease. Even when situated between these two extremes it can be very difficult, and sometimes even impossible, to transfer and reuse knowledge even if it is openly available. The barriers toward such transfers seem to be lower when the they take place within a community that share the same language, beliefs, judgements and values. When firms co-locate, a spatially defined community is usually formed that makes it easier for them to bridge communication gaps resulting from heterogeneous knowledge endowments. The innovative capabilities of firms are enhanced because co-location can provide them with an arsenal of instruments to obtain and understand even the most subtle, elusive and complex information of possible relevance developed because they were *separate firms* pursuing their individual agenda. Hence, the territorial configuration of firms might *in itself* influence the process of learning as co-location tilts the balance between advantages of specialisation and costs of coordination and interaction between and among firms.

The opposite side of locally embedded learning processes relates to globalisation, which has by now become a catchword for a number of phenomena that increase the international interdependence and restrain the room for domestic policies also at a regional level. The term may be misleading in that there are counter-tendencies making the local, regional, national and European arenas more important than before. But when it comes to inter-firm cooperation and the formation of networks, there is a tendency for linkages that go across national borders and even across continents to proliferate. This reflects the need to speed up innovation – by combining special capabilities located at different places – and to speed up market introduction on a global scale. Information technology has made it possible to extend networks over great distances and the codification of knowledge has been one element in this process. Another element is the tendency for knowledge residing in different settings to grow apart and become more specialised over time. New links will have to be established for firms to take full advantage of this growth in knowledge dispersed.

The domain of localised learning is simply bursting with new challenges for policy-makers as well as for researchers with an empirical inclination or holding an interest in theory. It is a domain where the object of study is characterised by inter-organisational cooperation, and also the scholars studying it will need a high degree of inter-disciplinary cooperation in order to come to grips with its complexity. As we have indicated in this paper, there are reasons to believe that Nordic scholars in general are particularly well-prepared to contribute to knowledge advancements in this field, situated as they are in a relatively advanced economic environment characterised by smallness and openness. Furthermore, economic geographers have presumably an especially important role to play here. Scholars in various disciplines have increasingly come to suspect that the specific spatial arrangement of economic activities into geographical agglomerations might also *in itself* somehow influence the creation of knowledge and, consequentially, economic growth. Actually, localised knowledge might always have been contributing to economic growth through enhanced learning processes but the turn towards a knowledge-based economy has certainly magnified the political interest in the phenomenon and sharpened the academic interest in understanding the nature of this proposition. Much novel work is already under way and more will surely emerge in the years to come, making us understand better what learning is all about and – perhaps more significantly – how learning processes relate to space and place.

Acknowledgement. This paper draws on a book written with several co-authors (Maskell et al. 1998). The work with the book, and as a consequence indirectly also the writing of this paper, rested on the collaboration with Heikki Eskelinen, Ingjaldur Hannibalsson and Eirik Vatne. This paper partly draws on a more extensive paper published in European Urban and Regional Studies (Maskell and Malmberg 1999). We are also grateful to Peter Dicken for allowing the inclusion of some arguments first formulated in Dicken and Malmberg (2001).

References

Allen, R.C. (1983) 'Collective invention', *Journal of Economic Behaviour and Organization* 4: 1–24.

Alvesson, M. (1993) 'Organizations as rhetoric: knowledge-intensive firms and the struggle with ambiguity', *Journal of Management Studies* 30, 6: 997–1015.

Amin, A. and Thomas, D. (1996) 'The negotiated economy: state and civic institutions in Denmark', *Economy and Society* 25, 2: 255–281.

Antonelli, C. (1995) *The Economics of Localised Technological Change and Industrial Dynamics*, Dordrecht: Kluwer Academic Press.

Archibugi, D. and Michie, J. (1995) 'The globalisation of technology: a new taxonomy', *Cambridge Journal of Economics* 19: 121–140.

Arrow, K. (1962) 'Economic welfare and the allocation of resources for invention', in R. Nelson (ed.) *The Rate and Direction of Inventive Activity. Economic and social factors*, Princeton, NJ: Princeton University Press.

Arthur, W.B. (1994) *Increasing Returns and Path Dependence in the Economy*, Ann Arbor: The University of Michigan Press.

Asheim, B.T. (1992) 'Industrial districts, inter-firm co-operation and endogenous technological development: the experience of developed countries', in *Anonymous Technological Dynamism in Industrial Districts: An Alternative Approach to Industrialization in Developing Countries?* pp. 91–142. New York and Geneva: UNCTAD.

Axelsson, B. and Easton, G. (eds) (1992) *Industrial Networks – A New View of Reality*, London: Routledge.

Aydalot, P. (1986) *Milieux Innovateurs in Europe*, Paris: GREMI.

Balassa, B. (1965) Trade liberalisation and 'revealed comparative advantage', *The Manchester School of Economics and Social Studies* 32, 2: 99–123.

Baumol, W.J., Nelson, R.R. and Wolff, E.N. (eds) (1994) *Convergence of Productivity. Cross-National Studies and Historical Evidence*, Oxford: Oxford University Press.

de Bernis, G.D. (1966) 'Industries industrialisantes et contenu d'une politique d'integration régionale', *Economic Appliquée* 19: 3–4 (July–December), 415–473.

Boldrin, M. and Scheinkman, J.A. (1988) 'Learning-By-Doing, International Trade and Growth: A note', in Anderson, P.W., Arrow, K.J. and Pines, D. (eds) *The Economy as an Evolving Complex System*. Redwood City: Addison-Wesley Publishing Company.

Brander, J.A. and Spencer, B.J. (1983) Export subsidy and market share rivalry, *Journal of International Economics* 18: 83–100.

Carlsson, B. (ed.) (1997) *Technological systems and industrial dynamics*. Dordrecht: Kluwer Academic Publishers.

Chandler, A.D. (1992) 'Organizational Capabilities and the Economic History of the Industrial Enterprise', *Journal of Economic Perspectives* 6, 3: 79–100.

Cooke, P. (1995) 'Planet Europa: Network approaches to regional innovation and technology management', *Technology Management* 2, 18–30.

Dahmén, E. (1950) *Svensk industriell företagarverksamhet. Kausalanalys av den industriella utvecklingen 1919–1939*, Lund: Industriens Utredningsinstitut.

Dahmén, E. (1988) 'Development Blocks' in industrial economics. *Scandinavian Economic History Review* XXXVI: 3–14.

David, P. (1992) *Knowledge, Property and the system of dynamics of technological change, proceedings of the World Bank Annual Conference on Development Economics*, (Published as Supplement to the World Bank Economic Review), Washington DC.

Demsetz, H. (1988) *The Organization of Economic Activity. Volume I: Ownership, control and the firm*, Oxford: Blackwell.

Dicken, P. (1998) *Global Shift. Transforming the world economy*, Third edition. London: Paul Chapman.

Dicken, P. and Malmberg, A. (2001) 'Firms in territories: A relational perspective'. Paper submitted for publication in Economic Geography.

Dierickx, I. and Cool, K. (1989) 'Asset stock accumulation and sustainablity of competitive advantage', *Management Science* 35, 12: 1504–1513.

Dosi, G. (1988) 'Institutions and markets in a dynamic world', *Manchester School of Economics and Social Studies* 61, 2: 119–146.

Dosi, G. (1990) 'Finance, innovation and industrial change', *The Journal of Economic Behaviour and Organization* 13: 299–319.

Dosi, G. and Orsengio, L. (1988) 'Coordination and transformation. An overview of structures, behaviours and change in evolutionary environments', in Dosi, G., Freeman, C., Nelson, R., Silverberg, G. and Soete, L. (eds) *Technical Change and Economic Theory*, London: Pinter.

Dreyfus, H. and Dreyfus, S. (1986) 'Why computers may never think like people', *Technological Review* 89, 1: 42–61.

Dunning, J.H. (1958) *American Investment in British Manufacturing Industry*, London: Allen and Unwin.

Elbaum, B. and Lazonick, W. (1986) (eds) *The decline of the British Economy*, Oxford: Clarendon Press.

Eliasson, G. (1996) *Firm Objectives, Controls and Organization. The Use of Information and the Transfer of Knowledge within the Firm*, Dordrecht: Kluwer Academic Publishers.

Eliasson, G. (1998) 'Industrial policy, competence blocks and the role of science in economic development'. *Research report*, August, Department of Industrial Economics and Management, Royal Institute of Technology, Stockholm.

Enright, M.J. (1994) 'Regional Clusters and Firm Strategy', unpublished paper presented at the Prince Bertil Symposium on The Dynamic Firm, 12–14 June, Stockholm.

Feldman, M.P. and Florida, R. (1994) 'The geographic sources of innovation: Technological infrastructure and product innovation in the United States'. *Annals of the Association of American Geographers*, 84, 210–229.

Foray, D. (1992) 'The Economics of Intellectual Property Rights and Systems of Innovation. The inevitable diversity', unpublished paper presented at the MERIT conference on 'Convergence and divergence in economic growth and technical change', 10–12 December, Maastricht.

Foray, D. and Lundvall, B.-Å. (1994) 'The knowledge-based economy: from the economics of knowledge to the learning economy', in papers presented at the OECD conference on 'Employment and Growth in a Knowledge-Based Economy', 7–8 November, Copenhagen, Paris: The Organisation for Economic Co-operation and Development.

Foss, N.J. (1996) 'Higher-order industrial capabilities and competitive advantage', *Journal of Industry Studies* 3, 1: 1–20.

Freeman, C. (1982) *The economics of industrial innovation*, London: Pinter.

Freeman, C. (1991) 'Networks of Innovators: a Synthesis of Research Issues'. *Research Policy* 20 (5).

Gereffi, G. (1994) 'The organization of buyer-driven global commodity chains: how US retailers shape overseas production networks', in Gereffi, G. and Korzeniewicz, M. (eds) *Commodity Chains and Global Capitalism*, 95–122. Westport, CT: Praeger.

Gertler, M.S. (1995) 'Being There: Proximity, Organization, and Culture in the Development and Adoption of Advanced Manufacturing Technologies', *Economic Geography* 71, 1: 1–26.

Gertler, M.S. (1997) 'The invention of regional culture', in Lee, R. and Wills, J. (eds) *Geographies of economies*, London: Arnold.

Gibbons, M. et al. (1994) *The New Production of Knowledge*. London: Sage Publications.

Grossman, G.M. and Helpman, E. (1991) *Innovation and Growth in the Global Economy*, London: MIT Press.

Hagedoorn, J. and Schakenraad, J. (1992) 'Leading companies and networks of strategic alliances in information technologies'. *Research Policy* (21).

Håkansson, H. (1989) *Corporate technological behavior – co-operation and networks.* London: Routledge.

Hayek, F.A. (1960) *The Constitution of Liberty*, Chicago: University of Chicago Press.

Hedberg, B. (1981) 'How organizations learn and unlearn', in Nyström, P.C. and Starbuck, W.H. (eds) *Handbook on Organizational Design – Adapting Organizations to their Environment*, Oxford: Oxford University Press.

von Hippel, E. (1994) 'Sticky information and the locus of problem solving: implications for innovation', *Management Science* 40: 429–439.

Hirschman, A.O. (1958) *The strategy of economic development*, Clinton Mass.: Yale University Press.

Imai, K.-I., Nonaka, I. and Takeuchi, H. (1986) 'Managing the new product development process: how Japanese companies learn and unlearn', in Clark, K.B., Hayes, R.H. and Lorenz, C. (eds) *The uneasy alliance. Managing the productivity-technology dilemma*, Boston: Harvard Business School Press.

Katzenstein, P.J. (1985) *Small states in world markets. Industrial policy in Europe*. New York: Cornell University Press.

Kline, S.J. (1991) 'Styles of innovation and their cultural basis', *Chemtech* 21, 8: 472–480.

Kline, S.J. and Rosenberg, N. (1986) 'An overview of innovation', in Landau, R. and Rosenberg, N. (eds) *The positive sum game*. Washington DC: National Academy Press.

Korkman, S. (1992) 'Exchange rate policy and the employment in small open economies', in Pekkarinen, J. et al (eds) *Social Corporatism: A Superior Economic System?* Oxford: Clarendon Press.

Lazaric, N. and Lorenz, E. (1998) *Trust and Economic Learning*. London: Edward Elgar.

Loasby, B.J. (1990) 'Firms, markets and the principle of continuity', in Whitaker, J.K. (ed.) *Centenary Essays on Alfred Marshall*, Cambridge: Cambridge University Press for the Royal Economic Society.

Lucas, R.E. (1988) 'On the mechanics of economic development', *Journal of Monetary Economy* 22: 3–42.

Lundvall, B.-Å. (ed.) (1992) *National Innovation Systems: Towards a Theory of Innovation and Interactive Learning*, London: Pinter.

Lundvall, B.-Å. and Johnson, B. (1994) 'The learning economy', *Journal of Industry Studies* 1 (2).

Lundvall, B.-Å. and Maskell, P. (2000) 'Nation states and economic development – From national systems of production to national systems of knowledge creation and learning', in Clark, G.L., Feldmann, M.P. and Gertler, M.S. (eds) *The Oxford Handbook of Economic Geography*, pp. 353–372. Oxford: Oxford University Press.

Lung, Y., Rallet, A. and Torre, A. (1996) 'Innovative activity and geographical proximity. Paper for the 36th European Congress for the European Regional Science Association', 26–30 August, Zürich, Switzerland.

Malmberg, A. (2000) 'Lokal miljö, agglomeration och industriell konkurrenskraft', in Berger, S. (ed.) *Det nya samhällets geografi*. Uppsala: Uppsala Publishing House.

Malmberg, A. and Maskell, P. (1997) 'Towards an explanation of regional specialization and industry agglomeration', *European Planning Studies* 5: 25–41.

Maskell, P. (1986) *Industriens flugt fra storbyen*. Köbenhavn: Arnold Busck Forlag.

Maskell, P. (1997) Learning in the village conomy of Denmark. The role of institutions and policy in sustaining competitiveness, in H.J. Braczyk et al. (eds) *Regional innovation systems – the role of governance in a globalised world*, London: University College London Press.

Maskell, P., Eskelinen, H., Hannibalsson, I., Malmberg, A. and Vatne, E. (1998) *Competitiveness, localised learning and regional development. Specialisation and prosperity in small open economies*. London: Routledge.

Maskell, P. and Malmberg, A. (1999) 'The competitiveness of firms and regions: 'Ubiquitification' and the importance of localised learning'. *European Urban and Regional Studies* Vol. 6: 9–25.

Massey, D. (1979) 'In what sense a regional problem?' *Regional Studies* Vol. 13: 233–342.

Menzel, U. and Senghaas, D. (1980) 'Autocentric development despite international competence differentials', *Economics – a biannual collection of recent German contributions to the field of economic science*, 21.

Mjøset, L. (1992) 'Comparative typologies of development patterns', Lars Mjøset (ed.) Contributions to the Comparative Study of Development, proceedings from Vilhelm Aubert Memorial Symposium 1990, vol. 2, *Institute for Social Research Report*, Oslo.

Morgan, K. (1997) 'The Learning Region: Institutions, Innovation and Regional Renewal', *Regional Studies* 31(5): 491–504.

Nelson, R.R. (ed.) (1993) *National Innovation Systems: A Comparative Analysis*, Oxford: Oxford University Press.

Nelson, R.R. and Winter, S.G. (1977) 'In search of useful theory of innovation', *Research Policy* 6: s36–76.

Nelson, R.R. and Winter, S.G. (1982) *An Evolutionary Theory of Economic Change*, Cambridge, Mass.: The Belknap Press of Harvard University Press.

Nonaka, K. (1991) 'The Knowledge Creating Company', *Harvard Business Review*, Nov–Dec.

North, D.C. (1994) 'Economic performance through time', *The American Economic Review* 84, 3: 359–368.

OECD (1992) *Industrial Policy in the OECD countries. Annual Review*. Paris: The Organisation for Economic Co-operation and Development.

OECD (1995) *Indicators of tariff and non-tariff trade barriers*. Paris: The Organisation for Economic Co-operation and Development.

Pavitt, K. (1987) 'The objectives of technology policy', *Science and Public Policy* 14, 4: 182–188.

Penrose, E.T. (1959) *The theory of the growth of the firm*, Oxford: Oxford University Press.

Polanyi, M. (1958) *Personal Knowledge. Towards a Post-critical Philosophy*, London: Routledge.

Polanyi, M. ((1966) 1983) *The Tacit Dimension*, London: Routledge.

Porter, M.E. (1990) *The competitive advantages of nations*, London and Basingstoke: Macmillan.

Prahalad, C.K. and Hamel, G. (1990) 'The core competence of the corporation', *Harvard Business Review* 3: 79–91.

Reed, R. and DeFillippi, R.J. (1990) 'Causal ambiguity, barriers to imitation and sustainable competitive advantage', *Academy of Management Review*, 15, 1: 88–102.

Rosenberg, N. (1990) 'Why do companies do basic research with their own money?', *Research Policy* 19: 165–174.

Rumelt, R.P. (1984) 'Towards a strategic theory of the firm', in Lamb, R.B. (ed.) *Competitive Strategic Management*, Englewood Cliffs, NJ: Prentice-Hall.

Saxenian, A. (1994) *Regional Advantage*, Cambridge, Mass.: Harvard University Press.

Schienstock, G. (1997) 'The Transformation of Regional Governance. Institutional Lock-ins and the Development of Lean Production in Baden-Württemberg', in Whitley, R. and Kristensen, P.H. (eds) *Governance at work. The Social Regulation of Economic Relations*, pp. 190–208. Oxford: Oxford University Press.

Schumpeter, J. (1934 (1959)) *The Theory of Economic Development: An inquiry into Profits, Capital, Credit, Interest, and the Business Cycle*. Cambridge, MA: Harvard University Press.

Spender, J.-C. (1994) 'The Geographies of Strategic Competence: Borrowing from Social and Educational Psychology to Sketch an Activity and Knowledge-Based Theory of the Firm', unpublished paper presented at the Prince Bertil Symposium. The Dynamic Firm, Stockholm.

Stewart, F. (1977) *Technology and Underdevelopment*, London: Macmillan.

Sykes, A.O. (1995) *Product Standards for Internationally Integrated Goods Markets*, Washington: The Brookings Institution.

Walker, R. (1988) 'The geographical organization of production-systems', *Environment and Planning D: Society and Space* 6: 377–408.

Weber, A. (1909) *Über den standort der industrien, teil 1*, (translated by Carl Joachim Freidrich and published 1929 under the title: 'Theory of the location of industries', Chicago: University of Chicago Press), Tübingen: J.C.B. Mohr.

Wernerfelt, B. (1984) 'A resource-based view of the firm', *Strategic Management* 5: 171–180.

Whitley, R. (1994a) 'Societies, firms and markets: The social structuring of business systems', in Whitley, R. (ed.), *European business systems*, London: Sage Publications.

Whitley, R. (1994b) 'Dominant forms of economic organization in market economies', *Organization Studies*, No. 2, Vol. 15, pp. 153–182.

Whitley, R. (1996) 'The social construction of economic actors: institutions and types of firm in Europe and other market economies', in Whitley, R. (ed.), *The changing European Firm*, London: Routledge.

Zander, I. (1992) 'Patterns of technological specialization in an integrated Europe', *Business and Economic Studies on European Integration*, Vol. 4, INT, Copenhagen: Copenhagen Business School Press.

Chapter 2

On the new economic geography of post-Fordist learning economies

Bjørn T. Asheim

The new understanding of industrialisation as a territorial process, and innovation as a socially embedded process, i.e. underlining the importance of 'non-economic' factors such as history, culture and institutions for economic development, represents a substantial contribution from heterodox economics (in particular evolutionary economics and economic geography) to the economic orthodoxy. The challenge of bringing territoriality (back) into economics focuses on learning as a localised process, pointing at the importance of historical trajectories, at innovation as an interactive learning process, involving a critique of the linear model of innovation, and at clusters as the most efficient material contexts for interactive learning, emphasising the synergy effects of agglomeration. According to Amin and Thrift, this forces a re-evaluation of 'the significance of territoriality in economic globalisation' (Amin and Thrift 1995, 8).

The global context

The globalising world economy is characterised by two (partly) contradictory developmental tendencies. On the one hand we can identify the *neo-Fordist* development path, originating as the new international division of labour in the 1970s, of world-wide sourcing based on the principle of *comparative advantage* of relative lowest input costs (i.e. the relative best access to, and most efficient use of, 'natural' production factors), and enabled by developments in transportation and communication technologies, and further stimulated by liberalisation and de-regulation of international trade and financial markets. On the other hand we have the *post-Fordist* development path of the learning economy, in which global competition is based on the far more dynamic principle of *competitive advantage*, resting on 'making more productive use of inputs, which requires continual innovation' (Porter 1998, 78).

Global competition in post-Fordist learning economies based on the principle of competitive advantage, refers to the productive use of localised and unique combinations of inputs, which is often the result of specific historical and technological trajectories in regions and nations. Thus, the post-Fordist development path represents a seemingly paradoxical situation: 'the enduring competitive advantages in a global economy lie increasingly in local things – knowledge, relationships, motivation – that distant rivals cannot match' (Porter 1998, 78), i.e.

what could be called 'the globalization of economic activity and the localization of industries' (Enright 1999, 1).

The concept of a learning economy describes a qualitative change in the development of capitalist economies. This change is represented by the transition from Fordism to post-Fordism. Thus, the crux of the question of the degree of reality in the rhetoric of learning economies lies very much in the view on whether such a transition is really taking place or not. If one argues along with Lundvall (1996), Jessop (1994), Piore and Sabel (1984) and many others, it seems obvious that such an important transition is taking place, and the only theme for discussion is the speed, size and consequences of the transition, and the way the changes in the economy effect the political and institutional set up. However, it should still be underlined that the transition to post-Fordism is not complete, as important sectors globally as well as in countries both in the developed and underdeveloped world are characterised by neo-Fordist development tendencies.

An important factor contributing to the generalisation of the experiences of industrial districts is the new theoretical understanding of innovation as basically a social process, which could be referred to as a bottom-up *interactive innovation model* (Asheim and Isaksen 1997), much more adapted to the workings of the 'learning economy', where *knowledge* is the most fundamental resource and *learning* the most important process (Lundvall and Johnson 1994), than the previous dominating linear model of innovation. This new perspective implies a more sociological view, in which interactive learning is looked upon as a fundamental aspect of the innovation process, which, thus, cannot be understood independent of its institutional and cultural contexts (Lundvall 1992).

Lundvall and Borras explicitly argue that they prefer the 'learning economy' to the 'knowledge-based economy'. However, as knowledge, according to Lundvall and Johnson (1994), is considered the most fundamental resource, the learning economy is of course a knowledge-based economy. Furthermore, in order to underline the dynamic and rapid change in the contemporary globalising economy it is necessary also to pay attention to *knowledge creation* as a process of equal importance to learning and forgetting. In this context, however, it is important to remember that knowledge creation should not be restricted to formal R&D activities, but should also include how firms (e.g. in traditional industries) 'are innovative in the way they handle and develop pedestrian activities such as production organisation, logistics, marketing, sales, distribution, and industrial relations' (Malmberg and Maskell 1999, 6).

One problematic aspect of the 'learning economy' has been its focus being mainly on 'catching up' learning (i.e. learning by doing and using) based on incremental innovations, and not on radical innovations requiring the creation of new knowledge. In a long-term perspective it will be increasingly difficult for the reproduction and growth of a learning economy to primarily rely on incremental improvements of products and processes, for example in the form of imitation, and not on basically new products (i.e. radical innovations) as a result of, for example, an invention, even if Freeman underlines 'the tremendous importance of incremental innovation, learning by doing, by using and by interacting in the process of technical change and diffusion of innovations' (Freeman 1993, 9–10). This would, in fact, mean that imitation was considered more important than (a 'real') innovation, which would be even more problematic if it was based on exogenous learning. According to Nonaka and Reinmöller, 'no matter how great the efficiency and speed of exogenous learning, it will not substitute for the endogenous creation of knowledge. The faster knowledge is absorbed, the greater the dependence on the sources of knowledge becomes' (Nonaka and Reinmöller 1998, 425–26). Thus, what is more and more needed in a competitive globalising economy is the creation of new knowledge through searching, exploring and experimentation involving creativity as well as more systematic R&D in the development of new products and processes.

Clusters and the competitive advantage of regions

A dynamic, processual understanding of competitiveness clearly implies that enterprises in order to keep their position in the global market, must focus on developing their own core competencies (which also includes new competencies) through transforming themselves into learning organisations. But internal restructuring alone cannot sustain the competitiveness of firms in the long run. As firms are embedded in regional economies they are very much dependent on a favourable economic and industrial environment in general, and knowledge infrastructures at different geographical levels specifically. According to Porter 'untangling the paradox of location in a global economy reveals a number of key insights about how companies continually create competitive advantage. What happens *inside* companies is important, but clusters reveal that the immediate business environment *outside* companies play a vital role as well' (Porter 1998, 78).

Porter emphasises that the reproduction and development of competitive advantage requires continuous innovation, which in a learning economy is conceptualised as a localised interactive learning process, promoted by clustering, networking and inter-firm cooperation.

Thus, a strong case is made today that regional clusters are growing in importance as a mode of economic coordination in post-Fordist learning economies (Asheim and Isaksen 1997, Cooke 1994). The main argument for this is that regional clusters provide the best context for an innovation based learning economy due to the existence of localised learning and 'untraded interdependencies' among actors. In general, 'geographical distance, accessibility, agglomeration and the presence of externalities provide a powerful influence on knowledge flows, learning and innovation and this interaction is often played out within a regional arena' (Howells 1996, 18). Close cooperation with suppliers, subcontractors, customers and support institutions in the region will enhance the process of interactive learning and create an innovative milieu favourable to innovation and constant improvement. This influences the performance of the firms and strengthens the competitiveness of the clusters, and is increasingly seen as an important aspect of fostering regional competitive advantage.

The theoretical basis for this reasoning is to be found in agglomeration economies. Recently a discussion has been initiated concerning which type of territorial agglomerations are the most important in explaining spatial patterns of innovation diffusion and economic development (Malmberg 1997). In both conventional and Schumpeterian-based regional economics, agglomeration economies are understood in terms of external economies, normally specified as 'localisation' economies, i.e. 'the presence of same-sector businesses and employees' (Harrison et al. 1996, 233) referring to economies external to the firm but internal to the sector, and 'urbanisation economies', i.e. 'a diverse complex of economic and social institutions' (Harrison et al. 1996, 233) referring to economies external to the firm as well as the sector. The idea is used as a functional concept describing an intensification of the external economies of a production system by territorial agglomeration, i.e. external economies internal to a region. Harrison et al. (1996) argue, based on findings from a study of metalworking firms in the US, that the diversity of urbanisation economies are far more important than the sectoral specialisation of localisation economies in promoting innovative firm behavior with special reference to the adoption of new production technique. In another study Kelley and Helper (1996) find that both diversity (urbanisation) and specialisation (localisation) play a role in explaining firm's adoption of innovations, with the former being the most important (Harrison et al. 1996, 254). According to Harrison (1997), building on the work of Kelley and her colleagues, 'certain sources of geographic clustering are more likely to affect how (and even to what extent) nonadopters of various information technologies learn from spatially proximate prior adopters than are other forms of agglomeration. For relatively inexpensive stand-alone technologies, being located within a dense complex of similar firms – "localisation" ... – matters. So does proximity to institutes and colleges granting engineering degrees and to more diverse pools of labor – thereby conferring the benefits of ... "urbanisation economies". For other technologies, urbanisation matters, whereas localisation (specialisation in the sector) does not. Moreover, firm size and business organisation matter, with the smallest firms tending to be the most likely to learn from their neighbors' (Harrison 1997, 262).

This leads Harrison (1997) to say that he has 'always understood agglomeration to be important – but contingent' (Harrison 1997, 261). However, an important question, which has to be taken into account in this discussion, is what is understood by 'agglomeration'. When Harrison maintains that 'localisation' is 'the essential property of industrial districts' (Harrison 1997, 262), this is, of course, correct, but by only pointing to localisation economies he ignores Marshall's specific emphasis on the territorial aspects of agglomeration and their importance especially for innovation diffusion (Asheim 1994). Furthermore, Harrison et al. (1996) make the reservation that they 'have addressed only one aspect of agglomeration – the diffusion of a particular innovation through information-sharing presumed to be facilitated by proximity' (Harrison et al. 1996, 255). They have not, for example, looked into user-producer relationships, to investigate whether proximity promotes interactive learning in networks, and the evolution of such networking into long-term, inter-firm cooperation 'that might enhance firm performance and regional economic growth beyond what would have been expected without clustering' (Harrison et al. 1996, 255).

In contrast to regional economic theory, Marshall attached a more independent role to agglomeration economies underlining the quality of the territorial based social milieu of industrial districts that only indirectly affects the profits of firms. Among such factors, Marshall emphasised, in particular: the 'mutual knowledge and trust' that reduces transaction costs in the local production system; the 'industrial atmosphere' which facilitates the generation of skills and qualifications required by local industry; and the effect of both these aspects in promoting (incremental) innovations and innovation diffusion among SMEs in industrial districts (Asheim 1994).

The emphasis on the importance of regional clusters can, furthermore, find support from modern innovation theory, originating from evolutionary economics, which argues that 'regional production systems, industrial districts and technological districts are becoming increasingly important' (Lundvall 1992, 3), and from Porter, who emphasises that 'the process of clustering, and the interchange among industries in the cluster, also works best when the industries involved are geographically concentrated' (Porter 1990, 157). In 1998 Porter argues even stronger that 'a vibrant cluster can help any company in any industry compete in the most sophisticated ways, using the most advanced, relevant skills and technologies' (Porter 1998, 86).

However, what is a cluster? In a recent article Porter defines clusters as 'geographic concentrations of interconnected companies and institutions in a particular field. Clusters encompass an array of linked industries and other entities important to competition. They include, for example, suppliers of specialised inputs such as components, machinery, and services, and providers of specialised infrastructure. Clusters also often extend downstream to channels and customers and laterally to manufacturers of complementary products and to companies in industries related by skills, technologies, or common inputs. Finally, many clusters include governmental and other institutions – such as universities, standards-setting agencies, think tanks, vocational training providers, and trade associations – that provide specialised training, education, information, research, and technical support' (Porter 1998, 78).

This definition is rather similar to the one Brusco uses when he refers to 'the progressive specialisation of all the firms working in the same sector in the same area' (Brusco 1989, 259) as characteristic of industrial districts. With reference to products, it is possible to distinguish between three categories of firms in an industrial district: firms having a direct connection with the final market, 'stage firms', and firms of the vertically integrated sector (Brusco 1990, 14). These firms can be linked in three different ways: vertically or convergently, when different stages of a process are involved; laterally, where the same stage in a like process is involved; and diagonally, when service processes are involved (Bellandi 1989, 137). In addition Porter adds organisations and institutions which resemble an 'industrial district Mark II', which Brusco calls industrial districts with considerable government intervention, representing a development from the original 'industrial district Mark I' without local government intervention (Brusco 1990). An important part of this extended cluster definition is the incorporation of governance structures, which, in general, refers to, 'the degree of hierarchy and leadership (or their opposites, collaboration and cooperation)' in a network (Storper and Harrison 1990, 10).

As a contrast, Porter's original cluster concept was basically an economic concept indicating that 'a nation's successful industries are usually linked through vertical (buyer/supplier) or horizontal (common customers, technology etc.) relationships' (Porter 1990, 149). These ideas are more or less the same as the ones Perroux presented in the early 1950s. Perroux argued that it was possible to talk about 'growth poles' (or 'development poles' at a later stage in his writing) in 'abstract economic spaces' defined as the vertical relationships of a production system as well as the horizontal relationships of a branch, i.e. firms which are linked together with an innovative 'key industry' to form an industrial complex. According to Perroux, the growth potential and competitiveness of growth poles can be intensified by territorial agglomeration (Haraldsen 1994; Perroux 1970). However, in my view there is a need to apply clusters in both conceptualisations, as it is a quite normal situation to find (geographical) clusters of specialised branches being part of a national (economic) cluster of the same branches (e.g. the Norwegian shipping cluster, which is a national economic cluster (Reve et al. 1992), but which, in part, is constituted by geographical clusters of specialised branches making up the Norwegian shipping cluster).

What this extension of the definition of the concept of cluster also indicates is a deepening and widening of the degree and form of cooperation taking place in a cluster. The original and simplest form of cooperation within a cluster can often be described as a *territorial* integrated input-output (value chain) relations, which could be supported by informal, social networking as is the case with Marshallian agglomeration economies, but which could also take the form of arms-length market transactions between a capacity subcontractor and the client firm. A typical example of this would be the original industrial district ('industrial district Mark I'). The next step of formally establishing inter-firm networks, is represented by a purposeful, *functional* integration of value chain collaboration as well as building up a competence network between the collaborating firms. A distinction between clusters defined as input-output relations and networks is that *proximity* is the most important constituting variable in the first case, while networking represents a step towards more *systemic* (i.e. planned) forms of cooperation, as well as a development from vertical to horizontal forms of cooperation, which more efficiently promotes learning and innovation in the systems. The development towards more systemic forms of cooperation is taken a step forward by establishing systems, either in the form of production or innovation systems, which are characterised by *system* integration, where the principle of integration is based on the system world of the economy and the state, which can extend across time-space. Or as Nonaka and Reinmöller put it, 'the concepts of clusters of industrial districts and networks are also attempts to describe interorganisational phenomena. Industrial districts are accumulations of interdependent companies located near each other (the condition of proximity). Networks are a concept focused on interorganisational relations. ... Unlike the concept of industrial districts, the concept of networks does not necessarily entail the condition of proximity' (Nonaka and Reinmöller 1998, 406).

In the promotion of innovation supportive regions the inter-linking of cooperative partnerships ranging from work organisations inside firms to different sectors of society, understood as 'regional development coalitions', will be of strategic importance. By a development coalition is understood a bottom-up, horizontally based cooperation between different actors within and between firms and organisations in a local or regional setting but also generally the mobilisation of the resources of society, to promote innovation, change and improvement (Ennals and Gustavsen 1999). The concept of development coalition incorporates all the previous forms of integration (i.e. territorial, functional and system integration), and adds *social* integration, as the formation of a regional development coalition takes place on a societal level of the system as well as the lifeworld, where the co-existence and co-presence of actors in space and time is of vital importance in constituting a 'learning region' (Asheim 2001). Generally, the innovative capacity at the regional level can be promoted through identifying 'the economic logic by which milieu fosters innovation' (Storper 1995, 203). This deepening and widening of the degree and form of cooperation constituted by a progressive organisational and institutional development from clusters to development coalitions within a region underlines the strategic role played by *social capital.*

Innovation as culturally and institutionally contextualised processes

Social capital can depend on the level of 'civicness' in the civil society as well as on the degree of formal organisation in the system world. According to Putnam, social capital means 'features of social organization, such as networks, norms, and trust, that facilitate action and cooperation for mutual benefit' (Putnam 1993, 35–36). Social capital represents an extension of the 'capital' concept from the classical economists use of *physical* capital (i.e. assets that generate income) and the neo-classical economics introduction of *human* capital, focusing on the importance of education and training of the labour force, to capture the role *social* and *cultural* aspects in a broad sense are playing in influencing economic performance. As such, social capital can be viewed as a structural property of larger groups (Woolcock 1998), as it is a common value to several people, and also represents a set of expectations, obligations, and social norms which govern the behaviour of individuals in society (Greve 1999). The characteristics of such social capital – within an individual organisation or within a region – will contribute to determine the collectiveness of learning and knowledge accumulation.

Strategic in this theoretical reasoning is the understanding of interactive innovation processes as culturally and institutionally contextualised. What this broader understanding of innovation as a social, non-linear and interactive learning process means, is a change in the evaluation of the importance and role played by socio-cultural and institutional structures in regional development from being looked upon as mere reminiscences from pre-capitalist civil societies (although still productive), to be viewed as necessary prerequisites for regions in order to be innovative and competitive in a post-Fordist learning economy.

This perspective precisely addresses the importance of the embeddedness of the economy in broader societal, non-economic factors for the performance of national and regional economies. The 'Marshallian' view of the basic structures of industrial districts predates the idea of 'embeddedness' as a key analytical concept in understanding the workings of the districts (Granovetter 1985). It is precisely the embeddedness in broader socio-cultural factors, originating in pre-capitalist civil societies, that represents the material basis for Marshall's view of agglomeration economies as the specific territorial aspect of geographically agglomerated economic activity. By defining agglomeration economies as socially and territorially embedded properties of an area, Marshall abandons 'the pure logic of economic mechanisms and introduces a sociological approach in his analysis' (Dimou 1994, 27). Harrison points out that 'the industrial district model posits a very strong form of the embedding of economic (business) relations into a deeper social fabric, providing a force powerful enough to provide for the reproduction of even so apparently paradoxical a practice as cooperative competition' (Harrison 1991, 34), and emphasises that this mode of theorising is fundamentally different from the one found in conventional regional economics or in any other neoclassically-based agglomeration theory (Harrison 1991).

One of the major contributions in the formulation of the neo-Marshallian approach to industrial districts by Italian industrial and regional economists was the strong focus on the social and territorial dimensions of the concept (Asheim 2000). Becattini, perhaps the most well-known of these Italian economists, has termed the Marshallian industrial district 'a socio-economic notion' (Becattini 1989), and has defined the industrial district as 'a socio-territorial entity which is characterised by the active presence of both a community of people and a population of firms in one naturally and historically bounded area. In the district, unlike in other environments, such as manufacturing towns, community and firms tend to merge' (Becattini 1990, 38). This contribution to the development of the theory of industrial districts is also recognised by Martin who maintains that these Italian economists 'differ significantly from their spatial agglomeration and regional convergence modelling counterpart in that their approach is firmly rooted in detailed empirical work on specific regions and stress the social, cultural and institutional foundations of local industrial growth' (Martin 1999, 79).

However, in other social sciences this perspective is further developed. Soskice (1999) argues that different national institutional frameworks support different forms of economic activity, i.e. that coordinated market economies have their competitive advantage in diversified quality production (Streeck 1992), while uncoordinated market economies are most competitive in industries characterised by radical innovative activities. Following Soskice, the learning economies of the Nordic model can be referred to as coordinated market economies in contrast to what he calls uncoordinated or liberal market economies, where the main determinant is the degree of nonmarket coordination and cooperation, which exists inside the business sphere and between private and public actors; as well as the degree to which labour remains 'incorporated' and the financial system is able to supply long term finance (Soskice 1999). In a comparison between coordinated market economies such as Sweden, Germany and Switzerland on the one hand, and uncoordinated ones such as the US on the other, he found that the coordinated economies performed best in the production of 'relatively complex products, involving complex production processes and after sales-service in well-established industries' (e.g. the machine tool industry), and that the US performed best in industries producing complex systemic product such as IT and defence technology and advanced financial and producer services, where the importance of scientific based knowledge from national innovation systems based on the linear model is significant (Soskice 1999, 113–114).

This could be further specified by Whitley's concepts 'proximate economic institutions' and 'background social institutions' (Whitley 1992). Proximate institutions refers to institutions which are directly integrated parts of the economic system, and, thus, represent important elements of the national institutional framework of the economy. Soskice (1999) argues convincingly that this framework must be seen as resulting from the historical evolution of – as well as critical 'interlocking complementarities' between – finance and governance, education, industrial and intercompany relations (Soskice 1999), creating different labour markets, educational characteristics (i.e. vocational versus formal or 'dual systems' (Whitley 1992)), transaction environments and levels of opportunistic behaviour, and different profit preferences (the time perspective of investments), thus, constraining the ability of management to allocate resources to learning. Background institutions, on the other hand, are factors which often show regional differences as they basically are part of the lifeworld dominated civil society. According to Whitley these factors are typically 'reproduced through the family, religious organisations and the education systems, and often manifests considerable continuity from pre-industrial societies' (Whitley 1992, 20). Such background social factors 'structure the general pattern of trust, cooperation, identity and subordination ... (that) ... underpin the organisation of all economic systems and form the background to industrialisation and the development of modern market economies' (Whitley 1992, 20). They can, thus, represent important elements in the constitution of localised competitive advantages. According to Porter, 'differences in national economic structures, values, cultures, institutions, and histories contribute profoundly to competitive success' (Porter 1990, 19).

Thus, what Soskice basically argues is that competitive strength in certain markets – e.g. production characterised as 'diversified quality production' – is based on problem solving knowledge developed through interactive learning and accumulated collectively in the workforce (Soskice 1999), which in turn represents a situation in direct conflict with unilateral control over work processes (a preference generated by certain finance and governance systems); while competitive strength in other markets – e.g. markets characterised by a high rate of change through radical and systemic innovations – is based on the institutional freedom as well as financial incentives to continuously restructure production systems in light of new market opportunities (Gilpin 1996). While coordinated market economies on the macro level support cooperative, long-term and consensus-based relations between private as well as public actors, liberal market economies inhibit the development of these relations but instead offer the opportunity to quickly adjust the formal structure to new requirements. Such institutional specificities both contribute to the formation of divergent 'business systems', and constitute the context within which different organisational forms with different mechanisms for learning, knowledge accumulation and knowledge appropriation have evolved (Asheim and Herstad 2000).

In addition, the coordinated market economies promotes long-term employment, and enables the individual worker to accumulate firm and industry specific skills and use this as a basis for hierarchical mobility based on non-transparent skills – in sum solving 'the relational requirements of diversified quality production' (Soskice 1999) by forming the institutional basis for the development of social capital (Asheim and Herstad 2000).

Thus, the institutional competitive advantage of the coordinated market economies seems to be found within a further development and upgrading of existing industries and technological trajectories (e.g. manufacturing industries), which are characterised by the interactive innovation model, and where long-term cooperation between workers and firms as well as between firms and between firms and the knowledge infrastructure is of strategic importance to promote technological development through interactive learning. This could also explain the seemingly paradoxical situation of low tech industries (e.g. the furniture industry) flourishing and reproducing their international competitive advantage in high cost countries such as Denmark, Germany and Italy, which all can be described as coordinated market economies.

Forms of knowledge and localised learning

In the perspective of looking at organisations and their innovative activities as culturally and institutionally contextualised, strategic parts of learning processes, thus, emerge as a localised, and not a placeless, process. This constitutes important parts of the knowledge base and infrastructure of firms and regions, pointing to the role of historical trajectories. In a similar way, Malmberg (1997) argues that 'one of the few remaining genuinely localized phenomena in this increasingly "slippery" global space economy is precisely the "stickiness" of some forms of knowledge and learning processes' (Malmberg 1997, 574; Markusen 1996).

However, localised learning is not only based on tacit knowledge, as contextual knowledge also consists of 'sticky', disembodied codified knowledge. Disembodied knowledge, referring to knowledge and know-how which are not embodied in machinery, but are the result of positive externalities of the innovation process (de Castro and Jensen-Butler 1993), is often constituted by a combination of place-specific experience based, tacit knowledge and competence, artisan skills and R&D-based knowledge (Asheim 1999). This implies that the adaptability of the contextual form of codified knowledge is dependent upon, and limited by, artisan skills and tacit knowledge. Thus, I agree with Lundvall and Borras, who claim that 'it is the constitution of new ensembles of codified and tacit knowledge which is in question rather than a massive transformation of tacit into codified knowledge' (Lundvall and Borras 1999, 33). In this context it is important to emphasise that 'whilst knowledge in the form of embodied technical progress can be exported independently of social institutions, such knowledge in its disembodied form cannot be absorbed independently of such institutions' (de Castro and Jensen-Butler 1993, 3).

Thus, the strict dichotomy normally applied between codified and tacit knowledge can be quite misleading both from a theoretical as well as from a policy point of view. This is especially the case if localised learning is primarily said to be based on tacit knowledge. A claim for the superiority of tacit knowledge on such a ground could lead to a fetishisation of the potentials of local production systems, not discovering the problems such systems could face due to their lack of strategic, goal oriented actions and strategies, which, basically, has to be supported by codified knowledge (e.g. formal R&D) (Amin and Cohendet 1999). The category of localised, disembodied knowledge represents a concept which would be able to grasp the important basis for endogenous regional development, represented by firms relying on localised learning, but building this localised learning on a strategic use of codified, R&D-based knowledge in addition to tacit knowledge.

This broad understanding of knowledge creation could be further substantiated by introducing differences with respect to the *origin* as well as the *character* of knowledge creation between industries (Laestadius 1998). Concerning the origin of knowledge creation one must distinguish between typical high tech industries, which is based on academic R&D, while new knowledge in medium and low tech industries more often is the result of 'improved craft and traditional engineering skills on the shop floor' (Laestadius 1998, 222).

Concerning the character of knowledge creation Laestadius (1998) makes the analytical distinction between *analytical* and *synthetical* activities. By analytical activities he refers to 'normal practice in the natural sciences. To a large extent, this consists of a narrowing of the focus to isolated phenomena and concentrating efforts on understanding and explaining the inner details of the system. This is very close to the understanding of the creation of new (R&D-based (my addition)) knowledge' (Laestadius 1998, 222–23). In contrast to this, synthetical activities 'are directed toward building and designing systems through integrating components into complex wholes. This usually necessitates the understanding of the subsystems, although the intellectual efforts are directed toward the system and its interfaces rather than its components' (Laestadius 1998, 223).

Disembodied knowledge, which is highly immobile in geographical terms, is generally based on a high level of individual skill and experience, collective technical culture and a well-developed institutional framework. Storper (1997) defines such contexts as 'territorialization', understood as a distinctive subset of territorial agglomerations, where 'economic viability is rooted in assets (including practices and relations) that are not available in many other places and cannot easily or rapidly be created or imitated in places that lack them' (Storper 1997, 170). This view is supported by Porter, who argues that 'competitive advantage is created and sustained through a highly localised process' (Porter 1990, 19).

Lundvall (1996) maintains that 'the increasing emergence of knowledge-based networks of firms, research groups and experts may be regarded as an expression of the growing importance of knowledge which is codified in local rather than universal codes. ... The skills necessary to understand and use these codes will often be developed by those allowed to join the network and to take part in a process of interactive learning' (Lundvall 1996, 10–11). Such skills required for knowledge interfacing within and between collective learning processes tend to be highly time-space specific. Interactive, collective learning is based on intra- or inter-organisational routines, norms and conventions regulating collective action as well as tacit mechanisms for the absorption of codified knowledge. This requires that the actors in question have close connections to the 'local codes', which collective tacit as well as disembodied codified knowledge is based on. Thus, depending on the actual architecture of a productive knowledge base, the ability to interpret local codes will be critical for the integration of the operations of a firm within an inter-firm network (Asheim and Herstad 2000).

Following this line of reasoning it could be argued that the combination of contextual disembodied knowledge, 'untraded interdependencies' and different organisational and institutional frameworks can constitute the basis for localised learning (i.e. specific regional and national technological trajectories based on non-substitutable and specialised, 'sticky' capabilities) in a globalising learning economy, and, thus, can represent important regional and national context conditions with a potentially favourable impact on their innovativeness and competitiveness (Asheim and Cooke 1998). This would represent an important modification of the argument that 'ubiquitification' (i.e. the global availability of new production technologies and organisational designs at more or less the same cost (Malmberg and Maskell 1999), as an outcome of globalisation and codification processes, in general tends to 'undermine the competitiveness of firms in the high-cost areas of the world' (Malmberg and Maskell 1999, 6).

Types of regional innovation networks and systems

Such a constellation of specific locational assets can be supported by regional innovation systems which must be understood in the context of creating a policy instrument aiming at a systematic promotion of localised learning processes in order to secure the innovativeness and competitive advantage of regional economies (Freeman 1995, Cooke 1995). According to Storper and Scott, 'a new 'heterodox' economic policy framework has emerged in which significant dimensions of economic policy at large are being reformulated in terms of regional policies' (Storper and Scott 1995, 513).

However, it is important, analytically as well as politically, to distinguish between different types of regional innovation systems. On the one hand, we find innovation systems that could be called *regionalised* national innovation systems, i.e. parts of the production structure and the institutional infrastructure *located* in a region, but *functionally* integrated in, or equivalent to, national (or international) innovation systems, which is more or less based on a top-down, linear model of innovation. On the other hand we can either identify *networked* innovation *systems* constituted by the parts of the production structure and institutional set-up that is *territorially* integrated in a particular region, and built up in accordance with a bottom-up, interactive innovation model (Asheim and Isaksen 1997), or innovation *networks*, which are *embedded* in the socio-cultural structures of a region, characterised by a 'fusion' of the economy with society (Piore and Sabel 1984), and based on bottom-up, interactive learning. To be able to talk about territorially integrated, regional innovation systems the national, functionally integrated, techno-economic and political-institutional structures must be 'contextualised' through interaction with the territorially embedded, socio-cultural and socio-economic structures (Asheim 1995).

The networked regional innovation system is different from the embedded innovation network due to the *systemic* dimension of the former, which requires that the relationships between the elements of the system must involve a degree of long-term, stable interdependence. This implies that it is based on *system* integration, i.e. 'reciprocity between actors or collectivities across extended time-space' (Giddens 1984, 28), and not on *social* integration, i.e. 'reciprocity between actors in context of co-presence' (Giddens 1984, 28). A further consequence of this is that networked regional innovation system cannot be *embedded* in the community, as embeddedness builds on *social* integration (Granovetter 1985). However, it is still an example of a bottom-up, interactive innovation model, and, thus, represents an alternative to regionalised national innovation systems. The systemic, networked approach to regional innovation systems brings together regional governance mechanisms, universities, research institutes, technology transfer and training agencies, consultants and other firms acting in concert on innovation matters (Asheim and Cooke 1999). As such it could be said to represent a step towards the formation of 'learning regions' understood as 'regional development coalitions' (Asheim 2001).

Examples of a regionalised national innovation system could be the R&D laboratories of large firms, governmental research institutes, technopoles or 'science parks', often located in the proximity of technical universities and based on the thinking of the linear model of innovation (Asheim 1995; Henry et al. 1995). In general science parks tend to have weak local cooperative environments, which result in a failure to develop inter-firm networking and interactive learning in the parks, and, in addition, have rather few linkages to local industry, while technopoles are characterised by a limited degree of innovative interaction between firms in the poles, and by vertical subcontracting relationships with external firms (Asheim and Cooke 1998). This all implies a lack of networking capacity and leads to questions about their capability for promoting innovativeness and competitiveness on a broad scale in local industries (especially the SMEs) in particular regions, as a prerequisite for endogenous regional development.

The best examples of territorially embedded, regional innovation networks are SMEs in industrial districts in the Third Italy, which build their competitive advantage on localised learning processes. Of significant importance in this context is the understanding of industrial districts as a 'social and economic whole', where the success of the districts is as dependent on broader social and institutional aspects (i.e. the socio-cultural embeddedness) as on economic factors in a narrow sense (Pyke and Sengenberger 1990). Bellandi emphasises that the economies of the districts originate from the thick local texture of interdependencies between small firms and the local community (Bellandi 1989), and Becattini maintains that 'the firms become rooted in the territory, and this result cannot be conceptualised independently of its historical development' (Becattini 1990, 40). The rationale for territorially embedded networks is, therefore, to provide a bottom-up, network-based support for the 'adaptive technological and organisational learning in a territorial context' (Storper and Scott 1995, 513). However, the weakness of such regional innovation networks is their innovative capacity as they basically rely on incremental innovations, and have a low capacity for generating radical innovations due to a lack of strong R&D-based research institutions in the regional knowledge infrastructure as well as in the dominating clusters of SMEs (Asheim 1996).

The networked regional innovation systems combine elements from the regionalised national innovation system and the embedded, regional innovation network. They represent a planned interactive enterprise-support approach to innovation policy relying on close university-industry cooperation. Large and smaller firms establish network relationships with other firms, universities, research institutes, and government agencies. Examples of such networked innovation systems can either be found in regions in Germany, Austria, and the Nordic countries, where this model has been the more typical to implement (Asheim and Cooke 1999), or in later stages in the evolution of industrial districts, which were previously characterised by territorially embedded, innovation networks. Emilia-Romagna could serve as examples of the latter type of development path towards the creation of networked regional innovation systems.

Challenges from globalisation and the 'new economy' and the future role of regional innovation systems

Faced by the challenges from globalisation and the emerging 'new economy', what is the potential and future role of regional innovation systems based on the interactive innovation model? Key questions in this discussion are partly how new the 'new economy' really is, and partly if, to what extent and in what way it may transcend the globalising learning economy.

In the ongoing globalisation process two parallel tendencies can be identified: A substitution of local systems with global systems as well as a transition from production systems to learning systems, which – taken together – represent a development from local production systems (e.g. industrial districts) to global learning systems, often orchestrated by transnational companies (TNCs). The first tendency is partly caused by the increasing importance of TNCs in the globalising network economy, and partly by the globalisation and codification of knowledge. As already referred to, some authors argue that as a result of globalisation and codification processes knowledge becomes increasingly ubiquitous, which implies that the competitive advantage of high-cost regions and nations are steadily being undermined. In this article it is maintained that much strategic knowledge, tacit as well as codified, is disembodied, and, thus, remains 'sticky', and that important parts of the learning process continue to be localised as a result of the enabling role of geographical proximity and local institutions in stimulating interactive learning.

The second tendency is a result of the increased knowledge intensity of products. However, firstly, knowledge intensity cannot be equated with R&D-intensity, and, secondly, the new view of innovation as an interactive learning process makes the traditional distinction of the linear innovation model between high-tech and low-tech sectors, based on the intramural R&D expenditures of the end product, irrelevant, as all branches and sectors can be innovative in a broader sense (Porter 1998). Furthermore, in order to better understand the complex interactions and relationships which characterise the innovation processes of firms in different industries within vertical disintegrated, global production systems of the post-Fordist learning economy, it would be more theoretically adequate and empirically relevant to apply an economic cluster perspective on the knowledge base of firms, where the whole value system of a firm or value chain of a product is taken into consideration, when the knowledge intensity of a product is determined, or the relevant knowledge infrastructure in support if its innovative activity is evaluated (e.g. fish farming where salmon as such cannot be considered to be a very advanced product, but a closer examination discloses that the knowledge base of the production to a large extent is R&D-based).

This contextualised view on innovation will also have implications for the evaluation of the impact of new technologies such as IT and bio-tech on the constitution of the so called 'new economy'. I will argue that the fundamental divide in the modern economy is the transition from Fordism to post-Fordism, and that the IT and bio-tech based 'new economy' more should be understood as a new techno-economic paradigm than as a fundamentally new way to conceptualise the capitalist economy, i.e. the same position as the definition of post-Fordism as a learning economy takes (Lundvall and Johnson 1994). According to Freeman and Perez (1986), the term 'new techno-economic paradigm' can only be used when the new technology has been diffused to all sectors of society. In general, this points to the importance of the diffusion process of new technology, which implies that it is possible to talk about the 'new economy', understood as a new techno-economic paradigm, characterising a society without finding any significant manufacturing of the carriers of the new economy, e.g. IT and bio-tech.

A striking example of this could be found through a comparison between Norway on the one hand and Sweden and Finland on the other hand. These three Nordic countries have the highest penetration of IT-technology when it comes to use of PCs, mobile phones, internet and IT-based services in general (e-banking, credit card use etc.). However, the wide diffusion of this new technology seems to be totally independent on the actual production, as Norway has next to no production, while Finland (Nokia) and Sweden (Ericsson) are among the world leaders. Thus, the big potential for exploiting IT-technology in value creating production is not primarily to be found in the establishment of new general based IT-activities (i.e. hardware and software production), but in the use of IT in upgrading traditional economic activity within industry, service and public administration in order to exploit the efficiency gains from the use of IT-technology through organisational innovations, which often requires the production of specialised software. This is typically carried out in the proximity of the industry it is aimed for (e.g. software for the furniture industry close to a region specialising in furniture production).

Diffusion (exploitation/utilisation) of knowledge is not dependent on techno-economic subsystems, but on the socio-institutional framework. Thus, in order to generate economic growth and increased employment, as a basis for achieving social cohesion, focus must be on the absorption capacity of societies through improving the potentials for (regional) knowledge production and learning in a society. This points to the importance of non-economic factors such as culture (social capital) and the organisational and institutional framework (e.g. educational policies securing a well educated population through an equal, free of cost and proximate access to high quality educational facilities, labour market regulations etc.) for economic performance.

Conclusion

Earlier research on regional innovation systems (Isaksen 1999) has on the one hand demonstrated that the innovative activity of firms is still based on regional localised resources such as a specialised labour market and labour force, subcontractor and supplier systems, a unique combination of different types of knowledge, local learning processes and spill over effects, local traditions for cooperation and entrepreneurial attitude, supporting agencies and organisations and presence of important customers and users. Thus we could conclude that the policy lessons from this research to a large extent would still be valid as long as it is relevant to understand the contemporary economy as a globalising learning economy. This is especially true with respect to the interactive model of innovation, which was considered the most relevant for both large and small manufacturing firms.

On the other hand the research revealed that the regional level is neither always nor even normally sufficient for firms to stay innovative and competitive, and pointed at the additional importance of innovation systems at the national and international level for firms in regional clusters. This tendency will undoubtedly be reinforced by the globalisation process and the emerging 'new economy', which will have consequences for the relevant types and scales of innovation systems in order to accommodate the changes and adapt and modify the systems. The combination of a value chain perspective on knowledge intensity and global learning systems requires a multi-level approach to innovation systems, i.e. that different forms of knowledge must be accessed at different parts of the knowledge infrastructure at different geographical scales. This will especially challenge the future role of regional innovation systems with respect to the capacity for upgrading the knowledge base of firms in regional clusters.

References

Amin, A. and N. Thrift (1995): 'Territoriality in the global political economy'. *Nordisk Samhällsgeografisk Tidskrift*, No. 20, 3–16.

Amin, A. and P. Cohendet (1999): 'Learning and adaptation in decentralised business networks'. *Environment and Planning D: Society and Space*, 17, 87–104.

Asheim, B.T. (1994): 'Industrial districts, inter-firm co-operation and endogenous technological development: the experience of developed countries', in *Technological dynamism in industrial districts: An alternative approach to industrialization in developing countries?* UNCTAD, New York and Geneva, 91–142.

Asheim, B.T. (1995): 'Regionale innovasjonssystem – en sosialt og territorielt forankret teknologipolitikk'. *Nordisk Samhällsgeografisk Tidskrift*, No. 20, 17–34.

Asheim, B.T. (1996): 'Industrial districts as "learning regions": A condition for prosperity?' *European Planning Studies*, 4, 4, 379–400.

Asheim, B.T. (1999): 'TESA bedrifter på Jæren – fra et territorielt innovasjonsnettverk til funksjonelle konserndannelser?', in Isaksen, A. (ed.), *Regionale innovasjonssystemer. Innovasjon og læring i 10 regionale næringsmiljøer*. STEP-report R-02, The STEP-group, Oslo, 131–152.

Asheim, B.T. (2000): 'Industrial districts: The contributions of Marshall and beyond', in Clark, G. et al. (eds.), *The Oxford Handbook of Economic Geography*, Oxford University Press, Oxford, 413–431.

Asheim, B.T. (2001): 'Learning regions as development coalitions: Partnership as governance in European workfare states?' *Concepts and Transformation*, No. 1.

Asheim, B.T. and A. Isaksen (1997): 'Location, agglomeration and innovation: Towards regional innovation systems in Norway'. *European Planning Studies*, 5, 3, 299–330.

Asheim, B.T. and P. Cooke (1998): 'Localised innovation networks in a global economy: A comparative analysis of endogenous and exogenous regional development approaches'. *Comparative Social Research*, Vol. 17, JAI Press, Stamford, CT, 199–240.

Asheim, B.T. and P. Cooke (1999): 'Local learning and interactive innovation networks in a global economy', in Malecki, E. and P. Oinäs (eds.), *Making connections*. Ashgate, Aldershot, 145–178.

Asheim, B.T. and S.J. Herstad (2000): 'Regional clusters under international duress: Between local learning and global corporations'. Paper submitted to special issue of *Industry and Innovation*.

Becattini, G. (1989): 'Sectors and/or districts: some remarks on the conceptual foundations of industrial economics', in Goodman, E. and Bamford, J. (eds.), *Small Firms and Industrial Districts in Italy*. Routledge, London, 123–135.

Becattini, G. (1990): 'The Marshallian industrial district as a socio-economic notion', in Pyke, F. et al (eds.), *Industrial districts and inter-firm cooperation in Italy*. International Institute for Labour Studies, Geneva, 37–51.

Bellandi, M. (1989): 'The industrial district in Marshall', in Goodman, E. & Bamford, J. (eds.), *Small Firms and Industrial Districts in Italy*. Routledge, London, 136–152.

Brusco, S. (1989): 'A policy for industrial districts', in Goodman, E. and Bamford, J. (eds.), *Small Firms and Industrial Districts in Italy*. Routledge, London, 259–269.

Brusco, S. (1990): 'The idea of the industrial district: Its genesis', in Pyke, F. et al. (eds.), *Industrial Districts and Inter-firm Co-operation in Italy*. International Institute for Labour Studies, Geneva, 10–19.

de Castro, E. and C. Jensen-Butler (1993): *Flexibility, routine behaviour and the neo-classical model in the analysis of regional growth*. Department of Political Science, University of Aarhus, Denmark.

Cooke, P. (1994): 'The co-operative advantage of regions'. Paper presented for the conference on 'Regions, institutions, and technology: Reorganising economic geography in Canada and the Anglo-American World', University of Toronto, September 1994.

Cooke, P. (1995): 'Planet Europe: network approaches to regional innovation and technology management'. *Technology Management*, Vol. 2, 18–30.

Dimou, P. (1994): 'The industrial district: A stage of a diffuse industrialization process – the case of Roanne'. *European Planning Studies*, 2, 1, 23–38.

Dosi, G. (1988): 'The nature of the innovative process', in Dosi, G., et al. (eds.): *Technical change and economic theory*. Pinter, London, 221–238.

Ennals, R. and B. Gustavsen (1999): *Work Organization and Europe as a Development Coalition*. John Benjamins Publishing Company, Amsterdam.

Enright, M. (1999): 'The globalization of competition and the localization of competitive advantage: Policies towards regional clustering', in Hood, N. and Young, S. (eds.), *Globalization of multinational enterprise activity and economic development*. Macmillan, London.

Freeman, C. (1993): 'The political economy of the long wave'. Paper presented at EAPE 1993 conference on 'The economy of the future: ecology, technology, institutions'. Barcelona, October 1993.

Freeman, C. (1995): 'The "national system of innovation" in historical perspective'. *Cambridge Journal of Economics*, 19, 5–24.

Freeman, C. and C. Perez (1986): 'The diffusion of technical innovations and changes of techno-economic paradigm'. Paper presented to the Conference on innovation diffusion. Venice, March 1986.

Giddens, A. (1984): *The constitution of society. Outline of the theory of structuration*. Polity Press, Cambridge.

Gilpin, R. (1996): 'Economic Evolution of National Systems'. *International Studies Quarterly*, 40, 411–43.

Granovetter, M. (1985): 'Economic action and social structure: The problem of embeddedness'. *American Journal of Sociology*, 91, 3, 481–510.

Greve, A. (1999): 'The role of social capital in the development of technology'. Paper presented at a conference on 'Mobilising knowledge in technology management: Competence construction in the strategising and organising of technical change'. Copenhagen, Denmark, October 1999.

Haraldsen, T. (1994): *Teknologi, økonomi og rom – en teoretisk analyse av relasjoner mellom industrielle og territorielle endringsprosesser.* Doctoral dissertation, Department of social and economic geography, Lund University, Lund University Press, Lund.

Harrison, B. (1991): 'Industrial districts: Old wine in new bottles?' *Working paper* 90–35. School of urban and public affairs, Carnegie-Mellon University, Pittsburg.

Harrison, B. (1997): *Lean and mean.* Guilford Press, New York.

Harrison, B. et al. (1996): 'Innovative firm behavior and local milieu: Exploring the intersection of agglomeration, firm effects, and technological change'. *Economic Geography*, 72, 3, 233–258.

Henry, N. et al. (1995): 'Along the road: R&D, society and space'. *Research Policy*, 24, 707–726.

Howells, J. (1996): 'Regional systems of innovation?' Paper presented at HCM Conference on 'National systems of innovation or the globalisation of technology?' Lessons for the public and business sector', ISRDS-CNR, Rome, April.

Isaksen, A. (ed.) (1999): *Regionale innovasjonssystemer. Innovasjon og læring i 10 regionale næringsmiljøer.* STEP-report R-02, The STEP-group, Oslo.

Jessop, B. (1994): 'Post-Fordism and the State'. In Amin, A. (ed.), *Post-Fordism. A reader.* Blackwell, Oxford, 251–279.

Kelley, M. and S. Helper (1996): 'Firm size and capabilities, regional agglomeration, and the adoption of new technology'. *Industrial Performance Center Working Paper*, MIT, Cambridge.

Laestadius, S. (1998): 'Technology level, knowledge formation and industrial competence in paper manufacturing', in Eliasson, G. et al. (eds.) *Microfoundations of economic growth. A Schumpeterian perspective.* The University of Michigan Press, Ann Arbor, 212–226.

Lundvall, B.-Å. (ed.) (1992): Introduction in *National systems of innovation.* Pinter, London, 1–19.

Lundvall, B.-Å. (1996): 'The social dimension of the learning economy'. *DRUID Working Papers*, No. 96–1, Aalborg University, Aalborg.

Lundvall, B.-Å. and B. Johnson (1994): 'The learning economy'. *Journal of Industry Studies*, 1, 2, 23–42.

Lundvall, B.-Å. and S. Borras (1999): *The globalising learning economy: Implications for innovation policy.* Office for Official Publications of the European Communities, Luxembourg.

Malmberg, A. (1997): 'Industrial geography: location and learning'. *Progress in Human Geography*, 21, 4, 573–582.

Malmberg, A. and P. Maskell (1999): Guest editorial: 'Localised learning and regional economic development'. *European Urban and Regional Studies*, 6, 1, 5–8.

Markusen, A. (1996): 'Sticky places in slippery space: A typology of industrial districts'. *Economic Geography*, 72, 3, 293–313.

Martin, R. (1999): 'The new "geographical turn" in economics: some critical reflections'. *Cambridge Journal of Economics*, 23, 65–91.

Nonaka, I. and P. Reinmöller (1998): 'The legacy of learning. Toward endogenous knowledge creation for Asian economic development'. *WZB Jahrbuch 1998*, 401–433.

Perroux, F. (1970): 'Note on the concept of growth poles'. In McKee, D. et al. (eds.), *Regional economics: Theory and practice.* Free Press, New York, 93–103.

Piore, M. and C. Sabel (1984): *The second industrial divide: Possibilities for prosperity.* Basic Books, New York.

Porter, M. (1990): *The competitive advantage of nations.* Macmillan, London.

Porter, M. (1998): 'Clusters and the new economics of competition'. *Harvard Business Review,* November–December, 77–90.

Putnam, R. (1993): *Making democracy work.* Princeton University Press, Princeton.

Pyke, F. and W. Sengenberger (1990): Introduction, in Pyke, F. et al. (eds.), *Industrial districts and inter-firm co-operation in Italy.* International Institute for Labour Studies, Geneva, 1–9.

Reve, T. et al. (1992): *Et konkurransedyktig Norge.* Tano, Oslo.

Soskice, D. (1999): 'Divergent production regimes – uncoordinated and coordinated market economies in the 1990s', in Kitchelt et al. (eds.), *Continuity and change in contemporary capitalis.* Cambridge University Press, Cambridge, 101–134.

Storper, M. (1995): 'The resurgence of regional economies, ten years later: The region as a nexus of untraded interdependencies'. *European Urban and Regional Studies,* 2, 3, 191–221.

Storper, M. (1997): *The regional world. Territorial development in a global economy.* The Guilford Press, New York and London.

Storper, M. and B. Harrison (1990): 'Flexibility, hierarchy and regional development: The changing structure of industrial production systems and their forces of governance in the 1990s'. UCLA, MIT/Carnegie-Mellon University, Los Angeles, Cambridge/Pittsburgh.

Storper, M. and A. Scott (1995): 'The wealth of regions'. *Futures,* 27, 5, 505–526.

Streeck, W. (1992): *Social institutions and economic performance – studies of industrial relations in advanced capitalist economies.* Sage Publications, New York.

Whitley, R. (1992): 'Societies, firms and markets: the social structuring of business systems', in Whitley, R. (ed.), *European business systems: Firms and markets in their national contexts.* Sage Publications, London, 5–45.

Woolcock, M. (1998): Social capital and economic development: Toward a theoretical synthesis and policy framework. *Theory and Society,* 151–208.

Chapter 3

Economy-culture relations and the geographies of regional development

Jørgen Ole Bærenholdt and Michael Haldrup

Discussions of the relationship between 'the economic' and 'the cultural' have recently attracted attention within contemporary human geography (Sayer 1997, Gregson et al. forthcoming, Ray and Sayer 1999). Some of this interest has concentrated on the rediscovery of regional industrial districts in Europe, North America and Japan during the 1980s (Piore and Sabel 1984, Leborgne and Lipietz 1988, Amin and Thrift 1994, Storper 1997). Some has come from studies of consumption and cultural economics (Lash and Urry 1994, Miller 1995).

While geographies of consumption have by and large been a neglected area of research, Nordic human geography has contributed specific new approaches to the study of the economy-culture nexus in relation to local and regional development. Furthermore, these approaches differ in a number of ways from approaches found in (mainly Anglo-American-dominated) international research.

In this chapter we would like to outline some of the distinct features of Nordic geography in relation to questions of local and regional development. We will do so by first outlining some of the recent debates within Nordic geography, then proposing a way of conceptualizing the link between economy and culture in relation to the issue of local and regional development; thirdly, we will explore the intersection between 'economic' and 'cultural' aspects of regional change in a number of East Central European and North Atlantic cases of localized coping processes within the context of social transformation and spatial restructuring. In the fourth and final section of the chapter, we will sum up the main lessons we think should be drawn for further research on regional and local development.

Debates in Nordic geography

While Nordic geography, like other geographical traditions, can be divided into distinct 'culturally' (or in fact socially) and 'economically' oriented traditions of research, it is notable that both Nordic traditions, in contrast to Anglo-American geography, have emerged out of the same concern with urban, regional or local development. One reason for this can be found in the different types of liberal regimes in the Anglo-American world and the social-democratic Nordic welfare states. As Andrew Sayer has pointed out, it is no accident that in more social democratic societies, where there is a stronger sense of the public or the common, such as the Scandinavian countries, a more anthropological and moral-political way of understanding culture (e.g. as 'life-form') which goes far beyond the stylization of life is still strong' (Sayer 1997: 25).

Hence, social and economic geographies in the Nordic countries have certain common points of reference. In this section we will outline how the economy-culture nexus has been discussed in economic and social geography respectively in Scandinavia.

In *economic geography* in Scandinavia in the 1990s, one important event was the 'rediscovery of the region'. There have been several studies of local business milieus embedded in specific social and cultural settings (Illeris 1992, Isaksen 1993, Asheim 1995, Maskell et al. 1998). These studies have asked how social and cultural phenomena give rise to different forms of networks and innovation systems on different geographical scales (Lundvall 1992). A distinct contribution made by Nordic economic geography has been based on the concepts of innovation, learning and knowledge in the work of Lundvall, who has also inspired international discussions (Storper 1997, Maskell et al. 1998). In Lundvall's work culture plays a significant role as a contextual framework for innovations. Thus Lundvall opens his book on *National Systems of Innovation* by defining learning as

> a socially embedded process which cannot be understood without taking into account the institutional and cultural context' (Lundvall 1992: 1).

Knowledge is perceived as a place-bound factor of production, and the need to understand how knowledge is produced is also acknowledged. However this does not necessarily involve the cultural content (Vedsmand 1998). In a similar way, Maskell et al. (e.g. 1998: 181) fully acknowledge the importance of 'culture' in one of the major recent works in Nordic economic geography. However the concept of culture lacks conceptualization. Sometimes it seems that the concept of culture simply replaces the concept of space, as culture is one of the few assets of production that does not seem to have been ubiquitized yet. Culture is becoming the factor used to explain the 'capabilities of the area', which also include the social construction of natural resources as localized capabilities (Maskell et al. 1998: 51ff). What happens is that 'economy' (competitiveness) more or less becomes an output of the tacit untraded dependencies embedded in localized cultures: spatial proximity generates trust generates cooperation generates competitiveness – so goes the argument. However it is a moot question whether local cooperation is crucial to all business sectors. Obviously, 'economy' and 'culture' can be well connected without being spatially fixed on a particular scale. The crux of matter is to conceptualize culture appropriately.

Although it has become common to pay lip service to the importance of culture in Nordic economic geography, culture is mainly becoming a black box for generating different spatial systems of innovation, networks and trust. How culture, networks and knowledge are actually being localized and reproduced as parts of particular geographies of regional development remains an open question in Nordic economic geography. Hence, it is symptomatic that cultural studies and ethnographic work are disciplinary and methodological fields which have not so far gained much attention in relation to studies of socio-economic development.

Having reached this preliminary point, we will turn to the state of *social geography* in Scandinavia in relation to questions of local and regional development. In this field culture has been approached ethnographically as modes of life ('life-forms') and social practices. Throughout the 1990s, this has led to a number of studies of work and everyday life in a multiplicity of local settings in Norway, Sweden, Denmark, the Faeroe Islands, Iceland, Slovakia, Ghana and Senegal (e.g. Bærenholdt et al. 1990, Löfgren 1990, Bærenholdt 1991, Sørensen and Vogelius 1991, Simonsen 1993, Haldrup and Hoydal 1994, Buciek 1995, Fosso 1997, Haldrup 1999, Juul 1999). These studies have had a variety of focuses ranging from individual career and life-path strategies in education, migration and everyday life to collective tactics oriented towards industrial change, settlement structure and resource management. It has however been a shared ambition to demonstrate the significance of specific ways of interpreting identity and practice in coping with societal change. Thus a frequent discussion in these studies has concerned how to conceptualize culture. Is culture a passive resource for interpretation consisting of accumulated experience? Is culture the main or even the determining factor, to take the line pursued by cultural studies? Or should culture rather be understood within broader frameworks of social theory?

There has been a tendency towards the last of these approaches, i.e. to draw on concepts of modernity and/or civilization processes (e.g. Negt and Kluge 1981, Elias 1989, Habermas 1981, Bourdieu 1990) in order to link structural transformations and everyday life. Interestingly, the concept of culture has played a modest role in Nordic social geography, and it has been argued that this strand of Nordic social geography has been more concerned conceptually with social practice than with culture (Simonsen 1999). While Nordic social geography therefore offers substantial sociological and methodological approaches to the study of practice within specific local contexts, the ability to relate these insights to problems of regional economic development has been limited.

As outlined above, the discussion of economy-culture relations in Nordic geography takes very different forms in economic and social geography. Whereas the concept of culture is under-theorized and therefore conceptually and methodologically diffuse in Nordic *economic* geography, the ability of Nordic *social* geography to link studies of social practice and structural transformation to questions of innovative performance has been limited. However, we do not see these differences as antagonistic. Economic and social geography in Scandinavia exhibit certain characteristics that may provide steps towards overcoming the division between approaches (Haldrup 1997, Gregson et al. forthcoming), and this has in fact been the ambition of some recent studies of local economic transformations and social practice (Aarsæther and Bærenholdt 2001, Haldrup 1999). In what follows we will propose a model of economy-culture relations which dissolves the false dichotomies from which much current human geography suffers.

The economy-culture nexus

In this section we will argue that culture and economy cannot be treated as separate spheres or levels, but are intermixed in dense networks of relations. Thus rather than talking about linking 'the economic' to 'the cultural', we are asking how the economy-culture nexus can be appropriately conceptualized. We will answer this question in two stages: first by presenting a model focusing on the intersections among social regulation, processes of (economic) innovation and (cultural) identity formation; and secondly by discussing some of the main theoretical assumptions underpinning the argument.

A central question for both the economic and social geography approaches has been how to understand the social embeddedness of practices. One way of opening up the black box of culture and spatiality in economic geography has been to adopt the concept of *social capital* that emerged from political-science studies of the process of regional government reform in Italy (Putnam 1993) and thus to understand economic development as consequences of localized culture. This argument resembles that of evolutionary regional economics. However the concept of network is not confined to business networks; instead it relates to the understanding that

> networks of civic engagement that cut across social cleavages nourish wider cooperation' (Putnam 1993: 175).

In this case socio-economic development is explicitly not validated as a cause of governmental success. Instead, civic engagement (conceptualized as social capital) is the cause of both socio-economic development and governmental success. However, there is a risk that this could lead us into more geohistorical, deterministic approaches. Economy-culture relations can hardly be understood without a focus on the social practices of networking and institutional regulations, both of which build on and (re)produce social capital. For this purpose we propose to use Bourdieu's definition of social capital as the resources to which social agents have access

> by virtue of possessing a durable network or more or less institutionalized relationships of mutual acquaintance and recognition' (Bourdieu & Wacquant 1992: 119).

This definition of social capital is more analytical and less normative than that of Putnam (see Bærenholdt & Aarsæther forthcoming). Furthermore, Bourdieu's complementary concept of *habitus* offers us a way of conceptualizing how social capital is (re)produced and mobilized as part of social practice (Haldrup 1999, Bærenholdt 1998). However, as Woolcock (1998) has convincingly argued, social capital must not simply be equated with informal social networks, but must also include the practices of institutionalized regulation, for example political institutions on different spatial scales (see also Asheim and Haraldsen, this volume).

Another question common to economic and social geography has been to ask how the interplay between economic and cultural practices is produced through practices that transform social structures (and thereby also the relevant forms of social capital). As Michael Storper has emphasized, the study of the interplay between economic developmental processes and various forms of social practice requires that

> we focus on how individual and collective reflexivity operate in the contemporary economy, through cognitive, dialogic, and interpretive processes, with the substantive goal

of understanding how relations of coordination between reflexive agents and organizations are established' (Storper 1997: 31).

Here, reflexivity has a double meaning. With Scott Lash (Lash 1994: 115), we understand *reflexivity* as a shared, social form of practice that includes both 'structural reflexivity', where practices transform social structures, and 'self-reflexivity', where agents reflect on the meaning of these very practices which are central to the formation of identity. In this view (economic) innovation and (cultural) processes of identity formation are two sides of the same coin. Innovation always include the (re)production of certain identities, while at the same time depending on such identities. Hence, reflexivity as we understand it encompasses three things: the formation of identity, the constitution of social practice, and innovation; and thus at the conceptual level bridges the gap between 'economic' and 'cultural' phenomena.

Figure 3.1   The economy-culture nexus

Innovation

R
E
F
L
E

Networking   SOCIAL   Practice   CAPITAL   Institutional
                                                                  Regulation

X
I
V
I
T
Y

Formation of Identity

The model focuses on the dynamic practices that are crucial to the understanding of economy-culture relations as a process. All four components – innovation, networking, institutional regulation and the formation of identity – are interdependent aspects of practice. The horizontal 'social capital' axis contains the stabilizing elements, while the vertical axis of 'reflexivity' contains the practices involving change. Social capital and reflexivity are background resources; it is only through the four types of practice that they are produced and used. Of course economy and culture are in reality more than the components of the model, where we focus on economy-culture relations. While economy also includes material resources and structures, and culture also includes the formation of more enduring cultural categories which enable and constrain particular forms of practice, we focus on the transforming practices.

In Figure 3.1 we present the concept graphically. As argued above, we do not understand the economy-culture nexus in terms of mutually exclusive concepts. On the contrary, what we are focusing on is the interrelationship between forms of social capital (spanning both informal social networks and institutional regulation) and forms of reflexive practice (spanning both economic innovation and identity formation). In this respect we would like to add a few words regarding the concept of social capital. In both traditional and modern economic sociology 'the social' has become tantamount to fixed structures or networks. This partly explains the deterministic tendency of much of the work done in the new economic geography and sociology (and justifies Granovetter's (1985) warning against 'oversocialization'). As Woolcock (1998) has pointed out in his discussion of approaches to social capital, it is left

> unresolved whether social capital is the infrastructure or the content of social relations, the 'medium' as it were, or the 'message' (Woolcock 1998: 156).

This neglect of the cultural aspect of the reproduction, negotiation and transformation of social networks and institutions is of course problematical. However, this neglect is related not only to the issue of 'embeddedness', but to the very concept of practice, which is by and large rooted in a behaviourist model of agency which excludes questions of meaning and identity. If networks are communicative, then they have to be based on life-worlds that are to some extent common to and negotiated by the actors – to present the problem in Habermasian terms (Habermas 1981, 1991). In a similar discussion of network theory, Emirbayer and Goodwin (1994) address this question by pointing to the absence of 'agency' in studies of social networks. Social relations must be symmetrically grasped as both discursive (linguistically and symbolically mediated) and non-discursive (material, bodily and interpersonal). Thus,

> *Human agency*, as we conceptualize it, entails the capacity of socially embedded actors to appropriate, reproduce, and, potentially, to innovate upon received cultural categories and conditions of action in accordance with their personal and collective ideals, interests, and commitments' (Emirbayer and Goodwin 1994: 1442–1443).

The dual analysis of both discursive and non-discursive worlds is crucial to our understanding of how these worlds intersect in the processes we study. The task is to understand the intersection of economy and culture without reducing either of these to the other. The acknowledgement of social capital and reflexivity in this context should lead to an understanding of the relationship between the 'cultural' and the 'economic' in human geography where the former is not reduced to an underpinning of the latter or vice versa. The task is then not simply to detect differences among the variant ways in which regional (local, national) economies are embedded culturally as regionally fixed systems; but also to ask how social capital and reflexivity enable practices that cope with the increasing speed of transactions within the new global capitalism. To put the question in another way, how do the reflexive practices of networking and institutional regulation, i.e. the whole process of producing social capital, form the basis for the specific coping strategies of local people, public bodies and businesses?

Looking at the approaches used in and around economic sociology and economic geography internationally, we find a great many studies of the relations among innovation, networking and institutional regulation. We also find many studies of the relations among the formation of identity, networking and institutional regulation in sociology and social geography. Generally, however, we find very few studies of the 'full perspective' of economy-culture relations. No doubt this is to some extent due to the methodological and resource/capacity problems involved in conducting studies of both innovation and the formation of identity. There seems to be no alternative to rather problematical large-scale correlation studies of indicators except intensive research using ethnography-like fieldwork approaches. It is important, however, to keep in mind that regional development is not confined to a particular scale of analysis, or to a particular approach to external factors.

The specific geographical and social settings of the economy-culture relation are mutually constitutive (cf. Sack 1986, Sayer 2000: 105ff), and it is only through the close examination of these settings (which need not be local any more than they are regional, transregional or global) that we gain insight into the economy-culture-nexus.

Economy-culture relations within local settings

In this section we will illustrate how the dynamics pertaining between cultural and economic elements of local and regional development work out very differently in a number of cases selected from our own research. The cases in the first section are based on studies of North Atlantic localities conducted in the 1990s, and have been selected because of their relatively successful coping strategies. Most of the studies referred to are connected to the same overall international interdisciplinary social-science project. In the subsequent section we will discuss two cases from East Central European localities that involve slightly more complex coping processes.

North Atlantic localities

Klaksvík is the central village in the northern part of the Faeroe Islands, which is at present a home-rule area within the Kingdom of Denmark. It is the second-biggest town, or the biggest village, of the Faeroe Islands. The population has been as much as 5000, but during the severe crisis in the Faeroe Islands in the 1990s, the population dropped to around 4500. Having developed historically from a number of smaller villages, Klaksvík is today a fairly concentrated settlement with a natural harbour in a fjord on the northern island of Bordoy. It is a fishing town, and is well known for its strong sense of identity, indeed for an almost armed confrontation with the capital Tórshavn and the Danish state in 1955. There is a strong religious influence from the Herrnhut (Moravian Brethren) community (locally called the 'Baptists'), which is further related to the dominance of certain families and the Conservative political party.

Storfjord in Northern Norway can hardly be said to be a clearly localized entity. It is a municipality consisting of scattered settlements and three partly contrasting villages located around the head of the beautiful Lyngen Fjord. The population is stable, around 1900 inhabitants, and the case has a specific interest inasmuch as half of the women are newcomers. Furthermore, the locality has at least three distinct ethnic groups: the Norwegians, the Sámi (Lapps) and the Kven (Finns). It is also a border locality, bordering on both Sweden and Finland.

Figure 3.2   Two localities in the North Atlantic

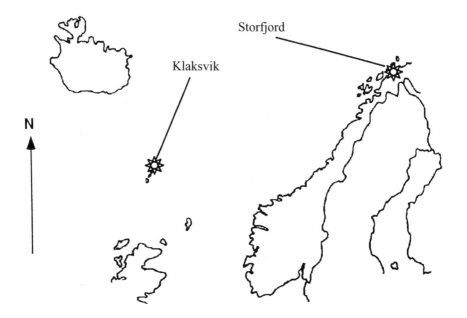

The coping processes in Klaksvík are typical of a strongly embedded local economy with relations to international fish markets, while the weakness of state regulation and the absence of linkages to national strategies is another specific characteristic (Hovgaard 2000). Klaksvík developed into one of the major localities for the development of the fishing industry in the Faeroes from the beginning of the 20th century (Haldrup and Hoydal 1994). Its history in this respect is linked literally and symbolically with a specific entrepreneur and his family. The municipality itself, local trade unions and in particular the local savings bank also played major roles in the development strategies pursued in Klaksvík throughout the 20th century. The many fishing vessels and fishing companies have had the major fish-processing plant 'Kosin' as the cornerstone of local development, although it has been closed down and reconstructed several times. In fact, people in Klaksvík have coped with several crises thanks to local innovations in the social organization of the economy, almost turning the lack of national linkages into a comparative advantage for the area over other Faeroese localities. While *institutional regulation,* apart from the strong local forms, is weak, Klaksvík is a case of strong connections between *networking* and the *formation of identity.* The municipality always acts as a background local regulator, but the central actors are to be found in the networks of local entrepreneurs and their supporters. The networks also include cultural activities as well as religious communities and families. The most crucial factor is probably the tradition of raising local capital when it is needed. This is done through the local savings bank as well as informally. The other important factor is the idea of keeping businesses in local hands. Klaksvík is not a case where there is much technological (i.e. product and process) innovation in the industries. The innovative work is more social in character, and this is strongly linked with the related reproduction of local identity: 'in Klaksvík the strong adherence to the local is a powerful source for managing crisis and transition' (Hovgaard, 2000). Reflexivity in Klaksvík is a collective – even a hegemonic – process of working within the local tradition. The key to Klaksvík's social innovations is the network of actors with strong reference to a common local discourse of identity. In Klaksvík most people identify with the traditions of local social innovation mediated through local networks. Meanwhile, there may be an important 'institutional' component in Klaksvík's advantage as the stronger fishing town in Faeroese society. One might ask whether the localist Klaksvík strategy will remain viable in the long run, especially in relation to the potential of national Faeroese economic development. Klaksvík could run the risk of either stifling national growth or becoming isolated with specific privileges, unless it integrates more firmly with national strategies and political culture.

The case of Storfjord is quite the opposite of the strong informal social embeddedness in Klaksvík. With respect to innovation, we find no development of big business, cornerstones or the like. The major 'cornerstone' is the public sector, where negotiations in the 1970s at the local, regional and national levels resulted in the placing of a major regional public laundry in the municipality. Historically, small-scale agriculture has been the major economic sector. Although it exists, agriculture is not a leading sector; many households combine activities and incomes from several sources including agriculture on the farms where they live. These combinations may include jobs in international firms where people either commute on a weekly basis along the major North Norwegian highway which runs through the municipality or are connected through IT networks, or they may combine these approaches. The highway running through the fjord scenery, and the 'Alpine' Lyngen Mountains also facilitate tourist businesses in the form of hotels, camping sites etc. Municipal public services are of high quality, and public-sector jobs are shared by many people as part-time jobs. Thus more people have access to stable incomes from the public sector. Meanwhile, Storfjord is also the southernmost municipality in the part of North Norway that has certain state-regulated tax allowances and other advantages which attract young people. It will already be clear from this that innovation processes in Storfjord have a great deal to do with *both networking and institutional regulation,* and that these two aspects of social capital work very much in concert. Government policies can indeed facilitate civil society in the form of local networks, if the actors in these networks know how to utilize the possibilities of funding and regulation by government bodies (see Woolcock 1998: 157). Interestingly, one finds no strong identification with Storfjord as such. Local identities are connected to the homes and small villages where some of the inhabitants grew up. Other identities are religious, and there are conflicts between different religious communities. Villages also struggle over the allocation of public services, and the result has been a decentralized service system which also provides local service jobs to each of the villages. Many strategies and identities are formed at the household level. Meanwhile, the municipality (and the parish council) work to a common agenda where issues are fought out and solutions found. It may be precisely 'the ability to live with conflicts' (Aure 2001) that explains the potential of Storfjord. It seems that this ability is also conditional on the acceptance of the common political identity and agenda of the municipality. This is no coincidence, since municipalities are a central element in the Nordic welfare states, especially in public service provision, the infrastructure and as a conduit for funding from national initiatives, where many local applicants compete for such funding. It is this mediation of networking and institutional regulation at the municipal level that makes locality a political unit in the still relatively strong welfare state of Norway. And it is through this mediation that the reflexive play of different strategies can take place. Of course some forms of political identity related to the welfare state and northern Norway have produced a kind of 'we' community, but there are no strong economy-culture ties at the local level. Storfjord is a case that illustrates the diversity of the late modern 'reflexive North' (Aarsæther and Bærenholdt 2001).

Figure 3.3   Two localities in East Central Europe

East Central European localities

The region of *Liptovsky Mikulas* includes two historically distinct but interconnected towns, Liptovsky Mikulas and Ruzomberok, located near the beautiful mountain resorts of northern Slovakia. The region has an occupational tradition dating back to the 12th century, and around 1770 industrialization began in leather manufacturing. From 1910 on the leather industry dominated the region with workshops concentrated in the regional capital Liptovsky Mikulas (1995 pop. approximately 33,000) and the nearby city of Ruzomberok. The 40 years of state socialist regulation had no significant effect on the industrial structure, although workshops were of course nationalized and combined. However, since 1989 Liptovsky Mikulas has emerged as one of the best-adapting regional economies, with a booming export-led consumer-product industry (mainly textiles) and an international orientation, manifested by its bid for the Winter Olympics 2002 (which ultimately failed).

Martin in Central Slovakia is located in what used to be the central rural area of pre-1918 Slovakia. During the 19th century the city became the main centre for the organization of the Slovak National Movement. This has had two significant consequences. First of all, the sparse industrialization of Martin, which eventually took place in the late 19th century, was tied to the National Movement and its main institution Matica Slovenska (also located in Martin), and took the form of the establishment of independent 'Slovak' financial institutions: printing houses, paper mills and educational institutions. Secondly, the city achieved a certain degree of cultural-linguistic hegemony, since the dialect of the region became the standard national language during the codification of Slovak. As a largely agricultural region, Martin received much attention from state socialist industrial planners from 1948 onwards. During the 1970s the engineering plant established in 1948 became the site of the headquarters of ZTS TS – the third-largest combine in Czech mechanical engineering, mainly producing tanks and other kinds of defence-related vehicles. The combine virtually took over all cultural, social, political and economic functions in the city, thus providing work, homes, schools, leisure activities and holiday homes for the approximately 60,000 inhabitants of the city (1995).

Liptovsky Mikulas and Ruzemberok has emerged as one of the most successful regional economies in post-socialist Slovakia (Smith 1998). What is immediately striking with regard to the *innovation* dimension is that no drastic structural changes are apparent. Despite a very strong 'western' orientation in the export structure, it is striking for example that ownership has only partially become private. The main textile manufacturer in the region, MAYTEX (located in Ruzemberok) is publicly owned, and even private manufacturers use publicly owned marketing companies as gateways to the western European market. This 'evolutionism' may reflect the fact that the consumer goods industry is much more flexible in its adaptation to market conditions. However, it also reflects a significant aspect of the institutional regulation of state socialist production in Liptovsky Mikulas. Whereas local industry, because of its relative sophistication in 1948, remained relatively untouched by the state socialist industrialization model, the gradual orientation towards the COMECON consumer market meant slow but steady technological modernization. MAYTEX gradually bought sophisticated production technology and became one of the technologically most sophisticated producers of synthetic fibres in Europe. The export-oriented strategy of the 1990s has continued along this path, and although outdated technology still coexists with more modern production equipment, this gradual *innovation* exercised through *institutional regulation* is a major explanation for Liptovsky Mikulas and Ruzemberok's successful coping with post-socialist transformation. However, one important element in this must be given special attention. In contrast to many other localities in East Central Europe (see below for example), no one manufacturer became dominant in the localities of Liptovsky Mikulas and Ruzemberok. This has had two consequences. First, no enterprise gained a dominant position in local politics, which meant that the relations between political and economic power were more associative and horizontal than one might expect from a state socialist 'command economy'. This meant that despite the good intentions of local politicians after 1989 to 'bring people together' by setting up meetings, no political agent (institution, enterprise, public body etc.) has emerged in Liptovsky Mikulas. Secondly, manufacturers (and export companies) in the region have been *networking* across different industries (textiles, leather, paper and pulp, telecommunications, tourism). Paradoxically, this has had the strange consequence that the *formation of identity,* which is mainly manifested at the household level, still works within the framework of the institutions of publicly owned post-socialist production, since the major manufacturers have maintained their commitment to housing and health-care provision. The case of Liptovsky Mikulas thus demonstrates how *institutional regulation* may go hand in hand with a very innovative, market-oriented local economy, parallel to the continuation of local cultural identities tied to the workplace and household. Quite another case is the locality Martin, approximately 50 km west of Liptovsky Mikulas.

Martin may be the archetypal case of a post-socialist 'lock-in' situation. Through the 1970s and 1980s the combine ZTS TEES, which almost completely dominated the employment structure of Martin, was rumoured to be one of the most innovative and technologically sophisticated machinery producers in East Central Europe. However the challenges of a general crisis in the heavy-armament industry (from 1988 onwards) and the general confusion following the collapse of state socialism, meant that innovation was stifled (primarily as a consequence of the lack of funding for research and development initiatives, managers in the industry say). The numerous institutions and agencies that were established in the years 1991–1994 with state and EU funding have by and large failed to have any significant influence on local socioeconomic development (Smith 1998). This does not mean, however, that nothing happened, or that the combine stayed the same – quite the opposite. From the very beginning of the transformation process, ZTS TEES in Martin experienced a creative explosion in *innovations in the social regulation of labour.* The different parts of the combine began a complex process of diffusion, reintegration, closure, new establishments etc., combined with many new forms of employer-employee relations (individualized payment systems, employee ownership or shareholding, neo-Taylorist sweatshops, self-paid holidays, reduction of working hours/salary, to mention some examples). In addition, all non-productive activities (schools, housing, holiday homes) were laid off. The combine headquarters in Martin eventually closed down in late 1995, leaving this myriad of independent and semi-independent enterprises. However, by this time the former top managers of the combine had emerged as the local political and economic elite, and it is interesting to take a quick look at their efforts to coordinate some sort of local development. In the political sphere there were intense efforts to establish some kind of local consensus on development issues, and these efforts were inspired by ideas about empowerment and the creative force of a reconstructed civil society (the great key concept at the time). While the district office succeeded in establishing western European networks that gave professional, moral and economic support to its initiatives, the local impact – indeed local knowledge – of these endeavours was virtually zero. Meanwhile, the new local economic elites were able to keep the machinery production running. This was financed through a system of 'mercantilist regulation', i.e. a barter system in which the trading companies set up by former managers of ZTS financed technology, salaries, raw materials and R&D expenses in exchange for products. While this form of financing was not locally confined, but expanded to other ZTS enterprises throughout Slovakia, some significant actors sought to reinvest their profits in the local machinery production. However, these efforts towards a 'capitalist' re-establishment of 'the corporation' (the former combine and its multiple offshoots) have not succeeded. Why is it that all attempts at *institutional regulation* have failed? An obvious answer is the conflicts within the non-formal networks involved. The innovative explosion of the early 1990s created numerous axes of conflict within the former combine management (between 'old guard' and 'newcomers'), within the working class (post-communist professional workers and national chauvinists), not to mention between these classes. These conflicts had their origin in a web of stories and narratives of 'who-did-what-and-why' conspiracies, thus emphasizing the central roles played by discourse in the reproduction and reconstruction of social networks (Haldrup 1999). In Liptovsky Mikulas, the relative continuity of the enterprise structure and commitments also meant a continuation of household-based and enterprise-based identities. But in the case of Martin, the explosion of organizational forms and the withdrawal from any kind of local social commitment have led to a fragmentation of identities and views of the kind of 'place' Martin should be (Haldrup forthcoming). The case of Martin thus emphasizes how reflexivity also plays a major role in the reproduction of a regional lock-in. Multiple identities do not necessarily give rise to regional development.

Conclusion

The overcoming of the divisions between the approaches of economic and cultural geography is not only relevant in the disciplinary context; it is also important in terms of broader societal trends. According to recent social theories (both economic and cultural), global capitalism is entering a new phase: learning processes constitute the basis for a distinctly new type of global capitalism in which social capital may be the most important asset (Lundvall 1999). Meanwhile, reflexivity is becoming a marked feature of the constitution of collective identities (Lash 1994).

UNIVERSITY OF HERTFORDSHIRE LRC

While we do acknowledge such trends, we would like to stress that the importance of social capital and reflexivity may not be such a new phenomenon. What is new is the ability of broader social science discourse to understand this. There is a growing awareness that neither economy nor culture can be understood as an isolated sector of society. Clearly, this awareness has traditions within economic sociology, anthropology and political economy. The cases presented in this chapter are all part of the historical geography of the older traditions of 'community', variously linked with 'local community' in 'Scandinavian welfare regimes' and with the 'combinate town' in 'real existing socialism'.

Following on from the discussion of the two local cases in the North Atlantic area, an obvious course would be to discuss the role of the locality as space and place in the Nordic context. It is characteristic of local development in Nordic countries like Norway, Iceland, Greenland, the Faeroe Islands and Denmark that local municipal politics are constitutive in producing the locality as a political space. In general, regional development at the local level is indeed a question of who is able to construct the locality as an economy and a culture in the context of the Nordic welfare state. Much the same can be said of our two East Central European cases, which document the role played by the various forms of social capital and how economy-culture relations are embedded in these. These cases call attention to how reflexivity and the discursive reproduction and manifestation of identity, social capital and innovation play a crucial role even in 'failed' coping processes.

On looking more closely at economy-culture relations (see Figure 3.1), we have found that such relations are important in explaining both success and failures in local coping. In this case the concept of social capital offers us an approach to understanding the intricate intersection of economic innovation and the cultural formation of identity through networking and institutional regulation. All the same, social capital does not by itself explain the dynamic processes of innovation and identity formation. What we need to stress is the associational or communal character of reflexivity (Lash 1994). Individual reflexivity is of little importance, as it may only lead to the disembedding of social relations that are crucial to practices of coping. Reflexivity based on a certain level of 'shared practice' may lead to solid innovation and identity formation connected to the production and use of social capital through networking and institutional regulation.

Interestingly, the case of Liptovsky Mikulas points to the importance of continuity in some form of public, institutional regulation that creates a framework for a variety of business activities. In spite of differences in scale, this case has similarities to that of Storfjord. In contrast, Klaksvík is a case of highly embedded economy-culture relations producing Klaksvík as an entrepreneurial locality within the framework of weak Faeroese national institutional regulation. And Martin is a case on a larger scale showing how highly embedded economy-culture relations locked into the former command economy are unable to transform the locality successfully because of centrifugal forces of reflexivity and the absence of sensitive institutional regulation. While Klaksvík may illustrate the 'cost' of having too much social capital (see Woolcock 1998: 158), Martin exemplifies how too much reflexivity in the transformation of social relations contributes to the stifling of innovation in other spheres.

From the Klaksvík case we saw the importance to local development of social innovation in the specific development of networking and identity formation. In the Storfjord case, innovative practices were very much a matter of the success of political negotiations at the municipal level and at the higher level of the Norwegian welfare state. Political innovations there have been more or less successful in coping with the multiplicity of local identities and innovations because of the explicit combination of networking and institutional regulation at the municipal and village level. Figure 3.1 could be elaborated by showing multiple practices of innovation and identity formation side by side. In this respect Liptovsky Mikulas showed interesting similarities to Storfjord: in both cases associative horizontal networking and institutional regulation were important in coping with multiple projects in the locality. Martin, however, was a case where this did not work, since the restructuring efforts were much more 'top-down', and Martin was embedded in the production of products that were quite simply hard to sell. Furthermore, restructuring efforts in Martin may have been 'too innovative' thus undermining possibly crucial stability in regional development. No general theory emerges from these comparisons, but we do learn something about the specificity of each case of regional development through such comparisons when the studies are structured by the same approach to economy-culture relations.

So far, we have outlined some generalized conclusions on the interrelationships among innovation, networking, institutional regulation and identity formation. However, deeper understanding and explanations of cases of regional development require intensive studies of the *specific content* of these practices. One central aspect that is elucidated by this approach is how local and regional economic development is always intrinsically linked to issues of social justice and cultural identity. All four cases presented here are examples of successful or failed coping processes, and at the same time stories of winners and losers. As such these cases also present complex lessons for planners, politicians or whoever wants to get beyond textbook examples of regional and local development. The approach to economy-culture relations in geographies of local and regional development presented here seems to be a useful analytical tool for understanding regional development, as well as the way dual processes of reflexivity and social capital are interwoven with the politics of space.

'Regional development' is often a confused concept that can cover many dimensions such as business development, living conditions, service provision, government and image. Most studies tend to focus on only one of these dimensions, although they can all be important dimensions of regional development understood as the spatial restructuring involved in social transformations. Furthermore, many studies take the territorial character of explanatory factors like culture for granted. We can see the problems in such tacit assumptions when we look more closely at the coping processes and practices that construct regional development. Rather than taking regional development for granted, we suggest a focus on the complex economy-culture nexuses in practices producing regional development.

Acknowledgements

We would like to thank those who made the many constructive comments on our earlier draft at the seminar on 'Economy-Culture Relations in Geography' at Roskilde University, November 2000. Thanks in particular to our discussion partner on this occasion, Esben Holm Nielsen, and to the editors of this volume.

References

Aarsæther, Nils and Jørgen Ole Bærenholdt (eds.) 2001: *The Reflexive North*, Copenhagen: Nordic Council of Ministers, NORD 2001:10.
Amin, Ash and Nigel Thrift (eds.) 1994: *Globalization, Institutions and Regional Development in Europe*, Oxford: Oxford University Press.
Asheim, Bjørn T. 1995: 'Regionale innovasjonssystem – en socialt og territorielt forankret teknologipolitikk?', *Nordisk Samhällsgeografisk Tidsskrift*, no 20: 17–34.
Aure, Marit 2001: 'Innovative traditions? Coping Processes among Households, Villages and the Municipality', chapter 4 in: Aarsæther and Bærenholdt (eds.): *The Reflexive North*.
Bærenholdt, Jørgen Ole 1986: *Livsformer og småbrug i Ungarn – et bidrag til udviklingen af en kulturgeografisk metode*, Publikationer fra Institut for Geografi, Samfundsanalyse og Datalogi, Forskningsrapport nr. 53, Roskilde Universitetscenter.
Bærenholdt, Jørgen Ole 1991: *Bygdeliv, Livsformer og bosætningsmønster i Nordatlanten, Om fiskeriafhængige bygder i Island og på Færøerne*, Publikationer fra Institut for Geografi, Samfundsanalyse og Datalogi, Forskningsrapport nr. 78, Roskilde Universitetscenter.
Bærenholdt, Jørgen Ole 1998: 'Locals versus Mobiles – Explaining Different Dynamics in North Atlantic Localities', chapter 11 in: *Coping Strategies in the North – Local practices in the context of global restructuring*, eds: Nils Aarsæther and Jørgen Ole Bærenholdt, Copenhagen: MOST and Nordic Council of Ministers, INS 1998:303: 201–221.
Bærenholdt, Jørgen Ole 2000: 'Circumpolar Coping Strategies – Embedding transnational cooperation in local practices in Greenland?', *Étude/Inuit/Studies*, vol 24(1): 79–96.
Bærenholdt, Jørgen Ole, Kirsten Simonsen, Ole Beier Sørensen and Peter Vogelius 1990: 'Lifemodes and Social Practice', *Nordisk Samhällsgeografisk Tidsskrift*, 11: 72–86.
Bærenholdt, Jørgen Ole and Nils Aarsæther, forthcoming: 'Coping strategies, social capital and space', *European Urban and Regional Studies*.
Bourdieu, Pierre 1990: *The Logic of Practice*, Polity Press.
Bourdieu, Pierre and Loic. J.D. Wacquant 1992: *An Invitation to Reflexive Sociology*, Cambridge: Polity Press.
Buciek, Keld 1995: *Arbejdet er guld værd – er guldet arbejdet værd? En analyse af arbejdsvilkår i ghanesiske minebyer*, Publikationer fra Institut for Geografi og Internationale Udviklingsstudier, Forskningsrapport nr. 109, Roskilde Universitetscenter.
Elias, Norbert 1989; *Über den Prozes der Zivilisation I-II*; Suhrkamp Verlag.
Emirbayer, Mustafa and Jeff Goodwin 1994: 'Network Analysis, Culture and the Problem of Agency', *American Journal of Sociology*, 99 (6): 1411–1454.
Fosso, Elia Janette 1997: *Industristeders arbeidstilbud og generasjoners forhold til utdanning, arbeid og sted – eksemplet Årdal*, upubl. Avhandling for dr.polit. graden, Institut for geografi, Norges Handelshøjskole og Universitetet i Bergen.
Granovetter, Mark 1985: 'Economic Action and Social Structure: The Problem of Embeddedness' in: *American Journal of Sociology* 91 (3).

Gregson, Nicky, Kirsten Simonsen and Dina Vaiou, forthcoming: 'Whose economy for whose culture? Moving beyond oppositional talk in European debate about economy and culture', *Antipode*.

Habermas, Jürgen 1981: *Theorie des Kommunikativen Handelns I-II*; Suhrkamp Verlag.

Habermas, Jürgen 1991: *Erläuterungen zur Diskursethik*; Suhrkamp Verlag.

Haldrup, Michael 1997: 'Hvor ligger Utopia? – kritik og geografi', in Löfgren A. and Moe M. (eds.): *Critical Perspectives on Society and Disciplin: the place of human geography in high modern society*, Trondheim: Paper from Department of Geography, University of Trondheim, New series A no. 5.

Haldrup, Michael 1999: *Postsocialistiske Understrømme – Arbejdere, teknokrater og habitusforandringer i postsocialismens Slovakiet*, upub. ph.d.-afh., Institut for Geografi og Internationale Udviklingsstuedier, Roskilde Universitetscenter.

Haldrup, Michael, forthcoming: 'Postkommunismens fragmenterede steder', in *Praksis, rum og mobilitet – socialgeografiske bidrag*, ed. Kirsten Simonsen, Roskilde Universitetsforlag.

Haldrup, Michael and Høgni Hoydal 1994: *Håb i krise – om muligheden af et menneskeligt fremskridt på Færøerne*, Research Report nr. 99, Publ. fra Institut for Geografi og Internationale Udviklingsstudier, Roskilde Universitetscenter.

Hovgaard, Gestur 2000: 'Comparing evidences – Explaining local coping strategies', chapter of draft PhD thesis, Department of Social Sciences, Roskilde University.

Illeris, Sven 1992: 'The Herning-Ikast textile industry: an industrial district in West Jutland', *Entrepreneurship and Regional Development*, 4 (1992): 73–84.

Isaksen, Arne (ed.) 1993: *Specialiserte produktionsområder i Norden*, Uppsala: Nordisk Samhällsgeografisk Tidsskrift.

Juul, Kristine 1999: *Tubes, Tenure and Turbulence: The effects of drought related migration on tenure issues and resource management in northern Senegal*; unpubl. PhD thesis, Department of Geography and International Development Studies, Roskilde University.

Lash, Scott 1994: 'Reflexivity and its Doubles: Structure, Aesthetics, Community' in Beck, Ulrich, Anthony Giddens and Scott Lash, *Reflexive Modernization – Politics, Tradition and Aesthetics in the Modern Social Order*; Polity Press.

Lash, Scott and John Urry 1994: *Economies of Sign and Space*, London: Sage.

Leborgne, Daniele and Allain Lipietz 1988: 'New technologies, new modes of regulation: some spatial implications', in *Environment and Planning D: Society and Space 6*.

Löfgren, Anders 1990: *Att flytta hemifrån, Boendets roll i ungdomars vuksenblivande ur ett situationsanalytiskt perspektiv*, Lund University Press, Meddelande från Lunds Universitets Geografiska Institutioner, avhandlingar 111.

Lundvall, Bengt-Åke (ed.) 1992: *National Systems of Innovation*, New York: Pinter.

Lundvall, Bengt-Åke 1999: 'Nation states, social capital and economic development – a system's approach to knowledge creation and learning', paper to be presented at The International Seminar on Innovation, Competitiveness and Environment in Central America: A Systems of Innovation Approach, San José, Costa Rica, 22–23 February, 1999.

Maskell, Peter, Heikki Eskelinen, Ingjaldur Hannibalsson, Anders Malmberg and Eirik Vatne 1998: *Competitiveness, Localized Learning and Regional Development*, London: Routledge.

Miller, Daniel (ed.) 1995: *Acknowledging Consumption: a Review of Recent Studies*; London: Routledge.

Negt, Oskar and Alexander Kluge 1981: *Geschichte und Eigensinn*, Frankfurt am Main: Zweitausendeins.

Piore, Michael and Charles Sabel 1984: *The Second Industrial Divide – Possibilities for Prosperity*, Basic Books.

Putnam, Robert D. 1993: *Making Democracy Work, Civic Tradition in Modern Italy*, Princeton: Princeton University Press.

Ray, Larry and Andrew Sayer 1999: *Culture and Economy after the Cultural Turn*, London: Sage.

Sack, Robert D. 1986: *Human territoriality: its theory and history*, Cambridge: Cambridge University Press.

Sayer, Andrew 1997: 'The Dialectic of Culture and Economy', chapter one in: Roger Lee and Jane Wills (eds.): *Geographies of Economies*, London: Arnold, 16–25.

Sayer, Andrew 2000: *Realism and Social Science*, London: Sage.

Simonsen, Kirsten 1993: *Byteori og hverdagspraksis*, Copenhagen: Akademisk Forlag.

Simonsen, Kirsten 1999: 'Difference in Human Geography – Travelling through Anglo-Saxon and Scandinavian Discourses', in *European Planning Studies 7 (1)*.

Smith, Adrian 1998: *Reconstructing the Regional Economy – Industrial Transformation and Regional Development in Slovakia*, Edward Elgar.

Smith, Adrian and John Pickles (eds.) 1998: *Theorizing Transition – The Political Economy of Post-Communist Transformations*, Routledge.

Sørensen, Ole Beier and Peter Vogelius 1991: *Livsformer og normativitet*, upubl. Licentiatafhandling fra Geografisk Institut, Københavns Universitet, vol. 1–3.

Storper, Michael 1997: *The Regional World – Territorial Development in a Global Economy*, New York: Guilford Press.

Vedsmand, Tomas, 1998: 'Viden som stedbunden produktionsfaktor – mod en ny teori om regional erhvervsudvikling', *Nordisk Samhällsgeografisk Tidsskrift*, 26: 37–51.

Woolcock, Michael, 1998: 'Social capital and economic development: Toward a theoretical synthesis and policy framework', *Theory and Society*, 151–208.

PART II
WELFARE STATE, PLANNING
AND HUMAN GEOGRAPHY

Chapter 4

Welfare states and social polarisation?

Frank Hansen

This article is about social geography. Social geography has often been defined negatively in relation to economic and political geography (Hamnett 1996). Therefore, it is not supposed to deal with the production even if the different social groups (types of families) in most cases are dependent on the production. The starting point is the already existing social polarisations and inequalities, and the studies are about the spatial/social segregation that is caused thereby. The political context, in terms of the welfare state's redistribution and the primary national differences in welfare regimes, are rarely brought into the analysis. This approach is invalid, as I shall argue in the following. The social inequalities are, for a majority of the population, created primarily in the world of work and change with respect to this. Therefore 'the economic' and the 'social' cannot be separated in such analyses. As already mentioned, 'the political' also influences the social inequalities that are created in society, and this is not only by means of welfare regulation. The regulation of work is very significant in the social inequalities, created as part of the world of work to which welfare regulation is directed. Finally, the 'cultural' aspect cannot be ignored either since family norms, social norms and legislation are extremely significant for different groups' access to education/work, for social rights and therefore for the social polarisation. Thus, social polarisation cannot only be illustrated from a socio-economic viewpoint. Due to the lack of social equality this perspective must be linked to a gender perspective, an ethnic perspective and so forth.

It is safe to say that concern for equality and equal opportunities is very strong in Scandinavia – both politically and academically. I will also claim that, until now there has been less public tolerance of phenomena such as unemployment, social polarisation and poverty than in many other countries, especially those dominated by a neo-liberal ideology. As will be shown this is, among other things, apparent in the differences between welfare regimes. We can talk about different national cultures regarding social equality and equal rights.

Thematically this article follows a Nordic tradition, as does the approach. The persistent claim that 'the social' cannot be understood independently from production is not new. The argument goes back to the strong focus on the study of production-based life forms as an important part of social geography (Bærenholdt et al 1990, Simonsen 1999). It also shows in the rather sceptical views in a large part of the Nordic discourse on the cultural turn of human geography. Class is not thrown out and forgotten, but thought of in a new way. 'The cultural' is interwoven into the study but is not made independent in relation to 'class-defined social positions'. In relation to the internationally dominating Anglo-Saxon geography this article should be read as an argument for a social turn of the subject but with strong emphasis on an inter-disciplinary approach to the studies of social and geographical polarisation. The aim is to create an outline to help understand the different regulation complexes' significance on the social polarisation, including the influence of different spatial scales, in particular the national one. The outline is constructed in steps. I begin by showing that the welfare state is indeed a significant factor on the social polarisation. In the next part a review of the discussions on welfare state regimes will be given. I criticise the regime approach but maintain it in a non-essentialist form where important aspects of the welfare state are seen as contingent in relation to the regime classification. I further argue that the study of welfare state regimes must include their concrete time-space configurations and the subsequent significance for the socio-spatial (re-)distribution of welfare. This part of the article also contains a short account of the connection between a given regime and social polarisation. The third part details the feminist critique of the theory. I include this discussion in order to show that the family is a fundamental, yet ignored 'producer and redistributor' of the social welfare and in addition that the family and family ideology have a large influence on the welfare state. At the same time, I emphasise that the family is an independent element in the understanding of social polarisation. The fourth part is a sketch of how to conceptualise work regulation. The latter is defined as an independent social-economic regulation complex that regulates the social polarisation processes within the work life. Therefore it is of great importance for the degree and the type of social inequalities that welfare regulation is directed at. As will be shown in the descriptions of welfare regulation and work regulation, it is also necessary to include a gender-based and an ethnic-based 'inequality–perspective' on the regulation. Different groups of society have unequal access to work and unequal rights in relation to work- and welfare regulation. These processes will briefly be touched in the fifth part that describes the regulation of rights and equality with special focus on gender inequalities. The final part is a summary, unifying the insights from the previous sections in a single model.

Poverty and welfare state regimes (WSRs)

Poverty can be seen as a consequence of the social polarisation. When we compare the degree of poverty in, for example, the EU-countries or the OECD countries, significant differences exist regardless of definitions of poverty (see Figure 4.1, OECD 1994, or Eurostat 1998). Since the differences cannot be regarded as a mechanical expression of GNP per capita, one way of explaining them is with reference to the development of the welfare state in the individual countries. 'There are, however, substantive differences amongst countries in the extent and generosity of the public social sector. Some studies analyse the relationship between the size of the welfare state and cross-national variations in poverty. Gustafsson and Uusilato, for example, claim that 'the bigger the welfare state the smaller the poverty rate'. Figure 4.1 is regarded as a statistical confirmation of that relationship (OECD 1994). As such, one can argue that the national welfare policies play an important role for the social polarisation in a country.

This explanation is (even though it is, as we shall see, far from the whole explanation) very reasonable. This especially shows to be the outcome if one starts from the past ten years' discussions on welfare-state regimes as they are defined and characterised by Esping-Andersen. He has – if any – set the agenda in these discussions (Esping-Andersen 1990, 1996, 1999). In addition to the traditional interest in the welfare state's significance for social security, he emphasises the welfare state's role in the social stratification. According to him, it is one of the definable characteristics of the three ideal-typical regimes (the liberal, the corporatist and the social-democratic) which he works with.

Figure 4.1   The social inequalities and welfare regulation in selected OECD countries

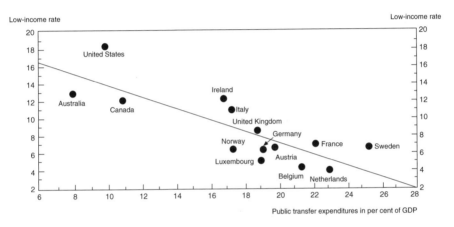

Note: Low-income rate defined as percentage of persons in families with incomes below 50 per cent of the median adjusted income.

Source: LIS micro data base; OECD social data base, 1994.

By a compound index measuring the degree of de-commodification, the independence from primary income, he seeks to grasp the welfare state's ability to secure a standard of living in connection with the loss of income: 'De-commodifying welfare states are, in practice, of very recent date. A minimal definition must entail that citizens can freely, and without potential loss of job, income, or general welfare, opt out of work when they themselves consider it necessary' (op cit. 1990: 23). According to him the degree of de-commodification corresponds to the division into welfare state regimes, (op cit. 1990: 51–54). The social-democratic regime (the Nordic countries) is the most de-commodified, the liberal one the least (USA, UK).

Considering this it is surprising that this discussion of welfare states has more or less been absent in social geography. One important exception is Hamnett (1994, 1998). He uses the concept of regimes to criticise the universalism in the 'global city thesis'. Different national welfare policies mean that phenomena such as social polarisation and poverty and their geography cannot be analysed without their recognition (Hansen and Jensen-Butler 1996, Hansen and Silva 2000). Therefore it is important that social geography is critically concerned with the welfare state regime theory and works with both comparative national studies and studies of the individual regimes/countries (see Hansen and Silva 1998: 1–2 for further clarification). In the following, I will give a short description of the three types of regimes, based mainly upon Esping-Andersen, concluding by positioning myself in relation to his approach.

Welfare state regulation, types of regimes and social polarisation

Welfare regulation is aimed at securing workers or citizens against social risks such as illness, unemployment and poverty and ensures them a pension when the pension age is reached. Briefly stated the welfare regulation must ensure families where there is no income or where the income is too low to maintain an acceptable standard of living. The regulation might have expanded into areas that cover different social and cultural citizen services for example the care of young and old. This element is not part of Esping-Andersen's typology. Welfare regulation consists of three types of regulation in relation to the market forces: The civil, the governmental, and one that is based on the social parties in the labour market (see Abrahamsson and Borchorst 1996 for a discussion of this). In the following description of the welfare-state regimes, the base is this tripartition. The civil regulation is primarily based on family subsidiarity even though it can also be determined via the legal system. But it also includes social networks within the civil society and voluntary organisations, among them church institutions. The systemic regulation is based on the entitlements of either the citizens or the workers and can be financed and administrated in different ways. It can be designed as a set of universal (citizen) rights and financed and administrated by the state, as seen in the social-democratic model. It can be based on workers' social rights and financed and administrated by the social parties in the labour market, as seen in the corporatist regime. Finally it can – as in the liberal regime – be a minimal, universal insurance that is administrated by the state but financed by the employers and insurance holders with financial aid from the state.

Welfare security normally consists of two systems. The primary and superior one, which is the 'safety net' that is supposed to deal with the majority of cases, and the secondary system which is concerned with those clients that fall through the first net. In all three types of regimes the state is responsible for the secondary system. The benefits there are clearly lower than those of the primary system.

The strengths of Esping-Andersen's typology lie in his stratification perspective; that is in his interest in the regime's significance for the socio-economic stratification (the class stratification). In other words, in the different stratification ideologies that are embedded and sustained by the social organisation of the regimes as expressed in its institutions. If the WSR contributes to the maintenance of differences in class and status in society, one can speak of a status-differentiated regime (a corporatist). The social-democratic regime is characterised as a conscious social redistribution. The liberal regime, on the contrary, has no social redistribution politics and is characterised by a status quo ideology (Esping-Andersen 1990: 55–78).

Table 4.1   The basic characteristics of the three welfare-state regimes

PRIMARY SYSTEM	CORPORATIST WSR	SOCIAL-DEMOCRATIC WSR	LIBERAL WSR
RESPONSIBILITY	The State	The State	The State
ADMINISTRATION	The unions and the employers' organisations	The State	The State
FINANCING	The unions and the employers' organisations; possibly little aid from the State	Primarily from the State, possibly together with employer	The unions and the employers' organisations, the State and other 'insured'
INSURED	Workers compulsory	Citizens rights	Insured members almost compulsory
STRATIFICATION IDEOLOGY	Status differentiated	Social redistribution	Status quo, flat rate
MOST IMPORTANT AREAS	Healthcare, unemployment, pensions	Healthcare, pensions, care services, unemployment insurance different system	Healthcare, unemployment, pensions
SECONDARY SYSTEM	State administered and financed Social security benefit unemployment help	State administered and financed Social security benefit	State administered and financed Social security benefits
THE ROLE OF THE FAMILY	Family subsidiarity e.g. GERMANY, not FRANCE	Based on the individual e.g. DENMARK	Based on the individual e.g. UK
TERRITORIALITY	Decentralised regional, local subsidiarity and redistribution e.g. GERMANY, not FRANCE	Decentralised rational solidarity and geographical social redistribution e.g. the NORDIC COUNTRIES	Centralised national solidarity and non-intended geographical social redistribution e.g. the UK

I regard – contrary to Esping-Andersen – other aspects of welfare regulation, for example priorities and compensation levels, as contingent and determined by concrete historical politics. This also applies to the family ideology and family subsidiarity that the welfare state is built on. By family subsidiarity I mean obligations among the generations and family members. I would also regard the welfare state's territoriality and its relation to the social geographical equalisation as contingent compared to the regime typology. The welfare state territoriality is more connected to different historical-geographical formations of democracy, i.e. federal versus national democracies and centralised versus decentralised democracies. Maybe one should speak of different territorial regimes also? Claiming that important properties of the welfare state are contingent in relation to the regime classification is the same as claiming that those properties do not necessarily follow the same geographical and temporal variation as the regime typology. Implicit in this understanding lies a critic of Esping-Andersen's use of the concept of ideal types, which is characterised by his empiricism and essentialism. I think it is important to discuss different types of regimes as ideal types bearing in mind that the characteristics of the regime are not sufficient to describe the welfare state in the individual country. On the other hand, I am critical of his view that the ideal type is a kind of empirical generalisation that can be changed as the empirical material changes (Esping-Andersen 1999: 73–74, 86–88). I regard a regime as a set of qualitative and durable institutionalised relations that are transformable only through radical reforms, and that characterise only certain essential aspects of the welfare state seen from an socio-economic inequality perspective. Hence I do not accept his tendency toward a 'totalising' essentialism in which all the relations within, and aspects of, the welfare state are subjected to the regime typology. The welfare state regime (WSR) must be regarded as a historically contingent social construction with a set of long time enduring institutions expressing a specific ideology of stratification.

An important, but overlooked, aspect of welfare regulation is its significance for the social redistribution between localities with varying social problems and financial resources. In order to examine this, it is necessary to focus on the administrative constitution of the welfare state, its connection to the political-administrative system, and to the social geographical politics of equalisation. This is especially important in relation to geography's interest in local social inequalities and the possibility of providing citizens with more or less equal conditions. This is an area where social geography can provide welfare research with an important insight. I have suggested that this aspect of the welfare state can be analysed through dichotomies such as: centralised/ decentralised administration and (with regards to financing) national solidarity versus regional/local subsidiarity. I also emphasise the necessity to question whether the processes of equalisation are intentional or unintentional. Welfare politics are thus played out on several geographical levels. In addition to those I have already mentioned, the EU-level is influential as well. The economic integration and the newly begun harmonisation of social politics influence the welfare politics of countries too. The politics of gender equality and the demand to have a social minimum benefit for all citizens in every country are good examples of this (see Hansen and Silva 1998 or Abrahamsson and Borchorst 1996).

It is extremely difficult to refer to an aggregated social polarisation since many different kinds of social polarisation are at force at the same time. They are between those in work and those out of work; between different groups of full-time workers; between men and women; between ethnic groups and between age groups. Taking this into consideration, it is evident that many relevant perspectives on social polarisation are possible, either individually or combined. Exactly because of this it might be meaningless to speak of an 'in toto' social polarisation. Seen from the perspective of social groups, it might be more fruitful to view the polarisation processes in relation to a specific group. This could, for example, be the low-income group, the unemployed labour force, the old-age pensioners, or another economically weak group. When I use the word polarisation it does not automatically mean that I view social differentiation as purely bipolar in nature, but rather I wish to emphasise the relativity and inequality of 'social positions', which the concept of social differentiation does not really include.

In the following account of social polarisation in relation to the three welfare state regimes, it must be stressed that I am only referring to certain important properties of this relation. For all three regimes it can generally be said that a polarisation will occur between those in work and those that are marginalised or excluded from the work life. The relative strength or degree of the polarisation will depend on the access to income compensation and the degree and duration of the compensation, in other words on conditions that are historically contingent. There will often – if not always – be a significant equalisation among the marginalised persons compared to their previous situation since there is a quantitative ceiling on the compensation, or because it is given on equal terms to all (i.e. 'flat rate'). If we look at rights and social inequalities in relation to compensation a different picture is drawn that reflects the properties of the regime.

In the corporatist regime these social inequalities and the social polarisation are especially caused by the fact that rights are linked to the worker and his or her status and success in the work life. As previously mentioned this causes a fundamental polarisation in relation to pensions and health insurance between those who are in work, and those who are not – for example housewives. Since the social redistribution takes place within professions and within the geographical area that is covered by the insurance company, one can further speak of a limited social redistribution that maintains status differences. Since the compensation is linked to the worker's success in the work life, the marginalised groups are in a worse position than those who have been working for several decades are. The social-democratic regime is founded on a social redistribution amongst the wage earners. One can speak of a consciously decided social redistribution, which also depends on the progressiveness of the tax system. This is only partly true for the state-supported unemployment insurance where the redistribution primarily takes place within the individual unemployment fund, professional group. With regards to the labour-market pensions the situation is totally the opposite since it is mainly those with the highest incomes that traditionally have had this type of pension. Since the level of compensation is highest for the low incomes, the social polarisation between them and those with higher incomes will be lessened in the case of unemployment, early retirement and old-age pension. Although the labour-market pension has a negative effect on this process. I must further stress that the level of compensation is not

100% so social accidents or old-age pension will always lead to a decline in income. This decline is particularly large for the labour-market groups that are extremely marginalised, as for example the long-term unemployed that no longer qualify for unemployment benefit. The liberal regime is built on a compulsory National Insurance where all contributions are the same, and everybody gets out the same. The level and the durability of the compensation are relatively low since it is designed to force people back into work, and low-income earners have to be able to afford to pay. Relatively speaking, in comparison to the two other regimes, this means that people who are hit by social accidents or who are going to pension are in a weaker position than those who are not or those who have supplemented their pension with private insurance. Since the level of compensation is highest for the lowest incomes the differences between the groups will be lessened if they are living on benefits unless the better off have supplementary private insurance. The most negative social polarisation occurs when people cannot afford to contribute to the national insurance or when they decide not to (married women) and are consequently assigned to the even lower public benefits of the secondary system. This is particularly true for those who are marginalised in the work life.

For a number of reasons it is not sufficient to describe welfare states as regimes. Some of them are hybrid like Portugal and maybe Holland. In addition the regime allows a certain variation in its characteristics, and a number of important aspects of the welfare state are contingent in relation to the regime typology. We are then dealing with country-specific properties of the regimes (or of hybrids of these). This can be illustrated using the four large Nordic countries. There is wide agreement that these four countries can be characterised as variants of the social-democratic regime. Despite this there are significant differences with regards to how the welfare state is financed, but not with regards to how it is administrated. In Norway, and particularly Finland and Sweden, the employers pay a considerably larger amount of the social expenses through social contributions than in Denmark. It is debatable though whether this is a social contribution from the employer or rather a 'wage tax', which he is merely collecting. In any case it is the state that dominates the regulation of welfare. With regards to the contingent qualitative and quantitative expansion of the welfare state under the Fordist expansion of the economy, Denmark and Sweden have been in the lead. Their social security and social service expenses were in relation to GNP in 1975, 23–24%, which is 4–6 percentage points higher than in Norway and Finland (see Figure 4.1 or Hansen and Silva 2000). The growth in expenditure continued after 1975 in all four countries mainly due to the consequences of the economic crisis and the growth in the number of pensioners. The growth has been largest in Finland and Sweden, the two countries that have suffered the most from the economic crisis. It is also these two countries that have most drastically cut down their welfare benefits (Abrahamsson and Borchorst 1996).

With regards to benefit types the Nordic countries are very similar. There is though a significant difference in the constitution of the pensions. In Denmark there is only one type of public pension – the old age pension, whereas the three other countries have an general supplementary pension, related to the labour market (Kosonen 1993). The Nordic welfare states are also amongst the most favourable to women's paid work and are therefore the least 'bread winner' dominated (Hernes 1987, Lewis and Ostner 1994). In this connection Denmark and Sweden have progressed the furthest with regards to the institutionalisation of public care for the young and old. Another frequently mentioned, almost constituting aspect of the Nordic welfare state is its aim to secure full employment. This is though a contingent aspect that, to a lesser degree applies to Denmark.

Figure 4.2　Social Expenditures in relation to GNP in the Nordic countries 1948–1993

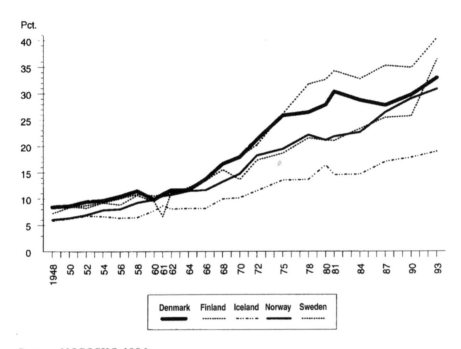

Source: *NOSOSKO 1996.*

Even though the welfare state's geographical formation is contingent in relation to the regime, it is true for all four countries that the welfare state is decentralised in the sense that the municipalities play a significant role and that a significant geographical equalisation is taking place. One can speak of a strong degree of 'municipalitisation' of the welfare state (Schou 1985).

Family ideology, family formation and the welfare state regimes

Already in the beginning of the 1990s a feminist critique of Esping-Andersen appeared (Sainsbury 1994, Lewis and Ostner 1994). It correctly pointed out that the regime theory was blind to the particular problems concerning women's social security. It failed to recognise the unpaid care work that takes place within the family, and it failed to incorporate the family ideology that laid the foundation of the welfare states. Concretely, this deficiency appeared for instance in the concept of de-commodification, that did not include the women who had never been commodified, and in the fact that the family's significance for welfare was generally ignored.

In her study of four case countries, Sainsbury shows that there are big differences in the perception of women's social rights, especially between Holland and Sweden in 1970. In Holland the women are primarily given their rights through the husband, whilst the opposite is the case in Sweden. She further points out that it is important to look at the rights connected to motherhood. Lewis and Ostner suggest in this connection a division of the welfare states into strong, moderate and weak breadwinner states, where the UK and Germany are placed in the first, France in the second and the Nordic countries in the third category (Lewis and Ostner 1994, Abrahamsson and Borchorst 1996).

Esping-Andersen accepts the feminist critique of his gender blindness and the lack of incorporation of the character of the women's social rights (Esping-Andersen 1999: 12, 46, 50, 51). He also accepts the criticism of the de-commodification concept: 'In any case the concept of de-commodification has relevance only for individuals fully and irreversible inserted in wage relationship' (op cit. 1999: 45). But he refuses to show interest in gender inequality and the perspective of equality. 'The objective is not to debate with gender theories but to understand the position of the changing family in the overall infrastructure of welfare production and consumption' (op cit. 1999: 50). The criticism on the contrary opens his eyes for the role of the family and for the necessity incorporating it as a significant element in his understanding of the welfare provision and the social security. He concludes that the household is a 'key source' in welfare production (op cit. 1999: 67). He reaches his conclusions partly through an analysis of how the family's role as care providers has diminished and partly through an analysis of the market's and especially the state's take-over of these duties. He calls this process a 'defamilisation' of the welfare society. Despite distinctive empirical deviations from the regime typology he maintains that the typology can include the family aspect. He does not argue that there is a casual connection. He is therefore caught in his empirical and 'totalising' understanding of the concept of ideal types.

It is surprising that he dismisses the gender perspective when he himself wishes to focus on the welfare state's stratification mechanisms. Why then only focus on class stratification and not on gender and ethnic stratification? In my opinion, the feminist criticisms point out that the relation between family ideology and the welfare state regimes is a contingent one. From his understanding of the concept of regimes, he would then have to abandon his theory. Maybe this is why he does not want to debate with the feminists? In this connection the question is whether it is at all possible, even desirable, to distinguish the family's importance from the family ideology's importance? If this is not done, it becomes clear that the national and regional discourses of the family are significant for the family's role as welfare producers. And the map of the family ideologies do not follow the map of welfare state regimes as it is shown by his own empirical data and by Lewis and Ostner's classification. One could also ask, what does it mean, 'to revisit the welfare regimes through the family's analytical lens'? (Esping-Andersen 1999). Do family members have a common set of lenses? Is it not the point in the feminist criticism that they precisely do not?

This does not change the fact that it is important to involve the family and the civil society in the discussions of the welfare society and the welfare state. In continuation of this it is surprising that what I call the family form is not given a more prominent role in the discussion. There are a number of studies of single parents, mainly women and their welfare situation in connection with studies of poverty. In the social-geographical literature this problem has especially appeared in connection with the studies of the situation for single mothers (the feminisation of poverty) but also in connection with men's and women's rather different socio-economic positions within the household (Winchester 1990, Hanson and Pratt 1995). In order to understand social inequalities and polarisation it is necessary to involve the differentiation and changes within family forms as an independent element in the analysis. The individual family is a self-regulating mechanism that needn't be subjected to the dominating family ideology in society. The differentiation into different social family forms is, analytically, an independent 'axis' of social polarisation. Seen in the light of the everyday life the family/ household should be the basic unity from which the study takes place. As Esping-Andersen points out 'The household is the ultimate destination of welfare consumption and allocation' (1999).

The regulation of the work life and the welfare state regimes

Already in 1990 Esping-Andersen mentions that the discussion of welfare regimes must also include labour-market regulation. His interest in this field grows through the 1990s where the employment rate's influence on stratification and employment problems in general becomes an increasingly important issue for him. In 1999 the welfare state's problem with 'the trade off between egalitarianism and full employment' is one of the main issues raised in his book (Esping-Andersen 1999). 'According to the mainstream analysis, exclusion in Europe and inequality in America are two sides of the same coin, namely the inevitable consequence of technology and the new global economy. What makes the difference is welfare statism and labour market regulation' (op cit. 1999: 96). This is why labour market regulation is up for discussion in a couple of the chapters. Starting from theories on industrial relations, he discusses labour market regulation through the trade unions and the system of agreement's influence on social inequality amongst wage earners. I will not comment on his conclusions, but regard his analysis as provisional. It is not sufficiently comprehensive and lacks a development of the necessary concepts to understand these very complex processes. And even though it causes some problems, especially with regards to the continental countries, he once again succeeds in maintaining the regime classification (op cit. 1999: 120, 122). As we shall see this is not valid since we here are dealing with contingency in relation to the regime classification.

I have therefore chosen to regard this mode of regulation as an independent complex and will adopt a wider approach to the subject by looking at labour regulation and not just labour-market regulation. In the following, I present a draft of my reflections on the contents and mechanisms at work in this kind of regulation. In addition to the work of Esping-Andersen my inspiration comes from studies of industrial relations and of labour-market segmentation and from comparative empirical studies (Boje and Toft 1989, Cousins 1999, Due-Madsen 1991, Ferner and Hyman 1998, Jensen 1995, Peck 1996, OECD 1993, 1997, EU 1999). For now I will leave open the question of possible regimes that might have a geographical overlap with the three welfare state regimes.

My point of departure is that, analogous to the welfare regulation, one can talk about three types of work life regulation (WR): the civil type and the two systemic ones. The latter ones work either as a regulation performed by the state or performed by a system of agreement between the unions and the employers' organisations. In line with Polanyi I do not believe that one can speak of unregulated labour markets (Polanyi 1944). The civil regulation will always be present and might even be dominant at least on some segments of the labour market. The civil regulation can be about all aspects of work. It works through norms and agreements, as they are determined in everyday life, in the interaction between the 'private' and the cultural public. The concept of civil regulation makes it possible to focus on the influence of social and cultural norms on regulation, also when they are 'hidden' in institutionalised agreements and in the legislation. Take for example the norms of women's right to work outside the home, of what typical women's jobs are, of equality of gender and so forth. At the same time it allows a distinction between the formal systemic agreements and norms and the concrete practices based on possibly deviant civil norms.

The systemic regulation normally will be a mix of the two mentioned forms, either dominated by the labour market organisations or by the state. In other words the state can participate in qualitatively different ways in the systems of agreement. WR organised by the two parties of industry is typically found in the Nordic countries. It is built on strong organisations, including a strong trade-union movement. State intervention is in this case very limited. WR with a strong state intervention is found especially in France and in the Southern-European countries that traditionally have a strong central state. In these countries there is a low degree of organisation, but the state has the right to enlarge local agreements in the individual industries to cover all, or the majority, of the labour force in the industry concerned. We can perhaps in this connection speak of two types of regimes: a social-democratic regime and a state-centred one. Between these two we find countries like Greece, Holland and Germany that can be classified as a kind of hybrid of the two systems. The state's possibility of expanding the agreements administratively is dependent on a wide support from the industry in question (OECD 1993). This partly corresponds to what Jensen calls the corporatist model (Jensen 1995: 38–39). In this model the state sets the rules for the collective bargaining and seeks influence on it through the tripartite talks. This model of WR demands that the organisations are pretty strong. If we add a liberal regime with very little systematic regulation or very individual oriented regulation one can talk about three types of regimes. The problem with the liberal regime is that even in the most liberal of countries such as the UK, a certain systemic regulation does take place albeit on a decentralised level, and the trade unions still play a limited role in the regulation (Edwards 1998). Please note that this classification does not correspond to Esping-Andersen's typology.

The classification into three regimes is even more problematic though. Only to a limited degree does it say anything about the work regulation's significance for social polarisation, and in addition only briefly touches the civil regulation. It is therefore necessary to link yet another aspect to the discussion of the systemic regulation, namely a further characteristic of the system of agreements that would say something about the social inequalities and the social polarisation that the WR helps to create. As Esping-Andersen expresses it: 'The greater the coverage, co-ordination and centralisation level, the more likely is it also that the bargaining will produce more homogeneous, across-the-board egalitarianism in terms of conditions' (Esping-Andersen 1999: 19). In saying this he points at something very central and important that is relevant for the stratification perspective. The degree of coverage describes the extension of systemic regulation and the relative dominance of the systemic rules and agreements over the civil (individual and decentralised) ones. But the degree of coverage does not necessarily say anything about the social polarisation since we cannot automatically suggest that civil agreements leave the wage earners in a worse position. They can do it if the civil agreements have been made to avoid (underbid, overbid) the norms and demands the systemic regulation lays down. In this case one speaks of a qualitative segmentation of the labour markets that give the wage earners essentially different wage and work conditions. In reverse, a high level of coverage does not necessarily lead to more uniform wage and work conditions. It can take form of a fragmentation with many different agreements. It is therefore very important to see whether mechanisms exist that co-ordinate the many agreements and thereby make them more homogenous. The co-ordination describes the processes where the rules and the mutual agreements for the individual groups are made more or less the same for large groups of wage earners that work in different industries. The mechanisms here can be common ballots, the replication of the collective bargaining from the leading industries, wage-drift compensation, legal measures etc. This concept can be difficult to distinguish from the concept of centralisation. In order to clarify the use of the concepts I would suggest that *co-ordination* is used to describe the level of aggregation of rules and agreements, in other words to describe the level the agreements are made on – i.e. on an individual, a company, an industry, an industry union level. I would then only use the concept of *centralisation* to describe the geographical spread of the rules and agreements, an aspect, which is often left out.

With regards to the civil regime one can safely say that it is characterised by a weak co-ordination and a strong decentralisation. The degree of co-ordination and centralisation must though be regarded as contingent in relation to the systemically dominated regimes. The historical development in the individual regimes and countries do in fact show very different tendencies (Ferner and Hyman 1998: introduction). This also counts for the Nordic countries. As Jensen says: 'If the differences in the collective bargaining's degree of centralisation in the EU-countries has to be explained, it is necessary to do it starting from the individual country's own historical development' and further, '...there have not been clear convergence tendencies...'(Jensen 1995: 46). In addition I do not believe that the concepts of co-ordination and centralisation in themselves are sufficient to describe the polarisation in wage and work conditions. In the scenario where people do not work under the same rules and agreements, the systemic labour market will always be divided into partial labour markets that have their own agreements. The social polarisation will therefore always be dependent on the solidarity between different professions that work under the same agreements, and between professions that work under different agreements in different partial labour markets. The solidarity between the professions, which must be regarded as a contingent factor, therefore becomes very important for the overall understanding.

At the same time it is important to realise that the WR is not reducible to questions of wage and work conditions, as most of the literature, because of its focus on the systemic regulation seems to imply. In order to get a better understanding of the whole WR it is therefore necessary to focus on the social polarisation processes that the regulation is directed towards. Work life regulation includes – in brief – norms, rules, agreements and legislation that regulate the work life and that influence the work differentiation, its hierarchisation, its qualification demands, its work conditions, its income differentiation and its marginalisation and exclusion from the work life.

Drawing inspiration from Hamnett, I believe there are at least four different 'axes' of social polarisation. I will call the first one the *employment differentiation*. It is concerned with phenomena such as employment, employment stability, part-time employment, unemployment, entitlements of early retirement and age pension, child labour and the discrimination in relation to all these phenomena. The next type I will call the *regulation segmentation*. It is concerned with the divide of the work life into segments that are characterised by the different types of regulation focusing on the relative strength of the systemic regulation. It is especially interesting in those cases where there is a large civil segment, which tries to underbid the systemic norms and agreements. One can also find discriminating systemic labour markets with regards to young people, the part-time employed ones, clients in activation programmes etc. The *work hierarchy creation* is the third polarisation axis. It is concerned with the dividing of work into jobs – in other words the pooling of work functions in a job – that demand different qualifications and that have different managerial competencies. The fourth type I call the *income polarisation*. It describes the income (and other goods) inequality and the income stability that is tied to the work life of all the people engaged in active employment. In addition it describes the transfer payments to those who are totally or partially excluded from the labour market. The objective of the forthcoming research is to relate the different regulation modes to the four different kinds of social polarisation. Some of these interconnections are exemplified in Table 4.2.

As in the discussion of welfare regulation, it is clear that the WR cannot only be analysed from the perspective of socio-economic positions. The polarisation and inequalities are at the same time articulated with other kinds of social polarisation and inequalities; they have to be put into relation with perspectives such as gender, ethnicity, age, part time etc. With regards to gender there is a substantive literature, within as well as outside geography, on the unequal opportunities between the genders with regards to work, segmentation of the labour markets plus wage and work conditions (EU 1999, Cousins 1999, Daly 1996, Sainsbury 1994, Bowlby et al 1989, McDowell 1989, Hanson and Pratt 1995). The literature on ethnicity is less comprehensive, but the research on this matter is experiencing a recent growth. (Hjarnø 1990, Jacobsen 2000, Madsen 2000).

Table 4.2   Different kinds of social polarisation and regulation – illustrated through examples

Polarisation dimension	Civil norms and agreements	Systemic norms, agreements, legislation, control, punishment
Employment differentiation	Work – and part-time work norms Family ideology Gendered work Prejudices about groups	Child labour, pension age, working hours, overtime, shift-work, division of labour, part-time job security, short-term contracts, access to unemployment benefits, work supplements
Regulation segmentation	Black work, tax evasion, discrimination, dignified treatment of others	Control, evasion punishment, citizenship demands, union membership agreement
Job hierarchy creation	Job qualification traditions Surveillance Promotion rewards	Job qualification demands, borderline agreements, transfer of credits, promotion
Income polarisation	Wage and payment in kinds	Minimum wage, premiums seniority wage, wage-solidarity unemployment benefit 'wage' during activation level of social security benefits

The Regulation of Social Rights and Equality (RRE)

As has been discussed in the previous part, it is necessary to focus on the norms, rules and legislation that define different social groups' rights from a perspective of equality. In all societies there are norms, rules and maybe even legislation on the rights, duties and equality of different groups. One can speak of civil norms or systemic norms, and they are practised in the work life as well as in welfare security and everyday life. The systemic norms are practised by different kinds of institutions and they influence the legislation. The civil norms are often norms that are taken for granted, and are hardly ever questioned. They can also be implicit parts of rules, agreements and legislation. Norms, agreements and legislation in this respect are about the differential treatment of gender differences, age differences, differences in sexuality, nationality differences and many more. Differences that make a difference. The individual groups can decide to make their situation visible and make it part of the public debate. This will normally happen through social movements. In this way the problem can become a political field in society. The result can be an institutionalisation like consultancy agencies, ombudsman and legislation. This development can be understood as a movement from a civil regulation mode to a systemic one, but it is important to emphasise that the systemic regulation does not just replace the civil one. It is rather a double regulation where a discrepancy between rules, legislation and civil practice takes place.

The regulation of social rights and the formation and change of equalities are tied to the geographical differences in the development of society, religion and culture. In the Western part of the world the ideas must be seen as tied to the emergence of modernity, the 'bourgeois' democracy and the nation state that originally privileged adult men who were property owners and who had a national citizenship. The civil rights are not essentially rights that are given to all adults who live in the nation state, and they do not apply to all spheres in society. Marshall, and many other people, forgets that to many groups in society these rights have been fought for, and very often still not achieved. Even today there can be a large difference between formalities and practice for many groups in society and in many ways. Smith is therefore right when she says that there is a radical potential in generalising the civil rights (Smith 1989). In this respect it might be possible to talk about a common western cultural inheritance; but having said that, however, it is important to stress that significant national and even regional differences do exist. The regulation of social rights and equality has geography, and these geographical differences matter. I have in the previous part of this article linked them to the nation-state and regional differentiations of the western culture, but also to supra-national institutions as the UN, the ILO and especially to the EU. These institutions represent important geographical scales with regards to this regulation complex. One of the areas where the EU makes a difference in social policies is the question of gender equality. And on a national-ethnical scale attempts to harmonise the protection of minorities are being made, as is a common policy for immigrants. It is important to emphasise that we are not speaking of *a* regulation complex but of many. Understanding the individual complex and its geography is an extremely complex affair and it demands a historical social-cultural analysis. At the same time I must emphasise that these hegemonic norms and rules on rights, duties and equality also influence the division of labour and the ideology in the individual family, but that it does not determine them. The individual family and the family members' positions and actions can be very different from the hegemonic norms and rules. This is an important point to make in relation to the conclusion in the next part.

An actual analysis lies beyond the scope of this article, and the following observations about the gendered regulation of social rights and equality are only meant to illustrate this complex. If we look at women's position in the family, the work life and in the welfare state, one cannot find a general equality in any of the OECD countries. At the same time we can observe large differences in these fields, among them (Cousins 1999, Esping-Andersen 1999, Rubery 1999, Sainsbury 1994, 1997). As previously mentioned, Esping-Andersen tries to show that the geographical differences in welfare rights and benefits with regards to this problem correspond to his regime classification. He does this purely empirically. This is problematic partly because the empirical data does not really fit and partly because he does not explain this congruence. Daly has followed his model and has added a fourth Southern-European regime based on a typology of different kinds of breadwinner welfare states (Daly 1996). The question is, whether we should be talking of a contingent historical classification where the countries' position can gradually change with historical and political changes, instead? In addition it is easy to point out deviations (see below). It is more stringent then to set up two ideal types – the breadwinner model (the regime) and the citizen model and from there conclude that all countries contain elements from the breadwinner ideology and that they lie on a continuum between the two poles (Sainsbury 1994, 1997). That would correspond with the classification in strong, medium and weak breadwinner models (Lewis and Ostner 1994). These studies underline that we are here dealing with contingent differences that do not correspond to the welfare-regime typology. For example, it cannot explain the differences between Portugal and Spain concerning women's position in the labour market and in the home; between France, Belgium and Holland or between England and Ireland, nor can it explain the likeness between England and Germany. This does not imply that there cannot be similarities between groups of countries as for example the Nordic countries as a consequence of collaboration and reciprocal learning processes. But even in this case it has been discussed whether one can speak of a single model (Rubery 1999: 23).

Conclusion: Construction of a provisional model

Social polarisation and social inequalities must be analysed from the perspective of the family, which as previously pointed out, is important for the production and distribution of welfare. The family should be seen as an antagonistic community of joint responsibilities and actions. It should however also be seen as a set of socio-economic positions (how much work, in which main segments, in which jobs, for what wage and supplemented by which benefits and social services). Further it is a set of members that are influenced by a family subsidiarity, a family ideology and a consumption pattern that might deviate from the hegemonic norms in society. In this way the family can be said to constitute its own socio-cultural regulation complex, which is an active part of the creation of social inequalities, and which is an independent polarisation axis. The family's size and form creates an inequality dimension itself.

As can be seen in figure three below, there are two additional socio-economic regulation complexes. The first is about the regulation of work life (WR). The 'normal' social inequalities amongst the population in the working age are created in the collision between the 'free market and management forces' and this regulation complex. Note that the definition of the working age also is a question of regulation. The regulation of work life is directed towards a number of different social polarisation axes which I, based on the literature, have provisionally determined to be four, concerning: the employment differentiation, regulation segmentation, job hierarchy creation and income polarisation.

The social polarisation in this part of the population will also depend on the welfare state's social security and service, in other words on the degree of access to social benefits, the compensation level of these and the duration of them. Note further that the regulation is not just a question of the structure's institutional set up, but that it also depends on the choices that are made in the families and on the family subsidiarity.

The other socio-economic complex (WSR) has, as previously mentioned, a key objective in correcting the social polarisation and inequalities that are created in the work life. Another key objective of the welfare regulation is the care of the pensioners and the children, to an extent, this is not seen as a family matter. Further it is the role of the welfare state to support working life by securing the health of the labour force, its availability to the labour market, its readiness to take up part-time employment and casual labour, its activation and retraining in connection with exclusion and so forth. The two socio-economic regulation complexes are in figure three therefore drawn overlapping each other. The arrows between them show their mutual influence.

Figure 4.3   Regulation and welfare

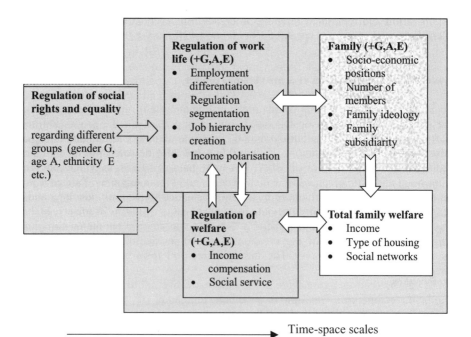

In all regimes and countries social benefits are provided for those who are ill, unemployed, on leave, or on different types of pension benefits etc. What differentiates the regimes is the way in which this redistribution interacts with the general redistribution in the society. In the liberal regime the ideology is that there should not be a large social redistribution. In the corporatist regime the redistribution must take place within professional groups thus maintaining a status differentiation in society; and in the social democratic regime this redistribution must be part of a large-scale redistribution in favour of the least well-off wage earners. The regulation in all regimes is designed to sustain a certain welfare level amongst the citizens in the form of income, consumption and service in connection with the loss of own income, or in connection with an insufficient income.

The preceding arguments also imply that, in theorising social polarisation it is necessary to recognise a number of socio-cultural regulation complexes (the regulation of social rights and equality RREs). As I have already mentioned this is due to the fact that different groups in society have different social rights and duties. From the perspective of these groups, the society does not provide social equality. Their rights are suppressed. In addition there are geographical differences in these rights that make a difference with regards to the social polarisation. That is why it will always be a misrepresentation to reduce social inequalities to only be about socio-economic positions and differences in family forms, as is done by Esping-Andersen and many others.

The approach should always consist of a combination of perspectives – an interactive fusion of perspectives that take into consideration the qualitatively different but mutually defined processes. The regulation of social rights and equality (RRE) can be said to interact with the WR and the WSR in a way that inscribes additional polarisation axes (dimensions) into the two socio-economic regulation complexes. In Figure 4.3 the inscribed RRE processes are illustrated by colouring all the boxes grey. Note that the regulation of social rights and equality also influences the family ideology and its form, but it does not determine it.

In other words one can possibly say that as soon as the socio-economic positions in the work life are populated with gender, age ethnicity etc., the picture becomes more complex, resulting in new kinds of social polarisation that link to the class polarisation. Therefore the regulation of social rights and equality must be dealt with in the study of WR. In the same way one can say that the regulation of social rights and equality adds to the welfare state regimes new polarisation axes than those already characterising them through the stratification ideology. Other types of inequality, for example gender-based or ethnicity-based, are also characteristic of the welfare state regulation.

References

Abrahamsson, P. and Borchorst, A. 1996: 'EU og Socialpolitik'. *Rådet for Europæisk Poltik Skrift* nr. 13. København.
Bærentholdt, J.O. mfl. 1990: 'Lifemodes and Social Practice'. *Nordisk Samhallsgeografisk Tidskrift* 11, Uppsala.
Boje, T.P. and Toft, C. 1989: *Arbejdsmarked og Segmenteringsteori*. Institut for Grænseregionsforskning. Åbenrå.

Boje, T.P. and Hort, S.E.O. 1993: *Scandinavia in a New Europe*. Scandinavian University Press, Oslo.
Bowlby, S. mfl. 1989: *The geography of gender*. In Peet, R. and Thrift, N. 1989.
Castles, F. 1996: *Need-based Strategies of Social Protection in Australia and New Zealand*. In Esping-Andersen (ed) 1996.
Cousins, C. 1999: *Society, Work and Welfare in Europe*. Macmillan.
Daly, M. 1996: 'Social Security, Gender and Equality in European Union'. Working Paper.
Due-Madsen, J. mfl. 1991: 'The Social Dimension: convergence or diversification of IR in the Single European market?' *Industrial Relations Journal*, 22.
Edwards, P. 1998: *Great Britain: from Partial Collectivism to Neo-liberalism to Where?* In Ferner and Hyman 1999.
Esping-Andersen, G. 1990: *The Three Worlds of Welfare Capitalism*. Polity Press, Cambridge
Esping-Andersen, G. (ed) 1996: *Welfare States in Transition*. Sage, London.
Esping-Andersen, G. 1999: *Social Foundations of Post-industrial Economies*, Oxford University Press, Oxford.
EU-kommissionen 1999: 'Women and Work'. *Employment and Social Affairs*. Belgien.
EUROSTAT 1998: *Social Portrait of Europe*. Belgien.
Ferner, A. and Hyman, R. 1998: *Changing industrial relations in Europe*, Blackwell, Oxford.
Hamnett, C. 1994: 'Social polarisation in global cities: theory and evidence'. *Urban Studies* 31: 401–424.
Hamnett, C. 1996: *Social Geography, a reader*. Arnold, London.
Hamnett, C. 1998: 'Social polarisation, economic restructuring and welfare state regimes'. *Urban Studies*, 33: 1407–1430.
Hamnet, C. m.fl. (eds) 1989: *The Changing Social Structure*. Sage, London.
Hansen, F. and Jensen-Butler, C. 1996: 'The Welfare State in Crisis: Local and Regional Effects'. *Regional Studies* 30: 167–187.
Hansen, F. and Silva, C. 1998: 'Transformation and Continuity in the Welfare States in Western Europe after World War II'. Paper to IGU Conference in Lisboa. København.
Hansen, F. and Silva, C. 2000: 'Transformation in the Welfare States after World War II: the cases of Portugal and Denmark'. *Environment and Planning C: Government and Policy* 18: 749–771.
Hansson, S. and Pratt, G. 1995: *Gender, Work and Space*, Routledge, London.
Hernes, H. 1987: *Welfare States and Woman Power*. Norwegian University Press, Oslo.
Hjarnø, J. 1990: 'Indvandernes situation på det danske arbejdsmarked'. *Politica*, 22.årg. 3, 320–331.
Jacobsen, V. 2000: 'Marginalisering eller integration? Indvandrere på det danske arbejdsmarked'. *Arbejdsliv* 2, Odense Universitetsforlag.
Jensen, C.S. 1995: *Arbejdsmarked og europæisk integration*. Jurisk-og Økonomforbundets Forkag, Danmark.
Kastrougalis, G. 1994: 'The South European Model of Welfare State and European Integration'. Mimeo, Roskilde Universitetscenter.
Kosonen, P. 1993: *The Scandinavian Welfare Model in the New Europe*. In Boje, T.P. and Hort, S.E.O. 1993.
Lewis, J. and Ostner, I. 1994: 'Gender and the Evolution of European Social Policies'. *ZeS-Arbeitspapier* 4. Universität Bremen, Bremen.
Madsen, P.K. 2000: 'Etniske minoriteter på arbejdsmarkedet–en sammenligning af position og integrationsindsats i fem europæiske lande'. *Arbejdsliv* 2, Odense Universitetsforlag.
McDowell, L. 1989: *Gender Divisions*. In Hamnett m.fl.
NOSKO 1996: *Nordisk socialstatistik 1946–1996*. København.
OECD 1993: OECD Economic Studies No. 21.
OECD 1994: OECD Economic Studies No. 22.
OECD 1997: OECD Economic Studies No. 29.

Peck, J. 1996: W*ork-place: the social regulation of labor markets*. Guilford Press, New York.

Peet, R. and Thrift, N. (eds) 1989: *New model of Geography*, vol 2. Unwin and Hyman, London.

Polanyi, K. 1944: *The Great Transformation*. Rinehart, New York.

Rubery, J. 1999: 'Overview and Comparative Studies'. In *Euro.Com. Employment and Social Affairs* 1999: Woman and Work.

Sainsbury, D. 1994: 'Women's and men's social rights: gendering dimensions of welfare states'. In Sainsbury, D. (ed.): *Gendering welfare states*. Sage, London: 150–69.

Sainsbury, D. 1997: *Gender Equality and Welfare States*. Cambridge University Press, Cambridge.

Schou, B. 1985: 'Den Kommunaliserede Velfærdsstat. Statslig Styring, Lokalsamfund og Kommunal-politik'. Rapport nr.38. *Institut for Samfundsfag og Forvaltning*. Arbejdspapir 1985/2.

Simonsen, K. 1999: 'Difference in Human Geography – Travelling through Anglo-Saxon and Scandinavian Discourses'. *European Planning Studies* 7: No 1.

Smith, S. 1989: 'Society, Space and Citizenship: A Human Geography for the "New Times"?' *Transactions of IBG* 14: 144–56.

Winchester, H.P.M. 1990: 'Women and Children Last: The Poverty and Marginalization of One-parent Families'. *Transactions of IBG* 15: 70–86.

Chapter 5

Does welfare matter?
Ghettoisation in the welfare state

Hans Thor Andersen and Eric Clark

We pose the question rhetorically. Of course welfare matters. The programs of the welfare state – in health care, housing, education and income security – impact on all, directly and indirectly. Our question is really more specific, and as the subtitle suggests is more accurately formulated: *Do differences in welfare state regimes make any difference with regard to processes of ghettoisation, segregation and social exclusion?* We raise the question because of recent developments in Scandinavian cities and in the Scandinavian welfare states (Abramsson and Borgegård 1998, Andersen 1998, Borgegård et al 1998, Lindberg 1999, Mishra 1999, Wessel 2000).

The Scandinavian welfare state differs in a number of ways from other welfare states (Esping-Andersen 1990), and differences in welfare states have been seen to account for differences in social polarisation and segregation (Musterd and Ostendorf 1998, Hamnett 1994, 1996, 1998): the more universal and generous the welfare state, the lower the level of social inequality and segregation. Yet, the patterns of segregation and social exclusion found in Scandinavian cities are remarkably similar to those of other countries with very different welfare state regimes. Have segregation and social exclusion become accentuated, despite favourable economic development and relatively generous welfare systems? How is it that ghettoisation takes place in advanced welfare states? Do the forces of globalisation and economic integration entail convergence of social and political conditions between countries – or will there still be room for localities to create their own balance between competitiveness and social justice? Are these indeed opposing goals requiring trade-offs? Are the emerging ghettos in Scandinavian cities taking shape in spite of the welfare system – or is the welfare system conducive to segregation and ghettoisation?

In the following we can only begin to address these issues. First we look into relations between globalisation, welfare state regimes, housing segmentation and social segregation in general. Then we focus on social inequality and segregation in Scandinavia in particular.

Globalisation

Globalisation is commonly understood to be a major force behind deep structural change in western societies (Sassen 1991, Friedrichs and O'Loughlin 1996, Dangschat 1994): rapid development and diffusion of high-tech, processes associated with deindustrialisation, fundamental changes in the labour market, liberalisation of trade and finance, growth in size of leading corporations, apparently declining importance of the nation state, emergence of new forms of organising urban politics, and increasing numbers of immigrants and refugees, to mention some of the more debated changes. We are aware there are many processes involved in what is commonly referred to as globalisation, and that the growing volume of empirical research operationalises globalisation quite differently depending on which process is in focus (Clark 1997, Clark and Lund 2000, Lund et al 2001). By globalisation we mean 'time-space compression' (Harvey 1989: 240), 'the annihilation of space by time' (Marx 1973: 524, cf Harvey 1982: chapter 12), 'the 'stretching' of social systems across time-space' (Giddens 1984: 181), and 'the intensification of consciousness of the world as a whole' (Robertson 1992: 8). This takes many guises, from transportation improvements ('the greatest of all improvements' according to Adam Smith 1976: 163) to major – not to say gross – reductions in turnover time (e.g. of chicken farming, from 120 days 75 years ago to 35 days today), from cheaper telecommunications to expansion of time-space routines. Globalisation is a generative term for many processes sharing to various extents the above mentioned common denominators, all of which entail *expansion over contextually given boundaries*. While specific contextually imbedded processes may reach some form of completion (or wane and reverse), globalisation with a capital G cannot be accomplished in any definite sense, for the simple reason that the annihilation of space cannot be accomplished (Massey 2001). Even the most enthusiastic champions of globalisation see through the rhetoric on the 'end of geography', concluding that the 'weight on mankind ... of geography – is bigger than any earthbound technology is ever likely to lift' (*The Economist* 1994).

Understanding the connections between globalisation, social change and segregation was initially quite simple (see Lovering 1997 for a discussion of 'simple stories'). Globalisation and related processes generate increasing numbers of low-paid jobs in sharp contrast to the smaller but growing numbers in well-paid positions in the successful sectors of the economy. This divide is etched into the urban fabric in the form of intensified social segregation, with social polarisation turning into spatial polarisation.

There is, however, a growing concern for understanding the causes of manifestly different social consequences of globalisation (e.g. Lash and Urry 1993, Hamnett 1996, Musterd and Burgers 2000). Social polarisation is not a necessary consequence of globalisation: institutional regulation of the economy bears on this relation. Social institutions, their organisation and constitutive elements, are important determinants of different social outcomes of globalisation (Amin and Thrift 1995). The welfare state in particular has emerged as a central institutional factor, without necessarily supplanting macro economic forces or links to labour market institutions and industrial relations. The relationships between globalisation and economic restructuring on the one hand and social stratification at particular locations on the other are multiple and complex (van Kempen 1994), and certainly include the role of public and other civil institutions.

Even if the full significance of these multiple and complex relations were mapped, the social geography of a locality cannot simply be read off. Many specific relations pertaining to the regulation of urban space, e.g. housing institutions involved in provision of and access to various types of dwellings, will influence the local consequences of supra-local processes. For instance, the volume, characteristics and spatial distribution of social housing is important, since allocation in this sector is not left to the market mechanism, which supposedly works the same regardless of context or place. When the peculiarities of local housing markets are combined with institutions and traditions, the resulting socio-spatial pattern of economic change appears more complex than the concept 'dual city' suggests.

Welfare

Some countries have managed better than others to deal with processes associated with de-industrialisation and the shift towards post-industrial conditions. Especially the extent of social exclusion and poverty varies markedly (OECD 1995). These differences are commonly considered to be the result of differences in industrial structure and competitiveness of the labour force. Recently, alternative explanations have been forwarded, most notably Esping-Andersen's (1990) study of national variation in systems of welfare provision. Subsequently, a broader interest has emerged in institutional impacts on social development in relation to major processes such as globalisation and the developing European Union (Brenner 1998, Harding and Les Gales 1997, Swyngedouw 1997).

Esping-Andersen argues that there are two key dimensions of welfare regimes: rights to welfare benefits, and the decommodification of welfare benefits. The first dimension has to do with who is entitled to receive welfare benefits. The extent of inclusion depends primarily on the financing of welfare services. Where funding is provided by an insurance fund (e.g. the German 'Krankenkasse') only members are entitled to welfare. In contrast, welfare services funded through taxation tend to be more universal. The second dimension has to do with the connection between financing and reception of welfare services. Some systems are based on co-financing or compulsory membership of welfare trusts, with close relationship between payment and services obtainable. In other systems, recipients may be completely disconnected from the costs of the services.

Based on these two dimensions, Esping-Andersen identifies three clusters of welfare regimes: the liberal or Anglo-Saxon welfare state, the corporate or continental welfare state and the smaller social democratic or Scandinavian welfare state. While the first cluster is characterised by modest and means-tested assistance, the latter two have more generous provision of welfare services. They differ however with regard to entitlement: the social democratic regime being inclusive of all residents, while the corporate regime limits welfare benefits to payers. Usually the system is funded through labour market contributions so that only those employed are included. Another important difference is ideological. Social democratic regimes have the political goal to provide equal support if needed, regardless of position in the labour market, income etc. The two other clusters of welfare states do not share this purpose.

A weakness of Esping-Andersen's analysis is that by focusing on pensions, sickness and unemployment benefits, which he says are the most important social welfare programmes, he ignores other important spheres of the welfare system, such as education and housing (Murie 1998). Especially housing is obviously of great importance for patterns of social exclusion and segregation. Another problem is typical of typologies, which tend to homogenise units within categories and emphasise differences between categories. There are for instance considerable differences between the Scandinavian countries with regard to provision of welfare services, and, though the Netherlands have much in common with Scandinavian countries in this respect, it is placed in the continental cluster of corporate welfare states.

Housing and segregation

Post-war suburbanisation radically changed the social landscape of most major Western European cities by creating deep geographical divides between socio-economic, demographic and ethnic groups. Those left behind in the inner cities were the poor, the unskilled workers, the singles, the elderly and immigrant groups. Thus the inner cities began a process of change which consolidated its characteristics of ethnicity and poverty (Andersen 1998). Moreover, the boom of the 1950s and following decades entailed considerable demand for labour, which was partly satisfied through immigration. As the wages of the immigrant workers were among the lowest and most of them expected to return to their home countries sooner or later, they themselves focused on the cheapest and thus poorest part of the housing stock. Thus segregation was generated by a combination of housing market structure and regulation on the one hand and broader economic and labour market developments on the other hand.

Kesteloot (1998) argues that this view does not constitute a universal explanation of segregation processes. There is rather considerable variation between cities. In a study of Brussels, Kesteloot identifies three structural mechanisms of segregation which transform social inequality into spatial segregation. The primary mechanism in the segregation of the poor is the lack of state intervention in the housing sector, allowing the market to distribute housing also among low income households. A second mechanism is social polarisation generated by changes in the labour market. When industries close and urban districts experience disinvestment, filtering takes place in the area's housing stock and poor households become geographically concentrated to the area. Thirdly, once established, segregation tends to maintain segregation or generate further segregation, partly due to the effect it has on limiting chances in the labour market.

Whinchester and White (1988) argue that groups which suffer from marginalisation will be limited in their choice of housing and residential location. They distinguish three dimensions of marginalisation which entail various degrees of exclusion and segregation: economic marginality (e.g. unemployed, welfare dependent), social marginality, which involves lack of 'acceptability' (e.g. ethnic minorities, refugees) and legal marginality (e.g. illegal immigrants, criminals and prostitutes). These are generally nested, so that while the first group only suffers from economic marginalisation, the second is hit by both economic and social marginalisation, and the third group faces economic, social and legal mechanisms of discrimination in the housing market.

Housing market deregulation, decreased investment in social housing, privatisation of public housing and tenure conversions during the 1980s and 1990s have in many cities led to a reduction in the number of cheap dwellings and thereby sharpened competition for housing. The location of marginalised groups is thus strongly influenced by processes in the housing sector (Andersen et al 2000). Especially the geographical location of various kinds of dwellings, how access to housing operates, and how (if) housing costs are regulated or subsidised, bear considerably on segregation of marginalised households.

A recent comparative analysis shows that ethnic segregation has increased in Western European cities (Musterd et al 1998). The studies show that this stems from similiar processes of economic and social change, immigration and urban restructuring, in spite of differences in welfare regimes. They also show that ethnic minorities are highly concentrated to certain inner city districts and newer peripheral housing estates. While the overall level of segregation (SI – Segregation Index) is 30–40 in most of the eight selected European metropolises, Brussels has a remarkably high level of segregation among immigrants from North Africa (SI=60). At the other end of the scale, the German cities of Frankfurt and Düsseldorf display a segregation index of 15–25. Both in British cities and in Brussels, immigrants are concentrated in specific areas of the inner city, where the oldest and cheapest housing is located. In contrast, in Stockholm and Amsterdam the concentrations of immigrants are located outside the city centre in newer estates. Musterd et al (1998) conclude that at least three major factors are relevant to understanding the present pattern of ethnic segregation: the urban planning and policy history of cities, the immigration history of cities, and the segmentation and functioning of the housing market.

Social inequality and segregation in Scandinavia

Before World War II the three Scandinavian capitals – Copenhagen, Oslo and Stockholm – were marked by relatively unregulated economies in the wake of rapid industrialisation. The inner cities developed into business districts, while the surrounding, densely built-up residential zones, mixed with factories and workshops, were inhabited by an expanding working class. Beyond these insalubrious zones, pockets of larger dwellings with better amenities were concentrated for the upper and middle classes. Urban development proceeded with few regulations. During this period social segregation directly reflected income, education and employment. Certain attractive locations with access to open land, lakes and woods at some distance from the city were developed into the first suburban areas. From the beginning, these areas consisted mainly of detached housing, populated by affluent citizens.

After 1945 urbanisation took a different course: The demand for governmental regulation during the crisis of the 1930s in combination with wartime regulation left a tradition of and strong political support for continued public influence on central welfare issues, including urban development and housing construction. The labour movement had formed strong unions and dominated national politics, establishing important preconditions for regulation. Public authorities became leading actors in urban planning, transportation and housing. Particularly in Denmark and Sweden, the massive expansion of the housing stock was promoted and supported by public sector planning and investment. The modern city was the rational city – i.e. well planned residential districts that included social institutions, shops, leisure facilities and green spaces, effectively connected to the central city and work places by fast and efficient public transport. An important element in this urban development was the rapid expansion of the welfare state, which managed to attain a remarkable degree of social equalisation in Scandinavia by providing services financed through a progressive tax system (see Table 5.1).

Table 5.1   Gini coefficients for selected OECD countries

Slovakia (1992)	0.19
Finland (1991)	0.21
Sweden (1992)	0.23
Norway (1991)	0.23
Denmark (1992)	0.24
Holland (1991)	0.25
Great Britain (1986)	0.30
USA (1991)	0.34
Russia (1992)	0.39

Source: Det Økonomiske Råd

The modern and well equipped dwellings became inhabited by young families of the working class and middle class. However, the more attractive districts continued being developed in the form of detached housing. This became the most attractive sort of housing and, with rapid post-war economic growth, also obtainable for the middle class and even segments of the working class.

   In terms of segregation, suburban expansion magnified the existing social division between attractive and less attractive districts and added a new dimension to the urban pattern: inner cities became the location of elderly, singles and low income groups. During the following decades both the inner cities and the non-profit housing estates in the periphery became residence for concentrations of poor households.

   Perhaps the most significant change during the post-war period in Scandinavian cities has been the marked increase in immigrant populations. Sweden imported labour during the 1960s and 1970s primarily from Finland, Turkey, Greece and Yugoslavia, but also from Poland and other neighbouring countries. Labour market immigration to Denmark and Norway started later, and came primarily from Turkey, Pakistan and Yugoslavia. Continued labour market immigration and Latin American refugees dominated immigration in the 1970s. 'Family reunions' of relatives to earlier immigrants added to immigrant populations in the 1980s and 1990s, as did refugees from the Middle East, Africa and Asia. Today, people with 'immigrant background' comprise 15–30% of the population in bigger Scandinavian cities. Due to ethnic segregation this figure reaches up above 80% in some residential areas.

The 1970s mark an important shift from general urban growth led by public investments towards more selective urban development dominated by private investments. In all three countries the expansion of the housing sector in the form of large, non-profit estates ceased. Instead, refurbishment of dwellings in the inner city (i.e. gentrification) and construction of owner occupied, detached housing in more remote parts of suburbia have characterised the last twenty years.

During the 1970s and 1980s, housing tenure became a major factor behind segregation. The spatial concentrations of different forms of tenure constituted a basic condition for this, but the segregation was magnified by tax systems that favoured ownership among high income groups and non-profit ('social', 'public') housing among low income households. While five municipalities in Greater Copenhagen have more than 50% non-profit housing, and eleven have more than 30%, ten municipalities have less than 20% and four have less than 10% of their housing stock in the non-profit sector. Instead these municipalities have a dominance of owner occupied housing and therefore a larger share of managers, self employed and married couples (Christoffersen and Even Rasmussen 1995). Similarly uneven spatial distributions of housing tenure are found in the three 'metropolitan areas' of Sweden (Stockholm, Gothenburg and Malmö) (Vogel et al 1990).

The spatial distributions of households by income and housing by tenure in Stockholm reveal a clear relation between income and housing tenure: the smaller the share of social housing, the higher the occurrence of high income households (Andersson et al 1997). High income households are nearly absent in social housing areas, particularly in the big estates from the 1960s and 1970s. This trend in social division by housing tenure is also evident in the Danish case, where owner occupation grew at the expense of private rental tenure. Consequently, the housing market has shifted from a more mixed situation to a polarised one as owner occupation has become a common form of housing among all socio-economic groups except unskilled workers and economically marginalised persons. The middle class abandoned rental housing, while this housing sector remains an important source of housing for workers and people outside the labour market (Christoffersen and Even Rasmussen 1995).

The relevance of socio-economic status and household types in different kinds of tenure at the local level is further emphasised by the marked changes in tenure composition in all three capitals. The share of private and municipal rental dwellings has decreased considerably in Copenhagen, Oslo and Stockholm, through urban renewal, 'flat break-up' and sale of public owned dwellings. In contrast, owner occupied and forms of shared ownership have become more dominant. This has been accentuated by shifts in municipal housing policies, as municipalities increasingly think in terms of attracting strong tax-payers, and develop local housing policies and plans accordingly (Lund 2000, Lund et al 2001). At the same time, segregation by income has increased markedly, with increasing numbers of housing areas with either very high or very low income ratios (the number of persons in the lowest 20% of the population by income, over the number of persons in the highest 20%) (SOU 1997:118). This pattern is perhaps more pronounced in Oslo, where rental units decreased from 51% of the housing stock in 1970 to 26% in 1995, while owner occupation grew from 13% to 35% (Børresen 1997, cf Wessel

1996). At the same time, the Gini coefficient of Oslo has increased markedly from 0.25 in 1986 to 0.34 in 1996 (Wessel 2000).

Social housing has become especially important for immigrants and people outside the labour market (Børresen 1997, Murdie and Borgegård 1998). The high-rise areas of the 'million programme' in Sweden (the construction of over a million dwellings during a ten year period, from 1965 to 1974, in a country with then about eight million inhabitants) and similar areas in Denmark and Norway, have become what is called 'belastade' (loaded, burdened, disadvantaged) or 'utsatta' (exposed, liable, vulnerable). These are the locations of ghettoisation, with extremely high percentages of population with 'immigrant background'. What 'native' population there is, is predominantly dependent upon welfare (SOU 1997:118). In some areas, as many as 40% of the school children are not able to qualify for entrance to upper secondary education, the labour market consequences of which are self evident.

Housing has always been a key issue for the labour movement and thus has been an integrated part of the Scandinavian welfare regime from the beginning. Financially favoured by the state, the sector had in practice to recognise social needs by providing housing for 'socially weak' households. This helped to integrate social groups during the early decades of the welfare state. In recent decades, however, the housing market changed from shortage to sufficiency. Consequently, vacancy rates among and accessibility to less attractive rental dwellings increased considerably. Marginalised groups – unemployed, welfare recipients, refugees – were channelled into the unattractive parts of the social housing market by authorities responsible for welfare and integration. By the 1990s, the bigger Scandinavian cities had developed ghettos very similar to those in most Western European metropolises. These are more often than not suburban high-rise estates (e.g. Rinkeby, Rosengård, Vollsmose, Gellerup), but a few ghettos remain in inner city private rental areas (e.g. Nørrebro, Grønland).

The successful housing policies of the welfare state from the 1930s to the 1970s have not been able to cope with the changing social conditions of the 1980s and 1990s. The very same characteristic that was once the pride of success – effectively providing decent housing for marginalised households – has become part and parcel of the process of ghettoisation. The welfare state reduces social inequalities and alleviates negative effects of the market. Pensions, medical care, unemployment benefits and the provision of non-profit housing are interventions that protect individuals from the 'raw forces of the market'. There is little doubt that the development of non-profit housing has provided a markedly higher quality of housing than the market could alone. However, despite the general improvements in quality, it has not prevented segregation. There are several reasons for this; in particular planning policy and taxation/rent reduction have been important. Urban planning in Scandinavia has been strongly influenced by functionalism, the separation of functions in order to avoid conflict between, say, housing and pollution from industry. Post-war urban development in the form of large uniform estates entailed a sharp division between various sorts of housing, some areas predominated by detached housing, others by multistory, non-profit housing. Nearly all Scandinavian cities ended up with large estates in the periphery.

Another instrument with which the welfare state provides decent housing for low income households is rent allowances. For other income groups, however, rents in non-profit housing can hardly compete with owner-occupied or tenant co-op housing. Due to tax reductions, middle and upper income groups have economic incentives to choose ownership housing. In addition, the 'social' environment in owner-occupied areas is generally considered more attractive.

At the core of the matter lies the question: 'under what circumstances are the processes driving polarisation mediated by a successful welfare state policy?' (Wessel 2000: 1963). Strong trade unions have been highly successful over the years and continue to play a significant roll in the welfare state. In recent years, however, they have repeatedly blocked policies such as trainee programs with reduced initial salaries, aimed at helping immigrants enter the labour market, in order to protect the principle of a high minimum wage. Likewise, strong housing policies formed by solidarity have been highly successful in upgrading housing conditions in Scandinavia. In recent years, however, the very housing that earlier lifted the housing conditions of the poor has become the new ghettos of the culturally different.

Conclusion

Scandinavia and its highly developed welfare state has reduced inequality to the lowest level within the OECD countries. Few countries have more equal income distribution or less gender inequality. This position has been obtained through a hundred years of struggle led by the labour unions, the social democratic party and other political organisations. During the last two decades, however, globalisation has posed challenges to the Scandinavian welfare state (Lindberg 1999, Mishra 1999).

Social polarisation and segregation, by income, education and ethnicity, has increased in Scandinavian cities since the early 1980s. Hard numbers in the form of Gini coefficients and segregation indices reveal this trend. National and local policies concerning immigration and 'integration' have not successfully counteracted segregation processes, and have in some ways contributed to them. The Scandinavian welfare states, like other welfare states, were constructed to counteract the social drawbacks of capitalism. However, the Scandinavian or social democratic version also intended to establish a high level of welfare services and protection in order to eliminate the 'underclass'. Scandinavian welfare states managed successfully to deal with the socio-economic problems associated with industrial capitalism, but the more complex socio-ethno-economic reality of post-industrial capitalism presents new and greater challenges. Huge suburban estates constructed in the 1960s and 1970s, once effective solutions to severe problems, have become separate social zones resembling those of other European cities – also called 'war zones' (Guston 1998).

Embedded in the Scandinavian version of welfare is a strong dimension of standardisation of social relations which leaves little room for deviation. In relation to immigrants and refugees this fact has become painfully obvious: despite high costs, integration remains a poorly understood goal. Lash and Urry conclude about Sweden that 'the price of institutions preventing underclass formation is an overregulated society in which minorities … are more effectively excluded from the occupational system' (1993: 146). It seems there are comparable mechanisms at work in the housing system. The Scandinavian welfare state regimes, so successful at eliminating the 'underclass' and limiting class segregation, have not been successful in hindering ghettoisation of new ethnic minorities. It seems the Scandinavian welfare state, once a model for others, is passing through a painful process of change. With international competitiveness in the global economy as influential political leverage, the solidarity component is shrinking in favour of the insurance component for what has been called the 'sustainable population' – good tax-payers who can cover their costs (Jørgensen and Warming 2000). Polarisation is however not a necessary outcome of globalisation, but must be seen in relation to local political forces of solidarity and (re)distribution of resources and life-chances.

References

Abramsson, M. and Borgegård, L.-E. (1998): 'Changing welfare states and social housing: consequences for spatial segregation' – reviewed, *Scandinavian Housing and Planning Research* 15: 149–173.

Amin, A. and Thrift, N. (1995): 'Globalisation, "institutional thickness", and the local economy', in P. Healey, S. Cameron, S. Davoudi, S. Graham and A. Madanipour (eds) *Managing cities*, 91–108. London, John Wiley.

Andersen, H.T. (1998): 'Social change and segregation in Copenhagen', *Geojournal* 46: 7–16.

Andersen, H.S., Andersen, H.T. and Ærø, T. (2000): 'Social polarisation in a segmented housing market', *Geografisk Tidsskrift* 100: 71–83.

Andersson, E., Borgegård, L.-E. and Hjort, S. (1997): 'Boendesegregationen i Stockholm under 1980'–talet. *Gerum*, Kulturgeografisk arbetsrapport, Umeå universitet.

Borgegård, L.-E., Andersson, E. and Hjort, S. (1998): 'The divided city? Socioeconomic changes in Stockholm Metropolitan Area 1970–94', in S. Musterd and W. Ostendorf (eds) *Urban segregation and the welfare state: inequality and exclusion in western cities*, 206–222. London, Routledge.

Børresen, K.S. (1997): *Bypolitik mod segregation*. København, Nordisk Ministerråd.

Brenner, N. (1998): 'Between fixity and motion: accumulation, territorial organization and the historical geography of spatial scales', *Environment and Planning D: Society and Space*, 16, 459–481.

Christoffersen, H. and Even Rasmussen, L. (1995) *Danskernes bomønster siden 1970*. København, AKF.

Clark, E. (1997) 'Globalizing cities?', in A. Lainevuo (ed) *Milieu construction*. Helsinki University of Technology, Milieu Construction Centre, Conference report S4/1997.

Clark, E. and Lund, A. (2000): Globalization of a commercial property market: the case of Copenhagen, *Geoforum* 31: 467–475.

Dangschat, J. (1994): 'Concentration of poverty in the landscapes of "Boomtown" Hamburg: the creation of a new urban underclass?' *Urban Studies* 31: 1133–1147.

Det Økonomiske Råd, København, 1996.

Esping-Andersen, G. (1990): *The three worlds of welfare capitalism*. Cambridge, Polity.

Friedrichs, J. and O'Loughlin, J. (1996): *Social polarisation in postindustrial metropolises*. Berlin, Walther de Gruyter.

Giddens, A. (1984): *The constitution of society*. Cambridge, Polity.

Guston, R. (1998): 'Frankrike har 1 081 så kallade krigszoner', *Sydsvenska Dagbladet*, 23 December.

Hamnett, C. (1994): 'Social polarisation in global cities: theory and evidence', *Urban Studies* 31: 401–424.

Hamnett, C. (1996): 'Social polarisation, economic restructuring and welfare state regimes', *Urban Studies* 33: 1407–1430.

Hamnett, C. (1998): 'Social change, social polarisation and income inequality in London 1979–1993', *Geojournal* 46: 39–50.

Harding, A. and Les Gales, P. (1997): 'Globalization, urban change and urban politics in Britain and France', in A. Scott (ed) *The limits to globalization*, 181–201. London, Routledge.

Harloe, M., Marcuse, P. and Smith, N. (1992): 'Housing for people, housing for profits', in S. Fainstein, I. Gordon and M. Harloe (eds) *Divided cities: New York and London in the contemporary world*, 174–202. Oxford, Blackwell.

Harvey, D. (1982): *The limits to capital*. Oxford, Blackwell.

Harvey, D. (1989): *The condition of postmodernity*. Oxford, Blackwell.

Hiebert, D. (2000): Ghetto, in R.J. Johnston et al. (eds) *The dictionary of human geography*, 312–313. Oxford, Blackwell.

Jørgensen, I. and Warming, M. (2000): 'Hvem skal bo i byen?', *SALT* 1: 23–25.

van Kempen, E. (1994): 'The dual city and the poor: social polarisation, social segregation and life chances', *Urban Studies* 31: 995–1015.

Kesteloot, C. (1998): 'The geography of deprivation in Brussels', in S. Musterd and W. Ostendorf (eds) *Urban segregation and the welfare state*, London, Routledge.

Lash, S. and Urry, J. (1993): *Economies of signs and spaces*. London, Sage.

Lindberg, I. (1999): *Välfärdens idéer: globalisering, elitismen och välfärdsstatens framtid*. Stockholm, Atlas.

Lovering, J. (1997): 'Global restructuring and local impact', in M. Pacione (ed) *Britain's inner cities: geographies of division in urban Britain*, 63–87. London, Routledge.

Lund, A. (2000): *Globalisering and urban forandring – en analyse af globalisering af erhvervejendomsmarkedet og urbanpolitiske forandringer i København*. Masters thesis, Institute of Geography, Copenhagen University.

Lund, A., Andersen, H.T. and Clark E. (2001): 'Creative' Copenhagen: globalisation, urban governance and social change, *European Planning Studies*, 9: 851–869.

Marx, K. (1973): *Grundrisse*. Harmondsworth, Penguin.

Massey, D. (2001): 'Politics, philosophy and space', lecture, Lund, April 6.

Mishra, R. (1999): *Globalization and the welfare state*. Cheltenham, Edward Elgar.

Murdie, R. and Borgegård, L.-E. (1998): Immigration, spatial segregation and housing segmentation of imigrants in metropolitan Stockholm, 1960–95, *Urban Studies* 35: 1869–1888.

Murie, A. (1998): 'Segregation, exclusion and housing', in S. Musterd and W. Ostendorf (eds) *Urban segregation and the welfare state*, Routledge, London.

Musterd, S. and Burgers, J. (2000): 'Global and local determinants of social exclusion: Amsterdam versus Rotterdam', in H.T. Andersen and R. van Kempen (eds) *Governing European cities: social fragmentation, social exclusion and urban governance*, London, Ashgate.

Musterd, S. and Ostendorf, W. (eds) (1998): *Urban segregation and the welfare state: inequality and exclusion in western cities*. London, Routledge.

Musterd, S., Ostendorf, W. and Breebaart, M. (1998): *Multi-ethnic metropolis: patterns and policies*. Dordrecht, Kluwer.

OECD (1995): *Income distribution in OECD countries. Evidence from the Luxemburg income study*. Paris, OECD.

Robertson, R. (1992): *Globalization: Social theory and global culture*. London, Sage.

Sassen, S. (1991): *The global city. New York, London, Tokyo*. Princeton, Princeton University Press.

Smith, A. (1976): *An inquiry into the nature and causes of the wealth of nations*. Oxford, Oxford University Press (orig. 1776).

SOU 1997:118 *Delade städer. Underlagsrapport från Storstadsutredningen.* Stockholm, Statens Offentliga Utredningar.

Swyngedouw, E. (1997): 'Neither global nor local: "glocalisation" and the politics of scale', in K. Cox (ed) *Spaces of globalization,* 137–166. New York, Guilford.

The Economist (1994) Does it matter where you are?, 30 July, 11–12.

Vogel J. et al (1990): 'Välfärd och segregation i storstadsregionerna. Underlagsrapport från Storstadsutredningen'. Stockholm, *Statens Offentliga Utredningar,* 20.

Wacquant, L. (1996): 'The rise of advanced marginality: notes on its nature and implications', *Acta Sociologica* 39: 121–139.

Wessel, T. (1996): *Eierleiligheter: framveksten av en ny boligsektor i Oslo, Bergen og Trondheim.* Dr. philos.-avhandling, Institutt for statsvitenskap, Universitetet i Oslo.

Wessel, T. (2000): 'Social polarisation and socio-economic segregation in a welfare state: the case of Oslo', *Urban Studies* 37: 1947–1967.

Whinchester, H. and White, P. (1988): 'The location of marginalised groups in the inner city', *Environment and Planning D: Society and Space* 6: 37–54.

Chapter 6

Geography, local planning and the production of space: A Swedish context

Jan Öhman

All kinds of research, especially within the discipline of geography science, meet society in some way. Theory and practice come together in day-to-day activities in the forms of firms, people, organisations, cities, traffic, planning and so on, which, in the end, constitute a whole society. Changes in different sectors of the economy, in politics, in the environment and in socio-economic conditions create needs for new types of knowledge. Of course we need not theorise all kinds of knowledge, but research has become a very important element in the constitution of modern societies. The ways in which research and society are connected differ among disciplines and countries. In Sweden, the discipline of social and economic geography has developed a close relationship to the welfare state and, especially, to the Swedish municipalities in the form of local planning. This is a relationship of longstanding tradition, established in the first half of the twentieth century, and, although the strength of this marriage has been variable, it must in an international comparison be seen as quite extensive.

Already at the beginning of the twentieth century there was a growing disciplinary specialisation within social and economic geography which was working with different aspects of planning. The movement towards planning has become increasingly important over time, and it will also come to influence various aspects of the discipline, among them, economic localisation theory, urban geography and social geography. Planning geography in Sweden has come to vary a lot in theoretical and methodological character, but it holds together in an effort, primarily concerning the choice of study object, of applying the discipline to planning. Sweden has, for most of the twentieth century, had a high and even rate of economic growth. Even though there were periods of recession, the country has had long-term, strong economic development. The changing of society in modern times and a spatial transformation of activities, population, enterprises, power and social relations, usually summarised in terms of the process of urbanisation, are indeed the framework for the development of a Swedish planning geography both from a theoretical and a methodological perspective. This was especially obvious during the 1960s and 1970s, when planning geography in Sweden had a rather strong position compared to other social sciences; this was partly because the research was quite successfully implemented in local, regional and national development. The main part of these efforts represented different aspects of an enlargement of the public sector by building new roads, hospitals, schools, universities, houses, ports and other forms of infrastructure for the evolving welfare state. There was also, during this time, active research on regional planning questions on different aspects of labour markets, industrial location, plant closures in different branches, decentralisation of manufacture industries and employment, the urbanisation process and socio-economic problems in medium-sized and large cities. As a consequence of this interest among geographers to take an active part in the planning of the society, Sweden, compared to other countries, came to have a high proportion of geographers involved in planning.

Viewed in retrospect and in a Nordic (Swedish) context, what can we then learn from these rather tight bonds between a discipline and the practice of that discipline in planning the society at a local, regional and national level? In the following, I will try to discuss some important phases of the growth and advancement of what I have called a human geography directed towards planning. In this chapter, focus is set on the renewal of planning, and how planning changed during the 1990s. I will call this new focus of municipal planning 'development planning', that is, planning that has in many respects abandoned the traditional orientation, with emphasis on physical planning and planning documents. In this chapter, therefore, the two following themes will be treated: a) social and economic geographic research and its relationship to the (local) planning of society, and b) municipal planning in Sweden, with a focus on the 1990s.

An early human geographer

In Sweden, compared to other countries, there was an early co-operation between human geographers and planners, architects, economists, and politicians at the local and national levels (Öhman 1994). One of the first instances of comprehensive co-operation arose as a consequence of the growth and expansion of Sweden's capital, Stockholm. In 1851 the city had a population of barely 94,000 inhabitants; it grew very rapidly, especially after the 1880s, and by 1930 it had a population of almost 605,000. Between 1881 and 1930 the population of Stockholm increased by 403,000 people, an expansion which, among other things, was accompanied by the building of new suburbs to accommodate the flow of people moving into the city.

It was from this background that the geography professor at the high school of Stockholm (now the Stockholm School of Economics), Hans Wilson Ahlmann in 1929 proposed to Stockholm's city council that an economic-geographic investigation of the suburbs of Stockholm be made. (Early predecessors to Ahlmann include Nelson 1918 and De Geer 1922). The main purpose was to show how 'modern geography can be done in such a way that it can serve practical purposes and contribute to the solution of current questions' (my translation, Ahlmann 1930). Within three areas of investigation – the inner differentiation of Stockholm, the chief outlines of the geographical development of Stockholm 1850–1930, and the traffic of goods to and from Stockholm – seven studies were published. Of these, one by William William-Olsson on the first theme claimed the most attention.

In his study of Stockholm, William-Olsson came to dispute earlier city studies that presented the city primarily as a part of the landscape. William-Olsson argued that a study of the shape of the city, its topographical site, geology, climate, vegetation, town plan, settlement and so on, are not the most essential factors

(William-Olsson 1937). Factors specific to the city, irrespective of the city and its relationship to other cities and the countryside, are determined by the stock of differential factors. The *inner* differential factors consist of the firms and the number of people competing for available dwellings in different areas of the city. The spatial result is the outcome of the needs of the firms and dwellers and of their ability to pay for certain locations. As a consequence of the character of the firms' and dwellers' needs and of the positions of power of both firms and dwellers, there evolves over time a spatial differentiation in the city consisting of areas where housing, public and private service production, industrial production and traffic occupies the territory of the city in question. The *outer* differential factors (the city's topographical site, geology, climate and vegetation) have only an indirect influence, guiding, accelerating and/or delaying the spatial differentiation. William-Olsson concluded:

> The separate buildings as well as the city habitation generally are only tools for the lives that are lived there. A palace is a palace only so long as the nobility are living there. Move them, and the palace may become a government office, a ruin, or something else (My translation, William-Olsson 1937: 6).

The study, which became William-Olsson's doctoral thesis, consists mainly of a grasping empirical survey and description of the differential factors and how they changed in Stockholm from 1850–1930. The concluding chapter discusses the relationships between the location of offices, downtown stores, theatres and so on, and there are some empirical generalisations about the specific situation in Stockholm. The specific situation is seen as both dynamic and orderly, mirroring demands and positions of individual and group economic activities in the city. It is a series of empirical generalisations formulated as statements resulting in concrete propositions on how to improve the city. William-Olsson argued for the importance of an increased knowledge of the specific (Stockholm) and the general (the differential factors) which should be a background to concrete actions when planning a society.

In many respects William-Olsson's study became a classic (Pred 1984: 101) and was followed four years later by the work, 'The future development of Stockholm' (*Stockholms framtida utveckling*) (William-Olsson 1941). The main purpose was to give the background to make a population projection for Stockholm. William-Olsson saw the relationship between the distribution of population and production in terms of a struggle. The development of production in time and space is decisive, depending on the social character of the labour force and the concrete results of consumption. In the analyses of Sweden's population distribution, the geographical environment, production, and population changes in time and space were of utmost importance. With respect to the driving forces behind the growth of Stockholm, William-Olsson argued that the manufacturing sector played a secondary role, and that quantitatively as well as qualitatively, political, administrative, financial and cultural activities had been more decisive for its expansion into a big city.

With the grasping empirical material that characterises most studies in this tradition, in 1941 William-Olsson drew several conclusions about future population trends, for example population growth during the period to 1970, including an empirical forecast of what later was named 'the turn-around' trend (William-Olsson 1941: 196–203).

Establishing a tradition: Central places and hinterlands

At the end of the 1940s the next important step was taken to develop a planning human geography. The discipline of human geography was constituted in 1948, and that year the research council of social sciences was established. In 1949 Gerd Enequist became professor of human geography at the University of Uppsala, and in 1950 she hosted a conference on behalf of the council of social sciences titled 'Central places and hinterlands'. The papers presented at the conference by Enequist, Bergsten, Godlund, Dahl and Hägerstrand clearly leaned towards social science (Enequist 1951) with a geographical planning ambition, and they were distinctly influenced by the work of Ahlmann and William-Olsson on Stockholm ten years earlier. The agenda of the conference was, among other things, to consider questions of the definition of central places, how to calculate the range of hinterlands, and different aspects of migration. The perspective presented in the conference papers on the relationship between central places and hinterlands was, in principal, an empirical/empiricist one expressing clear ambitions to generalise the central places as results of factors of, for example, centralised traffic, migration, the constitution of the labour market, innovations and central services (commerce, service, etc.). Grasping empirical data was presented in connection with these subthemes of central places and hinterlands. There was a deductive methodological ambition in several of the papers of the conference. This was expressed with reference to, among other things, the gravity model of Newton, the Pareto-function and chorological techniques to describe and analyse travel distances, traffic flows and, with the help of central place theory, to distinguish a national city structure and migration fields.

The separation between human and physical geography was reflected in the submitted papers, and physical geography was, on the whole, not seen as a strategic and important dimension in the study of relationships between central places and hinterlands. Somewhat drawn to a head, it can be argued that distance (between settlements, the length of migration, and between central places) is replacing the physical geography – a reduction of the natural and physical elements in geography with relationship between chorological objects.

The practice of the tradition

The meeting in 1950 became important because it made way for and contributed to the establishment of a tradition in which Swedish human geographers gained quite an important role in planning (Pred 1974, Arpi 1977, Olsson 1978, Asheim 1987, Christoferson and Öhman 1998, 2000). Characteristic of these early studies, as well as of those that followed, was that they were empirically extensive and focused primarily on spatial differentiation and the use of 'geostatistical methods'. The empirical skilfulness and accuracy that was thereby reached among Swedish human geographers came to be applied to the planning of society. During the period 1946–1954 several studies were published on the evolving tradition of a planning human geography, most of them directed towards a quantitative chorological perspective. These studies, together with economic geographical studies, marked a clear demarcation line against the tradition of (physical) geographical studies. Their focus has been directed definitively towards a study of the human influence on the changing society, and their research agenda includes few references to the integrated human and physical geography. Among the most important works in this 1946–1954 period of separation between human and physical geography were those of Kant 1946, Enequist 1947, Hägerstrand 1947, Enequist 1949, Hägerstrand 1949, Bergsten 1950, Bergsten 1951, Enequist 1951, Godlund 1951, Hägerstrand 1951, Kant 1951, Hägerstrand 1952, Hägerstrand 1953, Kant 1953, Pålsson 1953, Wendel 1953, Dahl 1954 and Godlund 1954. The Swedish economy grew very rapidly during the period 1949–1977, and had a historically unique and even growth rate. The economic-geographic consequences of this growth in the economic sphere were clearly reflected in works on migration, urbanisation, innovation, and the growth of the public sector (education, collective transportation etc.). The development optimism was apparent, as was the confidence in human geography as a discipline and in its ability to handle problems in the society and in relation to other social sciences.

The advancement of human geography

The planning tradition in human geography was established early into two spheres of work, theoretical and empirical. One part consists of the disciplinary work done at the universities, and the other part of the work done by planners. In many cases there is an exchange of persons and ideas between the two spheres which, among other things, means that people are moving between researching and teaching at the universities and working within authorities, departments, public investigations and so on, applying the discipline in concrete planning.

The applications are conducted in a variety of aspects of planning at the local, regional and national levels. They involve the use and development of many central themes within human geography, such as industrial location theory, regional development, territorial and administrative divisions, regional and town planning and spatial interaction theory (e.g., traffic, migration and economic flows). Some examples may illustrate this.

Swedish municipality reform started in 1952 and was conducted in a couple of instalments to reduce the number of municipalities from almost 2500 to about 280 in the late 1980s. One of the ambitions related to municipality reform was to change the borders of the municipalities to achieve a correction in the population size and central place structure according to Christaller's central place theory. The aim was for every municipality to have at least one central place with a minimum level of population (in 1975, 8000 inhabitants) to ensure a basis for, among other things, public service (Wallin 1968, 9–38).

Human geographers during the 1960s came to have a growing influence on both state and research reports in connection with governmental investigations, especially those concerning industrial location, regional development, urbanisation processes and structural changes in the economy. They had central positions in more than 20 public inquiries conducted by the government during the period 1963–1980. On a national level, human geographers also came to work with the Long Term Forecast (*Långtidsutredningen*) for example, and in connection with the population and housing census. Theoretical ambitions are commonly expressed in the research contributions to these state reports, for example, references to neo-classical economic location theory, and time-geography and behaviouralist models, although these reports do concentrate mainly on empirical issues, confirming how different phenomena varied spatially, usually with the use of statistical methods. In the state report, in many cases these empirical surveys are taken as a point of departure for the state to suggest measures concerning industrial support, relocalisation of public authorities, slowing the growth of the big cities, provision of regional transport support, methods to change the composition of the labour market in different parts of the country, environmental issues, differentiating regional production costs, etc.

As one example, in 1970 the Expert Group on Regional Studies (ERU) proposed a new central place system in Sweden based on several hierarchical levels. The basic element in the central place system was four hierarchical levels – big cities, big city alternatives, regional growth centres and service towns – and this categorisation had its theoretical and methodological origin in an interpretation of the rank-size rule. In terms of present and optimal hierarchy, there was a discussion of problems in the big cities as well as in the countryside (SOU 1970:3, 204–220). In association with the four hierarchical levels there was an attempt to define a regional hierarchical structure within this, with the support of regional political assets, and to try to decrease the imbalances between the regions with a combination of restrictive and/ or stimulating measures. The regional structure empirically proved by research becomes a regional political and ideological document.

In 1967 the government decided to establish extended investigation and planning at the county level. At the same time, new planning offices were built in the municipalities, as a consequence of the new and bigger municipalities that resulted from the municipality reform. This resulted in a huge demand for planners. Many of the recruited planners had been educated in the tradition of human geography directed towards planning. With this trickling down of the demand for some kind of planning geography, a great deal of work was produced at the regional and local levels as well, covering a huge range of topics, including industrial location, population threshold values, migration, birth rates, segregation, central business localisations, etc., usually with an ambition to forecast future development. These regional and municipal investigations were, in relation to those made at the national level, much more clearly directed towards empirical data and were largely lacking in theoretical ambitions.

The classical economic-geographical questions about space and place came in many studies to be replaced by prognosis and investigations of planning factors aimed at steering the society and its planning at the local, regional and national levels. Human geography came to have a great influence on all three levels, especially in the period of the late 1960s and 1970s. In the late 1970s a reorientation began in research with a less clearly spelled-out interest in problems concerning the different topics of planning. Theoretically this reorientation was directed towards a widening of the theoretical framework by relating the specific research to the whole discipline of human geography and by incorporating more of the theoretical perspectives that had evolved in other social sciences, for example, those of Marx, Weber, Keynes, Levi-Strauss, Frank, Durkheim and Rostow.

It has been argued that the more pronounced forms of quantitative human geography never got any real foothold in the departments of geography in Sweden. There are several reasons for this. One reason is that the massive development of planning institutions in Sweden coincided with the most intensive era of quantitative human geography. The planning offices evolving around the country came to recruit the majority of those who were most interested in quantitative models and techniques (as indicated by their dissertations, for example). The quantitative researchers very often chose to work at the newly established planning offices rather than to stay at the university. The application, and to some extent the development, of quantitative human geography moved from the university departments to the national, regional and some local authorities and organisations (e.g., the department of industry, the state industrial authority, regional office of counties, the National Land Survey Office, the Long Term Forecast, Statistics Sweden, municipal planning offices, county traffic planning offices, etc.)

At the same time, Swedish human geography had a tradition from the discipline's early work of the 1930s of using relatively uncomplicated quantitative methods to carry out research that focused on the planning of society. It made a path along the lines already laid down of how geographers primarily could be just human geographers (see the debate in YMER 1964 between David Hannerberg and William William-Olsson, and the discussion about the so-called school of Lund, Dahl 1964). Researchers who had a research interest in planning geography, such as Torsten Hägerstrand, Sven Godlund, Gunnar Törnqvist, Gunnar Olsson, Olof Wärneryd and others, all strove in different ways to make the quantitative methods part of a general science of society and to test them as instruments of a social science. This examination was primarily of a methodological character and was built on grasping empirical data, but it came later to be more and more theoretical and partly directed towards the status of the discipline's core. Some works also gained international attention (Whitehand 1985), especially the works of Hägerstrand and Olsson.

The disciplinary development of human geography in Sweden is characterised by an abundance of research topics and methodologies, which can be seen in part as a loss of larger comprehensive national research projects (except, for example, the nationwide urbanisation research programme during the 1960–1970s and the National Atlas of Sweden published in the 1990s). The more grasping and comprehensive programmes were conducted outside the university departments in association with government reports and public inquiries, within committees and by directions of different planning authorities. At the department level there developed more or less marked central points in the selection of disciplinary subject matters (towards historical geography, applied economic geography, time geography, 'rural research', etc.), while the research methods used generally showed less variation among the departments. This great variety and apparently undogmatic view of research methods was probably an effect of the separation of the discipline into areas of physical and human geography. This separation led to an increasingly evident integration of human geography into the social sciences; as early as 1949, Gerd

Enequist, professor at the department of geography at the time held her inaugural lecture on the subject 'The contribution of geography to the social sciences'.

But with the wide suit that the social sciences wore in Sweden during the period after the Second World War, the category of human geography, with its interest in different aspects of planning in society, was to develop into an applied discipline within the social sciences. It is apparent that the human geographers came to conceive of their mission primarily as a challenge to support the planning process at different geographical levels using empirical knowledge, and for a long period there was no theoretical challenge from other social sciences on the agenda. Spatial aspects of the changing society became the human geographers' speciality; due largely to the lack of theoretical interest, human geographers borrowed research methods used by sociologists, economists, political scientists and other social scientists. This engagement in inserting human geography into social sciences and linking it to the planning of society resulted in a lack of interest in the undivided discipline of geography and also only limited interest in the philosophy of human geography. In an examination of the Swedish Geographical Yearbook (Svensk Geografisk årsbok), Hägerstrand found that between 1944 and 1981 there were only two short articles published with the purpose of penetrating the basic questions of the discipline of human geography (Hägerstrand 1984, 16). Even though in other forums by the middle of the 1970s there was a discussion of the philosophy of human geography among Swedish geographers (e.g., see Olsson 1974, 1975), most researchers did not really see the need for a closer examination of the central theoretical questions of human geography. Human geographers in Sweden never really came to be a part of the quantitative drill, nor were they involved in grasping philosophical speculations. This was partly the result of a lack of a tradition penetrating the basic disciplinary questions in human geography, and partly a result of the fact that the university courses in human geography were so clearly devoted to preparing students for work in the planning sector (especially during the 1970s).

In the sphere of Swedish human geographers it was Gunnar Olsson who in the mid 1970s, and when he was professor at Nordplan (1977–1996), diverged by questioning and re-valuing the disciplinary subject matter, the research methods and the results of the planning geography. The critique was directed towards human geography as a social science and its disciplinary philosophy, containing both an epistemological and an ontological examination. Gunnar Olsson was therefore an early critic of the human geography as a social science and of its lack of understanding the charge of the social science, its too big engagements in the form of the spatial processes and the neglecting of its interlacing with the predecessors of power.

During the 1980s and 1990s there were some changes in the course of planning geography research. The research in this sphere of human geography was much more closely linked to other social sciences as sociology, political science and the economic group of sciences. At the same time the focus of the studied geographical level was moved from the local to the regional, national and international levels. The study of society and space was linked thematically to questions of dependency relations, private and public production, structures of resources, regional development and manufacturing, and spatial variations in employment. A perspective was developed in many studies with a grain of what can be called a 'society-geography' which was directed towards uneven development and questions about the process of urbanisation, cities and hierarchical city-systems, lifemodes and social practices, time-geography and planning, gender and manufacturing economic landscapes, service production in municipalities, territory and function, the state versus regional planning, industrial change and the local state, branch plant location, and, governance to mention but a few research topics (see e.g. Andersson et al. 1987, Berger 1991, Berger 2000). The literature in Sweden on these topics is quite extensive and we will now leave this broad perspective by focusing more directly on planning and the production of space.

By the late 1990s the growth and establishment of a human geography, with a clear subdivision directed towards planning in Sweden, was clearly a considerable part of the department's education and research. There has not been much of an academic critique of these relationships between, for example, research and planning. Is it possible, taking into account the above discussion, to formulate a perspective that would include both the discipline of human geography and the actual planning process as it evolved during the late 1990s? One way to arrange this marriage might be to incorporate the framework from, among others, Henri Lefebvre, David Harvey and the discussion of 'The production of space' and try to connect it to local planning.

Planning and the production of space

Municipal planning cannot be separated from the society of which it is a part, nor from its physical, social and economic context. It is also contextually formed in time and space according to the society in which it works. In addition, it mirrors those representations of society that exist among those participating in the different phases of the planning process (e.g., see Amdam and Veggeland 1991, Olsson 1996, Khakee 2000). In the last respect, planning, therefore, is an expression of an ideological position, because planning always entails choosing one or two alternatives among several physical, social and economic circumstances. The way in which planning is consequently expressed in specific societies therefore also becomes part of a political process, because the core and the aim of planning is to try to manage the development of the society towards, for example, social and economic goals. At a local level and with respect to the current overall uneven development, municipal planning has to handle this in a local context (e.g. see Pierre 1992, 1995, Wallenberg 1997). The spatial differentiation of social, economic and physical factors in a country like Sweden and the ways in which attempts are made to address them link the municipalities to the national and international level in efforts to overcome and manage the tensions that occur as a result of uneven spatial development (Putnam 1993, 181–185). And as, for example, Lefebvre frequently points out, because space must be seen as a product of the variation in space shaped in a process which, in its local result in a municipality, is part of an ongoing geographical uneven development, in the same time as 'the "object" of interest must be expected to shift from *things in space* to the actual *production of space...*' (Lefebvre 1991, 36–37). This production of space at the local level in terms of influences, planning and governing, is an expression of what Lefebvre would define as spatial practice, representations of space and representational spaces.

In an effort to link the tradition of a Swedish human geography directed towards planning to the municipalities and their situation in the late 1990s, a recent research project has been working with a framework to see municipal planning as a form of production of space (see Christoferson and Öhman 1998; Christoferson and Öhman 2000). On a theoretical level we argue that spatial practice in municipalities during the late 1990s in many ways is constituted by the people who live in the municipalities and their everyday lives, as men and women in their work, leisure hours, family life and in their dwellings, neighbourhoods and workplaces. In other words, these spatial practices are *lived* in everyday life. The spatial practices meet planning in a long sequence of primarily material expressions, as roads, water supply, refuse collection, public transport, borough parks, service supply, child care, schools, and so on. They also meet planning in the form of political and ideological symbols and representations, which for the individual citizen in Swedish municipalities in the 1990s, was a form of political disregard, a sign of political interest fading away and of a diminishment of local democracy. In the daily life of the individual, the space as lived space, something subjective, made up of memories and experiences and symbolically loaded, has in this way little identification with the architects' calculated 'planning space'. One can also see these spatial practices as an expression of the philosophy that 'geography matters' (Massey and Allen 1984), in that the everyday lives shaped in each municipality, taking into account the social, economic, political and geographical conditions, inevitably become part and parcel of the spatial practices (Simonsen 1993).

Representations of space are the conceptualisations of space made by planners, politicians, economists, researchers and others. These may be municipal plans and activities aimed at business in the municipality, employment, culture, tourism, information technology and EU issues. The basis of municipal planning in the 1990s was surveyed in an earlier book (Christoferson and Öhman 1998). Without excessive repetition of the framework in which we placed municipal social planning, we can say that this is seen as a process involving the attempt to manage social development by various means, a process that, to say the least, underwent comprehensive changes in the 1990s, with the direction changing towards what we call development planning. This interpretation of planning in, and in relation to, individual municipalities has been that, despite significant similarities in municipal exercise of public authority and production of service, there is major local variation in the planning of management and development issues. The geographical variations arise because conditions are unique in each municipality, with respect to political ideology, structure of the business community, geographical location, planning traditions and population development, to name a few of the more salient factors (see PLAN International 2001 for an overview). There is a clear tendency in contemporary Swedish municipalities away from the dominance of physical planning and towards development planning that expresses, and inherently is, a complex process. These attempts, which are becoming progressively more expansive in many municipalities, to bind together economic, social, political and structural transformations in a municipality in the form of a concept or vision – in the best interests of citizens of the municipality – represent an important shift in municipal planning during the 1990s. The survey reveals many different angles on the problem in the municipalities, as well as a variety of applications in various specific areas such as business, EU issues, IT, tourism and culture.

Representational space is Lefebvre's third definition of space. Representational space is 'space as directly lived through its associated images and symbols' which is found in an array of representational forms when municipalities sketch a picture of the municipality and e.g., the business community, culture, tourism and IT, in their activities, plans and, not least importantly, in their 'visions' (Lefebvre 1991, 39, see also Pred 1995). Since one aspect of planning is the attempt to steer the future in some desirable direction, it is strategically important for municipal planners, politicians, economists, etc., to attempt to convince and persuade others into believing in their vision of the future. In representational space – in the form of future representations of the municipality – the vision is pivotal, to attempt to visualise the plan, activity or vision. The institutions of social planning, in the broader sense, are creating representational spaces that underpin the identity, power and strategies of the agents involved.

On an overarching level social planning in Swedish municipalities has in the 1990s in a greater degree departed from extensive descriptions of actual conditions in the municipality. Increased importance has been given to how the individual municipality itself can be expressed as a representation of how the specific municipality can be described in terms of business community, culture, EU issues etc. But in planning focused more and more on conditions outside the municipality, municipalities have attempted to generalise the specific conditions of existing circumstances in the municipality by seeing business community, culture, EU issues etc. as expressions or representations of, general tendencies in a national and international world. This triad of how it *is*, the agents' *perception* of it and *beliefs* about it, provides an encompassing frame. As to how we, as individuals, behave differently in different situations and during different stages of our lives, it may be assumed that the nature of municipal social planning changes according to the municipal institutional, sectorial (business, culture, IT, etc.) and geographical context. The real problems in municipalities encounter the perceptions and beliefs about them in the guise of social planning.

Lefebvre writes that 'In the most modern urban planning, using the most highly perfected technological applications, everything is produced: air, light, water – even the land itself', thus expressing an ambition not unusual for the present reach and possibilities of social planning (Lefebvre 1991, 329). At the same time, there is also a belief in planning that is so all-encompassing that it may at least be considered important to more closely review and describe how this work was designed and directed in Swedish municipalities in the 1990s.

Renewal of municipal planning in Sweden: A few main features

In two earlier books, we reported an empirical mapping of municipal planning based on a survey of all Swedish municipalities (except for the three metropolitan areas) as well as case studies of seven municipalities (Christoffersson and Öhman 1998, and Christoffersson and Öhman 2000). A summary of the characteristics of Swedish municipal planning follows.

- On a general level, we can sum up by saying that perceptions of planning vary widely from municipality to municipality across the country.
- In slightly more than half of the Swedish municipalities, there are municipal planning departments that report to the local government. A scant 30 percent have chosen other solutions for planning and 17 percent have no planning departments at all.
- Slightly more than half of all Swedish municipalities have plans or programmes for the municipality's overall development. These plans are by and large written in general terms.
- Municipal activities are managed primarily through the budget and only to a lesser extent by means of long-term plans for each activity.
- It is unusual for municipalities to have adopted a common basis for planning.
- Most planners believe that for planning to be effective, consensus must be reached with those who will be affected by the issue.
- The comprehensive plan according to the Planning and Building Act tend to decline its share of total municipal planning.
- Working methods in the studied issues are highly characterised by dialogue with other parties.
- To improve the plan's chances to become a reality, more dialogue with other parties is necessary.

These results support the assumption that modern planning no longer fits the accepted image – that of planning as a general activity all over the country, similarly designed in all municipalities in the country, and resulting in a marked lack of differentiation among municipalities nor is planning the exclusive business of politicians and professional planners. There is extensive planning being done of a type not previously noticed. This planning is occurring in areas that the municipalities consider developable or where they believe there are urgent questions or problems in need of remedy. Much of this type of planning refers to activities that are not municipal assignment or the municipality's responsibility (see Schubert 1996, NUTEK 1998, Wallenberg 1997, SOU 1996, 169). Many municipalities also seem to be working with these issues in a process-oriented fashion, by striving to involve other players in the effort and to mobilise external resources for development projects in a wide variety of areas.

The concept of planning needs to be expanded and given meaning that is grounded in practical reality and in the context of political-geographical theory. In the concept of planning we should thus include activities that have a long-term orientation and purpose to achieve development in a particular, intended direction, even if the outcome of such efforts is not a planning document. We may also need to more expansively define the meaning of the planning document. In the process-oriented view of planning, the directive capacity of the planning document is toned down in favour of the working method, until it becomes a politically adopted document, and the planning document becomes instead a sort of manifesto over the (joint) effort that preceded the decision – devising a plan can become a pretext for starting a dialogue. Conceptually, this view fits easily into a perspective that sees planning as a structural process in which diverse mechanisms, including differentiated social conditions among Swedish municipalities, communicate the general terms for planning processes in the 1990s. There are also many examples of what could be called a post-modern development of municipal planning (see Pred 1995).

On the general level, municipal planning has very distinctly moved away from narrowly oriented physical planning towards planning characterised by flexibility in relation to the municipality's situation (Swedish Association of Local Authorities 1997, Nilsson 1995), and there are different forms of this planning. The common theme is that the process leading to the plan or action programme that the work is designed to produce is as important as the plan or action programme itself. A formal plan is far from always a topical question in the framework of development planning. Planning takes on the nature of a project, meaning that it is limited in subject area and in time, and frequently reinforced with temporary personnel hired for the project. Planning is directed outwards by involving several parties in the work, and the working method is process-oriented and aimed towards ensuring that those involved from the outside act in accordance with the objectives, providing expertise from their particular areas. There are a number of examples from different sectorial areas of this kind of development planning and, to sum up, it may be presumed that this working method reflects the real opportunities that the municipality believes it has to achieve the desired development. At the local municipal level, geographical differentiation is bringing about a variety of planning methods, a development that brought about extensive planning of a type that has not previously garnered much attention (Bernsand 1993).

Development planning is only to a slight degree guided by national interests. The initiative to begin planning, the subject field to which the planning refers, and the planning methods are designed entirely by individual municipalities.

Since the point of departure for planning is local conditions, the subject fields of planning differ from one municipality to the next, depending on what is considered developable. Planning may often be related to conditions linked to business and industry, tourism or the cultural sector. The aim in those cases is usually to make the municipality more competitive compared to other municipalities in attracting new businesses or to stimulate economic growth and create jobs. However, planning may also be aimed at trying to reinforce what is already there. Company networks, education and investments in IT are examples of such attempts. It may also involve planning that applies to certain geographical parts of a municipality, such as socially disadvantaged neighbourhoods where the municipality wants to reverse a downward spiral.

Development planning of some kind occurs in virtually all Swedish municipalities, at least within a couple of subject fields. The most common subject fields for development planning are those concerning IT, business and industry, employment and culture.

Development planning refers essentially to conditions outside the municipality's area of expertise, that is, areas where the municipality lacks the authority or ability to run a relevant municipal programme. This means that the intended development cannot be achieved without action by other parties, and that the municipality is dependent on involvement by those parties during the course of planning. Development planning is outward directed and predicated on cooperation with other agents. In practice, this means that the processes that begin in planning determine the prerequisites for achieving the intended results. The process leading to the decision is seen as more important than the decision itself when it comes to achieving concrete results in no less than 70 percent of Swedish municipalities.

Which parties are involved in the planning process depends on the matters at hand and the purpose. With respect to jobs and employment, for instance, the most extensive interaction is with public bodies like the employment service and social insurance office, but this shifts to the business community when the subject is commerce. By far the least involved are the public. One may also say that the less the subject lies within the municipality's field of action, the more necessary it becomes that planning is supported by other parties and other agents.

Now that major national projects aimed at improving public welfare are no longer predominant, the municipalities are increasingly playing the role of chief agent in public society with respect to local social development.

Since local conditions vary in highly significant respects among Swedish municipalities, differences among municipalities with respect to planning, as well as living conditions in general, will likely increase. Not least importantly, one may presume a correlation between local development and effective development planning in the municipality.

The wide variances among municipalities with respect to planning conditions and methods, divergent subject fields as the objects of planning, and diverse local conditions, preclude showing any all-encompassing model of the municipal planning process (see articles in PLAN International 2001). The complexity, incongruence and diversity of reality are not easily incorporated into rational models that describe, once and for all, the optimal approach to planning.

One discernible feature is that 'planning' cannot always be seen as synonymous with devising a plan, and that this plan is sharply distinguished from the subsequent execution phase. Implementation is often initiated while the plan is being drafted and the line of demarcation between 'preparing to act' and acting may begin to blur.

The societal changes in Sweden during the late 1990s have been seen by some as a shift from 'government' to 'governance' expressing an overall tendency to weaken the public sector and its tasks, financial resources and responsibilities in relation to the private sector. In the end this would result in a decline in the capacity to govern at different geographical levels at the same time, and the need would become greater to coordinate all kinds of structures and actions in society (Cars and von Sydow (2001)).

Enterprise that no longer functions seeks new paths. Planning that once was formalised and strictly politically aligned has gradually become largely ineffective. This type of planning has to a great extent been forced to give way to planning that is highly decentralised and more short-term and which includes distinct operative elements – but the picture is fragmented, and different forms occur side-by-side.

Conclusion

A few general aspects of society, planning and geography were addressed in the introduction to this chapter. In light of the review of planning-oriented human geography and changes in municipal planning in the 1990s, it may be appropriate to return in this conclusion to one of the fundamental issues. We can essentially discern two kinds of connections between planning and spatial influence. First, for companies, people, goods and services in production, space means that distribution and consumption are impossible without some kind of spatial transfer. The undertakings of municipal planning also entail an incredible number of spatial movements. Every decision generates a need for spatial movements. Decisions may also refer to investments in the space through infrastructure – roads, railways, telephone grids – but also more process-oriented and directed via transport subsidies, regional political means, agricultural subsidies, legislation, educational reforms, etc. Secondly, planning may attempt to counteract a certain transfer and depreciation of values in determined environments by simply supporting existing activities. Problems in metropolitan areas lead to investments in metropolitan areas to maintain investments already made. Similarly, rural areas are subsidised in order to preserve programmes and people in rural areas. Thus, planning has this dual role in relation to space: to facilitate movement on the one hand and to reduce movement on the other, in order to protect previous investments.

Essentially all exercise of power requires control over time and space, for both activities and individuals. There are many historical examples of this, ranging from the ancient city, the Hansa system, colonialism and multinational companies to discussions of an expanded European Union. History also teaches us that one of the most important driving forces in modern social development has been the attempt to use time to annihilate space. Through the 20th century, new production processes, means of transportation and communication technologies lessened the effect of necessary spatial transfers of goods, services, decisions and information. Basically to make money and make information and control functions more efficient, but nevertheless also to try and loosen the chains binding us to space (and time). The Swedish state and municipalities in the 20th century regularly and actively – and using planning for town structure, municipality reform, investments in the infrastructure, regional politics, decentralisation of state agencies, etc. – contributed to investments in space that changed the circulation. From a somewhat longer temporal perspective, there has been a tendency for the state, in concert with regional authorities and municipalities, to have as its initial overarching goal to distribute the population and buildings, primarily to the inland and northern parts of the country. That disposition changed beginning in about the mid-1960s towards attempting to preserve the existing spatial structure. Private enterprise, industry in particular, has had a more distinct spatially dynamic approach throughout the period, that of always making a considered effort to determine the optimal spatial localisation. Naturally, the differences between the actions of the state and those of private enterprise are considerably more complex and subtle. But the state's diverse spatial strategies are probably the logical outcome of its attempt to balance human needs throughout the country while doing what is necessary to try and make industrial growth and expansion possible through spatial mobility.

The renewal in municipal planning that took place during the late 20th century means that when the terms for the reshaping of society – meant here primarily in a geographical sense – change, the nature of planning will also change. Orientation has moved towards development planning, which, partly in new ways, is attempting to manage the transformation of the welfare state by more clearly attempting to utilise specific local assets of all types, as well as to emphasise the process rather than the plan. One of the effects on planning-oriented human geography in Sweden and the rest of Scandinavia is new standards for research, which could in very simplified terms be expressed as a greater need to contextualise processes rather than empirical outcome, local studies rather than national, and (post-)structural/ humanistic rather than empirical/positivistic.

References

Ahlmann, H. Wilson (1930) 'En ekonomisk-geografisk undersökning av nutida Stockholm med förorter'. *Ymer*.
Aldskogius, H. (1974) 'Samhällsgeografins vetenskapsfilosofiska och metodologiska problem under de senaste decennierna', 117–130. In: *Samhällsvetenskap på 70-talet*. Aldus.
Alvstam, C.G. et al (1979) 'Den disciplinära disciplinen – om geografi och ideologi', *HfKS* nr 2–3.
Amdam, J. and Veggeland, N. (1991) *Teorier om samfunnsplanlegging*. Universitetsforlaget. Oslo.
Andersson, R. et al (1987) *Maktutbredningen. Om resurser och beroenden i Sveriges kommuner*. Uppsala.
Arpi, G. (1977) 'Kulturgeografi. I Samhällsvetenskapliga fakulteten, Utvecklingslinjer och önskemål fram till år 2000. Uppsala.
Asheim, B.T. (1987) 'A critical evaluation of postwar developments in human geography in Scandinavia'. International Journal of Urban and Regional Research, no 4.
Berger, S. (ed) (1991) *Samhällets geografi*. Uppsala: Nordisk Samhällsgeografisk Tidskrift.
Berger, S. (ed) (2000) *Det nya samhällets geografi*. Uppsala: Uppsala Publishing House.
Bergsten, K.E. (1950) 'Agglomerationstendenser inom svensk bebyggelse'. *Svensk Geografisk Årsbok* 26: 45–60.
Bergsten, K.E. (1951) 'Sydsvenska födelseortsfält'. *Meddelanden från Lunds universitets geografiska institution, avhandlingar 20*. Lund: Glerups.
Bernsand, S. (1993) 'Efter marknadsyran – kommunernas nya uppdrag'. Stockholm: Kommentus.
Cars, G. and von Sydow, Å. (2001) 'Governance and partnership in Sweden'. *PLAN International*, Swedish Planning in time of diversity. Stockholm.
Christoferson, I. and Öhman, J. (1998) *Kommunal planering under 1990-talet – en studie av Sveriges kommuner*. Stockholm: Ascender.
Christoferson, I. and Öhman, J. (eds.) (2000) *Mot en kommunal utvecklingsplanering? – fallstudier av Sveriges kommuner*. Stockholm: Ascender.
Dahl, S. (1954) 'Västerås kontakter med landet i övrigt'. *Meddelanden från handelshögskolan i Göteborg Geografiska institution* no 42.
Dahl, S. (1959) 'Travelling pedlars in 19th century Sweden. *Meddelanden från handelshögskolan i Göteborg Geografiska institution* no 66.
Dahl, S. (1964) 'Reflexioner om ekonomisk geografi'. *Ymer* no 3.
Dahl, S. (1973) 'Kulturgeografi (Human Geography)', s 56–70. In: *Social Science Research in Sweden*.
Enequist, G. (1947) 'Sveriges mindre tätorter'. *YMER*, 241–285.
Enequist, G. (1949) 'Geografins bidrag till samhällsvetenskaperna'. *Ymer*.
Enequist, G. (ed) (1951) *Tätorter och omland*. Lund.
De Geer, S. (1922) 'Storstaden Stockholm ur geografisk synpunkt'. *Sv. Turist-föreningens årsskrift*.
Godlund, S. (1951) 'Trafik, omland och tätorter'. In Enequist, G. (ed.) *Tätorter och omland*, 50–72. Lund.

Godlund, S. (1954) 'Busstrafikens framväxt och funktion i de urbana influensfälten'. *Meddelanden från Lunds universitets geografiska institutioner*, avhandlingar 28. Lund.

Godlund, S. (1961) *Population, regional hospitals, transport facilities, and regions planning the location of regional hospitals in Sweden*. Lund.

Godlund, S. (1986) 'Swedish Social Geography'. In Eyles, J. (ed) *Social Geography in International Perspective*. London.

Hägerstrand, T. (1947) 'En landbygdsbefolknings flyttningsrörelser'. *Svensk Geografisk Årsbok* 23.

Hägerstrand, T. (1949) *Flyttningarna till och från Simrishamn*. Lund.

Hägerstrand, T. (1951) 'Omflyttningen och uppkomsten av kulturregioner'. In Enequist, G. (ed.) *Tätorter och omland*, 100–110. Lund.

Hägerstrand, T. (1952) 'The propagation of innovation waves'. *Lunds studies in geography. Ser B Human Geography, 4*. Lund.

Hägerstrand, T. (1953) 'Innovationsförloppet ur korologisk synpunkt'. Meddelanden från Lunds universitets geografiska institution, avhandlingar XXV. *Lund.*

Hägerstrand, T. (1970a) 'Tidsanvändning och omgivningsstruktur'. Bilaga 4 i SOU 1970:14 *Urbaniseringen i Sverige, en geografisk samhällsanalys*. Bilagedel 1: Balanserad regional utveckling. Stockholm.

Hägerstrand, T. (1970b) 'What About People in Regional Science?' *Papers of the Regional Science Association* vol XXIV.

Hägerstrand, T. (1972) 'Om en konsistent individorienterad samhällsbeskrivning för framtidsstudiebruk'. *Justitiedepartementet Ds Ju* 1972:25, Stockholm.

Hägerstrand, T. (1973) 'The Domain of Human Geography'. In Chorley, J.R. (ed) *Directions in Geography*. London: Methuen.

Hägerstrand, T. (1974) 'On Socio-Technical Ecology and the Study of Innovations'. *Rapporter och Notiser* no 10, Lunds universitets Kulturgeografiska institution. Lund.

Hägerstrand, T. and Lenntorp, B. (1974) 'Samhällsorganisation i ett tidsgeografiskt perspektiv'. In SOU 1974:2 *Ortsbundna levnadsvillkor*. Stockholm.

Hägerstrand, T. (1982a) 'Diorama, Path and Project'. *Tijdschrift voor economische en sociale geografie* vol 73 no 6.

Hägerstrand, T. (1982b) 'Likhet och närhet: om geografins ansvar för balansen mellan kunskapsperspektiv'. In Strand, S. (ed) Geografi som samfunnsvitenskap. *Ad Novas* no 19, Bergen.

Hägerstrand, T. (1984) 'Kulturgeografin i Svensk Geografisk Årsbok'. *Svensk Geografisk Årsbok.*

Hägerstrand, T. (1985a) *Time and Culture*. Paper, December 1985, Wissenschaftcentrum. Berlin.

Hägerstrand, T. (1985b) *Time-geography: Focus on the corporeality of man, society and environment. The Science and Praxis of Complexity*. The United Nations University.

Hägerstrand, T. (1989) 'Reflections on "What About People in Regional Science?"' *Papers of the Regional Science Association* vol 66.

Hägerstrand, T. (1990) 'En kulturgeograf ser på ämne och universitetsmiljö'. In Fridjonsdottir, K. (ed) *Svenska samhällsvetenskaper*. Stockholm: Carlssons.

Kant, E. (1946) 'Den inre omflyttningen i Estland i samband med de estniska städernas omland'. *Svensk Geografisk Årsbok* 22, 83–124.

Kant, E. (1951) 'Omlandsforskning och sektoranalys'. In Enequist, G. (ed.) *Tätorter och omland*, 19–41. Lund.

Kant, E. (1953) 'Migrationens klassifikation och problematik: några reflektioner'. *Svensk Geografisk Årsbok 29*, 180–209.

Khakee, A. (2000) *Samhällsplanering*. Lund: Studentlitteratur.

Lefebvre, H. (1991) *The production of space*. Oxford: Blackwell.

Massey, D. and Allen, J. (1984) *Geography matters*. Cambridge: University Press.

Nelson, K. (1933) 'En bergslagsbygd', *Ymer* 33.

Nelson, H. (1918) *Geografiska studier över de svenska städerna och stadslika orternas läge.* Lund.

Nilsson, Y. (1995) *Sverige och Europa – välfärd och kommunalt ansvar.* Svenska Kommunförbundet.

NUTEK, Närings- teknikutvecklingsverket (1998) *Bilder av lokal näringslivsutveckling. Intervjuer med företagsledare i större företag, politiker och chefstjänstemän som arbetar med lokalt näringslivsarbete.* R 1998:37. Stockholm.

Olsson, G. (1974) 'Servitude and Inequality in Spatial Planning: Ideology and Methodology in Conflict'. *Antipode.*

Olsson, G. (1975) *Birds in Eggs.* Ann Arbor.

Olsson, G. (1978) 'Identitet och förändring – eller om hemlängtan som ontologiska transformationer'. In *Regional identitet och förändring i den regionala samverkans samhälle.* Uppsala.

Olsson, G. (ed) (1996): *Poste Restante.* Stockholm: Nordiska institutet för samhällsplanering.

Öhman, J. (1994) 'Den planeringsinriktade kulturgeografin i Sverige'. In Öhman, J. (ed) (1994) *Traditioner i Nordisk kulturgeografi.* Stockholm: Nordisk Samhällsgeografisk Tidskrift.

Pålsson, E. (1952) 'Gymnasiums and communications in southern Götaland'. *Lunds studies in geography. Ser B Human Geography, 7.* Lund.

Pierre, J. (1992) *Kommunerna, näringslivet och näringslivspolitiken.* Stockholm: SNS Förlag.

Pierre, J. (1995) *Kommunal näringspolitik under strukturomvandlingen.* Stockholm: Svenska Kommunförbundet.

PLAN International (2001)

Pred, A. (1974) *An evaluation and summary of human geography research projects.* Stockholm: Statens råd för samhällsforskning.

Pred, A. (1981) 'Social Reproduction and the Time-Geography of Everyday Life'. *Geografiska annaler* vol 63 B, no 1.

Pred, A. (1984) 'From Here and Now to There and Then: Some Notes on Diffusion, Defusions and Disillusions'. In Billinge, M., Gregory, D. and Martin, R. (eds) *Recollection of a Revolution.* MacMillan Press.

Pred, A. (1995) *Recognizing European Modernities. A Montage of the Present.* London: Routledge.

Putnam, R. (1993) *Making Democracy Work.* Princeton University Press.

Schubert, G. (1996) *Kommunerna och tillväxten, möjligheter och faror.* Stockholm: Kommunförbundet.

Simonsen, K. (1993) *Byteori og hverdagspraksis.* København: Akademisk Forlag.

SOU 1996: 169 *Förnyelse av kommuner och landsting: slutbetänkande.* Stockholm: Fritze.

SOU 1970: 3 *Balanserad regional utveckling.* Stockholm.

Swedish Association of Local Authorities (1997) *Minska statens regelstyrning.* Stockholm.

Wallenberg, J. (1997) *Kommunalt arbetsliv i omvandling.* Stockholm: SNS Förlag.

Wallin, G. (1968) Småkommunerna på avskrivning. In Wallin, G., Andersson, H.G. and Andrén, N. *Kommunerna i förvandling.* Stockholm: Almqvist and Wiksell.

Wendel, B. (1953) 'A migration schema: Theories and observations'. *Lunds studies in geography. Ser B Human Geography, 9.* Lund.

Whitehand, J.W.R. (1985) 'Contributors to the recent development and influence of human geography: What citation analysis suggests'. *Trans. Inst. Br. Geogr.*

William-Olsson, W. (1964) *Behövs geografien? Ymer.*

William-Olsson, W. (1937) *Huvuddragen av Stockholms geografiska utveckling 1850–1930.* Stockholm.

William-Olsson, W. (1941) *Stockholms framtida utveckling.* Stockholm.

Ymer (1987) Regionalgeografi.

Chapter 7

Everyday life and urban planning: An approach in Swedish human geography

Ann-Cathrine Åquist

Everyday life is sometimes considered an important area of research in human geography, especially when human geography is seen from a gender perspective. In her presidential address to the Association of American Geographers, Susan Hanson (1992) argues that human geography has three core analytical traditions in common with feminism – everyday life, context and difference.

The aim of this article is to present some Swedish human geography research that takes everyday life as its point of departure. I will include some research conducted in other social sciences that has had an impact on human geographic thought in this field. Special attention is paid to time-geography since it can be understood as an approach that offers a specific perspective and methods for describing and analyzing everyday life. Much of the research presented here pertains to urban planning, wherein the perspective of everyday life can be used as a way of approaching planning issues. This perspective was taken, for example, in the development of master plans in Sweden in the middle of the 20th century. At the end of this article I will discuss the usefulness of time-geography as an alternative method of applying the everyday life perspective to urban planning.

First, I would like to address the question of the meaning of a *perspective* of everyday life. By perspective I mean something other than philosophy or theory. A perspective is a specific way of viewing the world, a specific point of departure. A perspective can be combined with various philosophies or theories. The perspective of everyday life focuses on the individual human being and her or his daily routines and activities in relation to the social and material surroundings, or, formulated differently, in relation to the time- and space-specific context. Taking this perspective as a point of departure opens up a view of the world that differs from the one that emerges when a sector of society (e.g., the economy) or a specific set of problems (e.g., environmental problems) are the departure points. However, in philosophy and the social sciences there are also *theories* containing specific understandings of the *concept* of everyday life, such as the French philosopher Henri Lefebvre's philosophical theory and the Danish ethnologist Thomas Højrup's theory of life-modes.

Perspectives of everyday life are not new, but this approach has become more frequently used in recent years. One thread goes back to the German philosopher Edmund Husserl, who founded phenomenology. His notion of the lifeworld can be understood as emerging from an everyday life perspective. Every individual is the center of his or her own lifeworld. It consists of our immediate experiences and actions in the world, in a pre-conceptual sense. Meaning is constituted in the lifeworld. Husserl used the concept of the lifeworld in his critique of science. He argued that science must recognize its subjective base in the lifeworld, where meaning is constituted in direct experiences (Skirbekk and Gilje 1987, Martel 1999). Anne Buttimer has elaborated the connections between phenomenology and human geography. In her article *Grasping the Dynamism of Lifeworld* (1976), she writes about the lifeworld as 'the culturally defined spatiotemporal setting or horizon of everyday life' (p. 277) and develops it in relation to the human geographical concepts of sense of place, social space, and time-space rhythms.

Another thread of the perspective of everyday life goes back to the women's movement in the Western world in the 1960s and the 1970s. Women argued that their experiences and the realities of their lives were concealed from the public world. 'The private is political' became a slogan. The theme was taken up by women's studies, which became a new field of research in the early 1970s. In the early days, the aim of women's studies was often formulated as the study and presentation of women's reality and experiences. The gender blind mainstream (social) science was criticized for obscuring the reality of women's lives and experiences. Some feminist researchers took as their point of departure an everyday life perspective in order to fulfill the aim of women's studies. This theme has been especially elaborated by the Canadian sociologist Dorothy Smith.

In the following I will present two theories of everyday life, developed by Henri Lefebvre and Dorothy Smith. I have chosen these two theories partly because they are more fully elaborated than most others. Further, Lefebvre's theory makes reference to urban life and urban planning. Some Nordic geographers have been inspired by his work in studies pertaining to everyday life. Dorothy Smith's theory can probably be useful in research on urban planning, even if Smith herself does not make such connections. Another reason for choosing Smith's theory is simply that I find it the most interesting.

Two theories of everyday life: Dorothy Smith and Henri Lefebvre

In his book *Critiques of Everyday Life* Michael Gardiner (2000) makes a distinction between two types of theories pertaining to everyday life. He designates some theories as taking a descriptive or analytic approach. Here, everyday life is presented as a non-contradictory and essentially unproblematic component of social existence. As one example, he mentions the phenomenologically inspired theory of the everyday developed by Alfred Schütz. The second type of theories forms a counter-tradition that not only describes or analyzes lived experiences, but tries to elaborate perspectives of everyday life as critical knowledge. One of the main objectives is to problematize everyday life. In these theories everyday life is given a historical dimension; it is understood as being bound up with the dynamics of modernity. Examples of this type, mentioned by Gardiner, are the theories developed by Henri Lefebvre and Dorothy Smith.

Henri Lefebvre

Henri Lefebvre wrote his critique of everyday life in the 1940s (1991/1947). He considers everyday life an essential, though overlooked and misunderstood, aspect of social existence. In his view, everyday life should not be dismissed as trivial and uninteresting compared to such human activities as politics, the arts, science or production, which are usually more highly valued.

> Lefebvre stresses that the everyday represents the site where we enter into a dialectical relationship with the external natural and social worlds in the most immediate and profound sense, and it is here where essential human desires, powers and potentialities are initially formulated, developed and realized concretely. It is through our mundane interactions with the material world that both subject and object are fully constituted and humanized through the medium of conscious human praxis. (Gardiner 2000, pp. 75–76)

In modern societies everyday life is closely bound up with the requirements and logics of the capitalist order. Examples of this are the distinctions between use-value and exchange-value, between working hours and leisure, and between public and private selves. Another example is the commodification of various aspects of everyday life. Everyday life has a routinized and commodified form, devoid of play and creativity. Out of people's feelings of alienation and unsatisfied needs in everyday life, a possibility for critique and emancipation is formed.

Lefebvre identifies a connection between people's everyday lives and the organization of time and space in society. This is especially experienced in urban settings. The dynamics of the city have specific routines organized in time and space. People's everyday lives are characterized by continuous adaptations and collisions with various structures of time and space (Simonsen 1993). Further, Lefebvre argues that there are connections between urban planning and everyday life. Urban planning creates forms in which everyday life takes place. He argues that in every urban planning project there is a concealed program for everyday life (Franzén and Sandstedt 1982).

Within Nordic Geography Lefebvre's theory of everyday life has inspired Kirsten Simonsen's study *Byteori og hverdagspraksis* (Urban Theory and Everyday Practice) (1993) and Jan Öhman's study *Staden och det varjedagliga utbytet* (The City and the Everyday Exchange) (1982).

The everyday world as problematic

In her book *The Everyday World as Problematic* (1987), Dorothy Smith aims at formulating a grounding for feminist social scientific inquiry. Her thinking is inspired by phenomenology and by Marxist theory. She argues for a beginning of inquiry outside and prior to textual discourses. A site for such a beginning is the everyday world. Smith argues that our world contains two layers. One layer is the world of ruling, which is primarily a world of texts and discourses. It is generalized and without a specific localization. Mainstream social science, mass media, the state and parliamentary politics belong to this layer. The other layer contains the everyday world. This is a particular and local world; every person is the center of her or his own everyday world. It is a world of concrete social practices. The everyday world is a basis for the world of ruling. It is like a 'service department' where we as human beings are reproduced. Smith gives an example of this divided world:

> When I went into the university or did my academic work at home, I entered a world organized textually (...) and organized to create a world of activity independent of the local and particular. ... But I went home or put down my books and papers to enter a different mode of being. I cleaned up after, fed, bedded down, played with, enjoyed, and got mad at two small children. I inhabited a local and particular world – the parks we would go to, the friends they had, my neighbors ... (ibid. p 6)

Smith argues that modes of understanding are created in the world of ruling, in the form of ideologies. These become tools for understanding both layers of the world. Smith's project is to develop a way of creating knowledge from a different point of view, from the everyday world. Here, the world is known otherwise; it is directly felt, sensed and responded to, outside discourses. This has a bearing on her feminist position. She argues that the world of ruling is a world dominated by men and men's perspectives. Women's work and activities are, to a greater extent than men's, contained within the everyday world. In order to make women's experiences and realities visible, the point of departure must be the everyday world. The aim is not merely to develop social scientific inquiries from women's perspective, but to address society and social relations from a standpoint outside the world of ruling. This is the standpoint where questions originate but answers are not necessarily to be found. In the world of ruling, social and economic processes that constitute the conditions for the everyday world are controlled.

In the following I will turn to a few examples of Nordic research on everyday life. I will first present studies by a research group consisting of Nordic women looking into concrete problems experienced by many women in the organization of everyday life. Their suggested solutions have a bearing on urban planning. After that, life-mode analysis is presented, a theory of everyday life that has been used by several Nordic geographers.

Examples of Nordic research pertaining to a perspective of everyday life

The research group for the new everyday life

During the 1980s some Nordic women researchers formed a network called 'Forskargruppen för det nya vardagslivet' (The research group for the new everyday life). The group had a feminist perspective and their research focused on urban planning from an everyday life perspective. Two anthologies were published: *Det nye hverdagslivet* (The New Everyday Life) (1984) and *Veier til det nye hverdagslivet* (Ways to the New Everyday Life) (1987). They defined everyday life in the following way:

> Everyday life consists of the basic actions that are repeated every day in order to maintain one's own and others' lives: cooking and eating, playing, caring for and raising children, helping and caring for sick people and others who cannot care for themselves, doing paid

work, caring for and maintaining bodies, clothes, houses and outdoor areas. (*Veier til det nye hverdagslivet*, p. 28)

The aim of the work in the research network was to develop new ways of organizing and integrating the most important parts of everyday life, which were considered to be: housing, care and work (*Det nya vardagslivet*, s 2). A model for such integration was found in the 'middle level'. The middle level is perceived in spatial terms and also as an organizational level between the households, the public sector and business, localized in the neighborhood. At the middle level, some tasks such as caring for children and the elderly can be performed, outside the household but within the neighborhood. This is supposed to make everyday life more integrated spatially and reduce the need for daily transport. Organizationally, these tasks are now carried out in households or by the public sector. In the institution called the middle level, work will be organized as community work, outside the formal labor market. People living in the neighborhood will themselves organize and control the work.

In the two anthologies published by the research group for the new everyday life, various issues connected to the researchers' everyday perspective are analyzed. There are articles about women's work within the formal and the informal sectors, the rationality of care, women's experiences of being unemployed, women's lives in relation to various urban structures, etc. The Norwegian sociologist Siri Nørve writes about identity and material structures of everyday life (Nørve 1984). She uses the concept of 'material structure' developed by the Norwegian sociologist Dag Østerberg (Østerberg 1985). He makes a distinction between the physical and the material, where the material is understood as physical entities formed within social relations. It includes concrete objects (cars, furniture, clothes, etc.) as well as spatial environments. For example, a certain city block is a physical entity designed and built within specific social relations – that makes it a material structure. Once such a material structure is established, it has certain influences on people living and moving in that environment. Nørve uses this understanding of material structure to argue that our identity is developed not only in relation to other human beings but also in relation to our material environment. Material objects and material space are included and drawn upon in agency, and in identity formation. Since women usually are responsible for the home and the housework, these probably are important to women's identity. By design and decoration of the home a woman tells the world something about herself. The same can be said about the food that she cooks, the presentation of meals, and the level of orderliness in the house. Nørve uses this theory to discuss the fact that few people live in collective housing, even though it is easier to organize a 'middle level' in such an arrangement. She argues that this form of living reduces opportunities to express identity thorough the material structure of the home and housework.

Life-mode analysis

The Danish ethnologist Thomas Højrup (1983) has developed a life-mode analysis, which has inspired several Nordic geographers. Influenced by Marxist theory, Højrup wanted to develop a type of analysis that focuses on various life-modes and exhibits the interdependence between life-modes and structural features of society. He regarded the focus on working life in Marxist theory as too restricted and wanted to include other areas of life in the analysis. In his theory three types of life-modes are developed: the independent life-mode, the paid work life-mode and the career life-mode.

People living in the independent life-mode are not engaged in paid work; instead they run small businesses like farms or shops, usually involving the whole family. There is no clear division between working hours and leisure time. Often people living in this life-mode do not have very much leisure time, but that is part of their way of life and a price of independence. The two other life-modes are both economically based on paid work, yet they differ from each other. In the life-mode of paid work there is a strict division between working hours and leisure time. The hours of paid work are endured while leisure time is spent on endeavors that make life worthwhile, for example, hobbies or family activities. Workers in manufacturing industries typically live in this life-mode. In the career life-mode the division between working hours and leisure time is again blurred. Formally there is leisure time, but it is often used for increasing one's competence for work, for example, studying scientific articles connected to work. The career is more important than leisure activities. This life-mode is typical for executives, medical doctors, academics, etc.

Højrup's life-mode analysis has inspired several Nordic human geographers. Ole Beier Sørensen and Peter Vogelius have studied working life (Beier Sørensen and Vogelius 1994). Pirkko Kasanen (1995) has used this type of analysis to study electronic-based home-work. Tora Friberg combined time-geography and life-mode analysis in her research on women's work (the latter study will be presented below).

After the presentation of these theories of everyday life I shall briefly summarize the main characteristics of everyday life, drawing on various theories and analyses by several researchers.

The characteristics of everyday life

The concept of everyday life has several dimensions and it can be defined in various ways. Charlotte Bloch (1991) has defined it as the activities through which we recreate ourselves at the same time as we contribute to the recreation of society (p. 31). This definition has much in common with Anthony Giddens' theory of structuration (Giddens 1979, 1984). In the theory of structuration, social practices in everyday life are understood as constituting society. Society and social relations are reproduced and transformed through the practices of everyday life. Bloch's definition looks much like the definition used by the research group for the new everyday life. Dorothy Smith adds some dimensions with her understanding of the concept; everyday life is lived in a particular and local world, different from the more generalized world of ruling, which is organized in texts and discourses .

One dimension of everyday life, mentioned by several researchers, is that we take our everyday lives for granted. (This aspect makes a phenomenological approach useful.) Birte Bech-Jørgensen (1997) argues that our everyday activities to a large extent pass unnoticed. Usually, we do not direct our attention toward everyday life;

we tend to carry out everyday activities without giving them much thought. This does not mean that we are unconscious of what we do. We can easily transfer our attention to everyday life, making it the focus of reflections and discussions (ibid.).

Another characteristic of everyday life is its routinization. Usually, we do the same things every day. From Monday through Friday our daily program looks much the same. Friday night often brings the start of another pattern, which dominates weekends. The routines of weekends are usually different from those of weekdays. A forming factor of everyday life is work, paid as well as unpaid. The time-schedule of paid work often directs the daily program. Those who work irregular hours do not have the same two patterns for the daily programs as those who work 'nine-to-five' Monday through Friday. Unpaid work, like cooking, cleaning, and doing laundry, as well as the caring for children and others, also forms the program of everyday life.

The daily routines give everyday life a certain time-organization, though these routines vary with the different phases of life. For example, a family's routine will vary according to whether the children are small, going to school, teenagers, young adults, etc. Everyday life also has a spatial organization (Bohm 1990). It is situated in space, in a specific place. Various activities are often localized to different places. Our workplaces for paid work are usually situated somewhere other than our homes. Children spend parts of their days in day care centers or schools. The housing segregation of urban areas is another aspect of the spatial organization of everyday life. We live our daily lives in concrete spaces/places created in the interaction of the physical and the social.

A distinction can be made between everyday life and its conditions (Bloch 1991). The conditions for everyday life can be the possibilities to get an education, a job, a place to live, or health care, but it can also include cultural phenomena like social norms, ideas about 'the good life,' etc. Economic and political circumstances influence the conditions of everyday life. Even the organization in time and space of an individual's surroundings is part of these conditions. Here, urban planning is important, since it influences the spatial organization of the city, the design and standards of housing, the relative localizations of various services in the city, the design of the transportation system, etc. For example, in a housing area planned as a neighborhood unit, conditions for everyday life go beyond single family houses. The specific conditions for everyday life can enable certain projects or activities, and they can obstruct others.

Having presented theories of everyday life and the characteristics of everyday life, I shall continue with a presentation of time-geography, which can be used as a method of study in this field.

Time-geography as a method for studying the everyday

Time-geography, founded by Torsten Hägerstrand (1970, 1982a, 1982b, 1985), opens up a certain perspective to the study of processes in time-space. The core of time-geography is the relationship of the individual to the surroundings. Emphasis is placed on the physical embeddedness of various processes. It is founded upon a physicalistic ontology, in which the world is regarded as a physical and concrete time-space context. Within this context, certain processes unfold in sequences of situations. In time-geography, processes consist of individuals' paths and projects in concrete time-space contexts. 'Project' pertains to the activities of individuals, while 'path' describes positions and movements of individuals in time-space.

Time-geography offers several advantages. For example, it gives a different view of the use of time compared to traditional time-use studies. Since paths and projects of individuals are followed in time-space contexts, time-geography illuminates how various activities are connected and where they take place, that is, their relative location. Another advantage is that the activities of an individual can be studied without being categorized from the start, for example, work, consumption, leisure. Nor is the study of activities restricted by being categorized as belonging to a certain sector of society, for example, the household, the public sector, the business sector.

From the point of view of constraints in time-space, an environment (e.g., a region, a city, a neighborhood) can be studied in terms of possibilities and restrictions presented to an individual in that environment. One example could be the study of individuals' actual access to various types of services, where not only the supply is analyzed but also the extent to which various services are within reach of individuals. One method for collecting empirical data often used in time-geographic studies is time-diaries, describing people's daily programs. Sometimes even time-diaries constructed by the researcher are used. Solveig Mårtensson (1979) used this method in her thesis *On the Formation of Biographies in Space-Time Environments*. She constructed several daily programs that were considered rather commonplace. The constructed daily programs were used to analyze whether it was possible to carry them out in three specific municipalities. This is a way to test actual surroundings, to discover the extent to which a specific time-space allows for certain daily programs to be carried out. However, more common in time-geographic studies is the use of actual time-diaries, written by people taking part in the study. (An example is presented below.)

The physicalist ontology in which time-geography is based gives it certain advantages but also has some shortcomings. A way of augmenting the usefulness of time-geography is to relate it to social relationships by way of the concept of the social institution (Åquist 1992). The concept is here understood in the following way: a social institution is a socially determined sphere for certain activities, for example, the family, the school, the church. An institution contains models for activities, or blueprints for projects. It also includes norms and rules for agency and conduct, based on various types of rationality. Further, it provides models or blueprints for roles. When an individual joins an institution, he or she is assigned a role. Along with the role come certain activities, or projects, and specific rules for agency and conduct. The content of a role often varies with age and sex. This understanding of social institution can augment the usefulness of time-geography by shedding light on the origin and characteristics of projects, as well as some circumstances governing the use of time. Most projects originate in an institutional context. This context also defines the character of the project. Projects are formed by the rules for agency and conduct prevailing within a social institution. The blueprints for roles of an institution bring about a distribution of projects among individuals. In this respect the institution also plays a part as one of the circumstances directing the use of time. Further, the rules of agency and conduct attached to an institution or to a role influence the use of time.

Another augmentation of the usefulness of time-geography has been the development, by geographers at the University of Gothenburg, of the use of time-diaries (Ellegård, Nordell and Westermark 1999). The use of time-diaries is a method for collecting empirical data that has long been used within time-geography. Time-diaries are kept by study participants, who are asked to write down their actual activities during one or more days. This gives a record of sequences of activities, their duration and, sometimes, where they take place. One example of the development of this method has been Åsa Westermark's use of 'reflecting diaries' in her study of the consequences of development aid projects for women in Bogotá, Colombia. As a supplement to traditional time-diaries, where daily activities are merely recorded, women taking part in Westermark's study were asked to write down their reflections about the various activities in which they took part, thereby revealing motives, feelings, needs, etc. This provided insights into the participants' personal views about their experiences.

A time-geographic study of women's everyday lives

In her PhD thesis, Tora Friberg (1990) uses life-mode analysis and time-geography to study women's everyday lives. She focuses on women's ways of coping with the need to integrate various responsibilities and tasks into a daily program: paid work, care for children and others, housework, leisure time. The study is based on interviews with thirty women, along with the time-diaries for two days. Even though all the women in the study are working mothers and consider that the norm, they set different priorities and organize their everyday lives differently.

In order to understand the differences, Friberg starts out from the life-mode analysis. However, her interviews and the time-diaries do not entirely fit into the model developed by Højrup and his associates. Friberg finds two groups of women who organize their everyday lives and think about their lives in accordance with two of Højrup's life-modes: the career life-mode and the paid work life-mode. Women living in the career life-mode consider their paid work, with its inherent career possibilities, important and try adjust family life to the requirements of the career. Women in the paid work life-mode think of their paid work primarily as a source of income. The work itself is not very satisfying, and the most important aspect of the work, besides the payment, is the companionship of their co-workers. But not all of the interviewed women fit into these two life-modes. There is a third group of women who live a form of life labeled the *balancing life-mode* by Friberg. These women try to balance their working life and their family life. They hold jobs that require education but do not normally lead to careers; they are, for example, teachers or nurses. They often work part-time when their children are small and plan to focus more on their jobs when the children grow up. They do not have an instrumental attitude to their paid work.

Even if women live in different life-modes, they have in common what Friberg calls organizational stumbling blocks. These can be colliding projects or other dilemmas or conflicts arizing from the various demands and responsibilities that women have to fit into a daily program. A common experience among the interviewed women is that sometimes projects crash because there is not enough time and energy to see them through, even if the projects are considered important.

Another thing all the women held in common is their wish that their children be safe and happy.

In the following I will turn to a more specific discussion of everyday life perspectives in relation to urban planning.

Urban planning from the perspective of everyday life

The idea of connecting planning issues to perspectives of everyday life is not new. It could be argued that much of the debate and planning of the Swedish welfare state in the middle of the 20th century was based on thinking related to everyday life. Urban planning of that period was also related to the everyday.

The Swedish context: A discourse on everyday life

In the 1940s and the 1950s, there was a political discourse on everyday life in Sweden, or at least a discourse that focused on parts of everyday life in a rather concrete way. It probably goes back to the political discussions of the 1920s and 1930s. A main problem at the time was low birth rates. In the Social Democratic Party this became interpreted as being caused by poverty. Alva and Gunnar Myrdal argued in their influential book *Kris i befolkningsfrågan* (The Crisis of the Population Issue) (1934) for this explanation. Poverty, high rates of unemployment, poor housing conditions and a severe housing shortage made it impossible for people to get married and have children. Here is a focus on the conditions of the everyday lives of 'ordinary' people. These conditions are understood as the explanation of the problem. The Social Democratic Party won the parliamentary election in 1932 and remained in power until 1976. During this period the Swedish welfare state was built. The construction of housing and urban planning became important tools in the building of the welfare state.

Within urban planning in the 1950s there was a line of thinking informed by an everyday life perspective. This comes through in my analysis of the master plan of the Swedish city of Örebro from 1955 (Åquist 2001b). The analysis is inspired by a statement of the French philosopher Henri Lefebvre, saying that in every urban plan there is a concealed program for everyday life (Franzén and Sandstedt 1982). The master plan of Örebro from 1955 concerns several issues that shape the conditions for the everyday lives of the population. Here, plans are made for the spatial organization of the city: transportation, localization of workplaces, housing, various types of services like schools, day care centers, post offices, sports grounds, churches.

Reading between the lines of the master plan, one can find a representation of everyday life – that is, the everyday life of a family with a bread-winning father, a home-making mother and children of school age. The family lives in a multi-family house in a housing area that has been planned as a neighborhood unit. The father goes to work, in the city center or in the adjacent industrial area, by bike or by bus. He probably comes home for lunch in the middle of the day. The mother can do most of her errands, on foot, using services within the neighborhood. If some of her errands require her to go to the city center, she can get there easily by bus. The children can walk to the nearby school, and the younger children stay at home with their mother. If the family has a car they use it to go out of town on weekends.

It is hardly surprizing that a plan from 1955 is based on this image of people's everyday lives. The family consisting of a bread-winning father, a home-making mother, and children was an ideal for many people, men and women, at the time. In Sweden, the 1940s and 1950s is sometimes labeled 'the era of the housewife.' In that period a majority of the married women were full-time housewives. In the periods before and after that, married women have to a larger extent worked outside the home (Hirdman 1983, Åquist 1987). However, the question of how well this type of everyday life suited all people might very well be raised.

During 'the era of the housewife' there was a discourse about the housewife's work and her situation in general. There were radio programs in Sweden in the 1950s on this theme. Various magazines, not only women's magazines, published articles about the work of the housewife. The weekly magazine of the cooperative movement, 'Vi' (We), surveyed its readers in 1949 on the contents of the magazine (Åquist 1987), and they presented the survey results in their first issue of 1950. The most common wish the readers expressed was for more information and advice for housewives. 'Vi' started a monthly supplement called 'Vi husmödrar' (We housewives). Every issue had a specific theme, such as cleaning, health, kitchen tools, suggested plans for the organization of the work of the housewife, etc.

In 1944 'Hemmens forskningsinstitut,' a research institute for the home, was founded in Sweden. Initiators were various women's organizations together with some women working with one of several public investigations on housing and the population issue (Lövgren 1994). The aim of the institute was to conduct research on the work of the housewife, studying both working methods and tools. One result of the research was regulations for the design of kitchens (counter height, light conditions, the relative placement of kitchen equipment and appliances, etc.). In 1957 the institute was taken over by the state and re-organized. The name was changed to 'Statens institut för konsumentfrågor' (The state institute for consumer issues). Maybe that was symbolic – housework was transformed into consumption, at the level of discourse.

This focus on the work of the housewife can be interpreted as a perspective of everyday life. It has to do with the individual and her daily activities in relation to a time- and space-specific context. Focusing on the family as a unit of consumption is different. That starts from an economic perspective. When the master plan of Örebro from the 1950s is compared to the current structure plans made by the municipality it becomes clear that the everyday life perspective of the 1950s is no longer used.

Putting everyday life in order

The Swedish historian Yvonne Hirdman (1989) has studied the period when the welfare state was founded, from the 1920s through the 1950s. She argues that the politicians focused on everyday life in the home and the private sphere, rather than on the conditions of working life. In the course of striving for 'putting everyday life in order' there was an understanding of how welfare must be seen in the context of people's everyday lives. Welfare has to do with 'the good life.' But who decides what is 'good'? Who decides what good housing is like, good and healthy food, good child care? Hirdman argues that politicians, supported by scientific experts, made value judgments about what was considered good. These were made without any inquiry into the values of the population. In fact, these values were not considered to be values; they were regarded as facts produced by social science and technology. Social engineering paved the road to the good society. Hirdman argues that, in their eagerness to create a welfare society, politicians and experts intruded upon the private sphere.

Changes in discourses

Since the 1950s and the 1960s the discourses in urban planning as well as in the welfare state as a whole have changed. Everyday life and its organization are no longer in focus. One illustration of this change relates to the argumentation behind the tax reform of the early 1990s. The Ministry of Finance investigated ways to increase the country's supply of labor power. It was found that a tax reform would encourage women in part-time employment to take on full-time employment – about half of all employed women were in part-time positions. But no consideration was given to the fact that most of the part-time employed women at that time had small children and spent more time doing unpaid work than paid work. So apart from taxes there were other restrictions on these women preventing their taking on full-time employment, and an awareness of the actual organization of everyday life would have indicated this.

Within urban planning in later years, it is difficult to discern a specific perspective from which various issues are seen, though new issues have emerged since the 1950s and the 1960s. Among the new and important issues are environmental problems. It is sometimes argued that urban planning, or land use planning, is an appropriate way of working toward sustainable development (e.g., Breheny 1992a). There is an international debate about urban form and sustainability, in which some researchers argue that the environmentally friendly city is a compact city, and others argue the opposite (Breheny 1992b, Jenks, Burton and Williams 1996, Åquist 2001a). Another important issue in urban planning is democracy and the involvement of citizens in the planning process. This was debated in the 1970s, as well, and was written into the Swedish planning legislation in 1987. It is still an issue since it has been difficult to find appropriate forms of citizen involvement in planning processes. In a recent study, Khakee (2000) found that planners and politicians support in principle the idea of citizen involvement in planning but in practice find it inefficient and difficult to organize.

I would like to argue for an approach to urban planning, based on an everyday life perspective, which is different from what was practiced in the middle of the 20th century. One important issue, which has changed since then, is the idea of the involvement of citizens in urban planning. Daily programs, a methodological tool developed in time-geography, could be used for this purpose.

An example of how the perspective of everyday life can be used in urban planning

Daily programs as a methodological tool for planning can take various forms. They can be *actual* daily programs describing the sequences of an individual's actual activities during one or more days. Actual programs illustrate the concrete organization of daily life. They are formed as a compromize between, on the one hand, our wishes and priorities, and, on the other hand, various demands related, for example, to working life and responsibilities for the family and the home. Also, the conditions for everyday life created by the surroundings in which people live influence the compromize of an actual daily program. It is a result of various wishes, demands, obstacles and possibilities. Torsten Hägerstrand, who founded time-geography, argues that for some purposes actual daily programs are not feasible because they do represent compromizes (Hägerstrand 1982a). For the purpose of studying concrete surroundings (e.g., a city, a neighborhood) as conditions for the organization of everyday life a more feasible method is to use *constructed* daily programs. With constructed programs the obstacles and possibilities in concrete surroundings for one or several types of daily programs can be studied. As mentioned above, Solveig Mårtensson (1979) used constructed daily programs in her study of living conditions in three Swedish municipalities. She starts from certain assumptions, for example that all daily programs include paid work and that the workplace is located in the center of the municipality. She then compares the possibilities to carry out certain constructed daily programs assuming various means of transport and various locations of the home. Following are the five constructed programs used:

Home – workplace – home
Home – workplace – grocery – home
Home – workplace – surgery – home
Home – workplace – library – home
Home – workplace – home – social participation – home.

A similar procedure can be used to study the obstacles and possibilities in a certain neighborhood or a part of a city as surroundings for various everyday lives. However, it requires a different spatial scale and more detailed daily programs. An example of what such an actual daily program can look like is the following. It comes from Tora Friberg's study of women's everyday lives (1990, p. 268).

The time-diary of Mia:

5:30	gets up, makes coffee
5:30–6:00	showers
6:00–6:30	reads the newspaper, has breakfast
6:30–7:00	makes breakfast for the children, wakes the children up
7:00–7:30	the children have breakfast
7:30–7:45	helps the children to wash and dress
7:45–7:50	Sandra goes to school
7:50–8:10	washes up, dresses Erika
8:10–8:15	bikes to Erika's day care center
8:15–8:26	stays at the day care center
8:26–8:32	bikes to work (arrives late!)

8:32–15:00	works
15:05–15:10	bikes to the day care center
15:10–15:20	talks to the staff, collects Erika
15:20–15:25	bikes to the after-school center
15:45–15:50	bikes home
15:50–16:15	plays with Erika, looks at the mail, makes the beds
16:15–16:35	talks to Sandra, plays with Erika
16:40–17:15	vacuums
17:15–17:50	makes dinner, fills the washing machine
17:50–18:20	has dinner, washes up
18:20–18:50	helps Sandra with her homework
18:50–19:30	takes out clothes for the next day, puts Sandra to bed
19:30–20:30	hangs the laundry, tidies the house, irons
20:30–20:45	has coffee with Per
20:45–23:00	watches TV, does crossword
23:00–	goes to bed

An everyday life organized like this needs short distances between the home, workplace, day care center, school and after-school center.

An analysis of a neighborhood, using actual or constructed daily programs, can have several purposes. It can be used for an inquiry into how well a certain neighborhood functions with respect to various daily programs – the assumption being that different social groups have different daily programs and demand different functions in the surroundings. The question may be, for example, does a certain neighborhood function well for elderly people? Or does it function well for families with small children? For teenagers? If not – what can be changed in the surroundings? Another purpose may be to compare qualities in different neighborhoods with the help of daily programs from several persons with different everyday lives. The method can also be used in the process of neighborhood renewal.

So far, actual and constructed daily programs have been discussed. A shortcoming of the method of actual daily programs is that they say nothing about what the person whose daily activities are recorded thinks about it – whether it corresponds to that person's idea of a good life or not. The use of *reflecting time-diaries*, as used by Åsa Westermark (Ellegård *et al* 1999) can help. Another way of including people's assessment of their everyday lives and its conditions is to use *ideal* daily programs. People taking part in studies or in planning projects can be asked to write down what they would prefer their daily programs to be like, thereby including the wishes and needs of citizens in a planning process at an early stage. Thinking in terms of actual and ideal daily programs may help people to concretize their wishes. This can be a method for involving citizens in planning processes.

Having discussed the usefulness of time-geography and different types of daily programs, I will return to Dorothy Smith's theory and its distinction between the everyday world and the world of ruling. The world of ruling is the sphere where power over decision making and resources is exercized. It is a sphere mediated in texts and discourses, which makes it different from the everyday world. Another difference is the universal character of the world of ruling. The everyday world is particular and concretely localized. Urban planning can be seen from the point of view of Smith's theory. Urban planning is a part of the world of ruling. Its content is mediated in texts and discourses. Within that world decisions are taken which have consequences for people's everyday lives since planning concerns the conditions of everyday life. If planners involve citizens, with their actual and ideal daily programs, in the planning process, a connection between the everyday world and the world of ruling can be made. The everyday world may be involved in the formation of its conditions.

Finally ...

There are various perspectives of everyday life, but they have some characteristics in common. They all have a certain holistic approach that is based on the individual human being. The world is seen as a whole, the way it appears to the individual, situated in a specific place, in time-space. Everyday life pertains to the mundane and concrete activities, the daily rhythms.

Taking an everyday life perspective is nothing new. Henri Lefebvre wrote about it in the 1940s, and, even earlier, similar ways of thinking existed within philosophy. It was used in urban planning in the middle of the 20th century as a planning tool. However, interest in perspectives of everyday life seems to have increased within the social sciences in the last two decades. One reason for this might be that it follows the increased interest in feminism and gender studies. Everyday life and gender are two perspectives that enhance each other. In human geography, time-geography can contribute to the development as a tool for the research of everyday life. In parallel, time-geography has been developed by, for example, reflecting time-dairies and distinctions between actual and ideal daily programs.

References

Åquist, Ann-Cathrine (1987): 'Hushållens tidsanvändning. En jämförelse mellan 1950 och 1983'. (The use of time in households. A comparison between 1950 and 1983) Mimo. Department of Geography, Univerisity of Oslo.

Åquist, Ann-Cathrine (1992): *Tidsgeografi i samspel med samhällsteori.* (Time-geography in asociation with social theory) Meddelanden från Lunds universitets geografiska institutioner, avhandlingar 115. Lund: Lund University Press.

Åquist, Ann-Cathrine (2001a): *Den miljövänliga staden – kompakt eller gles? En forskningsöversikt.* (The environmentally friendly city – compact or dispersed? A research overview.) University of Örebro, Centre for Housing and Urban Research.

Åquist, Ann-Cathrine (2001b): 'Urban change, planning and the organization of everyday life. The case of Örebro'. In: Andersson, Hari, Jørgensen, Gertrud, Joye, Dominique and Ostendorf, Wim (eds): *Change and Stability in Urban Europe.* Aldershot: Ashgate, pp. 193–210.

Bech-Jørgensen, Birte (1997): 'Symbolsk orden og hverdagskultur.' (Symbolic order and everyday culture) In: Christensen, Ann-Dorte, Ravn, Anna-Birte and Rittenhofer, Iris (eds): *Det kønnede samfund. Forståelser af køn og social forandring.* Aalborg: Aalborg Universitetsforlag, pp. 109–135.

Beier Sørensen, Ole and Vogelius, Peter (1994): 'En normbaseret livsformteori og analysen af arbejdets transformation.' (A norm-based theory of life modes and the analysis of the transformation of work) *Nordisk Samhällsgeografisk Tidskrift*, no 18, pp. 59–74.

Bloch, Charlotte (1991): 'I lust och nöd – om vardagsliv och känslor.' (For better or for worse – on everyday life and emotions.) *Kvinnovetenskaplig tidskrift* nr 2 1991, pp. 31–42.

Bohm, Kerstin (1990): 'Teorier om vardag och struktur.' (Theories of the everyday and structures), in: *Fysisk planlegging i forvandling: natur – struktur – hverdagsliv*. Rapport fra Nordplans 20–årssymposium Stockholm: Nordplan, pp. 73–106.

Breheny, Michael J. (1992a): 'Sustainable Development and Urban Form: An Introduction.' In: Breheny, Michael J. (ed): *Sustainable Development and Urban Form*. London: Pion. pp. 1–23.

Breheny Michael J. (1992b) (ed): *Sustainable Development and Urban Form*. London: Pion.

Buttimer, Anne (1976): 'Grasping the Dynamism of Lifeworld.' *Annals of the Association of American Geographers*, vol 66 nr 2, pp. 277–292.

Det nya vardagslivet. (The New Everyday Life) Forskargruppen för det nya vardagslivet, Nordiska ministerrådet, 1984.

Ellegård, Kajsa, Nordell, Kersti and Westermark, Åsa (1999): 'Att ta kontroll över sitt vardagsliv – kvalitativ dagboksmetod för reflektiv emancipation.' (Gaining control over one's everyday life – qualitative time-diary method for reflective emancipation) in: Lindén, Jitka *et. al.* (eds): *Kvalitativa metoder i arbetslivsforskning*. Stockholm: Rådet för arbetslivsforskning, pp. 108–131.

Franzén, Mats and Sandstedt, Eva (1982): 'Boendets planering och vardagslivets organizering – kvinnan, familjen och staden.' (Planning of housing and the organization of everyday life – woman, family and city), *Kvinnovetenskaplig tidskrift* nr 1 1982, pp. 6–15.

Friberg, Tora (1990): *Kvinnors vardag. Om kvinnors arbete och liv. Anpassningsstrategier i tid och rum*. (The everyday life of women, work and home: adaptation strategies in time and space) Meddelanden från Lunds universitets Geografiska institutioner, avhandlingar 109, Lund: Lund University Press.

Gardiner, Michael E. (2000): *Critiques of Everyday Life*. London and New York: Routledge.

Giddens, Anthony (1979): *Central Problems in Social Theory*. London: MacMillan.

Giddens, Anthony (1984): *The Constitution of Society*. Cambridge: Polity Press.

Hägerstrand, Torsten (1970): 'Tidsanvändning och omgivningsstruktur.' (The use of time and the structure of the environment.) Bilaga 4 i *SOU 1970:14 Urbaniseringen i Sverige, en geografisk samhällsanalys*. Bilagedel 1: Balanserad regional utveckling, pp. 7–37.

Hägerstrand, Torsten (1982a): 'Diorama, Path and Project.' *Tijdschrift voor economische en sociale geografie* vol 73 no 6, pp. 323–339.

Hägerstrand, Torsten (1982b): 'Likhet och närhet: om geografins ansvar för balansen mellan kunskapsperspektiv.' (Likeness and proximity: on the responsibility of geography for the balance between perspectives of knowledge) In: Strand, Sverre (red): *Geografi som samfunnsvitenskap*. Bergen: Ad Novas nr 19, pp. 182–189.

Hägerstrand, Torsten (1985): 'Time-geography: Focus on the corporeality of man, society and environment.' *The Science and Praxis of Complexity*. The United Nations University.

Hanson, Susan (1992): 'Geography and Feminism: Worlds in Collision?' *Annals of the Association of American Geographers* vol 82 no 4, pp. 569–586.

Hirdman, Yvonne (1983): 'Den socialistiska hemmafrun.' (The socialist housewife), in: Åkerman, Brita *et al* (eds): *Vi kan, vi behövs! – Kvinnorna går samman i egna föreningar*. Stockholm: Akademilitteratur, pp. 11–59.

Hirdman, Yvonne (1989): *Att lägga livet till rätta. Studier i svensk folkhemspolitik*. (Putting everyday life in order.) Stockholm: Carlssons.

Højrup, Thomas (1983): 'The Concept of Life-Mode. A Form-Specifying Mode of Analysis Applied to Contemporary Western Europe.' *Ethnologia Scandinavica* pp. 15–50.

Jenks, Mike, Burton, Elisabeth and Williams, Katie (1996) (eds): *The Compact City. A Sustainable Urban Form?* London and New York: E and FN Spon.

Kasanen, Pirkko (1995): 'Distansarbete som lösning eller problem – tolkningar genom livsformsteorin.' (Distance work as solution or problem – interpretations through life mode analysis) *Nordisk Samhällsgeografisk Tidskrift,* no 20, pp. 183–193.

Khakee, Abdul (2000): *Samhällsplanering.* (Urban planning) Lund: Studentlitteratur.

Lefebvre, Henri (1991): *Critique of Everyday Life.* Vol. 1 London: Verson (original 1947).

Lövgren, Britta (1994): 'Hemmen och samhällsplaneringen.' (Homes and social planning) *Bebyggelsehistorisk tidskrift* no 28, 1994, pp. 71–84.

Martel, Karol (1999): 'Lebenswelt och praxis. Om den sista fasen i Husserls fenomenologi.' (Lebenswelt and praxis) *Häften för kritiska studier* årg. 32 nr 4, pp. 3–21.

Mårtensson, Solveig (1979): *On the Formation of Biographies in Time-Space Environments.* Meddelanden från Lunds universitets Geografiska institutioner, avhandlingar nr 84.

Myrdal, Alva and Myrdal, Gunnar (1934): *Kris i befolkningsfrågan.* (The Crisis of the Population Issue) Stockholm: Bonniers.

Nørve, Siri (1984): 'Ta tingene alvorligt! Identitet og materiell i hverdagslivet.' (Take things seriously! Identity and the material of everyday life.) In: *Det nya vardagslivet.* Forskargruppen för det nya vardagslivet, Nordiska ministerrådet, pp. 137–147.

Öhman, Jan (1982): *Staden och det varjedagliga utbytet.* (The city and the everyday exchange) Uppsala: Geografiska regionalstudier nr 13 Kulturgeografisk institutionen, Uppsala universitet.

Østerberg, Dag (1985): 'Materiell och praxis.' (Materiel and praxis) In: Andersson, Sten (ed): *Mellan människor och ting.* Göteborg: Bokförlaget Korpen, pp. 7–24.

Simonsen, Kirsten (1993): *Byteori og hverdagspraksis.* (Urban theory and everyday practice) Akademisk Forlag.

Skirbekk, Gunnar and Gilje, Nils (1987): *Filosofihistorie 2.* (History of philosophy) Oslo: Universitetsforlaget.

Smith, Dorothy (1987): *The Everyday World as Problematic. A Feminist Sociology.* Boston: Northeastern University Press.

Veier til det nye hverdagslivet. (Ways to the New Everyday Life) Forskergruppen for det nye hverdagslivet, Nordiska ministerrådet, NORD 1987:61.

PART III
SPATIALITY, IDENTITY
AND SOCIAL PRACTICE

Chapter 8

Geography, space and identity

Jouni Häkli and Anssi Paasi

The last decade has witnessed a booming scholarly interest in identities, boundaries, and space (spatial metaphors and concepts) across the human and social science disciplines. This upsurge can partly be explained by the rise of ethnic and regional movements, immigration and displacement, and the breakdown of the geopolitical certainties of the Cold War era. All these changes have challenged the image of the world as a grid of separate territories with their own essential identities. However, factors 'endogenous' to the scientific discourse can also be discerned, such as the growing concern with globalization vis-à-vis localization, and discourses of the 'space of flows'. A major academic background for these tendencies has been the overall interest in the 'cultural' in social and political science.

Our purpose in this chapter is to provide an overview of the recent research on those aspects of spatial identities that are pertinent to the discipline of geography. Our starting point lies in the recognition of several simultaneous identity discourses, which emphasize different sides of the social construction of identity as related to social spatiality. We will first discuss the construction of places, regions and nations as centers for territorial identity. We then shed light on how geography, as (one specific) a scientific institution, has contributed to the construction of spatial identities and spatial imaginations. Finally, we will look at geography as location and/or context manifesting itself in the negotiation of spatial identities, i.e. we will scrutinize how 'geography' is both used and created by the proponents of regional administrative reform in Finland.

Our intention is, then, to illuminate what is at stake in the different ways of discussing 'territory' and 'identity', and thus increase our understanding of how geography is involved in the construction of hegemonic and other spatial identities. This will involve a critical evaluation of the (metaphorical) use of spatial language wielded in much contemporary sociological, socio-psychological, and cultural studies literature. In a paradoxical manner, by demonstrating how identity discourses often are both essentialist and 'banal', we also wish to contribute to an increasingly anti-essentialist understanding of spatial identities, where place, region and territory are not inevitably strictly bounded, nor exclusive categories but rather contexts where the particular and the universal intersect (Massey 1995). By looking at spatial identities in connection with major political institutions of the modern era, such as state territories and boundaries, we seek to account for some of the ways in which spatial identities and their construction are connected to social power.

In general, our research is related to constructionist approaches in social sciences. We share their aim to decompose categories and identities that furnish everyday understandings of the social world. This inevitably requires that we also try to reveal the relations of power that are hidden in spatial discourses and practices. In this regard our research will hardly find support among those institutional (and non-governmental) actors who are usually busy in constructing and reproducing such classifications! However, we are less satisfied with the ways in which (abstract) social theory has been able to address the spatiality of social life. As our contribution to social constructionist methodology we insist on contextualizing the processes of construction in geographical terms – both as discourses that make places, and as processes that stretch over space. As a concrete example of identity producing discourses and practices we will scrutinize the manner in which the Finnish provinces and counties have historically been constructed in popular and politico-administrative discourses, and how various institutions have constituted significant media for this process.

Spaces in identities

All identities can be said to have a spatial dimension because all individual and social action is spatially contextual – it literally 'takes place' somewhere. However, from all claims to collective particularity ('we'/'they') it is relatively easy to discern the ones that make a special reference to geographical spaces such as cities, places, regions, countries, or even continents. These spatial identities are interesting from a geographical point of view because they both depend on geographical classifications and depictions of the world, and are contextually situated in the geographical world that is understood and described through specific discourses, texts and 'identity talk'. Furthermore, the discipline of geography, as a particular body of spatial knowledge, has played an important role in the construction and institutionalization of modern spatial categories and identities (cf. Paasi 1996: 22–23).

At the outset, it is useful to make an analytical distinction between the identity of a region and people's sense of regional identity (or regional consciousness) (Paasi 1986). The former comprises aspects that distinguish one region from all others, and will include at least physical conditions, the region's history, and its economic, social, and political structures. Other important considerations are cultural features and dialects. These and other similar aspects form the distinctive basis upon which a certain symbolism arises, and the region is presented in various social and cultural practices and discourses.

These aspects are also implicated in the inhabitants' sense of regional identity, or regional consciousness, as this, too, reflects the history of the region, as well as its distinct characteristics. Yet, a consciousness of the particularity of one's homestead or region is not to be traced back only to individuals' own experiences and observations. At least equally important are the mechanisms through which the foundation is laid for a collective identity. The press and other media, regional literature, geography and history teaching in schools, and other such factors are essential, as they provide a basis for projecting, or representing, a certain 'imagined community' (Anderson 1991). It is through this imagined community that people who are strangers to each other can perceive themselves as 'we', as having a common past, present and future.

The larger the regional community, the more abstract and symbolic is the identity involved. National identity and the consideration of its significance is a separate matter, of course (cf. Paasi 1996, 1997). Everyone living in the modern world is an inhabitant of a particular state, which will attempt to determine the content of its citizens' national identity so as to ensure that an appreciable share of the loyalties of the various ethnic groups and nationalities living within its territory will be focused on that state as a whole. The most extreme 'ploy' open to a state wishing to assure itself of such loyalties is of course the use or threat of violence against its citizens. As acknowledged already by Max Weber, this is one of the legitimate rights of the state. Yet, national identities are not permanent 'things', and although the national iconography in terms of symbols and 'narratives' is often finite in nature, each generation interprets this 'reserve' anew and assigns fresh meanings to it, reflecting the international political environment in which they operate (Löfgren 1989).

One crucial aspect of a local or regional identity – whether national, provincial or other – is the relation between individual identity and social identity. Questions like 'who am I' or 'who are we' are always problematic, as identities and boundaries run closely hand in hand. Regional identities can be interpreted as narratives that explain who we are and where we come form, and it is particularly interesting to consider who finally defines the actual or imaginary features of 'us' and 'our region'. Whose identity is 'our identity'? That of the local or regional press? Or that of an advertising or business agency? Or that of some regional activist, politician or person in a high position?

For sure, every definition of a social identity contains an element of power which gains momentum from the fact that the definition of any imagined community – 'our' community – implies the construction of boundaries with the 'other'. Particular problems may arise, therefore, when identities are construed without any real interest in how individuals and social groups are actually building regional or local identities in their 'own narratives'.

The present, the past, and personal and social identities are bound up together in a complex manner, in which identity is rather a dynamic, continually changing process, than a static condition. As Breakwell (1986: 18) puts it,

> Current personal identity is the product of the interaction of all past personal identities with all past and present social identities. But the reverse is also true: current social identities are the product of the interactions of all past social identities with all past and current personal identities.

The intertwinement of contextuality, spatial identities, and geography is hard to analyse if we don't recognize the ultimate dependence of the constructions of individual and collective identity on language and its use in diverging social practices. Language is the medium which enables both the categorization of spatial and social phenomena, and the communication of these categories into the contexts and practices of everyday life. Geographers and the discipline of geography are, thus, one among many discursive contexts that give rise to spatial distinctions and definitions of collective identity. Particularly significant has been school geography because it has typically presented these distinctions as part of the 'normal order of things', i.e. it has contributed to spatial socialization where citizens learn the basic elements of their spatial world view and 'spatial vocabularies'. In identity discourses the spatial demarcations become fused with culture, ethnicity, and nation at various spatial scales that become 'nested' (Herb and Kaplan 1999).

If identities are 'language dependent', how, then, should we understand their relation to space? The idea of the contextuality of social life is one obvious avenue through which to address this question. All discourses take place somewhere, and importantly, serve some ends, in the broadest sense of the word. Thus, the contextuality of identity discourses does not only refer to the geographically variable settings of interaction, but also to the question of who is talking, from what position, and for what purposes. Identity discourses are not only rhetoric gestures: they manifest what has come to be called the politics of identity. The idea of identity, the very use of the word, actually makes the powerful claim that it is possible for us, as the collective addressed in identity discourses, to know who 'we' are, and who 'we' are not. Thus, while it can be argued that all identities are rooted and reproduced in the broad spectre of everyday social practices, it does not follow that identities can be treated as inherently benign cultural creations, as often seems to be the case (Jenkins 1996). Language is also a medium for social power, and therefore 'identity talk' is never socially innocent: it arises from, and feeds into stereotypical constructions of social groups, and is often tightly connected to powerful institutions.

It is precisely here that spatiality as geography enters the scene: collective spatial identities refer to the geographical world of regions, places, state territories, which represent a stable framework for individuals to literally move in and out of identifications in the course of their lives. 'Geography' enables and constrains identity talk both in the sense of being the image of the world's regional system, and as an academic discipline seeking to know the regional world. Yet, the stability of the geographical world is illusionary. Places, regions, and territories, too, are social constructions, and thus change over time (Häkli forthcoming). Geographers often take actively part in this construction, and thereby, knowingly or not knowingly, put themselves to the position from which different we's and they's are defined. Indeed, it seems that geography, space, and identity are intricately connected, but what actually is 'identity'?

Deconstructing 'identity'

The concept of identity has become common currency both within and outside the academia. However, while identity is definitely one of the keywords of current times (Schlesinger 1991), this was not always the case. The rapid rise of interest in identity in the social sciences is well illustrated by the fact that Raymond Williams (1976) did not include the concept on his list of social science keywords of the 1970s. But since the 1970s identity discourses have proliferated in social sciences, and to some degree replaced notions such as 'community value' or 'social organization' (Jenkins 1996: 105).

Yet, while identity has become a major concern in social and cultural studies, as well as in geography, it remains an extremely complicated category (e.g. Lash and Friedman (eds) 1992, Cohen 1994, Hooson (ed.) 1994, Dijkink 1996). Jenkins (1996: 9) notes that 'at the end of the twentieth century, the sheer volume of discourse about identity has reached new magnitudes'. Along similar lines Hall (1996: 1) points out that 'there has been a veritable discursive explosion in recent years around the concept of "identity", at the same time as it has been subjected to a searching critique'. This critique has been increasingly directed at any essentialist notions of integral, original, or unified identity.

How, then, should we approach this complicated and contested category? Some authors argue that the term applies to individuals rather than collectives (Schlesinger 1991). In psychological analysis identity is usually understood as a view of the self that people develop as acting agents, while being objects of their own and others' observations and interpretations. In this view identity is connected to the experience of individual particularity, and the key question of 'who am I' (Guibernau 1996: 72). However, identity cannot be analytically reduced to individual experience. The logical flip side of difference is similarity, which points to collective, or shared elements. Locality, region, nation, gender or ethnicity, for instance, may provide frameworks for the rise of collective identities. Even though their existence is dependent on embodied human beings who produce and reproduce such identities, their construction also requires both a set of social practices and shared discourses/ narratives that join people together (Jenkins 1996). Thus, it can be argued that in the final instance individual identities are always social identities.

Unsurprisingly, then, some analysts have attempted to build theories of the social construction of identities by addressing the classic question of the relationship between individual and society (e.g. Paasi 1991). In this effort the theories of structuration have provided useful avenues (Giddens 1984, Bourdieu 1991), and the research has often focused on the ways in which social identities emerge as the dialectic of internalization and externalization of social categories. Others have wanted to avoid essentialism in understanding identities, and argue that they are never unified but rather increasingly fragmented and fractured, never singular but rather multiply constructed across diverging intersecting and antagonistic practices, positions, and discourses (Hall 1996: 3–4). Yet, as Douglas (1986: 55) points out, 'for discourse to be possible at all, the basic categories have to be agreed on'. This is an important realization and aptly points to the connection between identities and social power.

Douglas (1986) goes on to note that 'nothing else but institutions can define sameness. Similarity is an institution'. The major function of institutions is to establish stable structures for human interaction, to reduce uncertainty, and increase ontological security (Giddens 1990). Institutions order social life, but, of course, vary a lot in nature. North (1990) points out that formal rules in a society may change rapidly as a consequence of political or judicial decisions, whereas informal constraints embedded in customs, traditions and codes of conduct are considerably more impervious to deliberate policies. However, both types of institutions have something in common: language, discourse, is the pre-eminent vehicle of the institutional order, in the form of performative communication, rules and laws, written records, narratives, etc.

When deconstructed, 'identity' seems to stand for established ways of 'reading', categorizing and representing the social world. However, this does not mean that identities could be explained away as mere feeble linguistic phenomena with no existence in more substantial sense. This is because identities have to be practiced before they can become fully meaningful in social life. They have to be performed to become actual (Jenkins 1996: 95). This is also the reason why identity discourses impregnate such institutional practices as education, the media, government, sport, and religion. It is precisely these and other concrete institutional settings that materialize the processes of identification, and turn spatial representations into institutionalized forms of identity discourse. In a word, they constitute a crucial basis for the spatial socialization process (Paasi 1996).

Identity and ideology

In discussing national identities Michael Billig (1995: 61) states that one should not ask 'what is identity' but rather 'what does it mean to claim to have an identity'. It is therefore crucial to reflect how discourses and representations of spatial identity are created and whose 'plots' dominate the narratives through which social groups are represented, and the ideas of 'we' are created. At stake here is how collective identities relate to social control, given that the representations of difference and similarity are linked with social power relations occurring on various spatial scales.

From this standpoint the idea of spatial identity comes very close to the concept of ideology, and specifically the ideology of constructing territorial inclusions and exclusions on different geographical scales (Paasi 1999). This is the case particularly when identities are generated and maintained by the existing states. In this sense ideology points to the process of producing meanings, signs and values in socio-spatial life, that is, to the process of signification (Paasi 1996). The link between ideology and discourses of spatial identity, and thus the social practices through which these discourses become materialized, is based on the fact that these discourses are crucial instruments of social integration and control. They are therefore also linked with the physical and symbolic violence practiced institutionally to maintain diverging forms of social order.

Ideology is not merely a set of ideas or beliefs, but rather a complicated set of social practices and rituals that manifest themselves in the institutional arrangements operating in modern societies. For instance, it is well known that national ideologies, discourses, and practices of national identity exist in numerous ways in contemporary societies. Without committing ourselves too deeply to the structuralist and economistic framework of Althusser (1984), we can nevertheless note that his examples of the ideological state apparatus provide a general framework which can be re-thought contextually on different scales and geographical contexts. He makes a distinction between various ideological state apparatuses: religious (the system of various churches), educational (private and public schools), the family, jurisdictional, political (the political system and parties), professional, communication (the media) and cultural (literature, art, sport). These together constitute the state ideology and give it a tangible form in and through social practice.

Along the Althusserian lines, we may think that the ideological apparatuses, which give rise to spatial identity discourses, are characterized by multiplicity and are located partly in the private sphere. Through these diverging institutions different ideas of space, boundaries and regions are produced and reproduced, and various constellations of power relations exist (cf. Newman and Paasi 1998). In the process, the use of language is central. The construction of social communities, their boundaries and identities, and their limits of exclusion and inclusion, occurs through narratives that aim at binding a group together and distinguishing it from other groups (Paasi 1999). Through social narratives people come to know and make sense of the social world, and constitute their identities (cf. Somers 1994, Campbell 1998).

It is important to note that ideological institutions are not autonomous, deterministic structures but rather operate, to employ the expression coined by Bourdieu (1998), in the field of symbolic economy, which – by contrast with 'rational' material economy – points to the exchange of symbolic goods and 'gifts'. Bourdieu reminds us that symbolic work is simultaneously both an act of 'form giving' and 'following the rules' and that each social group requires that when one's individual human dignity and 'basic values of the soul' are cherished, the human dignity of others will also be respected and the rules of the community accepted. The idea of symbolic exchange points to a specific social relation that converts power relations into moral ones (Paasi 1999). Importantly, symbolic exchange is possible only if participants have identical categories for observations and appreciation. People identify themselves with collective institutions only if they feel that they will also benefit from this symbolic communion. This is obvious at all spatial scales but particularly clear this is in the case of national, state-bound institutions, such as national education, legislation, health care, etc.

Identity and ideology converge, thus, not only on the level of institutional apparatuses, but also on the moral level, particularly as regards the idea(l) of 'community'. Cohen (1985: 14) has pointed out that the idea of community symbolises exclusion as well as inclusion, and carries a powerful symbolic load: it not only says how things are, but also how things *should* be. Thus, the construction of identity narratives is political action, and an expression of the distribution of social power in society. This harks back to the social (and spatial) divisions of labour – the degree to which people and groups are involved in the production of these narratives varies greatly.

Since spatial identities are narrative constructs, a rhetorical, persuasive element forms part of them. Spatial discourses and practices may be territorial (exclusion) while laying stress on internal integration (inclusion) at the same time. The limit between these practices is of course diffuse, and it is perhaps best to accentuate the simultaneity of the production of ideas regarding 'us' and the 'other', and the power relations that are involved in these practices.

In addition to being discursive, territorial identities also take shape on various geographical scales. They can be thought of forming a continuum from personal and local to larger territorialities. National identity is usually particularly significant. The broader the spatial scale is, the more symbolic and non-personal identities are from the perspective of daily life. Spatial identities are therefore flexible, which reflects their hierarchical nature and connection with practices and discourses, norms and values, which are not unambiguously local or non-local.

Spatial identity and institutions: Regional administration reform in Finland as an example

Contested territories

We will take one particular concrete example to show the ways in which regional identity has been historically bound up with symbolic domination, discourse, and community ideology. Attempts to reform the intermediate level government in Finland illustrate well the contested identity discourses and how different actors in society have had very different perspectives on these regions. The reform can be understood in terms of the intersection of two different identity discourses – one that 'ordinary' people may find attractive, and another that has the political-administrative practice as its proper context. Yet, it should be noted that in proposing a distinction between governmental and popular identity discourses we do not wish to view these in a simple oppositional relation, as they in fact constantly resort to similar language and images. As we argued above, a 'common' language is crucial for the operation of all institutions. Governmental agents use rhetoric persuasion, and appeal to popular ideas and identities to gain support, while people may routinely express their cultural identity and distinctiveness in territorial terms, even though at times the territorial dimension may be rather vague (Paasi 1986, Kaplan 1994, Häkli 1998b).

We will start from the fact that 'competing' types of region exist on the intermediate level in Finland. The provinces (*maakunta*) and counties, or 'administrative provinces' (*lääni*), have for a long time been crucial instruments of territorial governance and an important spatial scale for regional identification, along with the local-level administrative units (*kunta*). In the course of years both have had different connotations. In regionalistic discourse the 'county' has most often been perceived as 'a remote station' of state level administration, i.e. it has been interpreted as being constructed 'from above'. Counties (*lääni*) were, and still are, the instruments of the state in regional governance. A province, on the other hand, has been interpreted as an area born through the operations of ordinary people, i.e. 'from below'. Although the meanings of provinces and counties have been perceived differently, there has often been a considerable overlap in their areas (Paasi 1986). Provinces (*maakunta*) as cultural units have never become self-administrative units but they are often considered important from the point of view of regional (cultural) identity, and different actors have sought to define these areal divisions by resorting to identity discourses. The appeal of provinces as centers of regional identity, however, varies greatly from area to area in Finland.

A 'province' has traditionally referred to historical provinces, units corresponding to medieval castle counties. Their borders took shape gradually, when people began to utilize areas dividing inhabited regions as hunting land. The borders, based on customary law, were not particularly exact but they provided the basis for the shaping of the limits to the province (Paasi forthcoming). The division of labor, the constructing of centers and spheres of influence, as well as the strengthening of regional civil activity, establishment of regional associations, and the development of mass media that took place in the 19th century, created new 'functional areas' and, concomitantly, a new regional division, the present provinces. Provincial unions were formed as early as the 1920s to advance their interest and they began actively to create images for the provinces. For decades they acted in order to develop the regions' educational and financial conditions. Nature and landscape provided a material and symbolic basis for this work, together with cultural features (Paasi 1986).

However, people tend to identity themselves with local communities or urban metropolitan areas rather than provinces. There are several reasons for the insignificance of provinces for ordinary people. Apart from some exceptions, the current Finnish provinces are not particularly well established cultural and historical units. Since provinces have not had any specific administrative role in the Finnish system of governance either, they simply have lacked the political, financial, and administrative position that could accentuate the areas' importance in and through people's everyday life (Paasi 1986).

Hence the institutional context makes a difference. While administrative organizations often exploit various institutional practices to define and demarcate regions in a universal and universally applicable way, no such urge can systematically be found in the popular realm or in the context of daily life place formation. Subject to place bound sentiments and regional identities, but also economic interests, place marketing, and parochialism, the Finnish regions remain contradictory and contested realities. This is a crucially important assertion in that it prompts us to ask what is actually at stake when undefined and ephemeral identity discourses meet with the governmental strive for objective and universal identification of regions.

What eventually has become a whole series of regional administration reforms was first launched in Finland in the latter half of the 19th century. Since then as many as 34 initiatives have been processed by the state government (Pystynen 1993). The most authoritative attempts to carry out the reform have been made by state appointed committees. Over the period of 125 years, eight state committees have delivered their reports proposing a reform, and finally in 1994 more political power and administrative tasks were transferred from the state's district administration to 19 provinces.

The committee reports are a showcase of 'official' identity discourse. Inherently of and for political power, the committee reports have sought to contain and reduce the diversity that is manifest in the popular talks, for instance, about what it means to live in Osthrobotnia (Pohjanmaa) or what the Karelian people are like. One problem is that the idea of a province means very different things in different areas. Whereas Southern Ostrobotnia, for instance, has by tradition had a strong cultural and historical role in people's regional consciousness, some new provincial areas like Päijät-Häme or Keski-Suomi are relatively recent constructs that have more or less emerged as the spheres of influence of their urban centers (Paasi 1986). Yet, the institutional identity discourse is dictated by the need to territorialize space in a universally applicable guise in amidst conflicting economic, symbolic and political interests vested in popular identity discourses.

The difficulty of bridging this difference has been evident in attempts to institute new administrative regions in Finland. Setting up new regions has been arduous, and sometimes the conflicting interests have prohibited governmental decisions from being put into effect (Ylönen 1994). Unsurprisingly, to identify regions legitimately, the governmental discourse has resorted to an evolutionary conception of space. The idea of an organic cultural or economic-functional development of regions has elevated their essence from the mundane world of human interests up to the transcendental realm of 'community'. Thus, in the governmental identity discourse regions are made to exist and appear the same to everyone – as the inevitable outgrowths of history, culture, and human behavior (e.g. Committee report 1953, 1992). Yet, while the idea of a spontaneously built regional community may appeal to many 'ordinary' Finns, it nevertheless is an ideological discourse that tends to conceal its politics. This can be seen also in the fact that the regions suggested in committee reports have varied both in terms of their territorial shape and symbolism, particularly naming (Paasi 1986). After all, 'we' are not all the same, and even though 'we' should all be in favour of 'community', there is no such thing as unequivocal common good (e.g. Cohen 1985).

Constructing the 'community'

The construction of community occurs, again, in discourses that are located on the fuzzy area between official and private spheres and inevitably reflect the search for a common language, the language defining 'us'. Indeed it is possible to talk about a dialectic between the languages of integration and distinction: the former aims at homogenizing the contents of spatial experience and imaginaries, the latter strives to distinguish this homogenized experience from the 'other' (Paasi 1996: 15).Moreover, the encounters of governmental and popular identity discourses leave space for domination other than merely that connected to community ideology. One example has to do with the ways in which the discourse on regions is constructed. The protagonists of the regional government reform have tended to view the process in terms of the victory of people's regional identities over the state's administrative rule (e.g. Kirkinen 1991). Yet, contrary to this it can be argued that the governmental discourse, replete with expert jargon dealing with issues such as 'LFM-frames' and 'regional gateway-projects', has in fact handed the Finnish regions to a numerically small group of institutional actors. In other words, instead of bringing about a politico-administrative system of a 'more humane scale and quality', the conflation of governmental and popular identity discourses has turned from simple appropriation to outright (symbolic) domination.

This illustrates well the manner in which the official discourse on regions constructs its own realities which allegedly are more real than the contestable lived social spatiality (Häkli 1994, 1998a). Thus, the official discourses, following the logic grounded in institutional strategies, have actually *manufactured* the Finnish regions, as much as they have re-presented them. Moreover, the experts in committees have, at least up to 1950s, concomitantly drawn on traditional regional identity narratives and, by appropriating the popular identities, sought to create visions of homogeneous populations, mentalities and other cultural traits in the regions in question (Paasi 1986).

In all, discourses on regional identities represent the attempt to institutionalize a particular conception of ideal government: the alliance of spatial circumscription, organic community, and common good. Yet, paradoxically enough, in the governmental reports the indeterminate symbolisms and multiple geometries of the

Finnish regions are projected on the two-dimensional plane of the politico-administrative system. In Bourdieu's terms the process bears all the characteristics of symbolic violence: 'the power to constitute and to impose as universal and universally applicable within a given "nation", that is, within the boundaries of a given territory, a common set of coercive norms' (Bourdieu and Wacquant 1992: 112).

Importantly, the objectification and universalization of the Finnish regions has had consequences reaching far beyond the realm of symbolism, language or imagery. The conflation of institutional and popular geographs discloses a persistent search for renewed governmental legitimacy through popular appeal; a spatial platform from which new political action could spring, new institutions be established, new political structures forged, new economic relations built (Lefebvre 1991: 275). While inscribed on paper, the official identity discourse has always appropriated the symbolic power of popular identities, interests and material projects.

The 'provincialization' of regions

The meeting of institutional discourses and popular geographs is often a fertile ground for political reactions. This has been the case in Finland on several occasions. The members of parliament from certain regions, for instance, have often – in the spirit of regionalism – aligned their vote on administrative reforms in spite of their basically conflicting political opinions. The political dynamic of regional identity discourses has also become evident in defending the names of regions. A fitting illustration is the debate that emerged regarding the names of the forthcoming counties in 1997 when the number of existing counties was cut from 11 to five. This example shows the power and importance of naming in the construction of territorial identities.

While the spatial patterns of contemporary regional identities – or, in fact, the patterns of people's regional consciousness and discourse – can be mapped (e.g. Palomäki 1968), the different ways of using 'identity talk' among the larger population cannot be reached by means of standard questionnaires or Gallup interviews. Instead, it is necessary to study the broader processes of the production of space and territories. This means that the nuances of territory building and identity formation should be analysed sensitively, by using all kinds of textual materials (such as maps, literature, novels, newspapers, and depth interviews; see Paasi 1986, 1996).

These little nuances, which easily escape the analyst, are very important for an understanding of how different social actors make use of spatial categories in constructing identities and rationalizing political choices. Their analysis requires particular theoretical sensitivity and reflexivity. This is due to the fact that the popular identity discourses are not reducible to the governmental ones. This is where the notion of lived spatiality may be illuminating. Even if we acknowledge the fact that everyday life is discursive just like the practices of statecraft, and that popular identity discourses can assume a political meaning like their institutional counterparts, the notion of lived space points at the different contexts and ways in which identity discourses are constructed and used.

In the Finnish context, regionalism has emerged as an ideology manifesting itself in, for example, regional narratives in media and novels. Regionalism has been particularly strong in literature where the aims of the authors to build up a bond between the text and a particular territorial unit are often very apparent. The link between political and literary dimensions can be very close, too. It has been argued that in many European countries novelists have effectively created regional images and identities and have therefore also had a significant political role. Landscapes are one significant element in regionalist writings. This is based on the fact that most provinces have their unique landscape features, which the novelists can transform into meaningful narratives and contexts where the imagined/real worlds of their texts come alive. Most Finnish provinces have had their own novelists in the course of years that are typically linked with the regional life in cultural publicity. Hence Antti Tuuri in closely linked with Pohjanmaa (Bothnia), Heikki Turunen with Northern Karelia, Eino Säisä with Savo, Kalle Päätalo with Koillismaa, and Veikko Huovinen with Kainuu, etc. (Paasi forthcoming).

The Finnish regionalism and provinces are currently living a new renaissance. This is due to the fact that in 1995 Finland entered the European Union where questions of the images of regions and provinces are topical. As we found above, the position of provinces in the intermediate level government has also become stronger during the 1990s. Uniting the provincial unions and regional planning associations resulted in an association of provinces. One of their most important tasks is preparatory and programming work connected to the EU regional policy funding.

Also regional dialects have experienced a Renaissance in Finland over the last few years, and a number of associations supporting dialects have been established while provincial readers have been drawn up. Provinces are developing new images and they are being presented outwards more actively. Together with various institutions and organizations, provinces are also linked with numerous symbols through which they show their differences. In addition to traditional symbols, such as coats of arms, provincial birds, flowers, fish, and minerals have also been nominated in recent times.

Finnish regionalism has not been merely an artistic movement. As far as the major perpetual constituents of territorial identity are concerned, the role of media, particularly the role of newspapers is crucial. Provincial newspapers in the peripheral areas have been active promoters of regional identity. This is obvious in articles that put stress on the collective characteristics of the region, its landscapes or its people in comparison with other regions and their inhabitants. Articles may also present the region as a collective actor that struggles with other regions (Paasi forthcoming). These discourses provide strong basis for a 'we' feeling.

The importance of provincial newspapers as creators of time-space-specific regionalistic narratives is crucial on account of the fact that they have particularly wide circulation within their own provinces, to the extent that an 80 per cent coverage of the homes in the region is not a rarity. Newspapers provide a specific 'written identity' that seems to draw on rather fixed identity narratives that are linked with both the inhabitants and the region and its landscapes. In a comparative study on the emergence and identity of four Finnish provinces it was found that nature and landscapes are significant elements in the regionalistic writing style that regional press follows. These elements are part of broader regional thinking and often used as indicators of the represented regional or local uniqueness in the promotion and marketing of the region in the field of tourism, for instance (Paasi 1986).

Conclusion

In this chapter we have sought to map the various dimensions of spatial identity by first evaluating the meanings of the concept of identity and the links between identity and ideology. We then focused, as an illustration of the theoretical arguments, on the roles of spatial scales and narratives in the construction of identities of Finnish provinces and counties. These areas – that have overlapped in many cases – have been contested for more than 100 years, and a number of committees have been engaged in a fruitless struggle to create regional division that would satisfy the needs of political, social, and cultural actors operating at various spatial scales. The Finnish administration reform is a showcase of the ways in which governmental and popular identity discourses are conflated in the modern political practice. Needs and meanings which apply in politics and administration are discursively equated with 'everyman's' benefit and spatial imagination. While here approached through the Finnish context and in local circumstances, the case represents a routine procedure in modern societies dependent on the government by and through knowledge.

While spatial identities may be regarded as expressions of social consciousness and collective memory, the dimensions of identity and the meanings of history and heritage become much more complicated in everyday life. Even if identities may be strongly represented in the form of abstract or concrete 'official' symbols such as coats of arms, regional songs, memorial days, statues or certain 'local' buildings (museums, art galleries), the meanings of the symbols in everyday life may vary a lot. This is due to the fact that while symbols typically are institutionally engendered, they are always being interpreted in the contexts of daily life, where they receive their banal meanings. In this sense, individual experience mediates spatial identities (Cohen 1982). It is also obvious that the power of collective identitities does not emerge from any symbols as such, but from the fusion of social action and symbols in the practices and discourses thus spatialized. In this sense all spatial identities are rooted in particular forms of social life and thus are lived through, rather than with (Billig 1995).

Regional identification is weakened in the contemporary world by strong regional mobility – a phenomenon that is occurring at all spatial scales and has again increased in Finland. Less than half of Finns live in the municipality in which they were born, although there are great differences between regions. Before the reform of the counties in 1997, inhabitants living in the county of their birth varied from 86 per cent in Uusimaa to less than 60 per cent in Mikkeli and Kuopio. This means that the whole idea of a fixed regional identity is put under increasing pressure. Further, regional contexts and backgrounds are only one part of the complicated constellations of factors constituting identities – class, gender, sexuality, generation, or ethnicity may all be more significant elements for identity construction. Similarly, global cultural flows and internet, for example, may provide material for identity discourses that are not territorially bound. All this means that geographers should not take identities for granted, but rather they should contribute critically to existing discourses and reflect upon the complicated and contextual relations between the ideas of space, region and identity.

References

Althusser, L. (1984). *Ideologiset valtiokoneistot* (orig. Positions, 1976). Vastapaino, Tampere.

Anderson, B. (1991). *Imagined Community*. Verso, London.

Billig, M. (1995). *Banal Nationalism*. Sage, London.

Bourdieu, P. (1991). 'Identity and Representation. Elements for a Critical Reflection of the Idea of Region'. In Thompson, J.B. (ed.). *Language and Symbolic Power*. Polity Press, Cambridge, 220–228.

Bourdieu, P. (1998). *Järjen käytännöllisyy*s (orig. Raisons practiques. Sur la théorie de láction, 1994). Vastapaino, Tampere.

Bourdieu, P. and L. Wacquant (1992). *An Invitation to Reflexive Sociology*. Polity Press, Cambridge.

Breakwell, G. (1986). *Coping with Threatened Identities*. Methuen, London.

Campbell, D. (1998). *National Deconstruction: Violence, Identity, and Justice in Bosnia*. University of Minnesota Press, Minneapolis.

Cohen, A. (1982). 'Belonging: the experience of culture'. In Cohen, A. (ed.) *Belonging: Identity and Social Organization in British Rural Cultures*. Manchester University Press, Manchester, 1–17.

Cohen, A. (1985). *The symbolic construction of community*. Tavistok, London.

Cohen, A. (1994). *Self Consciousness. An Alternative Anthropology of Identity*. Routledge, London.

Committee report (1953). *Aluejakokomitean mietintö* (Report from the committee for regional division) no. 4.

Committee report (1992). *Maakuntaitsehallinnosta maakuntayhtymiin. Selvitysmies Kauko Sipposen ehdotus maakuntahallinnon kehittämisestä* (From provincial government to provincial associations: Governmental delegate Kauko Sipponen's proposal for the development of provincial self-government) no. 34.

Dijkink, G. (1996). *National Identity and Geopolitical Visions*. Routledge, London.

Douglas, M. (1986). *How Institutions Think*. Syracuse University Press, Syracuse, New York.

Giddens, A. (1984). *The Constitution of Society*. Polity Press, Cambridge.

Giddens, A. (1990). *The consequences of modernity*. Polity Press, Cambridge.

Guibernau, M. (1996). *Nationalisms*. Polity Press, Cambridge.

Häkli, J. (1994). 'Maakunta, tieto ja valta. Tutkimus poliittis-hallinnollisen maakuntadiskurssin ja sen historiallisten edellytysten muotoutumisesta Suomessa' [Region, knowledge and power. The emergence of and historical preconditions for the political-administrative discourse on provinces in Finland]. *Acta universitatis tamperensis* ser A, vol. 415.

Häkli, J. (1998a). 'Discourse in the production of political space: Decolonizing the symbolism of provinces in Finland'. *Political Geography*, 18(3), 331–363.

Häkli, J. (1998b). 'Manufacturing Provinces: theorizing the encounters between governmental and popular geographs in Finland'. In S. Dalby and G. Tuathail (eds.). *Rethinking geopolitics*. Routledge, London, 131–151.

Häkli, J. (forthcoming). 'In the territory of knowledge: state-centered discourses and the construction of society'. *Progress in Human Geography*, 24.

Hall, S. (1996). 'Introduction: Who needs identity?' In Hall, S. and P. Du Gay (eds.) *Questions of Cultural Identity*, Sage, London, 1–17.

Herb, G. and D. Kaplan (1999). *Nested Identities*. Rowman and Littlefield, New York.

Hooson, D. (editor 1994). *National Identity*, Blackwell, Oxford.

Jenkins, R. (1996). *Social identity*. London: Routledge.

Kaplan, D. (1994). 'Two nations in Search of a State: Canada's Ambivalent Spatial Identities'. *Annals of the Association of American Geographers*, 84(4), 585–606.

Kirkinen, H. (1991). *Maakuntien Eurooppa ja Suomi* (Finland and the Europe of the regions). Otava, Helsinki.

Lash, S. and J. Friedman (editors 1992). *Modernity and Identity*. Blackwell, Oxford.

Lefebvre, H. (1991). *The Production of Space*. Transl. by Donald Nicholson-Smith. Blackwell, Oxford.

Löfgren, O. (1989). 'The nationalization of culture'. *Ethnologia Europaea* 19, 5–23.

Massey, D. (1995). 'The conceptualization of place'. In Massey, D. and P. Jess (eds.) *A Place in the World? Places, Cultures and Globalization*. The Open University, Oxford.

Newman, D. and A. Paasi (1998). 'Fences and neighbours in the postmodern world: boundary narratives in political geography'. *Progress in Human Geography* 22, 186–207.

North, D.C. (1990). *Institutions, Institutional Change and Economic Performance*. Cambridge University Press, Cambridge.

Paasi, A. (1986). 'Neljä maakuntaa: maantieteellinen tutkimus aluetietoisuuden kehittymisestä' (Four provinces in Finland: a geographical study of the development of regional consciousness). *University of Joensuu Publications in Social Sciences* no.8. Joensuu.

Paasi, A. (1991). 'Deconstructing regions: notes on the scales of spatial life'. *Environment and Planning A* 23, 235–256.

Paasi, A. (1996). *Territories, Boundaries and Consciousness: the changing Geographies of the Finnish-Russian Border*. Wiley, Chichester.

Paasi, A. (1997). 'Geographical perspectives on Finnish national identity'. *GeoJournal* 43, 41–50.

Paasi, A. (1999). 'Nationalizing everyday life: individual and collective identities as practice and discourse'. *Geography Research Forum* 19, 4–21.

Paasi, A. (forthcoming). 'Finnish landscape as social practice: mapping identity and scale'. In Jones, M. and K. Olwig (eds.) *Nordcapes: Regional Identity, Diversity, Nature*. University of Minnesota Press, Minneapolis.

Palomäki, M. (1968). 'On the concept and delimitation of the present-day provinces of Finland'. *Acta Geographica*, vol 20, 279–295.

Pystynen, E. (1993). 'Maakuntaitsehallinnon ongelma Suomessa' (The problem of provincial self-government in Finland). *Kunnallistieteellinen aikakauskirja* 3/93, 211–223.

Schlesinger, P. (1991). *Media, State and Nation*. Sage, London.

Somers, M. (1994). 'The narrative construction of identity: a relational and network approach'. *Theory and Society* 23, 605–649.

Williams, R. (1976). *Keywords*. Fontana Press, London.

Ylönen, A. (1994). 'Keskusteluja Pirkanmaan tulevaisuudesta' (Discussions of the Pirkanmaa's future). *University of Tampere, Working papers of the Social Sciences Research Institute* 10.

Chapter 9

The embodied city: From bodily practice to urban life

Kirsten Simonsen

The paper that follows inscribes itself in the recent tradition of human geography that has been rather diffusely designated a 'cultural turn'. Besides a more or less sympathetic showdown with economistic tendencies in much work within the subject, it involves a rapprochement between what have earlier been seen as its social and cultural dimensions. I have elsewhere argued that this development of a social and a cultural geography in the Nordic countries has followed different paths from those of Anglo-American discourse, probably as a result of a closer marriage here between cross-disciplinary social sciences and the welfare state (Simonsen 1999). I will later return to the context of the present approach, but for the time being it will do to position myself in a new Nordic social and cultural geography.

More specifically, this paper has a twofold, although integrated purpose. First, I want to advocate an approach to human/social/cultural geography that takes its starting point in social *practice* – that is, an approach claiming that nothing in the social world is prior to human practice: not consciousness, ideas or meaning; not structures or mechanisms; and not texts, discourses or networks. This means that my main concern is with embodied or practical knowledge and its formation in people's everyday lives, with the world of emotions, desire and imagination, and with the infinitude of encounters through which we make the world and are made by it in turn. The starting point I advocate is not far from what Thrift (1996) calls 'non-representational thinking'. It is thinking which on the one hand takes a critical approach to theories that claim to 're-present' some naturally present reality. But on the other hand it also invites a degree of scepticism about some of the poststructuralist and 'linguistic' tendencies in the human/social sciences, because they often cut us off from one of the most interesting aspects of human practices, that is their embodied and situated character.

As a consequence of this interest in practice, my second aim with the paper is to discuss an aspect of the city that has remained hidden or at least undertheorized in the dominant currents of urban writing – that is *the embodied city*. This can be seen as a part of the general upsurge of interest in the body that we are currently experiencing in interdisciplinary and geographical enquiry; a development that in some sense makes the body a metaphor for studies that consider difference, domination and subversion to be central to the understanding of contemporary cultural spatialities (see e.g. collections from Duncan 1996, Ainly 1998, and Nast and Pile 1998). Still, not much of this literature locates the body and considers practical bodily interspaces, for instance the city. I therefore want to explore the possibilities in a few earlier contributions which, as I see it, have genuinely attempted to situate the body in the city. This should be considered part of thinking in terms of spatial scales, starting from the body as 'the geography closest in' and reaching out from there to other scales of social life.

But before moving to these issues, I want to reveal, to some extent retrospectively, how working in a Nordic context has informed the approach that I am advocating today. The paper is therefore organized in four parts. The first and briefest part will be an exploration of the Nordic background of my present approach. Then, in the second part, I want to outline what it means to have a starting point in practice, in particular in relation to the problem of subjectivity. In the third part the intrinsic corporeal and spatial character of practice will be discussed; and finally, in the fourth part, I want to draw some lines from that to the understanding of urban life. I would, of course, not see these ideas as exclusive in any sense, but only as one contribution among others to an improved understanding of the embodied city.

Some Nordic predecessors

When I reflect on the Nordic background that underlies my current interest in practice and the body, two lines of thought come to mind, each in some sense arising from the relationship between social science/geography and the development of the welfare state. One of these stems from a set of analyses and discussions of living conditions and modes of life (cultures) in the Nordic countries.

In the late 1960s and the 1970s quite a few geographers in all the Nordic countries were involved in social surveys and statistical analyses. The aims of these studies were to measure living conditions and the distribution of welfare amongst the Nordic populations, and they were conducted in order to produce a knowledge base for the politics of redistribution in the growing welfare states. However, the policies and the analyses did also provoke criticism, for example from the geographical margins of the Nordic countries. Most powerfully, the Norwegian sociologist Ottar Brox, on the basis of a study of post-war regional development in Northern Norway, mounted a severe attack on the homogenizing discourse involved in the social-democratic welfare project (Brox 1966). He exposed deep-lying conflicts between the regional planning of the central Norwegian state and the needs, values and systems of meaning within the local populations, thus giving voice to a 'central state/local culture' opposition. Even if this first attempt was based on a rather romantic view of small communities in Northern Norway, it effectively situated the question of cultural difference right in the centre of planning discussions and gained a wide influence in the social sciences throughout the Nordic countries. The debate was twofold: first, it questioned the objectivity and the materiality of the conception of living conditions and introduced dimensions of immateriality, imagination and possibilities for action; and secondly, it forced an idea of cultural difference into the discourse of homogeneous Nordic societies. And these were the questions to be theorized in the following years.

Most influential within geography, in particular in its more critical variants, was an approach first formulated by the Danish ethnologist Thomas Højrup (1983a, b).

With a point of departure in Althusserian Marxism he developed a concept of *life-mode* as a system of mutually dependent practices and ideologies, all assigning meaning to one another. True to the Marxist source, a specification of different life-modes in Western societies begins with modes of production and the meaning of work, thus suggesting that the question of cultural difference not only has a dimension of place, but also one of class. Although I was from the very start rather sceptical about this approach because of its economistic arguments and its strongly gender-biased analysis (see Simonsen 1993), I think the whole debate was an important contribution to Nordic geography. It did put cultural identity on the theoretical and empirical agenda, and it did so from a conception of culture closely related to social practice.

The other line of thought within Nordic human geography, which at a very early stage put the question of human day-to-day activity at the heart of the subject, was time-geography as formulated by Torsten Hägerstrand and practiced by a growing group of people during the 1970s and early 1980s (see e.g. Hägerstrand 1970, 1974, 1982). As in the above-mentioned works, this had close connections with the development of the Swedish welfare state; a lot of the work in the field was done in collaboration with planning agencies on different spatial scales.

Time-geography can be seen as consisting of three interrelated parts: an approach, a mode of description and a model (Åquist 1992). What is of primary interest in the present connection is the approach. At its core it is about the relationship of the individual to his or her surroundings, and it is mainly based upon identifying sources of constraints on human activity given by the nature of the body and the physical contexts in which activity occurs. This involves a concern with the capabilities of the human body, its means of mobility and communication, and its path through everyday life and the life-cycle – that is, with human beings understood as projects and paths in time-space contexts. In this way the routinized character of daily life is placed at the core of the effort, and Hägerstrand's now famous time-space diagrams can be seen as a geographical vocabulary aiming to describe what cannot be written, namely the movements and copings of everyday life.

Time-geography has been exposed to much critical discussion, most trenchantly when the focus has been on its physicalistic ontology (see among others Gregory 1985, Giddens 1984, Åquist 1992, Rose 1993). This is what turns Hägerstrand's 'musical score' of bodies and things into a *danse macabre* – 'an alienated world of bodies in autonomic motion' (Gregory 1994: 244). This is however not the point in the present connection. The point is that even if the core of the approach was somehow defective, time-geography made everyday life, bodies and bodily movement a legitimate geographical topic and introduced the idea of the 'situatedness' of interaction in time and space.

What this retrospective exploration shows is that working with everyday life and cultural identity is not a new endeavour in Nordic geography, even if the degree and the character of their treatment have varied from country to country and from institution to institution. The development of a 'geography of social practice' has however required a showdown with the tradition – a showdown basically ontological in character, abandoning physicalism and structuralism. Today, I prefer to consider these discussions to be over and done with, which is why I will proceed in the following to the presentation of my current approach.

Practice and subjectivity

During the last twenty years or so questions of subjectivity have broadly imbued geographical thinking in different ways. With inspiration from among other things structuration theory, poststructuralism, psychoanalysis and postcolonialism, a range of notions – such as self, body, agency, identity and subject – have been deployed to explore the role and the character of the individual in social settings (see e.g. Pile and Thrift 1995). What I am basically looking for in this contested terrain is a conception of the subject that considers it as multiple and dynamic, but only partially decentred. I accept the understanding of our identity as something complex and variable, but not ideas of ceaseless mutability and weightless choice. That means that popular notions of 'multiple identities' should be treated with some reservations. With Susan Bordo one can say:

> To deny the unity and stability of identity is one thing. The epistemological dream of becoming multiplicity – the dream of limitless multiple embodiments – is another. What sort of body is it that is free to change its shape and location at will, that can become anyone and travel anywhere? (1990: 44)

To adhere to these reservations, I start from the idea that the subject's understanding of the world comes from his/her everyday practices. As with many contemporary approaches in social theory, this proposition involves a rejection of the classic Cartesian notion of the subject as a unitary being made up of disparate parts, mind and body, which is universal, neutral and gender-free. In this view consciousness is a disembodied, immaterial unity with full reflexive access to itself, and the body in turn is a material object to which consciousness is attached. The dissociation from this notion has however followed very different paths. With a 'slogan' borrowed from Merleau-Ponty, the one I want to follow here can be formulated as 'Consciousness is in the first place not a matter of "I think that" but of "I can"' (1962: 137). That is, the subject is basically derived *in practice.*

One important source of inspiration for such an approach has been Heidegger's existential phenomenology – in particular as formulated in *Being and Time* (1962). In this work, 'Dasein' or human 'being-in-the-world' is described as an existential 'facticity' – as a practical, directional, everyday involvement. Our concern with the environment takes form through tools and articles for everyday use as well as useful products and projects – all together designated as 'equipment' (Zeug). 'Being-in-the-world' is then everyday skilful coping or engagement with an environment including things as well as other human beings. That means that our 'environment' does not arrange itself as something given in advance but as a totality of equipment dealt with in practice. It is important to state, however, that the use of the metaphor of equipment or tool does not lead to a reduction of the notion of practice to one of work, as seen in much Marxist literature. It is a much broader conception, as for instance when houses or flats are seen as equipment for living in a place.

Heidegger describes very simple skills – hammering, walking into a room, using turn signals, etc. – and shows how these everyday coping skills involve a familiarity with the world that enables us to make sense of things and to find our way about in our public environment. He thus demonstrates that the only ground we have or need to have for the intelligibility of thought and action is in the everyday practices themselves, not in some hidden process of thinking or of history (Dreyfus and Hall 1992). But the skills involved in these everyday practices are in themselves remarkable. Even in the most banal activities, extensive biological and cultural resources are mobilized.

A further development of such thinking is found in Merleau-Ponty's sensuous phenomenology of *lived experience,* where it is closely connected to the question of perception (1962, 1968). Merleau-Ponty's discussion of perception starts from a critique of two opposed strands of thought: empiricism and intellectualism. The former of these sees perception as a mere physical sensation and as a reflection of a pre-given, isolated object in the visual system. In so doing, it fails to recognize that perception always involves 'somebody' sensing something and that this somebody produces significance in the process. The other tradition, intellectualism, considers perception a conscious judgement or constituting act and therefore presupposes a pre-given, independent mind. In other words, intellectualism presupposes the subject of perception, just as empiricism presupposes the object. For Merleau-Ponty, on the contrary, perception is an opening-out to and engagement with otherness, a dialectical relationship of the body and its environment, which at the same time constitutes both subject and object. Therefore, perception is not in the first instance an 'experience' of objects, it is a conjunction and involvement with them, and the related mode of consciousness is a practical consciousness which is pre-reflective, pre-objective and pre-egological (Crossley 1996). We should thus speak neither of reflection nor observation, but of participation, and it is in this participation or practice that meaning and subjectivity are constituted.

Merleau-Ponty's favourite example is taken from football, and at the same time serves to highlight the importance of acquired cultural skills and routines. Football players don't reflect on the field and the rules of the game when playing, they are absorbed in the game. The players read the game and see openings, passes, 'off-sides' and goals – that is, different meaningful dimensions of the game. The point is that the significance of these elements is constituted, not reflectively but practically. The players have what Bourdieu has later called a 'sense of the game'.

It is this kind of thinking that is later sociologized and viewed in a historical/ structural setting by authors who formulate social theories of practice, such as Lefebvre (1958, 1961), Giddens (1984) and in particular Bourdieu (1977,1990). When Lefebvre writes about the importance of everyday life, Giddens about 'practical consciousness' as the basis of many of our day-to-day activities, and Bourdieu about 'habitus' as internalized dispositions for action and about people's 'sense of the game', the point is exactly this transcendence of the distinction between subjective and objective, coming from the inseparability of practice and subjectivity. What these authors also make clear is that practice should not be seen as isolated, intentional acts, but rather as continuous flows of conduct which are always future-oriented or part of a project.

One more dimension is important, however, considered in relation to the constitution of subjectivity and meaning – that is, the close connection between everyday practice and everyday language. The philosopher who has most thoroughly developed this relationship is Wittgenstein, in particular in his late work *Philosophical Investigations* (1953). Among other things, the relationship between language and social practice is explored in it, and, in accordance with the above,

Wittgenstein argues that meaning and significance cannot be ascribed to some kind of pre-given independent phenomenon; they are produced by human beings in the course of specific activities (Brock 1988).

Significance/meaning is constituted by the use of language, and being a language user is always connected to a practice and to a specific situation that in some sense has to be taken as given. What Wittgenstein provides with his philosophy of language is therefore at the same time a philosophy of practice – a phenomenological hermeneutics in which being a language user is in absolute concordance with being an acting and speaking person situated in a specific context. Language becomes a medium for social practice. As a consequence, Wittgenstein argued, in his thinking about human 'being', for a return to everyday life – to the life that we share through our language with one another – a strategy that brings us to yet another aspect of the relationship between practice, subjectivity and meaning; that is, that our understanding of the world is worked out in joint action and dialogue.

To develop this proposition it will be useful to dwell a little longer on language and on some of the authors mentioned above. Merleau-Ponty discusses how thought and language are two sides of the same coin and how both of them are social in character, but again it is Wittgenstein who makes the clearest contribution. He introduces the notions of 'language game' and 'form of life' to illustrate the significance of language and the relationship between language and practice. He says:

> Here the term 'language-*game*' is meant to bring into prominence the fact that *speaking* of language is part of an activity, or of a form of life (1953, I p. 11e)

The social character of these notions is further explored through what the philosophers call Wittgenstein's 'private language argument'; that is, a discussion of whether a person can develop a totally private language which only (s)he can understand. The argument goes like this: as language is developed through practical experience and learning, and as one cannot name an object without having a frame of understanding from which to do so, language can only exist *intersubjectively*. Without shared human activity no structured 'reality' or practical experiental basis exists that makes it possible to identify items for designation.

This demonstration of the intersubjectivity of language and practical language use has at least two implications. First, it means that the classical model of the sovereign subject grounded in reason can be transcended without therefore giving up notions of subject and subjectivity. The point is the constitution of subjectivity. In this respect, the 'private language argument' shows that self-consciousness has no primacy in relation to consciousness of the existence of 'other' people, since language – which is collective in character – serves as access to both. That means that intersubjectivity does not come from subjectivity, the constitutive process takes the opposite direction. And that is what has caused Crossley (1996) to characterize Wittgenstein's (and Merleau-Ponty's) thinking as 'radical intersubjectivity'.

The general argument then relocates the meaning of our talk from consciousness (imagination) to the public sphere (language, intersubjectivity) and relates it to the innumerable sets of language games that we play with one another as social beings. The notion of 'forms of life' is then invoked as a notion of culture – as concordant ways of living within which the language games are located and our utterances acquire meaning. The constitution of meaning is referred to networks of social practice, to the capability of acting within different social, temporal and spatial contexts.

Practice, body and space

Another characteristic of lived experience and social practice is that they are intrinsically corporeal. This statement stands in direct opposition to the already-mentioned Cartesian dualism of body (as material object) and mind (as an autonomous thinking subject). In order to challenge this dualism we can return to Merleau-Ponty, who in his analysis of perception introduces the notion of the '*body-subject*' for exactly this purpose. To Merleau-Ponty (1962), the lived experience is located in the 'mid-point' between mind and body, or between subject and object – an intersubjective space of perception and the body. In it, perception is based on practice; that is, on looking, listening and touching etc. as acquired, cultural, habit-based forms of conduct. Perception, from this perspective, is not seen as an inner representation of the outer world, but rather as a practical bodily involvement. It is an active process relating to our ongoing projects and practices, and it concerns the whole sensing body. This means that the human body takes up a dual role as both the vehicle of perception and the object perceived, as a body-in-the-world – *a lived body* – which 'knows' itself by virtue of its active relation to this world. The 'body-subjects' are not locked into their private world, but are in a world that is shared with 'others'. Consequently, to meet or to see the other is not to have an inner representation of him/her either, it is to be-with-him/her. This underlines the understanding of the world as a genuine human interworld and of subjectivity as publicly available; the subjects are sentient-sensuous bodies whose subjectivity assumes embodied and public forms. In this way, the concept of intersubjectivity can be amplified by one of 'intercorporeality' (Merleau-Ponty 1968).

However, the corporeality of social practices concerns not only the sensuous, generative and creative nature of lived experiences, but also how these embodied experiences themselves form a basis for social action. Bourdieu, for instance, talks about 'habitus' as embodied history, which is internalized as a second nature. As a result of this, social structures and cultural schemes are *incorporated* in the agents and thus function as generative dispositions behind their schemes of action:

Adapting a phrase of Proust's, one might say that arms and legs are full of numb imperatives. One could endlessly enumerate the values given body, *made* body, by the hidden persuasion of an implicit pedagogy which can instil a whole cosmology, through injunctions as insignificant as 'sit up straight' or 'don't hold your knife in your left hand', and inscribe the most fundamental principles of arbitrary content of a culture in seemingly innocuous details of bearing or physical and verbal manners, so putting them beyond the reach of consciousness and explicit statement (Bourdieu 1990: 69).

These considerations can support a social conception of the body which, like that of Shilling (1993), sees it as an unfinished biological and social phenomenon that is transformed, within certain limits, through social practices and participation in society. On the one hand, the body consists of features such as flesh, muscles, bones and blood, and exhibits species-specific capacities that identify us as human beings.

On the other, these features change for various reasons during our lifetime. This happens through aging, through care and nutrition and through the social practices and relations in which we participate. For example our upbringing, as shown in the above quotation from Bourdieu, is to a considerable degree concerned with body training and the disciplining of bodily practices. Furthermore, our bodies are regularly transformed by social practices. In this sense they become objects of labour, which are worked on just like other aspects of the natural and social world. These transformations often take place, consciously or unconsciously, in order to match social discourses of the 'normal/ideal' body form. The body, then, is definitely a social product, but it is not totally mouldable as suggested by some social constructionists. The body both facilitates and constrains social practices. To adopt a phenomenologically inspired conception, the body can be addressed as a combination of *facticity*, an existential condition and a basis for our understanding of ourselves and our environment, and *project*, a phenomenon in the process of becoming, dependent on our future-oriented practices and projects.

What we have seen so far, then, is that there is a givenness in embodiment and participation in nature, culture and society; but also that this givenness is indeterminate, capable of further determination or further development. More than anywhere else, the difficulties in comprehending this duality are exposed when we consider the gendered character of our bodies and social practices.

It is therefore no accident that in geography as in other social sciences the body has first appeared on the agenda in feminist writings. The problems involved in dualisms such as body/mind, nature/culture and essentialism/constructivism have been of particular importance here, not least because they have often been philosophically and culturally 'sexualized' (see e.g. Bordo 1993). The female body has been a metaphor for the corporeal pole of the dualisms, representing nature, emotionality, irrationality and sensuality. Images of the dangerous, appetitive female body, ruled precariously by its emotions, stand in contrast to the masterful, masculine will, the locus of social power, rationality and self-control. This cultural discourse has formed the basis of sexism and biological determinism, in which claims for the subordination and control of women have been made with reference to life sciences, in particular biology. The whole project of modern feminism can be seen as a showdown with this kind of biological essentialism.

The first reaction to this essentialism was in fact the introduction of a new dualism serving to disconnect social processes from biology; that is the dualism between sex and gender. In short, the strategy was to leave the body to biology and concentrate on social processes, and this has been of the utmost importance to the formulation of modern feminist research and politics. Gradually, however, quite a few people have found this dualism unsatisfactory, and other counter-formulations to biological determinism have been proposed. A quite dominant notion in the humanities and social sciences today, articulated for instance by the Foucault-inspired philosopher Judith Butler (1990), argues that sex is just as culturally, performatively and discursively constructed as gender, so the distinction between the two becomes irrelevant. This means that the strategy has changed from denying that biological facts can be the basis for social norms to denying the very existence of biological facts that are independent of social and political norms (Moi 1998). The body becomes a *tabula rasa* awaiting inscription from culture.

From my perspective, however, this solution is unsatisfactory too, because such a 'textualization' of the body gives free rein to meaning/discourse at the expense of attention to the body's material locatedness in history, practice and culture. A much more useful approach, respecting the materiality and historicity of the body as well as its gender, has in my opinion come from the Norwegian feminist Toril Moi (1998). She bases her understanding on a re-reading of Simone de Beauvoir, also drawing on Sartre and Merleau-Ponty. The starting point is Beauvoir's notion of the body as a '*situation*'. It is a situation amongst many others – such as class, race, nationality, biography, location etc. – but it is a fundamental situation because it forms the basis of our experiences of ourselves and of our environment. It is a situation which will always be a part of our lived experience. Following Sartre, Moi considers the situation to be a structural relationship between our projects (freedom) and the world (which includes the body). In this way, the understanding of the body involves exactly the doubleness of facticity and project that I suggested above. The meaning of a woman's body is connected to her projects in the world – to the way in which she uses her freedom – but it is also marked by all her other life-situations. There are countless ways of living out the specific burdens and potentialities of being a woman. The understanding of sex/gender put forward by Moi (and de Beauvoir), then, is both historical and open – it is always in a process of becoming, marked by our shifting and fluctuating experiences of ourselves in the world. The relationship between body and subjectivity is neither necessary nor accidental, it is *contingent*.

Part of the locatedness of the body referred to above is a matter of its situatedness in space and time, and this opens an avenue for an understanding of the relationship between the corporeality of practice and space. First, it can accentuate the 'place character' of space (see e.g. Casey 1993, 1997). The body is always in place; notwithstanding developments of 'placelessness', 'disembeddedness', mobility and 'hyperspace', we can't escape that fact. More important, however, is the way in which the body itself is spatial. To explore that we can once more turn to Merleau-Ponty. Initially, he states that the spatiality of the body is not a spatiality of *position*, but one of *situation*. This goes for temporality as well, and it means that we should avoid thinking of our bodies as being *in* space or *in* time – they *inhabit* space and time:

> I am not in space and time, nor do I conceive space and time; I belong to them, my body combines with them and includes them. The scope of this inclusion is the measure of that of my existence (Merleau-Ponty 1962: 140)

This means that active bodies, using their acquired schemes and habits, position their world around themselves and constitute that world as 'ready-to-hand', to use Heidegger's expression. And these are moving bodies 'measuring' space and time in their active construction of a meaningful world. This also accentuates the indispensable intertwining of matter and meaning. For Merleau-Ponty, the material world is not juxtaposed with an ideational one:

> Merleau-Ponty refuses to separate the ideational and the material. All ideas and meanings are necessarily embodied (in books, rituals, speech, buildings etc), he maintains, and all matter embodies meaning and derives its place in the human world by virtue of that

meaning ... In this sense then he calls our attention ... to *the embodiment of culture*, and he extends his argument against the abstraction of meaning and matter (Crossley 1995: 59)

Notwithstanding internal disagreements, I think Lefebvre (1991) can add something to this with his stronger emphasis on social practice and the production of space. He establishes a material basis for the production of space consisting of:

a practical and fleshy body conceived of as totality complete with spatial qualities (symmetries, asymmetries) and energetic properties (discharges, economies, waste) (Lefebvre 1991: 61)

An important precondition of this material production is that each living body both *is* and *has* its space; it produces itself in space at the same time as it produces that space.

Like Merleau-Ponty, Lefebvre assigns an important role to the body in the 'lived experience'. As a part of that, the body constitutes a practico-sensory realm in which space is perceived through sight, smells, tastes, touch and hearing. It produces a space which is both biomorphic and anthropological. The relationship to the environment is conducted through a double process of orientation and demarcation – practical as well as symbolic. These processes are connected in a conception of '*the spatial body*':

A body so conceived, as produced and as the production of space, is immediately subject to the determinants of that space ... the spatial body's material character derives from space, from the energy that is deployed and put to use there (Lefebvre 1991: 195)

When Lefebvre refers here to the energy of the body, it is not only a material/ biological notion. With reference to Nietzsche, he emphasizes the Dionysian side of existence according to which play, struggle, art, festival, sexuality and love – in short, Eros – are themselves necessities. They are parts of the transgressive energies of the body. Further, it is important to notice, this concerns not only the material and meaningful production of space, but also the capacity to transgress the 'everydayness' of modern life. It involves participation and appropriation of space for creative, generative, bodily practices, as formulated for instance in the 'right to the city' (Lefebvre 1996). The contributions from Merleau-Ponty and Lefebvre thus provide us with an understanding of the indispensable relationships among practice, body and space. What they don't appreciate to a satisfactory degree is the differences among bodies. Here, I have done this with the aid of Moi's/de Beauvoir's notion of the body as a situation. As a preliminary attempt to spatialize this notion, it is worth considering an original contribution from Iris Marion Young (1990) in which she explores the possibility of a specifically 'feminine' body comportment and relation in space. She displays a contradictory spatiality primarily based on the historical and cultural fact that women live their bodies simultaneously as subjects and objects. A woman in our culture experiences her body on the one hand as background and means for her projects in life. On the other hand she lives with the ever-present possibility of being gazed upon as a potential object of others' intentions. This ambiguous bodily existence tends to 'keep her in her place', and it influences her manner of movement, her relationship to her surroundings and her appropriation of space. Probably other deviations from the 'neutral' body – such as skin colour, age and sexuality – can in similar ways give rise to specific practical and symbolic spatialities.

What I have tried to establish so far, then, is the way in which practice and subjectivity are mutually constitutive. This constitution is radically intersubjective, and practice, body and space are inseparable. The relationship of 'body-subjects' to space can therefore never be a question of simple location; it is an active engagement with the surrounding world involving a production of meaning. The social body can then be seen as 'the geography closest in' – as a constitutive social spatiality reaching out towards other socio-spatial scales from local, urban and regional configurations to national and supra-national/global connections.

The embodied city

In the remainder of this paper, I want to extend the discussion with an attempt to sketch out an entry into the embodied city – a relationship between spatial bodies and the urban scale. That is of course only one of many possible perspectives on the city, but one that emphasizes the practical co-constitution of body and space proposed above. One article often cited in this connection is Grosz's (1992) interesting essay on 'Bodies-Cities' in which she points to the city as one ingredient in the social constitution of the body. That is, 'the form, structure, and norms of the city seep into and affect all the other elements that go into the constitution of corporeality and/as subjectivity' (1992: 248) In spite of the intention to deal with co-constitution, however, the idea of mutually defining relations seems to vanish from the argument in favour of an installation of the city as just one more element in the social construction of the body. Therefore, I prefer to start this discussion from another point; namely de Certeau's (1984) discussion of '*walking in the city*'.

What de Certeau is talking about here is practitioners of the city following the urban pathways, but at the same time producing their own stories, shaped out of the fragments of trajectories and alterations of spaces. It is a process of narration in which walking in the streets mobilizes other subtle, stubborn, embodied and even resistant meanings. With reference to Merleau-Ponty he writes:

> These practices of space refer to a specific form of *operations* ('ways of operating'), to 'another spatiality' (an 'anthropological', poetic and mythic experience of space), and to an *opaque and blind* mobility characteristic of the bustling city. A *migrational*, or metaphorical, city thus slips into the clear text of the planned and readable city (de Certeau 1984: 93)

Walking in the city, then, is one of those everyday practices or 'ways of operating' which make up the game of ordinary people, of 'the others', when they move along in a creative and tactical way in a network of already-established forces and representations. It is a spatial practice using and performing the urban system in a way that secretly influences the determining conditions of urban life. It is a *lived space* – a space of disquieting familiarity with the city. Here, the affinity with both Merleau-Ponty and Lefebvre becomes suggestive.

With inspiration from theories of ordinary language use, walking in the city is dealt with as a speech act. The act of walking, de Certeau argues, is to the urban system what the speech act is to language or to the statements uttered. Walking is a space of 'enunciation', in this sense having a triple function: it is a process of *appropriation* of the urban topographical system; it is a spatial *realization* or acting-out of place; and it implies *relations* among differentiated positions, that is, among pragmatic 'contracts' in the form of movements (or moves in relation to someone).

Altogether, this means that walking practices can't be seen only as simple movements, they rather spatialize. Their intertwined parts give their shape to spaces. They weave places together. In that respect, walking practices create a diversity of subsystems whose existence in some sense makes up the city. Different characteristics of use are at work in this process. While a pre-given spatial order can organize an ensemble of possibilities and interdictions, the walker actualizes some of these possibilities. S/he makes them exist as well as emerge. But s/he also moves them about and invents others, since the improvisation of walking privileges, transforms or abandons spatial elements. Thus the walker creates discreteness, whether by making choices among the signifiers of the spatial 'language' or by displacing them through the use of them. In this realization and appropriation of space, the walker also constitutes a here and a there; s/he constitutes a location and in relation to that a location of an 'other', thus establishing a conjunctive and disjunctive articulation of places. The whole 'rhetoric of walking' has a 'phatic' aspect; through contacts in meetings, followings, networks etc., it creates a fluid and mobile organicity in the city.

De Certeau's contribution is not only an account of the moving body's creative and tactical use of the city. Perhaps its most original part is the already-suggested relationship between spatiality and narrativity. A theory of narration is indissociable from a theory of practices, as its condition as well as its production (1984: 78). This is not simply about the built environment becoming text, but rather about the city becoming a collection of stories. Everyday stories tell us what we can do in it and make out of it – they are treatments of space. Different mental and symbolic mechanisms are involved in this weave of spatial and signifying practices – such as legend, memory and dream – and they organize the invisible meanings of the city. They make places habitable or believable, they recall or suggest phantoms and, altering functional identity by detaching themselves from it, they create the stories of 'the other' in places.

Even if de Certeau thus produces an understanding of urban life from 'closest in', his contribution is not a voluntaristic micro-sociology (see also Crang 2000). His moving bodies (or agents) are constituted against a monolithic vision of power – against imaginary totalizations produced by the eye. One of these is the panoptic and strategic discourse of planning and social theory which rationalizes the city and organizes it by speculative and classificatory operations. Another one is the imaginary discourse of media and commerce (de Certeau 1997). They create cities that are 'imaginary museums' and as such form counterpoints to cities at work. These imaginary entities are characterized by a growing eroticization, by a celebration of the body and the senses. But it is a fragmented body, categorized by virtue of an analytical dissection, cut into successive sites of eroticization. In this connection de Certeau even talks about speech and signification as 'denaturing' acts.

These arguments are close to the ones put forward by Lefebvre (1991) when he is linking the history of the body with the history of space and, to use Gregory's (1994) word, understanding the development of modernity and the modern city as a *decorporealization* of space. This process involves a logic of visualization and one of metaphorization; living bodies, the bodies of 'users' are caught up, not only in the toils of parcellized space, but also in the work of images, signs and symbols. These bodies are transferred and emptied out via the eyes, a process that is not only abstract and visual, but also phallocratic. It is embodied in a 'masculine' will to power and, metaphorically, abstract space and its material forms symbolize force, male fertility and violence.

As we have seen, however, the moving body serves both authors as a critical figure as well. It is not possible totally to reduce the body or the practico-sensory realm to abstract space. The body takes its revenge – or at least calls for revenge – for example in leisure space. It seeks to make itself known, to gain recognition as *'generative'*, thus appropriating or shaping urban space through everyday life, struggle (Lefebvre) or tactics (de Certeau). One problem in these formulations is the flavour of authenticity they tend to ascribe to the body and everyday life. By using the conception of the social body put forward above, I do however think that it is possible to avoid romanticizing the body and to understand the role of moving bodies in the constitution of and conflict over urban space as a historical, open-ended process.

The conception of the (spatial) body also suggests that the cultural embodiment of the city is gendered (and marked by other bodily ascribed identities). Young (1990) argued that feminine spatiality involves not only an experience of spatial constitution, but also one of being 'positioned' in space. That is why feminine existence tends to posit an enclosure between itself and the space surrounding it, such that the space belonging to it is constricted but is also a defence against bodily invasion. This is about power relations and in the last instance about fear of violence. For women being 'wise' is about not frequenting the city at specific times or in specific places, not wearing specific clothes etc. On the basis of her studies in Finland, Koskela (1997), however, stresses the importance of analysing courage as well as fear. She argues that women not only passively experience space but also actively take part in its production. Some women's confidence about going out produces space that is available to other women. Walking in the street can be seen as a political act: women 'write themselves onto the street' (1997: 316)

This discussion is part of the broader one of the gendered (and sexualized) character of the binary opposition between public and private space, one which has been central in both feminist geography and feminism in general. It is now a well-known story how the female body has culturally and historically been associated with private space and restricted in public space, and how this distinction has been reproduced in planning and urban design. What is also important, however, is to recognize how this distinction is also continually (re)negotiated, through collective actions, through dress and body language and through just 'being there' (see e.g. Duncan 1996, Valentine 1996, Koskela 1997).

The private/public dichotomy can be further deconstructed with the help of Lefebvre's incomplete ideas on 'rhythmanalysis' (1992), focusing on the spatio-temporal flows of living bodies and their internal and external relationships.

Lefebvre starts from the body and views the body-city relationship through a distinction and conjunction between two kinds of rhythms: 'rhythms of the self' and 'rhythms of the other'. The rhythms of the self are deeply inscribed rhythms, organizing a time oriented towards private and intimate life, while rhythms of the other are rhythms turned outward, towards the public. These two poles are connected in a multiplicity of transitions and imbrications: in apartments, houses, streets, squares and places; in family, kinship, neighbourhood and friendship relations; and in the city itself. The separation between private and public, then, is broken down with a starting point in the 'body-subject' and its senses, reaching out to the bustling world and linking the two. In a few essays Lefebvre discusses the rhythm of the city as a spatial temporality involving among other things flows of bodies, spectacles and sounds. But he also stresses a continuous conflict between tendencies towards homogeneity and diversity. That is, conflicts between rhythms imposed by political and economic centrality and the polyrhythmy of different cultures, languages and sexualities.

Obviously, rhythmanalysis is an incomplete project, but it ties up some of the threads that are spun in this paper and suggests a development of alternative methodologies to grasp the more opaque sides of urban life. It opens up a path to an understanding of urban life through alternating successions of interactive bodies during day and night. A paradigmatic dimension of such an understanding is difference – in culture, ethnicity, class, gender and sexuality – that is, experiences and encounters between different bodies in lived and perceived space. Furthermore,

> It is on the one hand a relationship of the human being with his own body, with his tongue and speech, with his gestures, in a certain place and with a gestural whole, and on the other hand, a relationship with the largest public space, with the entire society and beyond it, the universe (Lefebvre and Régulier 1996: 235)

Even if this seems something of an overstatement, in keeping with the above it suggests an interaction between different spatial scales with the body as 'the geography closest in'.

References

Ainly, R. (ed) (1998) *New Frontiers of Space, Bodies and Gender*, London/New York: Routledge.

Åquist, A-C. (1992) *Tidsgeografi i samspel med samhällsteori*, Lund: Lund University Press.

Bærenholdt, J.O., Simonsen, K., Sørensen, O.B. and Vogelius, P. (1990) 'Lifemodes and Social Practice – New Trends in Danish Social Geography', *Nordisk Samhällsgeografisk Tidskrift* 11, pp.72–86.

Bordo, S. (1990) 'Feminism, postmodernism and gender scepticism', in Nicholson, N.J. (ed) *Feminism/Postmodernism*, London: Routledge.

Bordo, S. (1993) *Unbearable Weight: Feminism, Western Culture and the Body*, Berkeley/Los Angeles/London: University of California Press.

Bourdieu, P. (1977) *Outline of a Theory of Practice*, Cambridge: Cambridge University Press.

Bourdieu, P. (1990) *The Logic of Practice*, Cambridge: Polity Press.

Brock, S. (1988) 'Livsform som syntese af det objektive og det subjektive. Om livsformsbegrebets status og genese hos Wittgenstein', *Philosophia* 17: 1–2, 89–106.

Brox, O. (1966) *Hva skjer i Nord-Norge?* Oslo: Pax.

Butler, J. (1990) *Gender trouble: Feminism and the subversion of identity*, New York: Routledge.

Casey, E.S. (1993) *Getting back into Place*, Bloomington/Indianopolis: Indiana University Press.

Casey, E.S. (1997) *The Fate of Place. A Philosophical History*, Berkeley/Los Angeles/ London: University of California Press.

de Certeau, M. (1984) *The Practice of Everyday Life*, Berkeley/Los Angeles/London: California University Press.

de Certeau, M. (1997) *Culture in the Plural*, Minneapolis/London: University of Minnesota Press.

Crang, M. (2000) 'Relics, places and unwritten geographies in the work of Michel de Certeau (1925–86)' in Crang, M. and Thrift, N. (eds) *Thinking space*, London/New York: Routledge.

Crossley, N. (1995) 'Merleau-Ponty, the elusive body and carnal sociology', *Body and Society* 1:1, 43–65.

Crossley, N. (1996) *Intersubjectivity. The Fabric of Social Becoming*, London: Sage.

Dreyfus, H. and Hall, H. (1992) (eds) *Heidegger. A Critical Reader*, Oxford: Blackwell.

Duncan, N. (ed) (1996) *BodySpace*, London/New York: Routledge.

Duncan, N. (1996) 'Renegotiating gender and sexuality in public and private spaces', in Duncan, N. (ed) *BodySpace*, London/NewYork: Routledge.

Flemmen, A.B. (1999) *Mellemromserfaringer. En analyse af kvinners frykt for seksualisert vold*, PhD dissertation from the University of Tromsø.

Giddens, A. (1984) *Constitution of Society*, Cambridge: Polity Press.

Gregory, D. (1985) 'Suspended Animation: The Stasis of Diffusion Theory', in Gregory and Urry (eds) *Social Relations and Spatial Structures*. London: Macmillan.

Gregory, D. (1994) *Geographical Imaginations*, Oxford: Blackwell.

Grosz, E. (1992) 'Bodies-Cities', in Colomina, B. (ed) *Sexuality and Space*, Princeton papers of Architecture, New York: Princeton Architectural Press.

Hägerstrand, T. (1970) 'What about people in Regional Science?' *Papers and Proceedings of the Regional Science Association 24*, pp. 7–21.

Hägerstrand, T. (1974) 'Tidgeografisk beskrivning – syfte och postulat', *Svensk Geografisk Årsbok* 50, 86–94.

Hägerstrand, T. (1982) 'Diorama, Path and Project', *Tijdschrift voor economische en Sociale Geografie* 73, pp. 323–39.

Harvey, D. (2000) *Spaces of Hope*, Berkeley/Los Angeles: University of California Press.

Heidegger, M. (1962) *Being and Time*, Oxford: Blackwell.

Højrup, T. (1983a) *Det glemte folk*, Copenhagen: Institut for europæisk folkelivsforskning/ Statens Byggeforskningsinstitut.

Højrup, T. (1983b) 'The concept of life-mode. A form-specifying mode of analysis applied to contemporary Western Europe', *Ethnologica Scandinavica*, pp. 15–50.

Irigaray, L. (1984) *Etique de la difference sexuelle*, Paris: Minuit.

Jónasdóttir, A.G. and von der Fehr, D (1998) 'Introduction: ambiguous times – contested spaces in the politics, organization and identities of gender', in von der Fehr, D., Rosenbeck, B. and Jónasdóttir (eds) *Is there a Nordic Feminism?* Berkeley: University of California Press.

Koskela, H. (1997) '"Bold Walk and Breakings": women's spatial confidence versus fear of violence', *Gender, Place and Culture*, 4:3, 301–319.

Koskela, H. (1999) *Fear, Control and Space. Geographies of Gender, Fear of Violence, and Video Surveillance.* Helsinki: Publicationes Instituti Geographici Universitatis Helsingiensis A 137.

Lefebvre, H (1958, 1961) *Critique de la vie quotidienne*, vol I and II. Paris: L'Arche Éditeur.

Lefebvre, H. (1991) *The Production of Space*, Oxford: Blackwell.

Lefebvre, H. (1992*) Élements de rythmanalyse: Introduction à la connaissance de rythmes*, Paris: Syllepse.

Lefebvre, H. (1996) (edited by Kofman, E. and Lebas, E.) *Writings on Cities*, Oxford: Blackwell.

Lefebvre, H. and Regulier, C. (1996) 'Rhythmanalysis of Mediterranean Cities', in Lefebvre, *Writings on Cities*, Oxford: Blackwell.

Longhurst, R. (1995) 'The Body and Geography', *Gender, Place and Culture* 2:1, 97–106

Lyngfelt, A. (1998) 'The dream of reality: a study of a feminine dramatic tradition, the one-act play', in von der Fehr, D., Rosenbeck, B and Jónasdóttir, A.G. (eds) *Is there a Nordic Feminism?* Berkeley: University of California Press.

Merleau-Ponty, M. (1962) *Phenomenology of Perception*, London: Routledge and Kegan Paul.

Merleau-Ponty, M. (1968) *The Visible and the Invisible*, Evanstone, IL: Northwestern University Press.

Moi, T. (1998) *Hva er en kvinne? Kjønn og krop i feministisk teori*, Oslo: Gyldendal.

Nast, H.J. and Pile, S.(eds) (1998) *Places through the Body*, London/New York: Routledge.

Pain, R. (1991) 'Space, sexual violence and social control: Integrating geographical and feminist analyses of women's fear of crime', *Progress in Human Geography*, 15: 415–431.

Parviainen, J. (1998) *Bodies moving and moved. A Phenomenological Analysis of the Dancing Subject and the Cognitive and Ethical Values of Dance Art*, Tampere: Tampere University Press.

Pawson, E. and Banks, G. (1993) 'Rape and Fear in a New Zealand City', *Area* 25: 55–63.

Pile, S. (1996) *The Body and the City*, London/NewYork: Routledge.

Pile, S. and Thrift, N. (1995) *Mapping the Subject: geographies of cultural transformation*, London/New York: Routledge.

Rose, G. (1993) *Feminism & Geography*, Cambridge: Polity Press.

Scott Sørensen, A. (1998) 'Taste, manners and attitudes – the bel esprit and literary salon in the Nordic countries c.1800', in von der Fehr, D., Rosenbeck, C. and Jónasdóttir, A.G. (eds) *Is there a Nordic Feminism?* Berkeley: University of California Press.

Shilling, C. (1993) *The Body and Social Theory*, London/Newbury Park/New Delhi: Sage.

Simonsen, K. (1990) 'Urban Division of Space – a Gender Category?', *Scandinavian Housing and Planning Research* 7: 143–153.

Simonsen, K. (1993) *Byteori og hverdagspraksis*, Copenhagen: Akademisk Forlag.

Simonsen, K. (1999) 'Difference in Human Geography – Travelling through Anglo-Saxon and Scandinavian Discourses', *European Planning Studies*, 7:1, pp. 9–25.

Thrift, N. (1996) *Spatial Formations*, London: Sage Publications.

Valentine, G. (1989) 'The geography of women's fear', *Area* 21. 385–390.

Valentine, G. (1996) '(Re)negotiating the "heterosexual street"', in Duncan, N. (ed) *BodySpace*, NewYork/London: Routledge.

Wilson, E. (1991) *The Sphinx in the City. Urban life, the control of disorder and women*, London: Virago Press.

Wittgenstein, L. (1953) *Philosophical Investigations*, Oxford: Blackwell.

Young, I.M. (1990) *Throwing like a girl and other essays in feminist philosophy and social theory*, Bloomington: Indiana University Press.

Chapter 10

Rural geography and feminist geography: Discourses on rurality and gender in Britain and Scandinavia

Nina Gunnerud Berg and Gunnel Forsberg

The contextual character of knowledge production

During the 1990s human geographers have increasingly acknowledged that knowledge per se is a social construction. Consequently, the contextual character of knowledge production and the ways dominant paradigms have influenced the construction of academic knowledge have been focused. How questions of authority, positionality, power and representation are bound up with the research encounter has been very much discussed. Influenced by feminists, especially Haraway (1991), and their ideas about knowledge as views from somewhere, rather than nowhere, not least feminist geographers have contributed to the position that takes a view of knowledge not as fixed truths, but rather as *embodied situated knowledges* produced within particular contexts and through particular interactions (McDowell 1992, Rose 1993, 1997, Bondi 1997). Also in rural geography such epistemological reflections have led to a heightened awareness about the situated nature of understandings and a critique of dominant paradigms within the sub-discipline (Philo 1992, 1993, Murdoch and Pratt 1993, 1994, Phillips 1994, Cloke 1994).

Our point of departure in this chapter is that British rural geography and feminist geography have produced academic discourses that in recent years have become, and still are, very influential on scholarship in Western Europe. What we want to do is to problematise the adoption of British concepts and theories into Swedish and Norwegian rural geography in general and in feminist rural geography in special. We do not claim that British rural and/or feminist geographers themselves do not realise the partiality of their knowledges, or that they claim that their knowledges have universal applicability. Neither do we suggest that they work to exclude other knowledges. What we want to do is to illustrate the partiality of British academic discourses by filtering British notions of rurality and gender through Scandinavian academic lenses, i.e. other situated knowledges. We do not argue that we shall *not* adopt theoretical frameworks across nations, rather that a reflexive awareness should permeate our theoretical exchange. What motivates our concern is the belief that researchers' understandings and conceptualisations do matter because it affects what we see and acknowledge as interesting or important.

A couple of years ago we, the authors of this article, realised that we shared some thoughts concerning theory import. We had both started to ask questions about when

173

and to what extent it is relevant to use concepts developed in British rural studies, gender studies and studies where the two fields meet in analyses of the restructuring of the Scandinavian countrysides. There is, in other words, a personal point of departure in this chapter. The above mentioned ideas about the sociology of knowledge have no doubt influenced us, but our own experiences from trying to grasp the central dimensions of our own empirical materials with the help of British theoretical frameworks are as important. Norwegian and Swedish discourses on rurality and gender do not always fit very well into the British discourses. We have chosen to illustrate the problem with the concept of *rural idyll*, because of its central position in international literatures on rural areas. Amongst the numerous publications on rural change in which the rural idyll is central to the analyses, there are some that are informed by gender perspectives and argue that the rural idyll is a gendered concept (Hughes 1997, Valentine 1997, Little 1994, 1997, Little and Austin 1996). We argue that the concept is conveying a *British* rural idyll and that the way it is gendered is British too. In our unpacking of the rural idyll, we suggest the concept '*gender idyll*' to illustrate our point. To make our theoretical discussion more concrete, we focus on the relevance of the concept of rural idyll in analyses of *migration into rural areas*, an issue we both have analysed in Sweden and Norway, respectively (see e.g. Forsberg 1994, 1996, Berg 1998).

Positioning ourselves in the theoretical landscape

The influence of postmodernism has during the last decade led to new approaches in both rural studies and gender studies. In line with ideas about deconstruction of established analytical categories, the categories of rural and urban areas are questioned within rural studies, and the categories of men and women (male and female, masculinity and femininity) are questioned within gender studies. Both fields, consequently, have changed their emphasis from generalisations about rural (or urban) areas and women (or men) to focusing on diversity and variety. This is reflected in the use of plural – ruralities/countrysides, masculinities and femininities. Deconstruction of established categories is in accordance with an approach to both rurality and gender as socially and culturally constructed which today dominate rural studies and gender studies respectively. Such an understanding places analyses of social representations of rurality and gender at the centre stage of research. It is within this theoretical framework that hegemonic social representation of the rural (like the rural idyll) and other more or less marginal ones (other countrysides) have come to play a central role within rural studies. Within gender studies hierarchies of masculinities and femininities are analysed. Implicit in thinking of different social representations as ranked is an awareness of the fact that power is bound up discursively in the very social and cultural constructs. As regards social representations of rurality they include for example attitudes about who does and who does not belong to the countryside. An example from gender studies is that representations of masculinities and femininities are bound up with ideas about what it is to be a real man and a real woman. It is within this type of theoretical framework we continue this chapter. We will, however, stress that seeing rurality and gender as social and cultural constructs by no means sees them as devoid of any material basis.

In the next section we turn to the concepts of rural idyll and gender idyll and research on urban-rural migration. The section serves to open the terrain which is explored and where we ask *why* British (feminist) rural geography's use of the rural idyll seem partial to us. Does it have to do with different discourses on the rural and the urban in Britain on the one hand and Sweden and Norway on the other? Are different discourses on masculinity and femininity in Britain and Norway/Sweden of significance? We end the chapter by discussing how we should deal with import of theoretical approaches.

Rural idyll, gender idyll and urban-rural migration

Conceptualisations of rurality and migration

The pros and cons of adopting concepts and theories developed in analyses of the British countryside in other empirical frameworks, as e.g. the Swedish or Norwegian countrysides, are visualised very well in analyses of the phenomenon of migration into rural areas. The British debate has been very much focused on the extent to which those moving into rural areas are motivated by a desire for 'rurality' in terms of rural living environment and lifestyle – rural idyll – as opposed to choosing, or even being forced, to move because of a geographical redistribution of elements important to their quality of life such as jobs, housing, services and safety (Champion 1998).

As we see it the debate is closely related to the discussion about *how to define rurality*, a topic that has occupied much space in rural studies. As opposed to traditional definitions of rurality that focus on employment and housing, service provision, land use and other measurable variables (functional definitions), more recent approaches see the rural as a mental construct (Mormont 1990). That is to say that the way the rural is experienced by those individuals who integrate visions of rurality into their daily lives is focused upon (Hoggart et al.1995). As Halfacree (1993) and Jones (1995) emphasise the rural as a social representation relates to lay discourses of rurality, i.e. the words and concepts understood and used by people in everyday talk. Attention turns, in other words, to how the rural is perceived which is important because behaviour and decision making – e.g. concerning migration – are influenced by people's perceptions of the rural. It is the understanding of rurality as a phenomenon which is socially and culturally constructed that has brought the concept of rural idyll into the debate about the reasons for migration into rural areas. The explanatory power of the rural idyll for migration to the countryside is, however, not our focus. What we want to concentrate on is rather the *underlying ideas* behind the focus on the rural idyll and their relevance in Norwegian and Swedish research on urban-rural migration and later on its constitutive elements dependent on place.

The understanding of rurality as socially and culturally constructed is no doubt an approach, which represents a step away from rural geographies' rootedness in economic geography towards more pluralistic perspectives, not least *cultural perspectives*. It is, therefore, more comprehensive than the traditional ones, but far from unproblematic. While rurality defined in functional terms easily could be measured and therefore made comparable across nations and regions, rurality understood as a social and cultural construct that varies in time and space is much harder to grasp and mediate. To re-present images of the rural is much more difficult than to describe the rural by use of e.g. a rurality index.

The debate over the reasons for urban-rural migration is, in addition to being related to how rurality is understood, also related to *how migration should be conceived of*. While migration was conceptualised mainly as goal-directed behaviour in traditional migration research a more complex conceptualisation has developed more recently (Boyle et al. 1998). It has been suggested that instead of stressing the purposeful and calculating character of migration, one should emphasise its location within the individual migrant's entire biography and seek to demonstrate the complexity of the seemingly simple act of migration and its embeddedness within the everyday context of daily life for those involved (Halfacree and Boyle 1993). It is recognised that migration is a *cultural experience* making concepts as cultural identity, sense of place and dislocation central to the analyses (Chambers 1994, Fielding 1992, Massey 1991, Gilroy 1993).

It is no doubt this 'cultural turn' in both rural studies and migration studies which lies behind the focus on migrants' ideas of the rural in explaining urban-rural migration found in a lot of British studies. Migration to rural environments is found to be informed to a lesser or greater extent by images of the idyllic rural (Halfacree 1994, Hughes 1997, Valentine 1997, Murdoch and Marsden 1994) and is considered to form *the* central dynamic in the ongoing shift from a productivist to a post-productivist era in the countryside (Marsden 1998). The term *post-productivist countryside* denotes an increasing use of rural space for non-agricultural purposes and the predominance of consumption interests over production interests, with *the rural as a space for residence* (Halfacree 1997). Idyll-type social representations of the rural are of course different across Britain, but on a national level the versions have ingredients as harmony, consensus, healthiness, simplicity, peace, safety, tradi-tion, community, domesticity, aesthetic quality (nice landscapes), and pastoralism in common.

> In Britain such images derive much of their power from the proximity of the countryside ideal to British national identity, and it has always seemed to enshrine those timeless qualities that makes this 'sceptred isle' forever 'England'. Rural land is considered a priceless part of the nations heritage. It has traditionally been a 'cosy corner' in which an 'Anglocentric' culture, one opposed to multiculturalism increasingly evident in many cities, could nestle down safe from harm (Lowe et al. 1995), (Murdoch and Pratt 1997: 51).

There are, in other words, forms of life and lifestyles associated with the British idyllic representations of the rural. Studies on urban-rural migration have shown that these seem tempting and make migration into rural areas an escape from the city, representing a new life strategy.

It should be mentioned, however, that this kind of explanation – although central in recent research – have been problematised among its adherents, for instance by Halfacree (1995) who argues that many migrants are quite capable of seeing through the 'chocolate box' stereotype of the village presented by the rural idyll. He claims, however, that it still has a place as a cognitive framework and may be capable of motivating people, even at a subconscious level. *'We may reject the myth but we all know of it.*' (op.cit. p. 14). Furthermore, Boyle and Halfacree (1998: 311) argue that there is a need to regard those migrating from urban to rural areas *'not as passive irrational dupes (of the rural idyll?) but as "responsible" human agents*'. It should be stressed then, that individual British studies differ in conclusions about to what extent idyll-type representations of the rural explain urban-rural migration. It is, consequently, the awareness of the fact that they might be important and the struggle to decide how such images are woven into migration decisions that is the characteristic of this approach.

Is such an approach then, including the concept of rural idyll, relevant in explaining urban-rural migration in Norway and Sweden? First, surveys in both countries show that there is a strong wish to live in rural environments (Hansen and Selstad 1999, Orderud 1998, Haaveraaen 1992, Nationen 1993, Forsberg and Carlbrand 1993, Borgegård, Håkansson and Malmberg 1995, Vartianen 1989, Amcoff, Forsberg and Stenbacka 1995, Stenbacka 2001, Amcoff 2001). Second, representations of the rural as idyll play, as far as we are concerned, an important role in popular discourses in all western societies, Norway and Sweden included, and is on a general level a consequence of urbanisation and modernisation. In Sweden and Norway, to which we restrict our discussion, literature, journals, newspapers, postcards, television programmes etc. confirm its existence and its resemblance with the British idyll-type representations of the rural. Harmony, consensus, healthiness, simplicity, peace, safety, tradition, community, domesticity, aesthetic quality and pastoralism are central elements in representations of the rural in both Norway and Sweden. The single elements need, however, to be unpacked to demonstrate that the striking resemblance is more or less superficial. It is also important to take into consideration regional and local representations within nations. The local level is important as the dominant meanings of the rural are negotiated at the local scale (Little and Austin 1996). It is also at the local scale that different individuals' and groups' constructions are highlighted. Our answer then to whether cultural perspectives and especially a focus on idyll-type representations of rurality are relevant in explaining urban-rural migration in Norway and Sweden is: yes, but 'the rural idyll' has to be unpacked and related to place since migrants' knowledge about rurality are contextual. So far only a few recent studies have focused on how images of the rural idyll are woven into migration decisions (Villa 1997, Berg 1998, Lysgård, Ryntveit and Karlsen 2000, Forsberg and Carlbrand 1993, Amcoff 2001, Stenbacka 2001).

Gendered ruralities

Suggesting the concept 'gender idyll' to illustrate that 'the rural idyll' is a gendered concept is based on an understanding of gender as a social and cultural construct that varies in space and time. We draw on recent feminist geography literature on the manufacture of gendered identities within space, in which both masculinity and femininity are recognised as social and cultural constructions that are multiple, fluid and contingent (WGSG 1997). Furthermore, we draw on feminist rural geography that argues that gender and rurality should be treated as unstable and interactive reference points (Whatmore et al. 1994). We suggest that the conceptualisation of the rural as idyll contributes to and builds upon particular notions of masculinity and femininity, i.e. prescribed and hegemonic gender relations that are re-presented as idyllic. The rural idyll so to speak incorporates a gender idyll that reinforces, or at least matches, its central elements, not least harmony, consensus, tradition, community and domesticity. But like the image of rural idyll itself, the included image of gender idyll is contextual, since gender, like rurality, is constituted in place. Our experiences of the gendering of the British rural idyll as partly different from the gendering of Swedish and Norwegian idyll-type representations of the rural have no doubt to do with the place-based constitution of femininity and masculinity.

In feminist rural studies in Britain the attention has first and foremost turned to femininity and the place that women have been assigned in the rural idyll (Hughes 1997, Little 1986, 1987, 1997, Little and Austin 1996, Braithwaite 1994). The constructions of femininity incorporated in the British rural idyll are more or less related to all the above mentioned elements of the image, not least community and domesticity. For example Hughes (1997:125) argues that

> *A particular construction of rural femininity has developed, linking womanhood and domesticity with notions of the organic community, a construction that has been reproduced within a range of contemporary writings about the rural.* Little (1997:155) notes that *There is an image of rural woman to which, clearly, not all women conform – and to which, perhaps, no woman conforms totally – but which nevertheless influences the behaviour, values and expectations of all rural women and men, and hence becomes incorporated in a very real sense within gender identities.*

Her empirical work shows that the expectation of women's role as wives and mothers has featured very significantly within rural women's identities and that internal and external beliefs about the appropriateness of women's involvement in childcare and family reproduction has been prioritised over employment. Furthermore it shows that the idea of women as 'community-makers' has assumed a central role in the identity of rural women. '

> .....the rural idyll is instrumental in shaping and sustaining patriarchal gender relations and....it incorporates, both consciously and unconsciously, strong expectations concerning aspects of household strategy and gender roles and consequently impacts on the nature of women's experience within the rural community. (op. cit. p. 102)

The intertwining of discourses on masculinity and rurality has by no means gained as much attention as the intertwining of discourses on femininity and rurality in British rural geography. The ideas of masculinity incorporated in the British rural idyll are, however, more or less implicit in the ideas of femininity. An image of the rural woman as the one in the household taking care of the children and carrying out the domestic tasks, as well as being involved in voluntary work in the rural community, brings about an image of the rural man as the breadwinner, often the farmer. The ideal gender relations incorporated in the British rural idyll might consequently be characterised as *complementary gender relations.* Although domesticity and community are elements in constructions of rural womanhood also in Norway (Brandth and Haugen 1996, Brandth 1995, Berg forthcoming) and Sweden (Bjerén 1995) as is breadwinning in constructions of rural manhood, there are important differences as regards what they convey.

Rural idyll in Britain and the Scandinavian countries

In this section we aim at unpacking the idea of rural idyll itself and compare the image in the Scandinavian countries with the image in Britain. Even though many of the main ingredients in the concept of the rural idyll are the same in Britain and the Scandinavian countries, they have a slightly different meaning in the different geographical, social and cultural contexts.

What then is understood by the 'rural idyll' in Norway and Sweden? Some significant elements in material basis are likely to be embedded in the construction of the concept. We will elaborate on some essential distinctions between Britain on the one hand and Sweden and Norway on the other, which in our opinion are of importance. Our hypothesis is that the pattern of settlement, the historical structure of land-ownership, the character of the industrialisation process and the accessibility to the countryside is worth taking into account when unpacking the idea of a rural idyll.

First, Sweden and Norway have low population densities, relatively speaking, even in the most densely populated areas. The average number of inhabitants per square kilometre is 20 in Sweden and 15 in Norway (SSB 2000). In most remote rural areas the number is even smaller. In the U.K. there are 241 inhabitants per square kilometre (SSB 2000). Another measure of population density is 'distance between inhabitants'. If people in Sweden were evenly distributed throughout the country, the distance to any other person would be 249 metres. The corresponding distance in Norway is even longer, 299 metres. Even in the most densely populated area in the two countries, the capital region of Stockholm, the distance would be as long as 68 metres. This can be compared to England where the distance would be 70 metres as average for the whole country. All countries in central and southern Europe would have distances between 50 and 150 metres. (Sveriges Nationalatlas 1991)

The consequence of this is that the bid-rent curve is steeper in the Scandinavian countries than in more densely populated countries, i.e. land prices fall drastically away from the city centres. Within commuting distance it is possible to attain a proper real estate without being too well off (Forsberg and Carlbrand 1993, Kåks and Westholm 1994). As a consequence of this, property as positional capital is not as powerful in the Scandinavian countryside as in the British countryside. British rural researchers have stressed that investments in the British countryside should be regarded as positional consumption because of the competition for land (Cloke et al. 1995, Urry 1995). Such a competition does not take place in Sweden and Norway except in very attractive sites in the archipelagos of the Stockholm, Gothenburg and Oslo regions. There are of course beautiful areas, enclaves of gentrification, where land prices are relatively high in the countryside of both Sweden and Norway, but the point to make here is that surrounding them there are vast areas of accessible property for people from different class-positions. This has a significant influence on the way people experience the rural idyll. Furthermore, the motives to move to the countryside and the idea of the rural idyll are first and foremost associated with democratic symbols like 'ordinary people', decent and reasonable places. The countryside is thus a place for 'everybody'. But in this concept of everybody, different groups of people are more or less excluded. One of these groups is the immigrants. Other groups are single parents, teenagers and people with physical disablement (Forsberg and Carlbrand 1993, Amcoff 2001).

Second, the historical land-holding system in the Scandinavian countries differs from the one in Britain. The dominance and long tradition of the 'family-farm' with self-owned farmers is a central element of the rural idyll in Sweden and Norway. Generally speaking agriculture, forestry and fishery as practised by independent individuals and families is associated with the Scandinavian rural idyll. The countryside is not a place for landlords and wealthy people of the aristocracy, but grandmothers' and grandfathers' old places, which many people still remember from their summer vacations. In Britain less than 7 000 persons owned 4/5 of all British land as late as at the end of the 19th century (Urry 1995). Although rural land now is predominantly under the control of owner-occupying farmers, the idea of the countryside as a home for the aristocracy remains. In Sweden and Norway agricultural labourers receiving allowance in kind were found only in some parts of the countries, i.e. in the high productive lowland agricultural areas. They contribute to the idea of a former class-society with inequality and injustice, but they have not formed the idea of the countryside as such. More than earls and landlords, the conception of traditional rural people are a male farmer and his wife. Even if the wife is looked upon as a 'farm wife' rather than a farmer, she represents a hard working and relatively independent person used to taking decisions of her own.

Thirdly, the prescriptive law in Sweden and Norway, giving people access to private open land for walking and picking berries and mushrooms should not be underestimated in this context. It gives people a feeling of belonging to the countryside. The woodlands and the pastureland are looked upon as part of people's natural surroundings and something available to everybody – not reserved for the wealthy few. On the contrary, the tradition to walk in land and woods has been widespread among working-class people and low-paid groups. Picking mushrooms and berries is a way to make the housekeeping money last longer. These activities, something between recreation and hard work, have traditionally been very popular among working-class women. Although the economic motive is less important today the activities are still popular as lingonberries, especially, almost count as national dishes in Scandinavia. Even hunting and fishing, predominantly men's activities, are as popular and almost as common among working class and upper class people (be that they hunt different animals and fish different fishes). Contrary to this, in Britain 'countryside recreation' has, according to Urry (1995), been driven by private property holders and organised as a middle-class amusement. A lot of today's uncultivated land in Britain is owned by great amusement and recreation companies and most of the urban working-class people have very restricted access to the countryside. Male professionals and managers are more likely to visit the countryside than blue-collar workers, women, disabled people, old people, ethnic minorities and single parents. We can then draw the conclusion that there are class-differences in the usage of the countryside due to legislation and tradition in Scandinavia and Britain. While countryside recreation in Sweden and Norway is spread among classes, it is understood as an occupation for the middle and upper classes in Britain.

Fourth, and related to the three aspects discussed above, is the way the countries were industrialised. The history and the geography of manufacturing must be taken into account. In a European perspective, Sweden and Norway, can be described as 'rural-based industrialised nations'/industrialised countryside nations'. While the industrialisation of Britain took place mainly in the cities and/or resulted in large urban areas growing up, the resource-oriented character of the manufacturing industries in Scandinavia, led to industrialisation in rural areas and resulted in small one-company towns. In these, industrial workers with one foot left in agriculture have not been unfamiliar until the recent past. In addition most working class families in the cities have had relatives – and consequently someone to visit – in rural areas. The generation growing up in today's service economy is the first one where the majority is uniquely urban without relatives living in the countryside.

Along with the growth of the rurally based industrialisation, grew the tradition of second homes in the countryside for the urban population. The summerhouse tradition in Norway and Sweden is just as much a characteristic of the working and lower middle class as for people with money. A rural summerhouse was considered a compensation for lack of surrounding nature and natural landscape in the block house apartment in the city. A notable part of the stock of summerhouses came into being by amateur carpentry (Nordin 1997). The summerhouse tradition can also be understood as a part of the Scandinavian social-democratic model – everyone has a right to a decent living and a nice place for recreation and comfort. Accompanying own-your-own home movements in the 1930s and 1940s, communal summerhouse areas for labourers were established. Norway and Sweden are among the countries in the world with the highest percentage of inhabitants owning a second home and a pleasure-boat (Meyer 2000). This is without doubt of relevance when analysing urban-rural migration and the idea of the rural idyll that people conceptualise.

Gender idyll in Britain and the Scandinavian countries

Complementary versus 'egalitarian' gender relations

In addition to what is discussed in the previous section, we will stress a fifth important aspect, namely the idea of a gender idyll as an inherent part of the rural idyll. In Britain there is a rather limited literature on gender relations in rural communities (Little and Austin 1996), but an entry into the publications reveals that the consensus of opinion is, as Little and Austin (1996: 102) put it: '.......*that the rural idyll is instrumental in shaping and sustaining patriarchal gender relations*'.

As mentioned most of the literature on gender and rurality focus on women and femininity. According to Braithwaite (1994) '*the stereotype of a rural woman is that of a family woman traditional and conservative absorbed in the care of the home*' (p. 12). Also Little and Austin stress the significance of 'the home' and 'the family' in the hegemonic construction of 'the rural woman' and argue that '*There can be no doubt that the woman of the rural idyll is the wife and mother, not the high-flying professional, the single childless business entrepreneur.*' (1996: 106). These citations are examples of conclusions drawn in British works on rurality and gender that make us argue that the British rural idyll is conveying complementary gender relations. Our impression is that the overall argument – that aspects of the rural idyll operate in support of traditional gender relations, prioritising women's mothering role and fostering their centrality within the rural community – dominate independent of whether the studies focus on farming women (or women farmers) (see e.g. Whatmore 1991) or on rural women more broadly (see e.g. Hughes 1997 or Little 1991).

In our opinion in Scandinavia it is necessary to distinguish between farm women (and men) and farming women (and men) on the one side and rural women (and men) more broadly on the other hand. Others' studies on the first mentioned category and our own (and others') studies on the latter indicate that the hegemonic construction that farm women and women farmers face are more in line with the British construction of the rural woman. Brandth (1994), for example, argues that although rural femininity is being reconstructed, domesticity is very important in constructions of the farm woman and the woman farmer. The gendering of the rural idyll appears to be less coloured by the idea of complementary gender relations when studied separate from farming, for example in connection with urban-rural migration. We do not argue that family, home and community are missing elements in the dominant construction of rural women outside farming, but want to suggest that they seem to be somewhat less important.

People moving from urban to rural areas often take the gendering of the rural idyll into account when considering migration. Some researchers argue that the prime reason for some migrants to move to the countryside is to get away from the pressure of modern living and to live more authentic rural lifestyles in which getting back to nature and the 'domestic' is central (Hughes 1997). It might as well be the case that people are hesitant to move to the countryside in fear of the 'traditional gender relations' they expect to face (Berg 1998). When settled in the rural environment, the gender idyll becomes present as a regulator of everyday lives.

Interviews with incomers – women and men – into post-productivist countrysides in Sweden and Norway indicate that the hegemonic rural gender relations facing them are characterised by family orientation on behalf of both men and women. The ideal is a dual income family with a part time working woman (in the service sector). The male breadwinner family is so to speak 'out'. The 'correct' way to be a rural woman is not to be merely a housewife. Correspondingly, the 'correct' way to be a rural man is to take a relatively large part in house work and child caring (Berg 1998, Stenbacka 2001). The prescribed gender relations should, consequently, rather be characterised as egalitarian. That is not to say that the 'correct' relationship between the genders are one of complete equality, but it is clearly not the traditional one with complementary gender relations that the British rural idyll incorporates. Vartdal (1999) finds that it actually may cause frustrations among rural household members not to live up to the norm prescribing egalitarian gender relations. Different characteristics and functions are prescribed to rural women and men also in Scandinavia and power relations are definitely embedded in the dominant construction of the rural idyll. A male nurse working part time who is not interested in hunting or fishing may experience that he is not regarded a proper rural man (Berg 1998). Our main point is that both femininity and masculinity seem to be much more compound in the Scandinavian gender idyll than in the British one, outside farming more than within.

Areas experiencing rural in-migration in Sweden are in fact characterised by gender relations of a more equal kind than in other parts of the country (Forsberg 1997). According to a study by Stenbacka (2001) rural in-migrants are of miscellaneous kinds, different in age, class, income, and education, but they have something in common, namely a family and household orientation. These couples look upon themselves as a rather equal working unit, they both have work and they both take care of their children and the housework. They are eager to relate to the prescribed norm of gender equality rather than gender complementarity. This corresponds with Berg's (1998) analysis of families who have migrated from urban to rural areas in Norway. At least the youngest households represent themselves as consisting of two rather equal partners.

In many British studies (see e.g. Cloke et al. 1995) men are found to be the decision-makers as regards the decision to move from urban to rural areas and women are dragged into country life more or less against their will – at least against their interests, since their job opportunities are reduced and they run the risk of getting caught into domesticity. Stenbacka (2001) is sceptical to this interpretation as the British studies neglect the value of home and house and take the women's position at the labour market as the only measure of the situation for women who have migrated to rural areas. To understand the gain and losses that women experience in relation to migration, it is necessary also to take other values than economy and work into account, according to Stenbacka. Even if women have a somewhat lower labour participation rate in rural areas than in urban, women might feel that they experience an enriching living standard for both themselves and their family members since they moved to the countryside, especially pronounced by non-professionals and low-educated women.

How to understand the Scandinavian image of gender idyll

As with the differences between the rural idyll in Scandinavia and Britain the differences as regards gender idyll can be scrutinised as connected to history, economy and social structure. What are then the unique characteristics of the Scandinavian gender relations?

First, there was an early and rapid growth of the two-earning family model. Only during a period of something like 30 years (between 1930 to 1960) the male breadwinner model with a 'housewife' dominated. In the mid 1950s 80 per cent of the Swedish married women and 90 per cent of the Norwegian married women were housewives (Leira 1996). During the 'housewife period' there was a project of professionalisation of domestic labour, so as to valorise women's work. Detailed quantitative research on what a scientific convenient household would look like was conducted. How many knives and forks are needed in families of different sizes? How many minutes shall it take to make a bed? How often should a floor be washed? This was a Fordist way to look at housework and it was also a way to integrate it as an internal part of productive and rational working life. In the 1960s, however, the breadwinner model broke down and women started to take up paid work. The 'professional housewife' came to be looked upon as the working man's 'luxury' (Forsberg, 1992). The fact that working mothers were more common at an earlier stage and has been more widespread in Scandinavia than in other western European countries (Leira 1996), no doubt contribute to the Scandinavian understanding of the gender idyll.

Secondly, the early social democratic penetration into society and its replacement of the church for moral guidance is also important. The correct way of family organisation according to the social democratic idea is a family where both man and woman are part of the labour market. The dilemma that this ideal implies for housework and childcare is solved by part-time work for women and nursing and day care for children. Consequently, a social democratic welfare state in which gender relations are supposed to be related to economy and profane organisation instead of the Christian understanding of complementary gender roles has developed. Interestingly enough, both the Scandinavian social-democratic model and the Christian church have a hierarchical organisation structure. Implicit in 'the Scandinavian Model' is a perception of men and women having different tasks in the family and in society, but it is not tasks of a divine order, rather of economic practice. Compared to other countries, the ideal gender relations in Scandinavia developed so as to focus very much on equality: a man and woman working side by side with almost equal responsibilities and obligations. Everyday practice is, however, not in line with this, but the official standpoint as well as lay discourses on gender relations are based on an equal gender idyll perspective.

Thirdly, and related to the above mentioned points, influences from modernist and feminist ideas advocated by Alva and Gunnar Myrdal in Sweden and Margarete Bonnevie and Mimi Sverdrup Lunden in Norway as early as before the Second World War are important. They took up the question of women's roles in general and women's right to take on waged work in special. In a situation where birth rates fell below mortality rates, it was argued that family reforms had to be carried out to stimulate family formation and childbirth.

Fourthly, the family farms are the icons of Scandinavian food producers. The stereotype of a family farm is one with mixed production structure, some forestry, some dairy production and some crops. In the traditional self-owner farm, husband and wife worked together, he as 'the Farmer', she as an important worker, not least in the dairy production. Some would say that the tradition of mountain pasture, where women only are together with the milk cows in the cottage during the whole summer, is one of the main reasons for Scandinavian women's 'equality' to men. Mountain pasture prevailed in parts of Sweden, but died out more or less during the sixties, in Norway it is still practised in some places. The gender idyll of the traditional family farm does, in other words, 'match' the social democratic model of gender idyll in that it conveys the picture of two people struggling together. It should be noted, however, that the representation of 'the Farmer' as a male taking care of outside work and the farm wife as taking care of mostly inside work clearly suggests complementary gender roles and domesticity as a central element in the construction of the farm woman's femininity.

The differences between the Scandinavian rural gender idyll and the British one, should, according to our opinion, be understood both as a result of the differences in the perception of the rural idyll discussed and the differences in the perception of the gender idyll discussed in this section.

Conclusions

In this chapter we have attempted to investigate British notions of rurality and gender through Scandinavian lenses. Our aim was to illustrate the contextual character of knowledge about rurality, femininity and masculinity. We chose the concept of 'rural idyll' as our focus because of its central position in British rural studies in the last decade and because of interesting analyses of the gendering of the British rural idyll by rural feminist reserchers. We suggested the concept of 'gender idyll' as a tool in our analysis of the notion of 'the rural idyll' in Scandinavia and Britain, respectively. We adressed also the underlying ideas behind the focus on the rural idyll in the British rural studies and discussed the potential of these in Scandinavian rural reserach with special attention to studies on urban-rural migration.

To take the latter first we identified an understanding of rurality and gender as social and cultural constructs that are multiple, fluid and contingent in the British studies. Furthermore, that gender and rurality are seen as unstable and interactive reference points. Taking these theoretical positions further we suggested that 'the rural idyll' incorporates a 'gender idyll', since it contributes to and builds upon particular notions of masculinity and femininity, that is prescribed and hegemonic gender relations that are represented as idyllic. The reason why it is important to analyse images of the rural is that they are woven into practices, decisions about where to live included. Such an approach which so far is rare in Scandinavian studies on urban-rural migration will undoubtly enrich the field.

We unpacked the rural idyll in Scandinavia and found that elements in the material basis are embedded in the construction. These are low population density and low land prices in the coutryside, the dominance and long tradition of the family farm, the prescriptive law, the industrialisation of the coutryside rather than the cities and the summer house tradition. All of them makes the construction rather different from the British one.

The gender idyll – which we see as an image included in the image of the rural idyll – was unpacked separately. Also the rural gender idyll should be analysed with regard to material basis. We found that the following factors make the gender idyll in Scandinavia different from the British one: the early and rapid growth of the two-earning family model, the strong social democratic influence, the modern feminist ideas presented into politics at an early stage and the traditional division of labour on family farms.

Our unpacking illustrated that the image of the rural idyll, the gender idyll included, are quite different in Scandinavia and Britain. It raises questions about how to deal with theory import. First of all we will stress that a reflexive awareness should permeate all theoretical exchange. As regards the concept of 'the rural idyll' we find it highly fruitful in Scandinavian research as long as one is acknowledging the situated nature of knowledge and the fact that relations of power are embedded within the social constructions of knowledge and discourses. Rural geographers, not least those studying urban-rural migration, should consider women's and men's subjective experiences as a valid way of knowing and understanding the rural. They should aim at highlighting and questioning a number of characteristics that have assumed a powerful role in the expectations and assumptions of women's and men's identities in rural communities since these influence decision making, e.g. concerning where to live. Urban-rural migrants in Scandinavia are no doubt influenced by lay discourses on rurality, femininity and masculinity, but we know, however, very little about the precise and variable power of them (Berg 1998).

Scandinavian and British academic discourses should learn from each other. In this case we have learned a lot from the British epistemological reflections concerning the situated nature of understandings. This knowledge in addition to our experiences with trying to grasp the essentials of our own empirical materials with the British theoretical tools was what made us go into the concept of 'the rural idyll' in the first place. Our respondents' stories about their migration from urban to rural areas or their practising of their new rural lives on an everyday basis could simply not be analysed with the concept of 'the rural idyll' as understood in Britain. Also Simonsen (1999) thinks that national academic discourses should learn from each other. Of course, that is what happens all the time, but a more reflexive awareness about when and how could enrich the exchange. Simonsen (1999: 21) for example ends her illustration of how the different directions an interest in cultural difference can take, due to difference in disciplinary tradition, social and political context and sociology of science by stressing that

> 'Scandinavian writers can learn from the serious treatment in the Anglo-Saxon discourse of the problem of representation and the fragility of knowledge claims' while 'the Scandinavian contribution can be the accentuation of the peopled character of culture'.

Widerberg (1992) writing about the development of gender studies in Norway claims that the Norwegian approaches are special in that their point of departure is empirical-political. Theories and concepts have developed bottom-up, and it is not the theories – at least not macro-theoretical perspectives – that have steered the research. This goes to a high degree also for Swedish gender studies, and we think that British feminist rural geography has something to learn from us. For example the concept of 'gender idyll' that we suggest here could be applicable in British studies.

The gender idyll is not just an integrated part of the rural idyll. It is part of the national models of social relations. We have illustrated here how it is part of the Scandinavian model of social relations, where the relations between the sexes have been perceived as equal. The concept of gender contract, developed within a Scandinavian feminist discourse (Haavind 1994, Hirdman 1988) is a concept that match 'gender idyll'. It is based on an understanding of gender as a relational concept, i.e. gender is shaped in relations between men and women and forms a cultural code. There is an 'agreement' as regards the 'correct' gender relations, that are continuously re-negotiated and re-interpreted (Haavind 1994). Especially in periods of structural changes the gender contract is changed (Forsberg 2001). The post-industrial period with its new migration flows have contributed to the development of a gender contract or gender idyll that can fit into the rural idyll without adapting traditional understanding of gender relations. The gender idyll in contemporary Scandinavia is a mixture of national arrangements and international and global inputs which makes it both specific and general. That is what make the unpacking of the rural idyll meaningful and theoretically fruitful.

Rura

References

Amcoff, Jan (2001): 'Samtida bostättning på svensk landsbygd'. *Geografiska Regionstudier,* nr 41. Kulturgeografiska institutionen, Uppsala universitet.

Amcoff, Jan, Forsberg, Gunnel and Stenbacka, Susanne (1995): 'Inflyttning och nybyggnation i Märardalens landsbygd'. Arbetrsrapporter nr 155. Kulturgeografiska institutionen, Uppsala universitet.

Berg, Nina Gunnerud (1998): 'Kjerringer og gubber mot (flytte)strømmen – ruralitet, kvinnelighet og mannlighet'. Paper til 18. Nordiske symposium for kritisk samfunnsgeografi, Holbæk, Danmark 24–27 September.

Berg, Nina Gunnerud (forthcoming): 'Discourses on gender in rural studies – the case of Norway'. In Baylina, M., Goverde, H. and de Haan, H. (eds.): *Rurality in the face of power and gender.*

Berg, Nina Gunnerud and Hans Kjetil Lysgård (forthcoming): 'Rural Development and Policies; the Case of Post-war Norway'. In Halfacree, K., Kovach, I. and Woodward, R. (eds.): *Leadership and Local Power in European Rural Development.* Ashgate, London.

Bjerén, Gunilla, (1995) 'Nordvärmländska livsformer i förändring, I Håkan Eles (ed), *Skogsfinnarna och Finnskogen,* Forskningsrapport / Högskolan i Karlstad. Samhällsvetenskap, 127–134.

Bondi, Liz (1997): 'In whose words? On gender identities, knowledge and writing practices'. *Transaction of the Institute of British Geographers* NS 22, 245–258.

Borgegård, Lars-Erik, Håkansson, Johan and Malmberg Gunnar (1995) 'Population redistribution in Sweden', *Geografiska Annaler* 77B, 31–45.

Boyle, Paul and Keith Halfacree (1998): 'Migration into rural areas: a collective behaviour framework'. In Boyle, Paul and Keith Halfacree (eds.): *Migration into rural areas. Theories and issues.* John Wiley and Sons, Chichester, 301–16.

Boyle, Paul, Keith Halfacree and Vaughan Robinson (1998): *Exploring Contemporary Migration.* Longman, Harlow.

Braithwaite, M (1994): 'The Economic Role and Situation of Women in Rural Areas'. Office for Official Publications of the European Communities, Luxembourg.

Brandth, Berit (1994): 'Changing femininity. The social construction of women farmers in Norway'. *Sociologia Ruralis* vol. XXXIV, no 2–3, 127–49.

Brandth, Berit (1995): 'Rural femininity and masculinity in transition'. Paper no 5, Senter for Bygdeforskning – Allforsk, Trondheim.

Brandth, Berit and Marit Haugen (1996): 'Bygdekvinner og feminisme'. *Landbruksøkonomisk Forum* Nr. 2, 5–17.

Chambers, I. (1994): *Migrancy, culture, identity.* Routledge, London.

Champion, Tony (1998): 'Studying counterurbanisation and the rural population turnaround'. In Boyle, Paul and Keith Halfacree (eds.): *Migration into rural areas – theories and issues.* John Wiley & Sons, Chichester, 21–40.

Cloke, Paul (1994): '(En)culturing Political Economy: A Life in the Day of a "Rural Geographer"'. In Cloke, Paul, Marcus Doel, David Matless, Martin Phillips and Nigel Thrift: *Writing the rural – five cultural geographies.* Paul Chapman, London, 149–90.

Cloke, Paul, Phillips, Martin and Thrift, Nigel (1995): 'The new middle classes and the social constructs of rural living', In Butler, Tim and Savage, Mike, *Social change and the middle classes,* UCL Press, London.

Fielding, Anthony (1992): 'Migration and Culture'. In A. Champion and A. Fielding (eds.): *Migration processes and patterns. Vol. 1 Research Progress and prospects.* Belhaven Press, London, 201–212.

Forsberg, Gunnel (1989): 'Industriomvandling och könsstruktur'. *Fallstudier* på fyra lokala arbetsmarknader. *Geografiska regionstudier* nr 20. Kulturgeografiska institutionen. Uppsala universitet. Uppsala.

Forsberg, Gunnel (1992): 'Kvinnor och män i arbetslivet', I Acker m fl. *Kvinnors och mäns liv och arbete.* SNS Förlag, Stockholm.

Forsberg, Gunnel and Carlbrand, Elinor (1993): *Mälarbygden – en kreativ region? En studie av Mälardalens landsbygd i förändring.* Forskningsrapporter från Kulturgeografiska institutionen, Uppsala universitet, nr 107.

Forsberg, Gunnel, (1994): 'Befolkningsomflyttningar på landsbygden'. Arbetsrapporter nr 55, Kulturgeografiska institutionen, Uppsala universitet.

Forsberg, Gunnel (1996): 'Är landsbygden en kvinnofälla?' I: Dokumentation från forskarsymposiet Kvinnor och män i dalog om regioneras framtid. *Working Paper* No 5b, SIR Östersund, 17–40.

Forsberg, Gunnel (1997): 'Rulltrapperegioner och social infrastruktur'. I: Sundin, Elisabet (ed) *Om makt och kön : i spåren av offentliga organisationers omvandling.* Rapport till Utredningen om fördelningen av ekonomisk makt och ekonomiska resurser mellan kvinnor och män. Fritzes, Stockholm.

Forsberg, Gunnel (2001): 'The difference that space makes. A way to describe the construction of local and regional gender contracts'. *Norsk Geografisk Tidsskrift* Vol 55, 1–5.

Gilroy, P. (1993): *The black Atlantic. Modernity and double consciousness.* Verso, London.

Haaveraaen, Morten (1992): 'Norske bostedspreferanser'. *Plan & Arbeid,* nr. 6, 2–6. Universitetsforlaget, Oslo.

Haavind, Hanne (1994): 'Kjønn i forandring – som fenomen og som forståelsesmåte'. *Tidsskrift for norsk psykologforening,* nr. 9.

Halfacree, Keith (1993): 'Locality and social representation: space, discourse and alternaive definitions of the rural'. *Journal of Rural Studies* 9, 23–37.

Halfacree, Keith (1994): 'The importance of "the rural" in the constitution of counterurbanization: evidence from England in the 1980s'. Sociologia Ruralis 34, 164–89.

Halfacree, Keith (1995): 'Talking About Rurality: Social Representations of the Rural as Expressed by Residents of Six English Parishes'. *Journal of Rural Studies* 11:1, 1–20.

Halfacree, Keith (1997): 'Contrasting roles for the post-productivist countryside. A postmodern perspective on counterurbanisation'. In Cloke, Paul and Jo Little (eds.): *Contested countryside cultures – otherness, marginalisation and rurality.* Routledge, London, 70–93.

Halfacree, Keith and Paul Boyle (1993): 'The challenge facing migration research: the case for a biographical approach'. *Progress in Human Geography* 17, 334–48.

Hansen, Jens Christian and Tor Selstad (1999): *Regional omstilling – strukturbestemt eller styrbar?* Universitetsforlaget, Oslo.

Haraway, Donna (1991): *Simians, cyborgs and Women; the Reinvention of Nature.* London: Free Association Books.

Hirdman, Yvonne (1988): 'Genussystemet – reflektioner kring kvinnors sociala sammanhang'. *Kvinnovetenskaplig Tidskrift,* 49–63.

Hoggart, Keith, Henry Buller and Richard Black (1995): *Rural Europe. Identity and Change.* Arnold, London.

Hughes, Annie (1997): 'Rurality and "Cultures of womanhood". Domestic identities and moral order in village life'. In Cloke, Paul and Jo Little (eds.): *Contested countryside cultures – otherness, marginalisation and rurality.* Routledge, London, 123–37.

Johannisson, Bengt, Persson, Lars-Olof and Wiberg, Ulf (1989): 'Urbaniserad glesbygd – verklighet och vision, Ds departementserien 1989: 22, Arbetsmarknadsdepartementet, Stockholm.

Jones, Owain (1995): 'Lay discourses of the rural: developments and implications for rural studies'. Journal of Rural Studies 11, 35–50.

Kåks, Helena and Westholm, Erik (1994): *En plats i tillvaron : studier av flyttning till landsbygden.* Falun : Dalarnas forskningsråd.

Leira, Arnlaug (1996): 'Fra statsfeminisme til statsfamilisme? Om mor og far, stat og marked i 1990-åra'. In Brandth, Berit and Kari Moxnes (eds.): *Familie for tiden. Stabilitet og forandring.*Tano Aschehoug, Oslo.

Little, Jo (1986): 'Feminist perspectives in rural geography: an introduction', *Journal of Rural Studies* 2, 1–8.

Little, Jo (1987): 'Gender relations in rural areas: the importance of women's domestic role'. *Journal of Rural Studies* 3, 335–42.

Little, Jo (1991): 'Theoretical Issues of Women's Non-agricultural Employment in Rural Areas, with Illustrations from the U.K.' *Journal of Rural Studies* 7/1–2, 99–105.

Little, Jo (1994): 'Gender Relations and the Rural Labour Process'. In Whatmore, Sarah, Terry Marsden and Phillip Lowe (eds.): *Gender and rurality*. David Fulton Publishers, London, 11–30.

Little, Jo (1997): 'Employment, marginality and women's self-identity'. In Cloke, Paul and Jo Little (eds.): *Contested countryside cultures – otherness, marginalisation and rurality.* Routledge, London, 138–57.

Little, Jo and Patricia Austin (1996): 'Women and the Rural Idyll'. *Journal of Rural Studies* 12:2, 101–11.

Lowe, P., J. Murdoch and N. Ward (1995): 'Networks in rural development', *Paper presented at the XVI Congress of the European Society for Rural Sociology*, 31 July–4 August, Prague, Czech Republic.

Lysgård, Hans Kjetil, Anne Kirsti Ryntveit and James Karlsen (2000): 'Å bo på landet – et valg av lisvsstil. En studie av Marnardal og Åseral'. *FoU-rapport* 15, Agderforskning, Kristiansand.

Marsden, Terry (1998): 'Economic Perspectives'. In Ilbery, Brian (ed.): *The Geography of Rural Change*, 13–30.

Massey, Doreen (1991): 'A global sense of place'. *Marxism Today*, June, 24–9.

McDowell, Linda (1992): 'Mutiple voices: speaking from inside and outside "the project"'. *Antipode* 24:1, 56–72

Meyer, Ronny (2000): 'Cognitive and behavioral aspects of people-place interactions in recreational boating. The case of locals, cabil dwellers and boat tourists in the Nøtterøy/Tjøme Skerries boating area'. Dr.polit-avhandling, Geografisk Institutt, NTNU, Trondheim.

Mormont, Marc (1990): 'Who is rural? Or how to be rural'. In Marsden, Terry, Phillip Lowe and Sarah Whatmore (eds.): *Rural Restructuring: Global Processes and their Local Responses*, Fulton, London, 21–44.

Murdoch, John and Terry Marsden (1994): *Reconstituting rurality: class, community and power in the development process*. UCL Press, London.

Murdoch, Jonathan and Andy C. Pratt (1993): 'Rural studies: modernism, post-modernism and the "post-rural"'. *Journal of Rural Studies* 9:4, 411–27.

Murdoch, Jonathan and Andy C. Pratt (1994): 'Rural studies of power and the power of rural studies; a reply to Philo'. *Journal of Rural Studies* 10:1, 83–7.

Murdoch, Jonathan and Andy C. Pratt (1997): 'From the power of topography to the topography of power. Discourse on strange ruralities'. In Cloke, Paul and Jo Little (eds.): *Contested countryside cultures – otherness, marginalisation and rurality.* Routledge, London, 51–69.

Nationen (1993): '300.000 vil flytte fra norske storbyer'. Nationen 20.12.1993.

Nordin, Urban, (1997): 'Skärgården i storstadens skugga : arbetsvillkor och försörjningsstrategier i storstadsnära glesbygdsområden : exemplet Stockholms skärgård under efterkrigstiden'. *Meddelanden från Kulturgeografiska institutionen vid Stockholms universitet*, 102, Stockholm : Kulturgeografiska institutionen.

Orderud, Geir (1998): 'Flytting – monster og årsaker. En kunnskapsoversikt'. *NIBR Prosjektrapport* nr. 6.

Phillips, Martin (1994): 'Habermas, Rural Studies and Critical Social Theory'. In Cloke, Paul, Marcus Doel, David Matless, Martin Phillips and Nigel Thrift: *Writing the rural – five cultural geographies*. Paul Chapman, London, 89–126.

Philo, Chris (1992): 'Neglected rural geographies: a review'. *Journal of Rural Studies* 8:2, 193–207.

Philo, Chris (1993): 'Post-modern rural geography? A reply to Murdoch and Pratt'. *Journal of Rural Studies* 9:4, 429–35.

Rose, Gillian (1993): *Feminism and Geography. The Limits of Geographical Knowledge.* Cambridge: Polity Press.

Rose, Gillian (1997): 'Situating knowledges: positionality, reflexivities and other tactics', *Progress in Human Geography* 21:3, 305–320.

Simonsen, Kirsten (1999): 'Difference in Human Geography – Travelling through Anglo-Saxon and Scandinavian Discourses'. *European Planning Studies*, Vol.7, No 1, 9–24.

SSB (Statistisk Sentralbyrå/Statistics Norway) (2000) Statistisk Årbok. Kongsvinger.

Stenbacka, Susanne (2001) 'Landsbygdsboende i inflyttarnas perspektiv: intention och handling i lokalsamhället', Geografiska regionstudier; 42 Uppsala: Kulturgeografiska institutionen, Uppsala universitet.

Sveriges Nationalatlas: 'Befolkningen'. Bra Böcker, Höganäs 1991.

Teather, Elizabeth (1994): 'Contesting Rurality: Country Women's Social and Political Networks'. In: Whatmore, Marsden and Lowe, *Gender and rurality, David Fulton Publishers*, London.

Urry, John (1995): 'A Middle-class countryside?' I: Butler, Tim and Savage, Mike, *Social change and the middle classes*, UCL Press, London, 205–219.

Valentine, Gill (1997): 'A Safe Place to Grow Up? Parenting, Perceptions of Children's Safety and the Rural Idyll'. *Journal of Rural Studies* 13, 137–148.

Vartdal, Barbro (1999): 'Bygdefamiliens moderne kvardagsliv'. Rapport nr. 6, Senter for Bygdeforskning, Allforsk, Trondheim.

Vartianen, Perttu (1989) 'Counterurbanisation: A Challenge for Socio-theoretical Geography', *Journal of Rural Studies,* 5(3) 217–225.

Villa, Mariann (1997): 'Det særeigne ved bygda'. *Landbruksøkonomisk Forum* nr. 4, 35–42.

Wahlström, Lage (1984): 'Geografiutveckling och geografisk utveckling … som om platser betydde något'. *Meddelanden från Göteborgs universitets geografiska institutioner* ser B nr 76. Göteborg,

West, C. and Zimmerman (1987): 'Doing gender'. Gender and Society 1:125–51

WGSG (Women and Geography Study Group) (1997): 'Feminist Geographies – explorations in diversity and difference'. Longman, Harlow.

Whatmore, Sarah (1991): 'Life Cycle or Patriarchy? Gender Division in Family Farming'. *Journal of Rural Studies* 7/1–2, pp. 71–76.

Whatmore, Sarah, Terry Marsden and Phillip Lowe (1994): Introduction: Feminist Perspectives in Rural Studies. In Whatmore, Sarah, Marsden, Terry and Lowe, Philip (eds.): *Gender and rurality*, David Fulton Publishers, London, 1–10.

Whatmore, Sarah, Marsden, Terry and Lowe, Philip (1994): *Gender and rurality*. London: David Fulton Publishers.

Widerberg, Karin (1992): 'Teoretisk verktøykasse – angrepsmåter og metoder'. In Taksdal, Arnhild and Karin Widerberg (eds.): Forståelser av kjønn i samfunnsvitenskapenes fag og kvinneforskning. Ad Notam Gyldendal, Oslo, 285–99.

Chapter 11

Choreographies of life:
Youth, place and migration

Anders Löfgren

Youth is a central concept in two rather different discourses on change in the Nordic societies. In the regional development discourse, youth is a pivotal age group. This discourse is based in disciplines such as regional economics, macro-sociology, chorological geography and demography. The mapping of the whereabouts and the migratory patterns of certain age groups is central in this discourse. A different discourse tries to understand the social and cultural role of youth in the Nordic welfare states, using the conceptual apparatus found in micro-sociology, cultural studies, psychology and specialized youth research. In the later discourse we can also find questions that pertain to space and place, e.g. what, where, when, how long, with whom and why? However, youth has been largely absent from the discussions on space, place and socio-spatiality in geography. If employed at all, the concept of youth has been dealt with as a given category or a social phenomenon somehow formed outside any socio-spatial processes. On the other hand, however rich and subtle in analysis, the perspective in 'new' cultural geography tends towards a collection of 'still life'-paintings of youth culture in various places (Jackson 1989, Skelton and Valentine 1998).

My main objective in this article is to suggest that youth can form an integral part of a socio-spatial conceptualization of the choreography of life in modern western societies. The frame-work coarsely laid out takes its main inspiration from the socio-cultural perspective of Nordic cultural geography (Fornäs 1995, Fornäs and Bolin 1995), contemporary youth and social(-isation) theory (Bærenholdt et al 1990), a critical use of some basic propositions in time-geography (Buchman 1989, Hägerstrand 1970 a,b, Hägerstrand 1982, Pred 1981, 1986) and theoretizations on life courses and generations. These inspirations are used to develop a conceptual 'toolbox' for the study of youth and its socio-spatial practices. The conceptualization takes its point of departure in two basic arguments about life in a modern world. The first argument is that a modern life course requires a choreography of life. This choreography organizes the answers to questions about what to do, when to do it, where to do it, with whom, in which order and why? The concept of choreography here has to be taken as general socio-spatial concept different from the one employed in dance, but sharing the basic trait of meaningful, planned, structured and conscious use of space. This concept of choreography differs from the phenomenological 'body-ballets' and 'place-ballets'(c.f. Seamon 1980). I do not employ a phenomenological method, and my interest is not focused on the everyday life and the life-world. However, both the everyday life and the life-world can be valid elements in a choreography of life.

The second basic argument is that when modernization and individualization erode the guiding forces of tradition in modern society, youth has to appear as a distinct life phase. To be adult is to be able to cope with the socio-spatialities of the modern world. We must develop competence for dealing with quite different socio-spatial contexts. Some contexts require a high competence, a level of coping we can call mastering. Modern youth may thus be seen as the result of a challenge to develop a mature adult life where the life course has an uncertain outcome (Mørch 1985, 1989).

From that, the article falls in three parts. First, I discuss a socio-spatial conception of youth from a perspective of modernity. In the second part of the article I try to develop this understanding specifically in a spatial sense through the ideas of 'home' and 'venturing'. And in the final part the concepts developed in these two sections are provisionally put into work in a discussion of the consequences for empirical work.

The socio-spatiality of the life course

The choreography of life is the result of both our self-conscious life projects and the structures we encounter in life. Basic social and cultural structurations such as class, gender and ethnicity provide powerful choreographic scripts of life. However, also the places and spaces we make use of in our lives are scripted. The interaction between all these scripts makes it necessary to choreograph our lives. This interaction can be studied at many scales, varying from the body all the way to the global. More and more often we are compelled to jump scales in order to grasp the connectivity in modern lives. Modernization is signified by an ongoing disembedding of time and space and a time-space distanciation or time-space compression.

One important effect of the modernization process is the erosion of tradition that results in a social and cultural disembedding *(freisetzung)* of our lives, a process laid out in the socialization theory of Thomas Ziehe (1986). This disembedding will cause a considerable stress on us, as we are forced to deal with a world that on the one hand promises increased ability to make choices and, on the other hand, requires an increased reflexivity about the context and consequences of any choice made. One can speak of an increased pressure to craft our lives as projects. A basic result of this pressure is a heightened subjectivity, not as an escape into a safe haven of oneself, but rather as a way of handling the stresses of a modern life.

Coping with this evolving disembedded, distanciated and compressed socio-spatiality is an aspect of the general well-being of any individual, and the level of coping is dependent on a resource base of living conditions. In other words, we must develop an ability to reembed time and space into our lives, into our life course. We have to learn to live with relationships stretching far beyond our everyday context as well as with complex expert systems guiding and enabling our agency (Giddens 1985, 1986, 1990). In order to cope we have to develop a constant reflexivity about our life. We have to be competent in dealing with the world 'out there', i.e. reaching out of our immediate environment, as well as competent in dealing with an everyday place that no longer is upheld and constructed only through tradition. In order to grasp the full meaning of socio-spatial coping we have to develop a set of theoretically informed but nevertheless concrete tools for the unpacking of modern lives.

The choreography of a life can be traced through the *biography*. This biography can be divided into the aspects of life that can be traced and recorded, the *life course*, and the narrative aspect of the same life, the *life (hi-)story*. A recorded life course and the narrative about the same life do not necessarily correspond to each other. The narrative does not have to reflect the life course in any simple way. The life course is in classic time-geography traced as a life path, a trajectory, in a time-geographic diorama at the scale of generations and lifetimes. What time-geography lacks, however, is a social theory. Thus time-geography becomes a 'dance macabre' in the words of Anne Buttimer (personal communication). Although acknowledging the inspiration, a choreographic perspective on life thus cannot employ most of the impressive conceptual apparatus of time-geography.

The conscious crafting of a life, the hallmark of a truly modern life, requires individuals to develop plans or perceptions of the coming life course. We can call it a *life project*. It is notable that Hägerstrand (1982) actually suggests the use of project in this way. In youth research, the concept of life project has also for a long time been part of everyday parlance. Especially during youth and young adulthood, the reflexivity of modern life and the ongoing cultural disembedding makes it a necessary exercise to imagine and try out life projects. The tacit guidance given by one single tradition is being eroded away, caving in to a rapid proliferation of competing cultural alternatives. More and more can be imagined as being possible to make or achieve, what Ziehe calls the make-ability[1] (machbarkeit) promised by modernization. However, we do not choose one project and stick to it, we have to develop it gradually as we gain experience and competence. Also later in life we can be forced to reconsider our life projects, such as in the 'mid-life' crisis of bewildered forty-somethings. As we try to force the actual life course and the narrative along the choreography of the life project we have to develop a regime of our life. We have to develop a *management of life*. As individuals we develop very different regimes, and we frequently relate to all kinds of ready made solutions offered to us through channels such as self help books on popular psychology, religion or 'common sense' mediated through parents, friends, teachers or peer pressure. But we must not disregard how such regimes also make use of popular culture spread by the global media industry, such as pulp fiction, soap operas, relational sitcoms and movie dramas. The success of this industry is based on its ability to give us parts and pieces of material to help us construct our life projects.

A basic instrument for comparison and simplification is to focus on reoccurring patterns in the choreography of real lives, the *life patterns*. Although modernization seems to give us an endless scope of choices and variations, it turns out that most choreographies of lives to a large extent are patterned. A major source of guidance and options are the more or less pronounced cultural *patterns of life* offered in the regimes mentioned above. The cultural disembedding does not require us to discard

---

[1]   A very awkward translation of the the german 'machbarkeit' or Scandinavian 'görbarhet' (Ziehe 1986).

traditional ways of living, but it requires us to actively choose and craft them. In order to be able to organize an understanding of life patterns and patterns of life we need analytical tools that break up the continuous conduct of life. This is much like how the historian breaks up the flow of history into epochs and events in order to be able to actually see the flow and to be able to interpret and retell it (Abrams 1982).

I want to suggest three main methods of breaking up choreographies of lives. The first method focuses on the *life phases*, such as childhood, youth, 'family life' and retirement. When a life phase transforms into another we frequently can discern a stage of *transition*, often linked to specific rites or rituals, *les rites de passage* in anthropological literature. These stages of transition are examples of medium length ranges of life that can be labelled a *situation*. The second method is thus to focus on situations such as the leaving of childhood, the leaving of home, the entering into marriage or the retirement. Also, the liminal experiences involved in these transitions can be seen as situations. Finally, a third method is to use the biographical notes and anecdotes in and of life, the *events*, such as birth, first day in school, the confirmation or bar mitzvah, the first date, graduation from school or university, the wedding or the last day at work before retirement. Both phases and situations are influenced by loosely scripted patterns of life, what we can call *cultural or social timetable*s for a particular sequence of life (Löfgren 1990). Events also have a tendency to be more or less scripted (Buchman 1989). These scripts all take the form of choreographic time-tables which lists answers to the questions of what, when, where, with whom, in what order and why?

The scripts in societies governed by tradition have been rather strictly laid out. The central feature of modernization is that the strict choreographies of the life phases are being eroded away. Youth are subjected to a mounting pressure to craft their own life project. The crafting of a mature adulthood requires more time until it has now evolved into a period spanning from the mid-teens to the late twenties. The modern youth phase has further been fragmented into sub-phases. The more simple division is into youth and young adults, and a more complex division can be into old children, youth proper (older teenagers), old youth and young adults. These divisions are not linked to ages or biophysical phases, but to increasing levels of challenges and corresponding levels of coping. If you do not develop a level of coping that is adequate in relation to context and the challenges you may encounter in adult life, more or less severe problems of identity and social integration can occur.

In order to cope with the increased subjectivity and reflexivity that is the result of structural changes in society, youth have to develop some sort of *orientation strategies* in order to meet the challenge. Ziehe has proposed several such strategies. To put it far too short; *ontologization* entails seeking a firm and stable ground for adult life, a strategy that seeks ontological security (Giddens 1990); be it religion, New Age, virulent nationalism or just to adhere to the values and norms of ones parents. *Potentiation* is a strategy where one seeks to enhance the intensity and potency of life; e.g. with music, sports taken to the extreme or the use of artificial stimulants. *Subjectivitization* and *aesthetization* try to overcome the erosion of tradition by making life into a project of self-expression, art and life-style.

The choreography of a specific life employs resources found both in the everyday environment and elsewhere. These resources, however, do not lie around for immediate use, they have to be actively attained and learned. Especially when it comes to resources not in the vicinity of your abode, this learning and acquiring comes when one embarks on *quests*. Quest here will be used in the meaning it has in the fantasy fiction genre, where the most famous quest is the one of Frodo the hobbit in Tolkien's epic saga *Lord of the Rings*. In this story as well as in the bulk of the other examples of this genre, the protagonist sets out on a quest. It can be to save the world from evil, to save himself[2] from evil, to claim what is rightfully his, to seek eternal wisdom or to find a lost father. The accomplishment of the quest also normally involves a lot of travelling in a fictional world[3] made up of an arsenal of mythical elements; from dragons to witchcraft. The quests can be quite different, but the often reluctant hero must go through several ordeals, confront antagonists, make many choices throughout the quest and has to gain competence in many things in order to accomplish the quest. *Even more central, there is no given recipe for success.* The outcome is never supposed to be certain. Any success is dependent on making the right choices along the course of the quest and making creative use of the competence gained on the way. In an analogy, I want to suggest that quests are important ways to learn to cope with the socio-spatiality of modern society.

The modern life includes quests such as for a body to live with, for love and for a workable identity. Although it may not seem like a quest in the sense used in the fantasy genre, to make oneself a Home[4] and to gain a certain authority over a place in the world has also become kind of quest. It may be easier to see Reach as a quest, e.g. the venturing out in order to see what's out there and in order to gain the competence of living in a world of time-space disembedding. I have borrowed the concepts 'Home and Reach' from Buttimer (1980), but I believe she would not readily accept my use of them. All these quests interact, making youth in itself a meta-quest. These quests all involve scripts, but the sheer multitude of conflicting scripts make it necessary to develop a reflexive regime of life. Finally, all interacting scripts are incorporated into a choreographed life-project.

The modern life has to an increasing part to be choreographed by the individual herself. However, when choreographing our lives we are not autonomous and unrestricted individuals. We are in many senses restricted in our choices. Most choices we cannot even imagine. Among the imaginable choices we have to rule out those that we know have no resources to make real. Another restriction is that many choices are made impossible by structural constraint, sanctions from others or by choices made earlier. All the classic structural constraints such class, gender, ethnicity, religion or disabilities are valid here. However, within these restrictions we always make choices. Our choices of patterns of life and cultural timetables are, to put it very bluntly, a reflection of identities and knowledge we develop. The statement that knowledge is situated has become almost a meaningless mantra. But in relation to the choreography of life, situated knowledge is the knowledge

---

2   The fantasy genre has its major appeal to young men. But I suggest that the romantic literature that is mostly read by young women also involves quests, although with different goals.
3   These quests most often take place in imaginary worlds, and these settings are charted and mapped in the novel (or series of novels).
4   Note that I do not see people belonging to places, but rather places belonging to people.

constructed and used in a situation. Similarly, it is possible to talk about an 'eventual' knowledge as passing as the event. Finally, the knowledge relating to the life-story and the life-course is storied or 'emplotted'.

Youth, home and venturing

Place and 'home'

The disembedding of lives and the increasing number of scripts for life implies that a life project is not limited to one place, one region or one nation. The relation between place and life has become reflexive and open for negotiations. A place is distinguished from other places by its script/s. Living in Manhattan is understood as being different than living in Malmö, most youth from the central area of Norway still uses the regional identification of being a 'trønder' to distinguish themselves from other Norwegians. In short, places, regions and even nations still are experienced as requiring different scripts for life. One must not forget the importance of scale in this relation. We frequently refer to Home both when we mean home-town or nation of birth. The script of Home is related to different scales (Mack 1993, Smith 1993).

In the present connection, my particular interest is the way in which scripts of Home are related to place, and I propose three themes at stake in this relationship.[5] These are respectively Home as the model and guardian of social order, Home as the foundation of social integration and Home as the root of authenticity. Each of these themes contains many facets, and they are not to be understood as unambiguously positive. This becomes even more apparent if one tries to capture the deeper meaning of Homelessness. Being without a Home implies more than just not having a personal space where to sleep. Homelessness also conveys notions of being outside the legitimate social order (Veness 1992); being 'matter out-of-place' (Douglas 1993) and being inauthentic.

Home is a script for that which makes you 'feel at home' in place, for how life should be lived there and for whom which are entitled to a particular place. However, these scripts are becoming less coherent. There are four major strands of development that reflect a challenge to places as Home in (high-) modern society. These are respectively; the abandonment of Home altogether, the moveable and multiple Home/s, the increased defence of Home, and the conscious construction of Home. These challenges interact and are not mutually excluding, and thus they affect us in many concrete combinations.

The first challenge is quite simply that Home, as a meaningful concept in the choregraphy of life, is in danger of withering away in modern society. While for a long time we have known that capital has no Home, this seems to be more and more the case for labour, civil society and culture as well. This may plunge people into a state of gigantic global Homelessness, a whirlpool of life where social order and

---

[5] In doing that, I of course do recognize that the two concepts are not synonymous. The connection expresses the particular interests followed in this chapter.

integration as well as authenticity cannot be sustained. But in a particularly illuminating example, Doreen Massey (1992) shows how her London community is constructed literally as a cross-roads of many different strains of culture and experiences from all over the globe. As I interpret her account, this community has come far in what we can call the co-construction of place.

All places are constructed, but the question is who and/or what it is that constructs places. When living in a place, we often choreograph our life as if the place was something constructed for us rather than by us? Quite literally, places are physically designed and constructed, and architects, planners and local political institutions are among those that influence these processes of construction. All those that have a relation to a place, however, take part in a process of co-construction of this place. The Kilburnites in Massey's account acknowledge a social order, a social integration and an authenticity that is not linked to roots but to 'routes'. We can actually re-create a global sense of place where disembedding forces can successfully be countered by active strategies for the co-construction of places. It may not create a global sense of Home, but the account of Massey indicates that it is possible to re-embed life into places, regions and nations without necessarily relying on the script of Home.

Another interpretation of Massey would be that the safety and protection of a social order, social integration and cultural authenticity is not necessarily linked only to a given place. It can equally be based in ones place of choice. Here the challenge to given scripts of Home is *the movable and multiple Home*, the ability to live ones life like a human 'tumbleweed',[6] anchoring oneself to places that offer and require particularly good scripts for a particular life project. A home of choice is a Home, but it is highly co-constructed as a part of a conscious choreography of life. In order to grasp this particular kind of co-construction we can utilize the example of gay/lesbian communities. In life stories that gays and lesbians tell the search for a place to settle and develop an adult gay or lesbian life is often narrated very much in the form of a quest (Cant 1997). Communities with a large gay/lesbian constituency can be found both in large American urban metropolises, as well as in smaller settings (Castells 1983, Godfrey 1989, Jackson 1989, Chauncey 1994, Bell and Valentine 1995, Adler and Brenner 1992, Stryker and van Buskirk 1996, Lauria and Knopp 1985, Lloyd and Roundtree 1978). The famous Castro in San Francisco is a key example of the former kind. Many explanations have been given for the rise of the Castro. However, the most intriguing question remains that of how these communities are sustained. The literature on the subject points in many directions, but of relevance in the present connection is the role these communities play in the specific choreography of life of gay men and lesbians. Places like the Reeperbahn in

---

6   The tumbleweed is a metaphor lent from the classic western movies in which a certain kind of bush is always blowing around outside the flapping saloon doors. This specific specie is mostly a dry tangle of branches, but when the occasional rain comes, it sets root and lives through a stage of being an ordinary rooted plant. When the drought comes back, the roots die and once again the tumbleweed enters its phase of being blown around the dusty landscape.

Hamburg or San Francisco's Polk Street[7] area are often integrated in a choreography of life only as places of week-end relief or occasional visits. The main force sustaining communities like the Castro, on the other hand, is the migrants moving in seeking the experience a social order, a social integration and claims of authenticity that values gayness and lesbianism as positive qualities in the life project. By far, most of these in-migrants are youth or young adults. In fact the main choreographic move in life that gives meaning to a gay or lesbian life project in modern America may be moving to a community like the Castro.

The example of gay and lesbian youth has implications for many other youth looking for a place to live their life. The major urban centres in the Nordic countries attract large number of youth moving in from more rural areas. This migration may be interpreted solely in terms of the search for more options in education and employment. However, there is also strong element of more options for realization of specific life projects. When youth in the Nordic countries are asked about why they leave their home place, the answers often quote the larger supply of scripts for their life projects in the larger cities.

Returning to the concepts of Ziehe and Giddens; the orientation strategy that strives to re-establish an ontological security as a way to counter cultural disembedding frequently employ the concept of Home. The ontologization of Home develops into defensive scripts. The defence of Home is often used in the rhetoric of the nationalist and racist right. The power of this rhetoric lies in the clever use of the script of Home. It becomes harder to dispute the resistance to immigration from foreign countries, as this is equal to preventing unwanted squatters from settling in your living room. Xenophobia is not so much about being afraid of the foreigners themselves, but more so about being afraid of foreigners taking over in ones Home. In the end, the worries about Home turn migration and cultural mixing into a problem itself. Concerns about the way society changes ends up in longings for an almost neo-feudal society where the given Home is seen as the place where one should be living ones life. Where some youth move to the cities to develop their life projects, others thus develop a strong place attachment as a central script in their life project.

In the classic study 'Learning to labour' (Willis 1977) we meet the 'lads' from a British Midland industrial town, aptly named Hammertown. Their resistance to school is preparing them for the traditional male working class culture of their hometown, providing them with a quite useful local symbolic capital. Knowledge derived from books and teaching is spurned as feminine, useless and unrewarding, and most important, something that is not useful script for their Home. Gunnar Jørgensen (1994) gives another example of the same processes of defensive scripting, this time from the western parts of Norway. The fairly small town, given the alias Bygdeby, has seen some changes as a local university college and other regional institutions have been established. He identifies two distinct youth cultures in the town; an anti-school culture much similar to the lads of Hammertown, and a culture of middle-class school achievers. The anti-school culture is showing a staunch attachment to Bygdeby. They don't ever want to move out of there and are

---

[7]   A seedy street of porn shops and bars, not that different from the red light districts such as Reeperbahn in Hamburg.

hesitant even to leave for shorter trips. In other words, they wanted to be 'at home', and they wanted Bygdeby to be *their* home. The students at the college made this less easy as they visibly brought the outside into the public space of Bygdeby. The students were perceived as intruders. The school-achievers, on the other hand, came from a middle-class culture that on the whole was much less bound to Bygdeby. They were often looking forward to travelling and/or studying abroad, and kept in touch with what was going on in the metropolises of the world, London, New York or Los Angeles. The school achievers furthermore seemed to be able to be at home wherever they would choose to settle.

Another reflection of the challenge to Home is the conscious scripting of Home, illustrated by the mission style developments in California's Orange County. These homes are not only supplied with water, electricity and conveniences, but also with a kind of simulacra history. In gated communities the social order and integration of the community is literally built into the physical space, as strict rules are applied as to who can live there and how they should live their lives inside the community. The gated communities take the conscious scripting of Home quite far. The gay-lesbian city communities are less extreme examples of this scripting of Home. What they have in common is the way the arenas of life are reconstructed to fit a certain preferred choreography of life. This is a development that has not gone very far in the Nordic countries, and certainly this is most important for other life phases like family life and retirement. Lately, however, efforts have been made in consciously scripting rural communities in such a way that they may become more inviting to youth seeking life projects that have been seen as 'urban'.

Venturing

The way to discover the world is by Reaching out, by venturing. Venturing has always been a part of the process of maturing, of becoming adult. In many societies, the young men are sent away quite literally to find their adulthood. The medieval travel of the journeyman, 'gesällvandringen', is another example. In the 16th, 17th and 18th centuries, the young men of the aristocracy were also sent out to venture around on long journeys, first on the continent and then around the globe in the age of imperial colonialism. Maybe needless to say, this venturing was highly gendered and almost exclusively male. The story of the modern youth has been markedly biased towards young men (Bjerrum-Nielsen and Rudberg 1991). In part this reflects a historic inequality between men and women, where modern youth as a way to deal with the challenge of modernity first developed among the young men of the bourgeoisie and then gradually spread to young men from other classes and to young women (Mørch 1985, 1989). It also, however, in part reflects a tendency to focus on mostly male youth sub-cultures. In modern western society the venturing out to experience and to learn is less gendered. Still, however, in venturing one should expect differences between the scripts for young men and women. The yearning for direct experience of what it is like elsewhere is one of the responses to the time-space distanciation youth encounter everyday. There is a world out there to be experienced first-hand rather than through media. This modern form of venturing takes longer, and requires a more reflexive approach.

The first steps in venturing often come with the tour downtown or into town on Saturday evening. The bright lights of the inner city are something quite different from sheltered and/or deprived lives in the suburbs or in the countryside. Being in the city makes you feel more grown up. Gradually you learn the codes that enable you to gain entrance to the places not intended for you, but for the older and more experienced ones. These codes include the use of style as well as other sub-cultural elements like music and slang (Hebdige 1984, Skelton and Valentine 1998). The hanging around in the malls of Middle America and Common Europe has a similar purpose.

The next step in the venturing process is going out of town; on holiday, visits to friends and relatives or study-tours. These trips are often organized and/or made with a purpose not originating from the youth themselves. They soon learn, however, how to corrupt and bend the rules set out, thus making the trip a worthwhile experience. Being abroad for the first time tends to be a special threshold experience. The success of any trip as a venturing quest is dependent on the knowledge and competence gained in how to be 'verdensvant' or wordly, to have been around and to know things.

For a larger and larger proportion of youth, the venture to a place of higher education; a university, a liberal arts college or an art school is a similar threshold experience, the first taste of being on your own. Most develop strategies to cope, but we must not overlook the possibility of some not being able to cope. For some this experience ends up in loneliness, desperation and a general bewilderment. More and more youth also see some odd years abroad as au-pair, exchange student or just working as a necessary experience. It gives them knowledge of languages as well as of cultures, making them more competent in being reflexive back home. They don't want to leave for good, but they see being abroad for some time during youth as an asset in their adult life.

The ultimate experience in the venturing quest is back-packing around the world. The back-packers form a distinctive group of anti-tourists, and they develop a hierarchy of places to go to, with the venture to places where no tourist has been before at the top of the priority list. They are in search for the undisturbed and the authentic, and are quite contemptuous of the modern mass-tourism that sends charter-tourists off to every corner of the world. But of course the irony of it all is that the sheer numbers of these back-packers effectively prevents most of them becoming anything else than mass tourists.

Another point to be made here is that one should not focus on travel as such, as one then risks ignoring the environmental bubble that often follows modern travelling. Going on a holiday trip to an average resort do not constitute reflexive venturing as such. Most resorts and most major tourist attractions are shaped in such a way that going there offers more relaxation than reflexivity. Going to Disneyland can be a reflexive venturing, but it can also be just a day off in an amusement park. Venturing has to be understood in relation to the intention and the outcome of a trip. One travels for personal enjoyment, but one ventures to gain competence and experience necessary in a world of time-space-distanciation. However, these two aspects may be interacting and it is only in the narrative mirror of the life history one discovers the reflexive venturing.

A fairly new development in this relation is venturing through means of new information and communication technology. Venturing in material space is supplemented by possibilities to venture in cyber space. Does this cyber-venturing replace physical journeys, or is it a distinctly different form of venturing? Quite certainly the new media of information will increase the erosion of tradition, and multiply the options when crafting a life project. But will this diversity be reflected in real choreographies of life? In the end, answers to these questions have to be settled by concrete research.

Some implications for empirical studies

In the discussion to follow, I draw selectively both on empirical work that I have previously conducted myself (Löfgren 1990, 1997) and on other studies contributing to the understanding of the socio-spatial practices of young people (Ainley 1991, Jones 1995, Goldscheider and Goldscheider 1993, Killeen 1992, Young 1987, Werner 1988). Furthermore, on the bases of my conceptual developments I suggest roads to follow in future research.

Leaving home

Housing is an important but 'wobbly' pillar in the structure of the Nordic welfare edifice. The 'echo-generation' of the post-war 'baby-boomers' created an unusually large cohort of young people in the mid to late 1980s, especially in the largest urban regions. Surveys of the housing preferences of youth presented a chaotic picture, but reached some consensus on the fact that most youth preferred a small flat of their own when leaving home (see Löfgren 1990). Another general pattern was that youth saw the small detached house in a suburban or small town setting as the ideal family dwelling when eventually settling down to an adult life. This mirrors both how legitimate the idea of youth having their own home had become, *and* the prevailing ideological importance of home ownership.

Leaving home should not be seen as a sudden event, but rather as a situation in the choreography of life. Leaving home is not only about moving out from one dwelling into another; it is central to the process of becoming an adult and richly embedded in the social and cultural structures of modern society. Although leaving home as a scripted situation is delimited, leaving home as a concrete process can stretch out for more than 15 years in the modern western society. The patterns of leaving home in both rural and urban areas were relatively stable up until the turn of the century. In the 20th century we have witnessed two major developments. First the practice of sending ones children away as servants and/or apprentices to other households at a relatively early age, was abandoned in favour of a pattern where youth stayed on at home until marriage. This is still a major pattern in many parts of Europe. The second change has been the increasing numbers of young people that leave home to form independent single households in their own right. This last process started with the proliferation of rooming and lodging houses and specially designed youth/students residences for youth living away as students and apprentices. This development came about in order to meet the demand in an increasingly mobile post war period in the Nordic countries. In the early years after the war ended, youth did not have any legitimate claim to homes of their own.[8] Gradually, though, this has changed, and very much so in the Nordic welfare states. In other words, youth had gradually been entitled to have housing preferences. It has become widely accepted, not only as legitimate, but also as quite normal in the choreography of the life project to form more or less short-lived households before settling down in a family.

Leaving home is of crucial importance for the 'take off' of the modern life project. Most often, leaving home is a kind of upwardly mobile career in a hierarchy of housing alternatives. The actual biographies do differ a lot, as well as the prospects of being able to realize ones yearnings. However, leaving home is scripted by major cultural timetables for the choreography of life between the actual event of moving out from ones parents and the day of oneself becoming a parent. The cultural timetables for leaving home can be structured around some key elements. The basic movements are made up of the actual housing arrangements, but important *rites de passage* and events further structure the timetable. Choices of education and employment are important, as well as all kinds of falling in love and falling out of love. Different quests, like the urge to venture out in the world, also have to be taken into account.

The scripts given by cultural timetables will always be dependent on context, both in space and time. Leaving home in the Nordic countries differs from leaving home in Italy or the US, the leaving of home in the 80s was different than in the context of today. Here I must add a small note on the difference and interaction of cohort and generation. Many life courses following approximately the same time-space paths, taken together, constitute a cohort. A cohort is a taxonomic collective that is fairly empty of meaning. Cohorts can, however, constitute the base for generations, for life histories that share common experiences and accounts. A generation shares something or has something in common; what Raymond Williams called a 'shared structure of feeling' (Taylor et al 1996). This sharing is not restricted to historical experiences (such as the Vietnam War or the crumbling of the Soviet bloc) but also includes a socio-spatial aspect. A generation shares common scripts of patterns of life and cultural timetables for situations such as leaving home. The generation leaving home in the Nordic countries of the 80s shared some common scripts for the situation of leaving home. But it was as a large cohort that this generation had an impact on the housing market.

I have reconstructed the scripts for the choreography of the leaving of home (Löfgren 1990), based on nearly 50 interviews with youth in the age range of 18 to

---

[8] Quite early in the century the long distances in most parts of Scandinavia had created a demand for arrangements for pupils/students living away. The solution was something rather similar to a boardinghouse located close to the secondary schools, teachers colleges and other educational institutions. These 'homes' were most often run by a warden, and were rather strictly organized (different floors for girls and boys, curfews and the like). In the 50s and 60s the expansion of the universities and colleges created a similar demand for student accommodations. Also, different types of boarding-houses were used for the young unmarried migrants that migrated to industrialized regions with a rapidly expanding labour market.

25, conducted in a medium sized city in Sweden. The basic structural elements of the choreography of the situation were the actual reasons for moving out and the quests for education, employment, love and relationships, among others. The cultural timetables in this context included one of forced or *hasty maturity* (leaving home early, short or no further education, and relatively early establishment of a family life). Another was one of *security* (leaving home late and after having completed education and/or gained a first steady employment, and establishment of a family at a fairly average age). Less coherent was the mainstream *extended youth period* (leaving home as a long process with a mix of further education, temporary employment and unemployment, travels and stays abroad, and also a late formation of family life). Finally, one timetable was that of being *forever young*, being much similar to the extended youth-period timetable, but without the family formation as the ultimate goal.

These cultural timetables could be linked to questions about where to live in urban regions, e.g. whether in the inner city or the suburbs. The suburban or place-bound setting was scripted into the timetables of *hasty maturity* and of *security*, albeit for differing reasons. The lure of the inner city life during the youth period was clearly scripted into the timetables of *mainstream/extended youth period* and of *being forever young*. The three main timetables, however, ended within the same suburban script, a nuclear family living in a detached house. The urban region thus becomes a circulating system, where youth grew up in suburban areas, moved into the city centre and then back again when it was time to establish a family.

A decade later, the scripts of the 80s still survive. However, due to changes in the general economy and in the housing market, these scripts have become less easy to follow. During the last 10 years the Nordic welfare states have gone through a process of restructuring. Resources and services provided by local, regional and national government have become more 'lean'. The age group between 20 and 30 is most exposed to this process. The living conditions for the young adults have worsened both in absolute and relative terms, compared to other life phases and to earlier cohorts in the same life phase (Hagquist 1997). If this marks a general trend of young adulthood being a period of relatively weak living conditions, a time stamp of an economically harsh decade on a cohort or a relative deprivation that will follow a generation remains to be seen.

Youth and migration

Youth migration, mostly in the form of youth leaving small towns and rural areas, is a reoccurring theme in regional research and regional development policies in several Nordic countries. The research often takes its point of departure in perceptions that the migration as such is the problem to be addressed. The main question regarding youth and migration thus has been the plight of the places and regions with a strong outward migration loss of youth. In the Nordic countries it is quite consistent that most small towns and rural areas have a heavy net loss of migrants in the age span of 18 to 25. This gradually reduces the cohort sizes. This may lead to a reduced population if the loss is not countered by an equal or larger net gain in migration. In fact, most of these places experience net gain in migration in the age span 30 to 40. The loss is, however, not balanced by the gain. In the end, the result is a slow thinning out of the population. This thinning out of the population in already small peripheral communities can evolve into an elongated spiral of decay. Services close down due to a too small population base, resulting in the loss of job opportunities, which in turn may force even more youth to leave. The causes of this gradual thinning out are complex, but a major focus has been on youth migration. How can this migration be stopped or even reversed, and how should one go about making those leaving come back?

Various remedies surface in public debate, including 'Return back home' campaigns, incentives in the labour market and a special focus on education. National policies of education and equal opportunity in the Nordic countries encourage and sustain a scholarly culture of internationally convertible symbolic capital. Contrarily, in some traditional agrarian Nordic communities symbolic capital was in parochial currencies. Knowledge was not necessarily unique, but knowledge was learned through participation in the local production and consumption and was acknowledged locally. Up to this day, much of the symbolic capital needed to find work in many rural areas has been in local currency, whether in an agricultural village, a fishing community or a one-company town. Regional development policies put much emphasis on such local symbolic capital, but this is not sustained by the national policies. It has also been suggested that the attraction of the bigger cities could be countered by offering a wider variety of resources in education, culture and leisure, such as opening art schools or establishing cafés serving a decent mocha latte. Housing has attracted less attention, yet housing is an important aspect. In the periphery there is available housing, but it is often too big and only adapted to a nuclear family life with steady income and stable patterns of everyday life. The small lodging room is often the only alternative for youth in these places.

Many worries about youth migration from rural areas end up in an ideological battle between urban and rural as distinct dichotomies, with Norwegian discourses as the most distinctive example. The battle makes use of all kinds of images and narratives, and the ideological content often clouds the real question involved, e.g. how youth shape their life projects. As we all use images and narratives retrieved from the store rooms of culture, the narratives of the life story and the life project may very well include images of urban and rural settings. But it emerges in the narratives youth retells to researchers that most youth do not actually think in terms of urban or rural as such, but rather in terms of specific conditions, resources and scripts different places have to offer. Furthermore, they are well aware that most places have both advantages and disadvantages. Finally, many life projects include moving from smaller places to big cities when young, but also returning to live in a smaller place once becoming adults. But this does not have to be the place of their childhood. Urban and rural, as such, is thus of little use when trying to understand the reasons for young people leaving rural areas. Rather it is necessary with concrete research into the conjunctions of the resources and scripts of places and regions and the aspirations and yearnings of youth in their life projects.

Another dichotomy employed in the Nordic literature when discussing youth in socio-spatial terms is a rather simple dualism of 'local' and 'global'. Some are said to have local orientation, others a global or cosmopolitan one (Dahman 1982). Local frequently become connected to inertia and traditional roots, global something linked to footloose and cosmopolitan lifestyles. But many youth defy this distinction by both being anchored in the local context *and* having a global outlook. The concepts of 'local' and 'global' do not incorporate the need to gain competence in socio-spatial coping, and thus the simple dualism of local and global is rendered inadequate. I want to argue that in order to fully cope with modern life, we need *both* competence in reaching out (being global) and competence in making a Home (being local) somewhere in the world. Furthermore, living conditions cannot be neatly divided into local or global. The school, for example, is physically local, but the content of education does not need to be local. The use of telecommunications and field trips as well as the curriculum can make the school quite global. Most popular culture is on the other hand produced for a global market and distributed as mass culture, but reception and actual consumption takes place locally.

The living conditions encountered in the youth period affect both the way life projects are shaped and the actual outcome read out from biographies. Places, regions and nations offer quite different living conditions, and living conditions change over time. However, I suggest that the point of departure should be the life projects of youth rather than a specific place or region. This perspective implies that living conditions are rules and resources that individuals employ when trying to choreograph their life projects. The rules and resources needed and the ones available are related to the arena or arenas that are choreographed into the life course. Any study of youth in any context must be theorized so it can accommodate the mobilization of rules and resources for the management of various life projects. All this implies that living conditions cannot be studied only as objective 'facts' found in different places, regions and nations.

I want to suggest that rather than being two opposing categories, local and global should be understood as two different dimensions of socio-spatial coping. These dimensions give many more possible positions than just 'local' or 'global'. Furthermore, it is rarely discussed how local or global orientations are attained and sustained. If one employs the framework I suggest in this article, these orientations could be linked to substantial structures like class and gender without being reduced to them. As Beck puts it, class is still a central aspect of our society but class relations have become individualized (Beck 1987). However, only concrete research can establish which relationships exist in any specific place at any specific time. Such research must operate with a multi-level design that includes at least four types of data.

The first group consist of long interviews with individual youth and where the life project is in focus. What narratives of their life do youth present and what are the important aspects regarding places to live and how to live there? In order to put these narratives into a context of available cultural timetables, scripts and patterns of life it is essential to also conduct group sessions/focus groups, which comprise the second set of data. A third set of data includes interviews with local key informants such as teachers, youth workers, local resource persons and even parents. This material is used to frame the data from the first two layers of research in a local context and history, including scripts, discourses and local knowledge. Finally, available hard data on living conditions, migration and resources must be used as a framework for the interpretation of data from the three first layers.

Concluding remarks

The proposed conceptual toolbox is put together with tools from various disciplines and traditions, and the use of any of the tools in isolation may not give inherently new knowledge. The perspective can however be of value when confronting questions that pertain to the conjunction of spatial, demographic and socio-cultural processes of change. When studying youth migration, local youth culture, youth and housing or the role of youth in regional development, the suggested toolbox first and foremost offers a different framework for interpretation of both quantitative and qualitative data. The question is not where youth are, but why are they there?

In this global whirlpool world of ours, how should we choreograph our life projects so that we can cope with modernization? Where do we find authenticity, order and social integration? Here we can see two very different prospects which are both less than inviting. One is a continuing erosion of tradition and a rapid globalization that leads towards the annihilation of Home as a meaningful concept altogether. This would indicate choreographies that put all emphasis on developing competence in venturing and in dealing with time-space distanciation. At the other extreme we find the revival of the Home as the central and commanding anchor point for life projects. There is some circumstantial evidence pointing towards this prospect. It is clearly visible in the growing strength of localist, regionalist and nationalist ideologies with markedly reactionary outlooks. But as indicated above, there is also evidence that points to a possible way forward somewhere in between these extremes, a way that is valid for youth in particular. If youth succeed in developing choreographies of life that can accommodate 'routes' as well as 'roots' (Hall 1995), then, maybe, youth may develop successful (modern) lives.

References

Abrams, Philip (1982) *Historical Sociology*. Bath: Open Books.
Adler, Sy and Johanna Brenner (1992) 'Gender and Space: Lesbians and Gay Men in the City'. *International Journal of Urban and Regional Research*, vol. 16, 24–34.
Ainley, Pat (1991)*Young people leaving home*. London: Cassel.
Bærenholdt, Jørgen Ole et al. (1990) 'Lifemodes and Social practice'. *Nordisk Samhällsgeografisk Tidskrift*, vol. No.11, 72–86.
Bech, Henning (1988) *Når mænd mødes*. København: Gyldendal.
Bech, Henning (1989) *Mellem mænd*. Viborg: Tiderne Skifter.
Beck, Ulrich (1987) 'Beyond status and class: Will there be an individualized class society?' In Meja, C. (ed.) *Modern German Sociology*. New York: Columbia University Press.
Bell, David and Gill Valentine, (eds.) (1995) *Mapping desire: geographies of sexualities*. London: Routledge.
Bjerrum-Nielsen, Harriet and Monica Rudberg (1991) 'Ungdom, kön och modernitet'. In Löfgren, Anders and Margareta (eds.) *Att förstå ungdom; Indentitet och mening i en föränderlig värld*. Symposion Stockholm/Stehag.
Boyd, Nan Alamilla (1997) '"Homos invade S.F." San Francisco's History as a Wide-Open Town'. In Beemyn, Brett (ed.) *Creating a place for ourselves*. New York: Routledge.

Buchman, Marlis (1989) *The Script of Life in Modern Society. Entry into Adulthood in a Changing World*. Chicago: The University of Chicago Press.

Buttimer, Anne (1980) 'Home, Reach and the Sense of Place'. In Buttimer, Anne and David Seamon (eds.) *The human experience of space and place*. London: Croom Helm.

Cant, Bob, (ed.) (1997) *Invented identities. Lesbians and gays talk about migration*. London: Cassell.

Castells, Manuel (1983) *The city and the grassroots*. London: Longman.

Chauncey, George (1994) *Gay New York*. NYC: Basic Books.

Dahman, Donald C. (1982) 'Locals and cosmopolitans. Patterns of social mobility during the transition from youth to early adulthood'. The University of Chicago, *Dept of Geography Research Paper* 204.

Douglas, Mary (1993) 'The Idea of a Home: A Kind of Space'. In Mack, Arien (ed.) *Home. A Place in the World*. NYC: New York University Press, 261–281.

Fornäs, Johan (1995) *Cultural theory and late modernity*. London: Sage.

Fornäs, Johan and Göran Bolin, (eds.) (1995) *Youth culture in late modernity*. London: Sage.

Giddens, Anthony (1985) 'Time, space and regionalisation'. In Gregory, Derek and John Urry (eds.) *Social relations and spatial structures*. London: Macmillan.

Giddens, Anthony (1986) *The constitution of society*. Cambridge: Polity Press.

Giddens, Anthony (1990) *The consequences of modernity*. Cambridge: Polity Press.

Godfrey, Brian J. (1989) *Neighborhoods in transition. The making of San Fransisco's ethnic and non-conformist communities*. Berkeley: Unversity of California Press.

Goldscheider, Frances K. and Calvin Goldscheider (1993) *Leaving home before marriage: ethnicity, familism and generational relationships*. Madison: University of Wisconsin Press.

Hägerstrand, Torsten (1970a) 'Tidsanvändning och omgivningsstruktur. Bilaga 4 i SOU 1970: 14 *Urbaniseringen i Sverige, en geografisk samhällsanalys*. Bilagedel 1: Balanserad regional utveckling. Stockholm.

Hägerstrand, Torsten (1970b) 'What about people in regional science'. *Regional Science Association Papers and proceedings*, 7–21.

Hägerstrand, Torsten (1975) 'Survival and arena. On the life-history of individuals in relation to their geographical environment'. *Monadnock*, Clark University,Worcester, Mass., vol. 49, 9–29.

Hägerstrand, Torsten (1982) 'Diorama, path and project', *Tijdschrift voor economische en sociale geografie*, vol. 73 (1982), No.6, 323–339.

Hagquist, Curt (1997) *The living conditions of young people in Sweden*. Göteborg: Dept. of social Work, Göteborg University.

Hall, Stuart (1995) 'New cultures for old'. In Massey, Doreen and Pat Jess (eds.) *A Place in the World? Places, Cultures and Globalization*. The Open University Press/Oxford University Press.

Hareven, Tamara K. (1993) 'The Home and the Family in Historical Perspective'. In Mack, Arien (ed.) *Home. A Place in the World*. NYC: New York University Press, 227–260.

Hebdige, Dick (1984) *Subculture – the meaning of style*. London: Methuen.

Jackson, Peter (1989) *Maps of meaning*. London: Unwin Hyman.

Jones, Gill (1995) *Leaving home*. Buckingham: Open University Press.

Jørgensen, Gunnar (1994) 'To Ungdomskulturer. Om vedlikehold av sosiale og kulturelle ulikheter'. *Bygdeby*, Vestlandsforsking, Sogndal 1/94.

Killeen, Damian (1992) 'Leaving home: housing and income – social policy on leaving home'. In Coleman, John C. and Chris Warren-Adamson (eds.) *Youth policy in the 1990s. The way forward*. London: Routledge. s189–202.

Lauria, Mickey and Lawrence Knopp (1985) 'Toward an anlysis of the role of gay communities in the urban renaissance'. *Urban Geography*, vol. 6, No.2, 152–169.

Lloyd, Bonnie and Lester Roundtree (1978) 'Radical feminists and Gay Men in San Francisco'. In Palm, Risa and Richard Lanegran (eds.) *An invitation to geography*. New York: McGraw-Hill.

Löfgren, Anders (1990) *Att flytta hemifrån. Boendets roll i ungdomars vuxenblivande ur ett situationsanalytiskt perspektiv*. Lund: Lund University Press.

Löfgren, Anders (1997) 'Living in the real world! The role of home in the life projects of youth'. *Young*, vol. 5, No.2, 17–30.

Mack, Arien, (ed.) (1993) *Home: a place in the world*. New York: New York University Press.

Massey, Doreen (1992) 'A Global Sense of Place.' *Marxism Today*, vol. No. June 1991, 24–29.

Massey, Doreen (1993a) 'Power-geometry and a progresive sense of place'. In Bird, Jon et al (eds.) *Mapping the futures. Local culture, global change*. London: Routledge, 60–69.

Mørch, Sven (1985) *Att forske i ungdom. Et socialpsykologiskt essay*. København: Rubikon.

Mørch, Sven (1989) 'Youth reproduced and investigated'. 2nd Nordic Youth Research Information Symposion Savonlinna, Finland.

Pred, Allan (1981) 'Power, practice and the discipline of human geography'. In Pred, Allan and Gunnar Törnquist (eds.) *Space and time in geography*. Lund: CWK Gleerup *Lund studies in geography* B48, 30–55.

Pred, Allan (1981) 'Social reproduction and the time-geography of everyday life'. *Geografiska Annaler*, vol. No.63B.

Pred, Allan (1986) *Place, practice and structure*. Cambridge: Polity Press.

Seamon, David (1980) 'Body-Subject, Time-Space Routines and Place-Ballets'. In Buttimer, Anne and David Seamon (eds.) *The human experience of space and place*. London: Croom Helm.

Simonsen, Kirsten (1999) 'Difference in Human Geography – Travelling through Anglo-saxon and Scandinavian Discourses'. *European Planning Studies*, vol. 7, No.1, 9–24.

Skelton, Tracey and Gill Valentine, ed. (1998) *Cool Places. Geographies of Youth cultures*. London: Routledge.

Smith, Neil (1993) 'Homeless/global: Scaling places'. In Bird, Jon et al. (eds.) *Mapping the futures: local cultures, global change*. London: Routledge, 87–119.

Somers, Margaret R. and Gloria D. Gibson (1994) 'Reclaiming the Epistemological 'Other': Narrative and the Social Constitution of Identity'. In Calhoun, Craig (ed.) *Social Theory and the Politics of Identity*. Oxford/Malden: Blackwell.

Stryker, Susan and Jim Van Buskirk (1996) *Gay by the bay*. San Francisco: Chronicle Books.

Taylor, Ian, Karen Evans and Penny Fraser (1996) *A tale of two cities. Global change, local feeling and everyday life in the north of England. A study in Manchester and Sheffield*. London: Routledge.

Veness, A.R. (1992) 'Home and homelessness in the United States'. *Environment and planning D: Society and Space*, vol. 10, 445–468.

Werner, Karla (1988) *Mer än tak över huvudet*. Stockholm: BFR T2:1988.

Willis, Paul (1977) 'Learning to labour'. Gower Publishing Ltd.

Young, C.M. (1987) 'Young people leaving home in Australia: The Trend towards Independence'. Australian Family Formation Project, *Canberra monograph 9*.

Ziehe, Thomas (1986) *Ny ungdom. Om osedvanliga läroprocesser*. Malmö: Norstedts.

Ziehe, Thomas (1989) *Kulturanalyser – ungdom utbildning modernitet*. Stockholm/Stehag: Symposion.

PART IV
NATURE, LANDSCAPE
AND ENVIRONMENT

Chapter 12

In search of the Nordic landscape: A personal view

Kenneth R. Olwig

This essay is concerned with the contemporary renewal of what I have defined as a particularly 'Nordic' conception of landscape as polity and place. To comprehend this renewal it is necessary to go back in time to its modern origins in nineteenth century pan-Scandinavianism. Insofar as this conception of landscape developed in contestation with conceptions of landscape as pictorial scenery, produced in the process of constructing a unified nation-state, particularly in Germany, it is necessary to delineate the origins and logic of this concept of landscape as well. This scenic conceptualization of landscape remains relevant because it continues to thrive, in various forms, particularly in Germany. Finally, because the nation-state emerged out of earlier state formations under which the scenic conception of landscape initially was developed, it is also necessary to go back to the Renaissance origins of this form of landscape. The pictorial conception of landscape, fostered by the Renaissance state, also continues to thrive, particularly in Britain, where it is a key concept in the British 'new' cultural geography. As agents, researchers participate, reflexively, in the creation and re-creation of the conceptual foundations of their disciplines. I have, in recognition of this, structured this essay around my own personal experience as an epistemological archaeologist, unearthing the Nordic landscape.

Personal prologue: Finding Norden in America

I grew up in a Scandinavian neighborhood on Staten Island in New York City. The tensions between Norway and Sweden, attendant upon Norwegian independence, were still in living memory, ever present in jokes, taunts and sneers ('A thousand Swedes,' the Norwegian kids would yell to the Swedish kids, 'ran through the weeds, chasing one Norwegian'). Norwegian nationalism was still rife, one scout leader even flew the Norwegian flag at camp (we were in 'nature,' and nature was Norwegian), and a fellow scout had the royal name, Harald Harald Haraldsen. There was a constant stream of immigrants as neighbors sent back for a spouse from the home country, or sent home to their native villages for young blood to work in their businesses – usually one of the building trades. I had friends from both Norway (Torfinn) and Iceland (Ejgil) who knew virtually no English when they entered my class at school. The neighborhood Swedish grocery was perfumed by the big wooden barrels of pickled herring, the lingon berries in the corner and, at Christmas, the lute fish under the counter. Though she died at the time of my birth, my grandmother's Swedish presence was still felt in the meatballs my mother made. However, when asked I preferred to say I was Danish, like my mother's father, to avoid problems with the Norwegians. It didn't hurt, of course, that the name Olwig is Norwegian in origin.

My neighborhood was no Scandinavian ghetto. The neighbors across the street were German, my father was the virtual foster child of French speaking Belgian Jewish World War I refugees and my best friend next door was of Italian and Polish background. Though we were remarkably conscious of the national differences separating we Scandinavians from each other, contact with the other ethnic groups also made us aware of our Scandinavian similarities. We all liked to keep our distance in both physical and social space. We spoke relatively slowly and quietly, we didn't gesticulate, we were tall and phlegmatic and we had nothing to do with gangs or the Mafia. I was always safe when I walked home from school in the shadow of Lance Olsen's enormous body. We were s(t)olid protestants, but we were also divided into a myriad of national Lutheran churches and protestant sects (many had fled to America to escape the iron control of the Norwegian and Swedish state churches). But there were also those who sought to bring us together in an ecumenical Lutheran church, like the one to which my scout troop was attached. In this way a kind of pan-Scandinavian identity developed amongst us, not unlike the pan-Italian identity which had developed amongst the Italian immigrants – that, in turn, helped foster Italian unity back home. This pan-Scandinavian identity was particularly apparent in Minnesota, with its large Nordic population, where I took a Masters degree in Scandinavian/Nordic studies and a doctorate in Geography. You can experience and study Norden as a whole in America in a way that is difficult to do in Norden itself.

Creating a Nordic identity

On Staten Island, we created our own cultural identities, depending on the context. We could be Danes/Norwegians/Swedes, Scandinavians, Staten Islanders, New Yorkers and sometimes Americans, depending on the situation. It was a bit of a shock to come to Denmark and find myself identified as an American who spoke an unknown language called 'American' (I thought I spoke English). Until recently most Europeans would probably brand us as being 'inauthentic,' but in today's post-national society there is an increasing awareness that national and ethnic identities are largely a social construction, and that they are multifaceted and complex, developed through an interplay between European states and their colonial others (including America) (Anderson 1991). This does not mean, as the recent rise of national chauvinism in Europe illustrates, that these national identities are not real to those who share them. We do not, furthermore, create these identities out of thin air. They are the stuff of history, art, and *landscape*. Landscape, as shall be seen, is an expression of both history and art, and it has long played a role in the creation of regional and national identities (Olwig 2002). A Nordic identity, likewise, does not need to be constructed out of thin air. There is plenty of stuff, much of it landscape, from which to shape such an identity (Olwig 1992, Olwig 1995). What is meant by landscape, however, depends upon the sort of identity with which you wish to identify. In the following I will outline an approach to landscape which helped foster a Nordic identity, and which might be called a particularly Nordic approach to landscape. I will contrast this with other ideas of landscape, also present in Norden, which shaped particular nation-state identities, and therefore ultimately worked to divide and dissolve Norden. Landscape is by no means a narrowly geographical concept; it belongs to society at large. In this treatment of the concept I will discuss geography and geographers, but only in the context of the larger discursive field of Nordic and national narratives that frame this discourse, and only as geographers have contributed significantly to that discourse.

Since, at the behest of the editors, I have begun with a personal statement, I suppose the best way to explain my argument might be to continue a bit longer in this personal vein. It all started in 1965–66 during a year of study abroad as a college junior, at Rødding Højskole, in Sønderjylland. This stay was arranged by a Nordic organization called *Scandinavian Seminar*. I was hereby plunged, unwittingly, into a core of issues related to Nordic identity. Rødding Højskole was the first *Folkehøjskole* (People's College), something that became a Nordic institution, and Rødding was located in Sønderjylland, the territorial subject of Pan-Scandinavianism's first cause célèbre. Sønderjylland was the 'landscape' name of the ancient Jutish/Danish landscape territory that marked the boundary to Germany, and the Holy Roman Empire, to the south. Sønderjylland was a landscape in its original Northern European sense of the term, where it was used to refer to a polity and its place, not to scenery. The crux of this conflict, I later discerned lay in the contestation between these two ways of conceptualizing landscape, and this is why this essay focuses upon the tension between the two.

The landscape name of Sønderjylland competed with the German name of 'Schleswig,' that had been given to Sønderjylland, with its mixed Danish, Frisian and German population, when it was formed as a Duchy, controlled by German nobles under the suzerainty of the Danish monarch. Nineteenth century German nationalists saw this territory as being inextricably linked to the culturally German Duchy of Holstein, and they saw both territories as rightfully belonging to the emerging unified state of Germany. Rødding Højskole was born in 1844 of the endeavor to strengthen the Danish/Scandinavian identity of the region. When Bismarck's troops decided to settle the issue by force in 1864, the blood of Nordic volunteers was shed in a fruitless attempt to defend the Nordic identity of this territory. Later, in 1920, a plebiscite returned the northern portion of Schleswig to Denmark, after which it regained its ancient Danish landscape name of Sønderjylland.

I developed some appreciation of the identity politics involved in the struggle over Jutland from Johannes V. Jensen's (1873–1950) writing, which made the ancient history of these landscapes come alive (Jensen 1963 (orig: 1898–1910), Jensen 1964 (orig: 1919–1922)). The writing of Martin A. Hansen (1909–1955), on the other hand, brought out the existential dilemmas experienced by a modern individual searching for place identity in a placeless post-war world (Hansen 1950, Hansen 1952, Hansen 1953, Hansen 1959). For both authors landscape was much more than scenery, it involved identity with place and polity. Neither, furthermore, was a narrow nationalist. Jensen was both a Jutland regionalist and, like Hansen, Nordic in orientation (Kristensen 1974). Hansen, in turn, led me to the work of the early nineteenth century Jutland author, Steen Steensen Blicher (1782–1848), who was a Jutland regionalist, a pan-Scandinavianist and something of a geographer, concerned with both the material and the cultural development of his Jutland homeland (Olwig 1984).

The particularity of Nordic landscape

The Rødding experience made me aware of a Nordic way of thinking about landscape and place that was different both from the British pictorial scenic approach, celebrated today by British 'new cultural' geographers (Cosgrove and Daniels 1988, Setten 1999), and from the layered, blood from soil, approach that had developed in Germany in service of its national cause. Much of what makes the Nordic approach special, I would argue, derives from the peculiar status of Norden itself. Nineteenth century pan-Scandinavianism might have led to the development of a unified Nordic nation-state, which occurred as a consequence of similar movements in Italy and Germany, but this did not happen in Norden. Here the pan-Scandinavianists needed to deal with the reality of two different, well-consolidated state formations (Sweden and Denmark) in a situation in which there was relatively little need for political amalgamation in the face of a mutual external enemy. In Germany, by contrast, there was a situation in which a myriad of relatively weak mini-states, dominated by one nascent nation-state (Prussia), were in confrontation with the well consolidated state apparatus of France. This means that the forces behind the construction of German and Nordic identity, and the conception of landscape mobilized in this construction process, were quite different from each other. There was not the same impetus, in Norden, to create a uniform national ethnic and racial identity, tied to the soil of a particular area of territory, as there was in Germany. Norden also developed differently from Britain.

Britain was constructed as a state during the seventeenth century, largely through a process of imperial appropriation centered on London. A unified, blood and soil ethnic/racial identity never really developed in Britain, but a sense of unity linked to territorial bonding within the physical landscape of the British isles, did supply the basis for a unified British identity as a state (Olwig 2002). Norden, however, was not so neatly unified by a bounded geographic body as Britain, and Norden, furthermore, was divided by two powerful states, each of which had imperial relations to other areas within Norden. Norway had become appended to Denmark much as Scotland had become appended to England, but Denmark lost Norway in the early nineteenth century, just at the time nationalism was becoming a potent force in Europe. Sweden gained Norway at this time, but lost Finland. The Swedish State continued to harbor dreams of leading a great northern empire that, like Britain, would have shared a somewhat bounded geographical territory. Finland remained, however, within the sphere of the Russian Empire until gaining independence in 1917, and the Swedish grip on Norway, with its emerging sense of national identity, was too weak for Sweden to succeed in fully incorporating Norway within a larger imperial state. The result was that both Norway and Sweden eventually emerged as two new sovereign states within Norden, and this process of devolution was to continue with the independence of Iceland and with persistent national rumblings on the part of the Faeroese and the Greenlanders.

As a result of historic circumstance Norden did not develop, like Germany, into a unified nation-state rooted in blood and soil. Nor did it develop into a unified imperial state, like Britain, bound by the physical landscape of a geographical body, but with a weak sense of unified ethnic and racial identity. Norden, instead, dispersed into separate sovereign states, that shared a Nordic identity based upon a common culture and sense of history (Olwig 1992, Olwig 1995). This Nordic identity, however, developed in a tensive relation with forces operating to generate separate nation-state identities within the differing Nordic countries. These separatist nationalistic tendencies were thus kept in check by pan-Scandinavistic feelings, fostered by the historical and cultural ties between the Nordic countries. They were also kept in check by the existence of well-developed central state apparatuses and ideologies, rooted in Renaissance absolutism, that had become well established prior to the rise of nationalism. These state formations neither needed the aid of nationalism to establish their power (as was the case with the greater German state), nor were they, as mercantile states, fully comfortable with the individualistic liberalism that drove nineteenth century nationalism.

The peculiar status of pan-Nordic identity, vis-à-vis other 'pan' identities in Europe, was reflected in the role which the notion of landscape came to play in Norden. The search for the roots of Nordic identity necessarily led back to historical eras prior to the formation of the well defined states that subsequently divided Norden. The result was that older, pre-state, conceptions of landscape that largely died out, or were subordinated, elsewhere in Europe, persisted in Norden. They persisted, however, in contestation with more modern notions of landscape, developed largely in Germany, that were mobilized in the creation of nation-state identities throughout Europe. I will illustrate the differences between these conceptions of landscape, and their importance for the practice of Nordic geographers, through an analysis of the work of two key, internationally prominent, nineteenth century geographical thinkers. They are the Danish geographer Joachim Frederik Schouw (1789–1852) and Dano-Norwegian-German geologist and natural philosopher Henrik Steffens (1773–1845). Both these thinkers could be termed 'proto-landscape geographers' in that the modern notion of what constitutes an academic geographer in general, and a landscape geographer in particular, was just emerging at this time. Schouw is widely recognized as a geographer by geographers today (though botanists call him a botanist), whereas Steffens is usually identified as a geologist, even though prominent geographers of his day regarded him as a major inspiration for their discipline (Olwig 1996, Olwig 1999). The discursive field, identified with landscape geography today, was then just forming through the efforts of people like Schouw and Steffens. Their discourse combined the topics and concepts we now link together in landscape geography, but for them, they formed no pre-given unity. They examined the relation between geology, botany, territory and human society, and they were concerned with the relation between nature and culture, and the visualization of that relation. Reading their work we inevitably think of landscape today because they participated actively in the discourses that produced our modern concept of landscape (Olwig 2002). For them, however, this was one term in a field of concepts that only later was to jell as landscape geography. I will first present Schouw's position, and then that of Steffens. I will then relate their two modes of conceptualizing landscape to the context of present day geographical research in Norden.

Joachim Frederik Schouw

The Author of 'The Earth, Plants and Man' is so well known to all who made any acquaintance with Physical Geography, that no apology seems necessary in presenting a work of his to English readers – the less when it is one so entertaining and instructive as the present (Schouw 1852: preface).

By 1852, when Joachim Frederik Schouw published his *The Earth, Plants and Man* in *Bohn's Scientific Library*, the same prestigious series which published Alexander v. Humboldt's *Cosmos*, his geography had gained a world-wide reputation. He was known as a natural scientist for his brilliant work in plant-geography, but he was probably best known for his writing in the area of 'physical geography,' a term which then did not designate a specialized natural science, but a broad study concerned with the interaction between society and the environment. He had also gained an international reputation through the publication, in many languages, of his highly successful school texts. At a time when geography was often identified with environmental determinism, Schouw argued that society was determining its environment, often with destructive consequences. By emphasizing the role of politics and economics in creating environmental problems, he might rightly be termed a proto-political ecologist.

Schouw's geography, I would argue, represents an early example of a particularly *Nordic* approach to landscape. He gave it an international status that attracted the attention of geographers like George Perkins Marsh, who drew upon the ideas of Schouw, and the work of Nordic geographers more generally (he read the Nordic languages), in developing his pioneering work on the need for environmental conservation *Man and Nature: Or, Physical Geography as Modified by Human Action* (Marsh 1965 (orig. 1864), Olwig 1980, Lowenthal 2000). Schouw, I have elsewhere argued, exercised a direct influence upon his nephew, Enrico Dalgas, founder of the Danish Heath Society. Dalgas followed in his uncle's footsteps by opposing the status quo argument that the Jutland heaths, and their natural environment determined the regional identity of the Jutlanders. He argued that there were social and political reasons for the deterioration of the Jutland soil, and the reclamation of the Jutland heaths, that he spearheaded, proved that a reversal of the social and political situation could also reverse the ecological situation (Olwig 1984).

Schouw, as noted, saw a natural connection between scientific and social concerns. This may reflect an educational background in which he first completed a legal degree (a common education amongst the leading intellectuals of his day), before taking up the natural sciences. This combination of interests was reflected in his engagement as the leader of the proto-democratic regional Assemblies of the Estates, both in Jutland and on Zealand. These were instituted, beginning in the 1830s, by the Danish monarchy, in response to pressure for more representative forms of government by German liberals in the duchies of Schleswig-Holstein. The combination of political and scientific interests was also shown in Schouw's later role as a key figure in the promulgation of Denmark's new democratic constitution of 1848, which simultaneously marked the end of absolute monarchy (Olwig 1999). Schouw, however, was not a nationalist, but rather a (leading) pan-Scandinavianist, heavily engaged not only in the struggle for Sønderjylland, but also in the shaping of a Nordic polity, particularly amongst Norden's natural scientists. Schouw's early

Figure 12.1   *There is more to this map than meets the eye.* **The text for this map reads, in translation: 'Sketch for a Physical-Geographical Map of Denmark, Holsteen and Lauenborg. It has been drawn by Captain O.N. Olsen and published by The Society for the Proper Use of the Freedom of the Press, 1837.' J.F. Schouw was the leader of this society and he bore the brunt of the scandal the publication of this map caused. The scandal owed to the map's use of the ancient Danish 'landscape' name of** *Sønderjylland* **for the area officially known by the German name of Slesvig (as spelled in Danish), which formed part of the duchies of Schleswig-Holstein (as spelled in German). The original is in the collection of the Danish Royal Library.**

research in Italy brought him into contact with the Nordic community in Rome, and this, together with his field research in Norway, provided an important basis for his later pan-Scandinavian scientific and political engagement. Schouw, however, also knew Europe well as a respected contributor to European geography (Schouw 1832) – he was no provincialist. As a pan-Scandinavianist, Schouw opposed narrow nationalism, and the attendant environmental determinism of national romantics such as Henrik Steffens. Schouw wrote, in response to this determinism:

> Denmark's nature is therefore not Scandinavian in the narrow sense, it is more similar to the German than to the Norwegian or Swedish. But then one should also conclude that the Danish people are more German than Scandinavian? This would be so if it were the case that it were true that a people's character is determined by or is significantly dependent upon the nature of that land which the people inhabit. But even though this view is very widespread and continually taken as given by philosophers, historians, natural scientists and poets, it is nevertheless a misconception which has only become so common because the relationship between nature and man is still in need of scientific treatment. With regard to this subject conclusions have been drawn with a superficiality which would not be tolerated in any other science (Schouw 1845: 8).

Schouw argued against the idea that society was determined by nature. Quite the contrary, he pointed out, different nationalities can share similar environments (as in Switzerland) and similar nationalities can share divergent environments (as in Scandinavia). For Schouw, the character of such societies:

> . . . has its soil, its intellectual soil in *History*, out of which it springs, – has its intellectual climate in *Language*, in which it lives and moves (Schouw 1845: 15).

At the time Schouw wrote the above words he was deeply involved in the revival of Danish representative political institutions through his engagement as leader of the regional Assembly of the Estates in both Viborg, Jutland and Roskilde, Zealand. This was a time when freedom of speech was tightly controlled by the state, and Schouw was a central figure in the battle for this freedom. Language was fundamental to the debate practiced at the Assembly of the Estates (the word 'parliament' comes from the French word for speech), where Schouw became a controversial figure because of his penchant for speaking his mind. Viborg was the ancient site of the Jutland '*Landsting,*' the judicial assembly of the *ting* (*thing* or *moot* in English) that had shaped the Jutland 'landscape law' which was foundational to the rule of law in Denmark. The political activists of Schouw's day were conscious of the historic parallels between the activities of the ancient *Landsting* and the modern Assembly of the States (the Danish parliament is now again called a *ting*). The 'landscape law' of Jutland, and similar polities throughout Scandinavia, amply illustrate Schouw's point concerning the role of history and language in shaping the constitution of a land's identity as a landscape – a place shaped, both socially and physically, by a polity.

The text of the 'landscape laws' of Norden, as some of the earliest documents written in the vernacular, subsequently became a repository not only of law, but of language. As repositories of custom, law and language, these laws provided inspiration to those who sought to revive the common cultural and social institutions of the Nordic peoples. The landscape districts of Norden thus literally grew out of the intellectual soil of history, and had their intellectual climate in language, as it came to expression in the articulation of the customary laws through which the land was built and shaped. I would argue that this conception of landscape as a polity (e.g. Sønderjylland), constituted through social practice, gave rise to approaches to landscape, like that of Schouw, that are fundamentally opposed to environmental determinism and to the blood and soil nationalism that it fosters. The existence of differing landscape polities, each with its own history and cultural expression, violates the uniformity fostered by the nation-state, as well as the inviolability of state boundaries. The landscapes of Norden have more in common between them, culturally and socially, than the nation-states that divide them. I will return to this fundamentally Nordic approach to landscape in the conclusion, but before doing so I will outline the development of an alternative, predominantly German, approach to landscape, that has competed with the Nordic approach outlined above. This approach owes some of its origin to the breakup of the Danish imperial state, and therefore is of intrinsic relevance here. A key figure in the development of this notion of landscape was Henrik Steffens.

Henrik Steffens

When Schouw referred to the 'widespread and continually taken as given' ideas of environmental determinism spread by 'philosophers, historians, natural scientists and poets,' he was probably thinking of Henrik Steffens (1773–1845) – who was engaged in all these activities. Steffens was the product of the Danish imperial state. His father (a doctor and public servant of the Danish state) was from the culturally German Duchy of Holstein, his mother was from the ancient landscape of Zealand, Denmark (his cousin was the Danish religious and educational reformer, N.F.S. Grundtvig, founder of the *højskole* movement) and he himself grew up in Norway. Steffens moved to Denmark for his secondary education and early university studies in botany, before moving to Germany for his doctoral studies in geology. The emergence of nationalism as a political force during the late eighteenth century raised important issues for Steffens concerning his personal identity as the subject of a unified Danish state, in much the same way as the nationalism forcing the breakup of the Yugoslavian state has shaken the identity of those who saw themselves as Yugoslavian, rather than Albanian, Bosnian etc. Steffens' extraordinary memoir, *Was ich erlebte: aus der Erinnerung niedergeschrieben* (Steffens 1840–45, Steffens 1840–1844, Steffens 1874 (orig. 1840–1844)), gives a vivid impression of this University of Copenhagen student's dilemma when he was forced, for example, to choose between a New Year's party held by the Danish or one held by the Norwegian students, and of his difficulty dealing with the jibes he received when he tried to go to both. He was deeply hurt by the vehement anti-German sentiments that began to emerge at the turn of the century, and the taunts he received for having written his doctoral dissertation (still regarded as a geological classic) in German. He did not, himself, feel a conflict between his Norwegian, Danish and German identities, but he was being forced to choose sides. He had hitherto been comfortable with multiple identities, each appropriate to a given context. He was a child of

Norway, but as a citizen he was Danish, and as a geologist and natural philosopher, he was German.

Steffens would have agreed with Schouw that Denmark's nature is similar to much of Germany's. His geological studies had taught him how strata of rock and soil were built up layer by layer, and his botanical studies showed him how well attuned plants were to the physical geography of the uppermost layer. His personal experience as a romantic wanderer in the beech forests of both Zealand and Holstein, where he found rocks embedded in the soil that were reminiscent of those in Norway, strengthened his perception of a unity of nature growing up out of the rock and soil. This unity also encompassed Steffens himself as an outgrowth of this nature and as an experiencing subject (Steffens 1840–45: v. 1, 279, v. 3, 267, 309). Steffens' experiences and studies therefore brought him to a conclusion opposite to that which Schouw reached. As Steffens put it:

> It is weak language to say that through the influence of physical conditions human actions assume their character. Man is *wholly* a product from the hands of nature. Only in his being this wholly – not partly, but wholly – do we confess that in him nature centers all her mysteries. And so it became plain to me that natural science is bringing a new element into history, which is to become the basis of all knowledge of our race. History and nature must be in perfect concord, for they are really one (Steffens 1874 (orig. 1840–1844): 100).

Steffens found resonance for his ideas amongst the philosophers of the emerging German Romantic Movement. Geology then enjoyed something of the same influence upon the metaphysics and philosophy of his day as physics does today. Steffens' geology lent substance to the speculations of such romantic philosophers as Friedrich Schelling (1775–1854) (Steffens 1840–45: v. 4, 81), and it also brought him into contact with the artistic circles identified with the nature mysticism of the landscape artist Caspar David Friederich. Steffens thrived in this intellectual environment, becoming one of the leading natural philosophers of his day. He brought these new ideas back to Denmark, and Norden more generally, in a series of historic lectures held in Copenhagen in 1803. These were attended by everybody who was anybody in the intellectual circles of the Dano-Norwegian capital of Copenhagen, and they marked the breakthrough of romanticism in Norden. Steffens gave expression to an emerging concept of landscape as pictorial scenery, built up in layers, as on a stage, in which nature is the foundation for culture. It was within this scenic space that nature and culture were bound into a single national unity. As he put in one of these lectures:

> Just as the individual human's existence is a string of incidences that have as an internal unifying principle the inner being of the individual itself, in the same way the history of nations consists of a string of changing events, that involves not only that of the single individual, but all of mankind. . . . In this eternal reciprocal interaction, in which the internal creative principle is unknown to us, the whole of mankind has a compelling effect upon the single nation and the nation has a compelling effect upon each single individual. . . . Through this interaction of the whole upon the individual, and the individual upon the whole, is generated an identical picture-history, which presupposes the entirety of nature as the foundation for all final existence, and all of humanity as the expression of this interaction itself. The expression of the coexistence of all these individuals' interaction in history and nature is *space* – eternity's continually *recumbent* picture. But the whole *is*

only an eternal chain of changing events. Yes it *is* this constant alternating exchange, this eternal succession of transformations itself. The constant archetype for these changes is *time* – eternity's constant moving, flowing and changing picture (Steffens 1905: 91).

Steffens' lectures marked a turning point in the career of the young poet, Adam Oehlenschläger (1779–1850), who gained fame throughout Europe. One of his poems now forms the text of the Danish national song, *There is a Lovely Land*, and it illustrates quite well the role of pictorial landscape in the nationalist use of romanticism. Each verse in the song takes place within a different landscape scene, each illustrating the step by step progress of Danish society from primitive Viking society to a modern nation-state. It is notable how this song differs from the Danish Royal anthem, *King Christian Stood at the High Mast*, written a generation earlier by Johannes Ewald (1743–1781). The royal anthem makes the monarch the embodiment of national identity, whereas *There is a Lovely Land* focuses not upon the monarch, but on the physical landscape that produces a people of a particular character. 'As long as the beech reflects its top in the waves of blue,' we are told, 'Our ancient Denmark shall remain.'

Figure 12.2   This sketch is of a painting from 1842 by the national romantic painter J. Th. Lundbye (who died in a war with the Germans over the national status of Schleswig-Holstein). The painting is called, in translation: 'Danish Coast.' It clearly shows the layered character of the landscape as conceptualized by Steffens. The image of a grove of beach trees (a tree that is heavily laden with Danish nationalist symbolism), reflecting in the sea, is central to the national song composed by Adam Oehlenschläger.

The implications of this conceptualization of landscape were made apparent in a speech on 'Danishness' held by another figure that attended Steffens' lectures, Oehlenschläger's brother-in-law, the physicist and natural philosopher, Hans Christian Ørsted (1777–1851). Ørsted's speech begins with a warning against an exaggerated cultivation of Danish culture as expressed in language. Danishness is an expression of the evolution of the Danish people within the framework of the physical nature of Denmark. It is not something that is easily disturbed by the whims of history. It is most certainly not something that found greater expression in some distant past, as some unnamed critics are said to claim. 'The Danes,' he proclaims, are living in a 'shining' present and 'have never been more Danish than now.' The result is a 'development which is in equal parts harmonious and genuinely Danish: loving, peaceful, and moderate' (*kjærlig, rolig, maadeholden*) (Ørsted 1836: 211). According to Ørsted, 'the character of the Danish people is in complete concord with the natural position of the land of their birth' (Ørsted 1836: 212):

> The Danish land has a friendly nature, the grand is revealed here seldomly except in the heavens and the sea, and the horrible is nearly excluded, only the sea shows itself at times in all its terribleness. But there are an endless number of points from which the Dane has either a grand or a smiling view over the blue surface. Our green fields and richly clad beech trees have never lacked deserved praise (Ørsted 1836: 213).

It was this 'land' which the ancient Danes chose to dwell in because it appealed to them:

> Surrounded by this nature the folk have now lived and developed for hundreds of years, shouldn't one expect a concord between them? . . . . Pray the Dane never be ashamed of these qualities (Ørsted 1836: 213).

Ørsted and Oehlenschläger, like Steffens, wished to preserve Denmark as a 'whole state,' including Schleswig-Holstein, and thus they emphasized the unifying landscape, with its peaceful contours. Steffens, however, was eventually to return to Germany, where he helped spark a more militant nationalism, directed against the Napoleon, Denmark's ally. For Steffens the Prussian State and the German people came to form a necessary unity (Steffens 1840–45: v. 6, 127).

The historical background for Steffens' landscape concept:
From landscape as polity to landscape as scenery

I have now distinguished between two approaches to landscape. The first was rooted in the ancient Nordic conception of landscape as a polity and the place shaped, both physically/visually and socially, by its laws and practice. The second is a pictorialized scene in which it is the physical environment that shapes the people who act out the drama of its existence upon its scenic surface. In the first conception, society is made up of nested polities, amalgamated within larger political associations, and in the other it forms the basis for thinking of the state as a unity of folk and territory (Olwig 2001). In the first, the emphasis is upon the representative legal institutions that develop out of the need to regulate relations within a society and between this society and its environment. In this sense of landscape, customary law and social practice shape the land as polity. In the second sense, the landscape is represented by a pictorial image, which encompasses a spatial structure, bonding the individual and the nation, as well as a temporal process of development from nature to culture. These two modes of representation grew out of the Renaissance contestation between the state of the regent (or lord) and the parliamentary representative body of the estates, concerning which was to be the legitimate expression of the polity. An historian gives the following description of this contestation:

> The *Land* comprised its lord and people, working together in the military and judicial spheres. But in other matters we see the two as opposing parties and negotiating with each other. Here the Estates appear as the 'Land' in a new sense, counterposed to the prince, and through this opposition they eventually formed the corporate community of the territorial Estates, the *Landschaft* [*landscape* in modern English]. At this point the old unity of the *Land* threatened to break down into a duality, posing the key question that became crucial beginning in the sixteenth century: who represented the *Land,* the prince or the Estates? If the prince, then the *Landschaft* would become a privileged corporation; if the *Landschaft*, then it would become lord of the *Land* (Brunner 1992 (orig. 1965): 341).

The scenic/pictorial representation of landscape emerged from the need of the state of the monarch/prince to represent its legitimacy in a way that could compete with the representative polity of the '*Landschaft*'/landscape (Olwig 1996, Olwig 2001, Olwig 2002).

Against the landscape of a polity built on custom, the Renaissance State of the monarch/prince could offer a state built on 'natural' statutory law based on the absolute principles of Roman law and the church. These principles were founded upon the natural spatial laws of geometry and mathematics, as still reflected in such terms as 'ruler,' 'regent,' 'justice,' 'right.' These were ancient principles, that had long legitimated the rule of European regents, by which the regent lay down the straight lines according to which his temple and state were to be drawn. According to Emile Benveniste, 'This is a concept at once concrete and moral: the "straight line" represents the norm, while the *regula* is "the instrument used to *trace* the straight line", which fixes the "rule"' (Benveniste 1973: 312). R*enaissance* regents strove to facilitate the r*ebirth* of this ancient order, based on geometrical conceptions of a natural, god given, order. This effort was greatly facilitated by the early fifteenth century rediscovery of Ptolemy's classical Greek work on geography, and with it the basis for the modern map, based on geometry. The development of surveying and mapping techniques in turn facilitated the mapping and regulation of the 'land' under the regent's domain into *reg*ions, thereby facilitating a transition in the meaning of *land* and *landscape* from designations for a polity, to the designation of a geometric area of territory or property (as in six acres of *land*) owned by the individual regent, or one of his minions (Olwig 1993).

The Renaissance development of the techniques of surveying and mapping not only contributed to the practical control of the apparatus of the state; it also contributed to the ideological justification for that control. This was because these techniques also enabled the construction of perspective pictorial, mirror like, representations of the land. The miraculous illusion of 3D space created by the geometries of perspective further contributed to the impression of godlike rule cultivated by Renaissance rulers through the use of such 'landscape' representations as the backdrop for theatrical productions.

Renaissance regents and ruling elites, beginning in Italy, spent great sums on the construction of a new form of theater with a perspective scenic backdrop. In this theater the throne of state was strategically placed so as to give the regent a commanding view of the scene just at the point where the lines of perspective converge, creating the maximum illusion of spatial depth. These theaters created an image of the larger 'theater of state' ('theater' became a favorite metaphor of the time, applied from everything to atlases to battlefields) under the powerful controlling gaze of the regent. When the English parliament challenged the authority of King James to establish himself as the regent of a British state, uniting England/ Wales and Scotland, the King thus responded with elaborate theatrical productions in which he was represented ruling wisely, with his commanding gaze, over landscape scenes of a united Britain.

Landscape scenery was used to visualize Britain as a physical geographical body, equivalent to the body politic of the regent, under him as its head of state. The regent was placed, within the theater of state, in a kind of spatial limbo. As a privileged individual agent he is located at a distance from the landscape scene upon which he gazes, at the same time as he is a corporal presence within the body politic, staged upon the landscape scene. This use of landscape scenery to represent and legitimate state power was by no means limited to Britain. James' theater was the construction of Inigo Jones, the Royal surveyor/architect who, though trained in Italy, and English by birth, came to the British court through the efforts of James' wife, Queen Anne of Denmark, who headhunted him from the court of her brother, King Christian IV of Denmark. Theater was well established as means of representing and legitimating power over the polity at the courts of Anne's family members in northern Europe, and throughout Europe more generally (Olwig 1996, Olwig 2002). James, I believe, was inspired by the success of his Danish in-laws in uniting Norway with Denmark and Schleswig-Holstein, something he wished to do vis-à-vis Scotland and England– Wales. It was only natural that he bring in expertise, from the courts of his in-laws to help him architect the theater of a unified British state.

The reconfiguration of the landscape picture

The spatial structure of James' and Jones' theater of state is not unlike the pictorial conception of the nation-state delineated by Steffens, two centuries later. Steffens' picture, however, has been reconfigured so that it is now no longer the regent, but the bourgeois individual, who occupies a limbic position. This figure, as an individual, is located in an external position to the pictorial scene, but is nevertheless incorporated, through a process of interaction, into the spatial frame of the nation. The idea of picturing gained a special valence at this time in German history, when leading elements of society, including Steffens, were seeking to build a territorial unified state under the guidance of a class of educated bourgeoisie. The word for picture *Bild* referred, at this time, not only to a graphic depiction, but was also identified with words like *Bildung* and *bilden* which suggested the idea of creativity, growth and development, and which were related to the English word *build* and the

Scandinavian *bygge* (as in: 'With law shall the land be *built/bygge*). It is also the root of words used to describe the quality of personal development (*gebildet*) which was vital to the development of a bourgeois, individualistic, German identity, and which might be translated as 'education' or 'cultivation' (*Bildung*) (Grimm and Grimm 1855: Bild, Markus 1993: 13–15). For Steffens the interaction between the individual, the nation and nature is quite literally an *imag(e)inative* pictorial process of *Bildung*. This 'picture' posited the infinite potentiality of future development in time and space that was dialectically rooted in the nature of an ancient Germanic past rooted in the geologic foundation of the soil (Steffens 1840–45: v. 5, 306–332). This idea was reinforced in the case of landscape picturing by the fact that the suffix *schaft* in *Landschaft* is related to the word *schaffen* which means to create, or shape and thus is somewhat synonymous with the idea of *Bildung* as a creative process (Olwig 1993).

Steffens' reconfiguration of the conception of landscape, as a spatialized unity of the individual citizen and the national collectivity, appealed to those seeking to build a bourgeoisie nation-state based on the liberalistic ideals of the time. These ideas, by the same token, did not appeal to the guardians of the Danish absolutist state, who sought to maintain the regent's central position within the theater of state. They made Steffens *persona non grata* in Denmark-Norway, forcing him to return to Germany, where he became an ardent German patriot (Steffens 1840–45: v. 3, 292, v. 6, 113, 151). Steffens' banishment from Denmark-Norway points, I believe, to significant differences between Scandinavia and Germany that were to affect the way landscape was conceptualized. As noted, Scandinavia, unlike Germany, remained divided into sovereign states under separate sovereigns and a well-established state bureaucracy. There was never a realistic possibility for the development of a monolithic Scandinavian (or Nordic) state founded on the monolithic national unity of individuals within the uniform space of a single national territory. The result was that German national romantic ideas, like those promoted by Steffens, were only of limited appeal in Norden. They might appeal to the national liberals, but they would not appeal to the guardians of the monarchical states, with which liberal democracy was forced to cooperate, and they did not, as has been seen, appeal to the pan-Scandinavianists.

Nordic landscape geography

Academic geography grew to prominence in Germany as part of the process of nineteenth century nation-state building, in which it served both practical and ideological needs. It served the needs, on the one hand, of a state bureaucracy that wished to form a picture of the physical and social circumstances of the different lands that were amalgamated within the emerging unified German State. It also, as has been seen above, provided a means of linking a newly constructed unified nation-state identity to a particular territorial body of soil. The laws governing the German geographers' *Landschaft* were those of a determinant nature which could readily be applied to the nature of the soil out of which the national/ethnic blood of a unified German nation flowed. This pictorializing of landscape was central, as noted, to the whole notion of education as the *Bildung*, through which the nation-state would be built, and it was thus of central importance in the schools.

German geography provided an important impetus and model for the development of geography in Norden, where it also played a role, particularly as a school subject, in the development of Norden's differing nation-states. Since this essay focuses upon the 'Nordic' conception of landscape, I will not detail the history of landscape geography developed on the German model here (Framke 1979, Hansen 1994), but it is important to recognize its presence in Norden during the rise of the nation-state. The tensive relation between these two modes of thinking about landscape is key, I believe, to the reflexivity that characterizes Nordic landscape geography. It is this reflexivity that creates an awareness of the role of language and history in shaping our concepts. They are not given by nature. This is illustrated, I believe, by the parallel reception of German ideas about landscape in Anglo-America.

German landscape geography, particularly through the influence of the early work of Carl Sauer in America, also became influential throughout the English speaking world in the course of the early twentieth century (Sauer 1925). Sauer, however, further developed his notion of landscape, particularly through the influence of the work of George Perkins Marsh who provided a means of thinking about landscape that emphasized human social and political agency, and conceptual reflexivity, rather than the determinism of a foundational environment. Students of Sauer's, such as Yi-Fu Tuan and David Lowenthal (who wrote a biography of Marsh for his doctoral dissertation), continued this reflexive line of thinking about landscape. Marsh, as noted earlier, was influenced by Schouw, and by his broad reading in Nordic geography, and it was through Lowenthal and Marsh that I became aware of this parallel Nordic tradition (Olwig 1976, Olwig 1980).

The renewal of Nordic landscape geography

The closing decades of the twentieth century witnessed something of a reversal in the role earlier given the nation-state in Norden. Globalism, and increased integration into a larger Europe, favored the down-playing of the nation-state and created conditions fostering the re-construction of historical regional identities. The new Europe has also, however, brought a cosmopolitanism that has alienated some, bringing about a reactionary revival of nationalism in some circles, while simultaneously creating a counter-awareness of larger, non-nationalistic, cultural and political identities, such as those that characterize Norden.

The 'Nordic' approach to geography, that I have identified with Schouw, is characterized by a concern with history, custom/law, and language and culture as they work together in forming a landscape polity and its geographic place. I have focused upon the ideas of Schouw for heuristic reasons, but he was part of a large and diverse pan-Scandinavian movement, and it is clear that he was not alone. Each of the geographers I include below as renewing this 'Nordic' approach would, I am sure, cite a different pantheon of predecessors that have inspired their work. One should, furthermore, be careful not to limit oneself to predecessors amongst geographers. The idea of landscape belongs as much to literature and art as to geography. I have mentioned the Danish authors Martin A. Hansen, Johannes V.

Jensen and Steen Steensen Blicher, but each country and region invariably has similar writers, not to mention painters. A good case in point would be the influence of the writer Selma Lagerlöf (1858–1940) upon the perception of the Värmland landscape (and the landscapes of Sweden more generally) would be a good case in point (Bladh forthcoming).

The 'Nordic' approach to landscape is concerned, to an important extent, with the empirical historical study of the development of particular polities and how these polities shaped the environments of the places where they dwelled. Such approaches are also, due to their interest in the shaping force of a polity and its culture, concerned with the way polities perceive and conceptualize landscape. Landscape is thus not a concept given by nature, but something that is created and constructed, consciously and unconsciously, by polities. There is thus both an empirical and a reflexive theoretical/philosophical dimension to this approach to landscape. This has been illustrated through the example of Schouw's empirical and theoretical interests, including his critique of the approach to landscape exemplified by Steffens.

The history of Norden precedes that of the modern Nordic states, and transcends the boundaries of those states. An historical approach therefore tends to seek out the political formations, such as those of the 'landscape' polities, that preceded those of the state, and thus tends to share archaeology's interest in early history. An important point of departure for an historically grounded study of Norden is thus the landscape polities – variously known as *landskap* (Swedish), *landskab* (Danish), *fylke/lag* (Norwegian) – that eventually were amalgamated into the differing Nordic states, but which continue to maintain a somewhat separate cultural identity (the Aaland Islands, in fact, still maintain a somewhat independent legal identity). These landscape polities, as I have noted, provided the legal traditions that were later incorporated as the legal foundation of the state. The landscape was not, however, the only form of polity of interest to this form of geography. Sub-units of the landscape such as the 'bygd' (of particular interest in Norway), the village and the hundred are all examples of polities that provide a useful point of departure for historical studies going back beyond the origins of the modern state (Jones forthcoming). Such studies, in turn, provide a useful background for studying developments since the origin of this state. In the following I will name a number of those who represent primarily contemporary examples of 'Nordic' landscape geographers. The list is personal, and by no means complete, but it provides a starting point for further exploration in this area.

An example of what I have termed a 'Nordic,' historical approach to landscape is Ulf Sporrong's studies of the basis in custom and law for the settlement patterns in the Swedish *landskap* of Dalarna. His approach helps explains the particular identity of Dalarna within Sweden up to this day, as well as the similarities between Dalarna and places outside the borders of the modern Swedish state (Sporrong and Wennersten 1995, Sporrong 1998). The same concern with the continuity of law characterizes Michael Jones' study of terrestrial uplift on the eastern Baltic coastlands of Finland (Jones 1977). The work of Sporrong, Jones, as well as that of Garbriel Bladh and Thomas Germundsson, illustrates how approaches to landscape as polity and place can be combined with approaches which take scenic, terrestrial forms into account (Jones 1991, Germundsson and Riddersporre 1996, Germundsson forthcoming). Bladh's work on Finnish communities on the Swedish-Norwegian borderlands illustrates how this approach tends to transcend the boundaries of the nation-state. My own studies of the 'ideological' landscape of Jutland, Denmark, combine an interest in Jutland as an ancient polity with an interest in the ways in which perceptions and conceptions of the nature of Jutland, and its once extensive heathlands, have been continually constructed and reconstructed, throughout the centuries. These perceptions and ideas have, in turn, exerted considerable influence upon the shaping and reshaping of the Jutland environment (Olwig 1984, Olwig 1986). Ari Lehtinen's studies of the northern forests of Finland likewise build upon an historical understanding of changing perceptions and conceptions of this area as a polity, and the way they relate to changes in the use and abuse of its environment (Lehtinen 1991, Lehtinen 1992). Though he has not been as interested in the physical and visual environment, Anssi Paasi's historical interest in the construction and reconstruction of Finish regional identities also belongs within this geographical tradition (Paasi 1996, Paasi forthcoming).

Geographers with a reflexive interest in landscape as an historical expression of language, also belong, I would argue, within this Nordic tradition. Here, I would include Bjørg Lien Hanssen's study of state authority's attempt to evaluate and classify the landscapes of Norway, and Tom Mels' analysis of the ideological construction of Swedish nature as preserved in national parks (Hanssen 1998, Mels 1999). Michael Jones and Karoline Daugstad's analysis of the differing uses of the word landscape by Norwegian administrators and researchers should also be included here (Jones 1991, Jones 1988: 1328, Jones and Daugstad 1996). Daugstad's work on the perception of the Norwegian summer farm as a feminine domain also belongs within this category (Daugstad 2000). This approach to landscape provides a useful antidote to the tendency to essentialize the landscape as the natural embodiment of national values, that comes from the layered scenic approach. This is a growing issue, as noted earlier, because of the rising interest in heritage, a subject that has been of great concern to Mats Widgren (Widgren 1997). This very process of reflexivity, that leads the geographer to examine the construction of the territorial identities that become reified as heritage, also leads to an awareness of the relativity of the way we think about landscape, and the Nordic focus of that interest. Nordic approaches to landscape geography are by no means applicable only to the study of Norden. Widgren, as I write this, is thus doing fieldwork in Africa, and my next book is about the relationship between Nordic, German, British and American ideas of landscape (Olwig 2002).

A reflexive approach to landscape requires that one not just study different empirical examples of landscape, or applications of the concept in concrete situations, but also examine the meaning of the concept itself (Olwig 2000). Through such work new ideas of landscape are conceived and reconceived, and new constructions put into practice (Jones and Olwig forthcoming). There is no Nordic essence, nor an essential Nordic landscape geography. Norden is not given, it is what our predecessors have made of it, and what we make of it. The idea of Norden has not had the same institutional support as that of the nation, and for this reason much of Norden's history, and the Nordic idea of landscape, remains untold – though we do have the Nordic Council, and *Nordisk Samhällsgeografisk Tidskrift*. Books published in Norden about Norden, or Nordic Landscape, are few and far between (Hastrup 1992, Karlsson 1992, Linde-Laursen and Nilsson 1995). Work needs to be done to reconstruct that history. In some ways it is easier to see Norden from the outside, where national identities become weaker, and common denominators stronger. The more cosmopolitan our world becomes, however, the more we all become outsiders, and the more we are able to reflect on the value of our more local identities. This might explain the renewal of interest in Nordic landscape.

References

Anderson, Benedict (1991). *Imagined Communities: Reflections on the Origin and Spread of Nationalism*, revised. London, Verso.

Becker-Christensen, Henrik (1981). *Skandinaviske Drømme og Politiske Realiteter: Den politiske skandinavisme i Danmark 1830–1850*, Aarhus, Arusia.

Benveniste, Emile (1973). *Indo-European Language and Society*. Elizabeth Palmer, London, Faber & Faber.

Bladh, Gabriel (forthcoming). 'The "Landskap" of Värmland and its Regional Landscape Identity'. *Nordscapes: Thinking Landscape and Regional Identity on the Northern Edge of Europe*. Michael Jones and Kenneth R. Olwig, Eds. Minneapolis, University of Minnesota Press.

Brunner, Otto (1992 (orig. 1965)). *Land and Lordship: Structures of Governance in Medieval Austria*. Howard Kaminsky and James Van Horn Melton, trans. Philadelphia, University of Pennsylvania Press.

Cosgrove, Denis and Stephen Daniels, Eds. (1988). *The Iconography of Landscape*, Cambridge, Cambridge University Press.

Daugstad, Karoline (2000). *Mellom romantikk og realisme: Om seterlandskapet som ideal og realitet*, Trondheim, NTNU.

Erslev, Edvard (1886). *Jylland: Studier og Skildringer til Danmarks Geografi*, Copenhagen, Jacob Erslevs Forlag.

Framke, W. (1979). *Rager den tyske geografis udvikling den faglige diskussion i Danmark?: Et debatoplæg*, Aarhus, Geografisk Institut, Aarhus Universitet.

Germundsson, Tomas (forthcoming). 'Scania – Flows of History and Flows of Traffic: Competing Regional Identities in An Old "Danish" Landscape'. *Nordscapes: Thinking Landscape and Regional Identity on the Northern Edge of Europe*. Michael Jones and Kenneth R. Olwig, Eds. Minneapolis, University of Minnesota Press.

Germundsson, Tomas and Mats Riddersporre (1996). 'Landscape, Process, and Preservation'. *Landscape Analysis in the Nordic Countries. Integrated Research in a Holistic Perspective*. Margareta Ihse, Ed. Stockholm, Swedish Council for Planning and Coordination of Research. Report 96:1: 98–108.

Grimm, Jacob and Wilhelm Grimm (1855). *Deutsches Wörterbuch*, Leipzig, S. Hirzel.

Hansen, Fran (1994). 'Landskabsgeografi med eksempler fra Danmark og Finland'. *Traditioner i Nordisk kulturgeografi*. Jan Öhman, Ed. Uppsala, Nordisk Samhällsgeografisk Tidskrift: 71–81.

Hansen, Martin A. (1950). *Løgneren*, Copenhagen, Gyldendal.

Hansen, Martin A. (1952). *Orm og Tyr*, Copenhagen, Gyldendal.

Hansen, Martin A. (1953). *Dansk Vejr*, Copenhagen, Hasselbalch.

Hansen, Martin A. (1959). *Af Folkets Danmarkshistorie*, Copenhagen, Gyldendal.

Hansen, Viggo (1970). 'Hedens Opståen og Omfang'. *Danmarks Natur: Hede, Overdrev og Eng*. T.J. Meyer and Arne Nørrevang, Eds. Copenhagen, Politken. **7**.

Hanssen, Bjørg Lien (1998). *Values, Ideology and Power Relations in Cultural Landscape Evaluations*, Bergen, Department of Geography.

Hastrup, Kirsten, Ed. (1992). *Den nordiske verden*. ed., Copenhagen, Gyldendal.

Jensen, Johannes V. (1963 (orig: 1898–1910)). *Himmerlandshistorier*, Copenhagen, Gyldendal.
Jensen, Johannes V. (1964 (orig: 1919–1922)). *Den Lange Rejse*, Copenhagen, Gyldendal.
Jones, Michael (1977). *Finland, Daughter of the Sea*, Folkestone, Dawson – Archon.
Jones, Michael (1988). 'Progress in Norwegian cultural landscape studies'. *Norsk Geografisk Tidsskrift 42*; 153–169.
Jones, Michael (1991). 'The elusive reality of landscape. Concepts and approaches in landscape research.' *Norsk Geografisk Tidsskrift* 45 : 229–244.
Jones, Michael (forthcoming). 'Landscape – morphology or community? The role of land rights, customs and local institutions in shaping the Nordic landscape'. *Nordscapes: Thinking Landscape and Regional Identity on the Northern Edge of Europe*. Michael Jones and Kenneth R. Olwig, Eds. Minneapolis, University of Minnesota Press.
Jones, Michael and Karoline Daugstad (1996). 'Cultural landscape under administration – a conceptual analysis'. *Landscape Analysis in the Nordic Countries*. Margarete Ihse, Ed. Stockholm, FRN: 162–188.
Jones, Michael and Kenneth R. Olwig, Eds. (forthcoming). *Nordscapes: Thinking Landscape and Regional Identity on the Northern Edge of Europe* eds., Minneapolis, University of Minnesota Press.
Karlsson, Svenolof, Ed. (1992). *The Source of Liberty: The Nordic Contribution to Europe* ed., Stockholm, The Nordic Council.
Kristensen, Sven Møller (1974). *Den Store Generation*, Copenhagen, Gyldendal.
Lehtinen, Ari (1992). 'Questions on Environment and Democracy within Northern Boreal Forestry: The Finnish Forest Conflict Becomes and International Issue'. *The Environment and International Security*. A. Hjort af Ornäs and S. Lodgaard, Eds. Uppsala, EIS (EPOS), Uppsala University: 67–78.
Lehtinen, Ari Akusti (1991). 'Northern Natures.' *Fennia* 169 (1): 57–169.
Linde-Laursen, Anders and Jan Olof Nilsson, Eds. (1995). *Nordic Landscapes: Cultural studies of place* ed., Copenhagen, Nordic Council of Ministers.
Lowenthal, David (2000). *George Perkins Marsh: Prophet of Conservation*, Seattle, University of Seattle Press.
Markus, Gyorgy (1993). 'Culture: The Making and the Make-Up of a Concept (An Essay in Historical Semantics).' *Dialectical Anthropology* 18 : 3–29.
Marsh, George Perkins (1965 (orig. 1864)). *Man and Nature: Or, Physical Geography as Modified by Human Action*, Cambridge, Mass., Belknap Press.
Mels, Tom (1999). *Wild Landscapes: The Cultural Nature of Swedish Natural Parks*, Lund, Lund University Press.
Merriam-Webster (1995). *Collegiate Dictionary*, Tenth Edition. Springfield, MA, Merriam-Webster.
Olwig, Kenneth (1976). 'Menneske/natur problematikken i geografi.' *Fagligt forum: kulturgeografiske hæfter* (9): 5–15.
Olwig, Kenneth (1986). *Hedens natur: Om natursyn og naturanvendelse gennem tiderne*, Copenhagen, Teknisk forlag.
Olwig, Kenneth (1992). 'The European Nation's Nordic Nature'. *The Source of Liberty: The Nordic Contribution to Europe*. Svenolof Karlsson, Ed. Stockholm, The Nordic Council: 158–182.
Olwig, Kenneth Robert (1980). 'Historical geography and the society/nature "problematic": the perspective of J.F. Schouw, G.P. Marsh and E. Reclus.' *Journal of Historical Geography* 6 (1): 29–45.
Olwig, Kenneth Robert (1984). *Nature's Ideological Landscape: A Literary and Geographic Perspective on its Development and Preservation on Denmark's Jutland Heath*, London, George Allen & Unwin.

Olwig, Kenneth Robert (1993). 'Sexual Cosmology: Nation and Landscape at the Conceptual Interstices of Nature and Culture, or: What does Landscape Really Mean?'. *Landscape: Politics and Perspectives*. Barbara Bender, Ed. Oxford, Berg: 307–343.

Olwig, Kenneth Robert (1995). 'Landscape, *landskap*, and the body'. *Nordic Landscopes: Cultural studies of place*. Jan Olof Nilsson and Anders Linde-Laursen, Eds. Copenhagen, Nordic Council of Ministers: 154–169.

Olwig, Kenneth Robert (1996). 'Recovering the Substantive Nature of Landscape.' *Annals of the Association of American Geographers* 86 (4): 630–653.

Olwig, Kenneth R. (1999). 'Joachim Frederik Schouw – Dansk Geograf?'. *Danske Geografiske Forskere*. Sven Illeris, Ed. Frederiksberg, Roskilde Universitetsforlag: 27–39.

Olwig, Kenneth R. (2000). '"Historical Aspects of Multifunctionality in Landscapes" – Opposing Views of Landscape'. *Multifunctional Landscape: Interdisciplinary Approaches to Landscape Research and Management*. Jesper Brandt, Gunther Tress and Bärbel Tress, Eds. Roskilde, Centre for Landscape Research: 133–146.

Olwig, Kenneth R. (2001). 'Landscape as a Contested Topos of Place, Community and Self'. *Textures of Place*. Steven Hoelscher, Paul Adams and Karen Till, Eds. Minneapolis, The University of Minnesota Press: 95–119.

Olwig, Kenneth R. (2002). *Landscape, Nature and the Body Politic: From Britain's Renaissance to America's New World*, Madison, University of Wisconsin Press.

Ørsted, H.C. (1836). 'Danskhed, en Tale.' *Dansk Folkeblad* 1 (53, 54): 209–216.

Paasi, Anssi (1996). *Territories, Boundaries and Consciousness. The Changing Geographies of the Finnish-Russian Border*, Chichester, John Wiley & Sons.

Paasi, Anssi (forthcoming). 'Finnish Landscape as Social Practice: Mapping Identity and Scale'. *Nordscapes: Thinking Landscape and Regional Identity on the Northern Edge of Europe*. Kenneth R. Olwig and Michael Jones, Eds. Minneapolis, University of Minnesota Press.

Rerup, Lorenz (1991). 'Fra litterær til politisk nationalisme. Udvikling og udbredelse fra 1808 til 1845'. *Dansk Identitetshistorie: Et yndigt land 1789–1848*. Ole Feldbæk, Ed. Copenhagen, Reitzel. 2: 325–390.

Sauer, Carl O. (1925). 'The Morphology of Landscape.' *University of California Publications in Geography* 2 (2): 19–53.

Schouw, Joachim Frederik (1832). *Europa. En let fattelig Naturskildring*, Copenhagen.

Schouw, Joachim Frederik (1845). *Skandinaviens Natur og Folk: Et Foredrag holdt den 22. November 1844 i det Skandinaviske Selskab*, Copenhagen, C.A. Reitzel.

Schouw, Joachim Frederik (1852). *The Earth, Plants and Man*, London, Henry G. Bohn.

Setten, Gunhild (1999). 'Den 'nye' kulturgeografiens landskapsbegrep.' *Nordisk Samhällsgeografisk Tidskrift* (29): 55–71.

Sporrong, Ulf (1998). 'Dalecarlia in Central Sweden before 1800: a Society of Social Stability and Ecological Resilience'. *Linking Social and Ecological Systems. Management Practices and Social Mechanisms for Building Resilience*. Berkes-Folke, Ed. Cambridge, Cambridge University Press.

Sporrong, Ulf and Elisabeth Wennersten (1995). *Marken, Gården, Släkten och Arvet: Om jordägandet och dess konsekvenser för människor, landskap och bebyggelse i Tibble och Ullvi byar, Leksands socken 1734–1820.*, Stockholm, Stockholms Universitet.

Steffens, Henrik (1840–45). *Hvad jeg oplevede*, Copenhagen, C. Steen.

Steffens, Henrich (1840–1844). *Was ich erlebte: aus der Erinnerung niedergeschrieben*, Breslau, Max und Komp.

Steffens, Heinrich (1874 (orig. 1840–1844)). *German University Life: The Story of My Career as Student and Professor*, Philadelphia, Lippincott.

Steffens, Henrik (1905). *Indledning til Philosophiske Forelæsninger i København 1803*, Copenhagen, Gyldendal.

Widgren, Mats (1997). 'Landskap eller objekt: Kring kulturminnesvårdens problem att hantera landskapets historia'. *Landskapet som historie.* Mats Widgren and Jan Brendalsmo, Eds. Oslo, NINA.NIKU. 4.

Chapter 13

Samhällsgeografi and the politics of nature

Ari Aukusti Lehtinen

Introduction: Environmental turn in geography

The 'cultural turn' in human geography, broadly launched in the 1980s, challenged the widely applied critical realism of earlier approaches. Textual orienteering, maps of the mind, narrative and linguistic emphases – all more or less inspired by different variations of social constructionism – forced the critical geography of structures and structurations to face the strength of heterogeneity and polyvalency in research practices. Suddenly, there was no way back to foundational overviews and solid stances. The powerful subject of geography was questioned. Some geographers identified themselves as nomads with mobile study positions and they increasingly focused their interests on socio-spatial flows and fluidities. The renewal was, in no way, a simple metamorphosis with unisonic applause from all the corners of human geography.

Inger Birkeland (1998: 227) argues, while referring to the cultural renewal in Anglophonic human geography, that *'in the process from the 'old' to 'new' cultural geography, the culture-nature relationship has been lost in favour of a society-space relationship'*. She also continues that in the Nordic context, for some reason, even *'the cultural turn has been met with a remarkable silence'*. Birkeland's conclusion is basically convincing, and it is easy to derive from the geographical literature to which she is referring. The avantgarde of the 'new' human geography has intensively elaborated on the socio-spatial aspects of geographical imagination, whereas the task of re-conceptualising nature has been more or less ignored (see e.g. Gregory 1994: xi), perhaps to be finally found at the turn of the century (Eden 2001). In addition, as Birkeland argues, several of the new cultural reorientations by the Western colleagues have undoubtedly remained rather unexamined in Northern Europe. The label of 'half-human geography' (Gregory 1994:124; Hottola 1999: 209) describes also the Nordic setting while underlining the particular silences in the various fields of (post)feminist geography (see also Koskela 1999).

Both of the critical remarks of Birkeland, however, can be critically weighed, too. First, it is not difficult to find evidence that the cultural turn has had a remarkable impact on the culture-nature of human geography and, at a closer look, it also seems evident that the environmental question has been profoundly included in the renewal of human geographies (see e.g. Gosgrove 1984, Olwig 1984, 2002, Smith 1984, Katz and Kirby 1991, Short 1991, Buttimer 1992, Burgess and Harrison 1993, Demeritt 1994, 2001, Zimmerer 1994, Massey 1995, Harvey 1996). Second, the Nordic human geographers soon reacted to and participated in the cultural turn but with striking internal variance: some adopted quickly the new codifications while others warmed slowly. Many remained sceptical. In general, the gradual reformulation of the Nordic *'samhälls- och kulturgeografi'*[1] took place. The apparently slow and rigid dynamics of the Nordic renewal resulted in frustration among the younger geographers, Birkeland included (see Nynäs 1990, Lehtinen 1990b), but it also secured a firm basis for developing hybrid conceptions and stances which could help to grasp the interconnections between the ('old') societal and ('new') cultural concerns. These interconnections, as will be shown below, appealed strongly to geographers who had an interest in environmental issues or, more generally, in interrelations of culture-nature.

The search for hybrid re-conceptualisation roots back to Bruno Latour's critique of modern scientific practices. *'[We] need to get rid of all the categories like those of power, knowledge, profit or capital, because they divide up a cloth that we want seamless in order to study it as we choose'* argues Latour (1987: 223) and points out a need for radical reorganisation of our way of identifying subjectivity in connection to the environing world, including its organic content and material foundations. The modern world view has, according to him, been entangled in abstractions that in fact refer to portions of collective associations and relations which cannot be cut into pieces without losing their intrinsic dynamism and heterogeneity. Therefore we remain conceptually ignorant of the interrelations of which we as individuals and cultures are indelibly constituted.

Geographically speaking, the modern mind has remained silent on the actual 'land- and lifescapes' we inhabit corporeally and through myriads of practical co-productions of culture-nature. In this article, the 'categories' (including those listed above by Latour) are not abandoned but instead situated in their specific spatio-temporal settings. For example, the differences between landscape, *landskap* and *maisema* are considered crucial when aiming at understanding the 'deep spaces' (Smith 1984, Gregory 1994, Häkli 1997, Hottola 1999) of culture-nature in the Nordic context. This reflects the (post)constructionistic dependency underlined here: the concepts we use refer to earlier respective statements within a particular discursive continuum and this is something we cannot avoid and purify ourselves from. We can only endeavour to increase awareness of these dependencies (see Lynch 1993: 107–113, Kotilainen 1997: 95). In addition, some hybrid-like formulations, as culture-nature and local-global, are systematically used in this study in order to remind us of the practical co-existence and vestedness of the poles

---

[1] *Samhällsgeografi*, literally societal geography (*samhällsgeografi* in Swedish, *samfunnsgeografi* in Norwegian, *samfundsgeografi* in Danish, *yhteiskuntamaantiede* in Finnish), refers here to Nordic critical human geography launched during the 1970s in connection to the radical leftist orientation among the students and younger university teachers. The Nordic connection is renewed annually in the Symposiums for Critical Human Geography, and by publishing the journal *Nordisk Samhällsgeografisk Tidsksrift*. On the other hand, *kulturgeografi* covers a broader spectrum of approaches within Nordic geography, initially constituted as the part of geography that studies the human impact on the landscape – distinguished from physical geography, or *naturgeografi* concentrating on the (paleo)ecological or geomorphological origin and structure of the landscape.

to which these dual conceptions refer. The hybrid stance is hence taken here as an inspiring way of noticing and underlining the actual interconnections between the artificially distanced spheres of 'land and life'. This way of looking at the world is familiar to Nordic *samhällsgeografi* as will be shown later in this article, and Latour is by no means alone in pointing at the crucial dependencies between the things divided by the key categories of modernisation (see e.g. Haraway 1991, Buttimer 1993, Tuan 1998, see also Berglund 1997b, Berg 1999).

The view adopted in this article is less dramatic than that of Birkeland's. It is argued here that – both due to and despite the cultural turn – human geographies have gradually and increasingly become informed by the layered existence of socio-cultural and eco-social hybrids, and this holds true especially in the Nordic countries. Occasionally, the Nordic geographers have constructed fruitful comparative settings – Nordic interpretations – based on both Continental European and Anglophonic debates (see some early formulations: Olwig 1980, Jensen and Simonsen 1981, Paasi 1984, Asheim 1985a, Olsson 1985, Vartiainen 1984, 1986a, b, 1987, Simonsen 1985, 1988, 1991, Åquist 1989, Baerenholdt et al. 1990, Karjalainen and Vartiainen 1990). In a similar manner, we can talk about several waves of the environmental turn within Nordic human geography, featuring such key concepts as territorial structure *(territorialstruktur)*, landscape *(landschaft, landskap, maisema)*, terrestrial nature, nature compressions *(natursammenhaenge)*, northern natures, recreational natures and culture-natures, and including also inspiring comments on such popular (late) modern projections as ecological modernisation, risk management and biopolitics. These concepts and approaches have gained a specific Nordic articulation (see e.g. Nielsen 1976, Buch-Hansen and Nielsen 1977, Vartiainen 1979, Axelsson et al. 1980, Olwig 1984, 1996, Baerenholdt 1989, Hansen 1990, Jones 1991, Vartiainen and Vesajoki 1991, Nynäs 1992, Ossenbrügge 1993, Bladh 1995, Lidskog 1998, Berg 1999, Kortelainen 1999, Simonsen 2000, Vepsäläinen 2000).

In the Nordic context, the longest traditions of culture-nature debate within (poststructural) human geography can be found in Denmark, where inspiring programmes have been initiated in the field of landscape studies (Olwig 1984, 1996, Hansen and Buciek 2000) and as part of the research programme on lifemodes (Baerenholdt 1989, 1991). In Norway, historical geography of landscapes is well developed in Trondheim (see Jones 1991, Setten 2000, Jones and Olwig 2002), whereas in Oslo the culture-nature formulations range from environmental feminism (Birkeland 1994, 1999, 2002) to environmentalism within economic *samfunnsgeografi*, increasingly inspired by cultural interdependencies of nontraded origin (Saether 1998, 1999). The long history of human geographical research on culture-nature in Sweden is internationally well known (see Hägerstrand 1985, Buttimer et al. 1992, Sandberg and Sörlin 1998, Christiansen et al. 1999), which is especially due to major outlines in historical landscape research (e.g. Sandell 1991, Westholm 1992, Bladh 1995, Sjöberg 1995) and in studies on modernisation and resource use (de Souza 1989, Lundqvist 1994) as well as in lifestyle studies (e.g. Hallin 1993, Svanqvist 2000). In addition, some scholars from closely related disciplines have made important geographical contributions (see e.g. Sörlin 1988, 1999, Hjort af Ornäs and Lodgaard 1992, Hjort af Ornäs 1996, Granfelt 1999).

The Finnish human geographical studies of culture-nature have a long history, too, rooted in the classical works of J.G. Granö, Väinö Tanner and Ilmari Hustich.[2] These initial approaches were later read in the light of explicit socio-cultural theory by younger colleagues (Vartiainen 1979, 1984, Paasi 1982, 1986, Karjalainen 1986) and they were also connected to the rise of environmentalism in Finnish social sciences (Raumolin 1981, Massa 1984, Lehtinen 1987, 1991). The gradual establishment of Finnish geography as a discipline with a social scientific status (see Vartiainen 1988) resulted soon in several new openings in culture-nature research with explicitly poststructural orientations. The most energetic formulation took shape in connection to the studies of the various spheres of 'urban natures' (Karvinen 1995, Nevalainen 1995, Häkli 1996, Kortelainen 2000, Vepsäläinen 2000, Virtanen 2000), which was soon accompanied by a constructionist re-reading of rural and marginal natures (Tanskanen 2000), topically in the context of organic farming (Kumpulainen 1999, Silvasti and Mononen 2001). The globalisation of environmentalism was also reflected in the studies of environmental consciousness and ethics (Kotilainen 1996, Rytteri 2000, 2002), accompanied by multiethnic and gender sensitive analyses of postcolonialism and interculturalisation (Hottola 1999: 188–222, Pehkonen 1999, Lehtinen 2001a, Möller and Pehkonen 2002). Thematic explorations of the culture-nature hybrids were also published at the turn of the century (Kortelainen 1999, Lehtinen 2000). In addition, Finnish geographers received support for their theoretical elaboration from the scholars of closely related disciplines, e.g. from environmental anthropology (Berglund 1997a,b), ecology and environmental policy (Haila and Levins 1992, Haila and Heininen 1995) and environmental sociology (Rannikko 1997, 1999 a,b).

During the last decade the Nordic human geography of culture-nature has become increasingly integrated with the Anglophonic schools but even then it has kept its specific Nordic intonation, coloured by contacts to the Continental streams of thought. The Nordic environmental turn is broadly connected to the politicisation of natures, which is integrally linked to the current contested networking of socio-spatial identifications and community activities stretching from individual (embodied) and local practices (landscaping) up to global projections and rankings (certificates of sustainability). The culture-nature practices are critically evaluated as questions of domination and empowerment, both within the spheres of intimate and intersubjective discourses, as well as in relation to the industrial-technological change within the local-global continuum. In addition, these questions have

---

2 Väinö Tanner (1881–1948), J.G. Granö (1882–1956) and Ilmari Hustich (1911–1982) carried out influential anthropo-geographical studies which in their own way questioned the position of Finnish geography exclusively among the natural sciences. Tanner (1929) was interested in the authentic ethno-cultural naming of places and land forms as a method for deeper understanding of symbolic and aesthetic landscapes, whereas Granö (1997, orig. 1929) looked for the perceptional categories of landscapes through the spectrum of all the five senses. Hustich (1960) in turn studied the regularities and particularities of culture-nature as part of the societal dynamics (Paasi 1982, Massa 1984, Lehtinen 1991, Susiluoto 2000). According to Paulo Susiluoto (2000), Väinö Tanner could be even seen as the first of the Finnish geographers in the genre of human geography (broadly understood as we do today).

repeatedly been re-worked through the more general debate on the changing role of the material processes of nature in the discourses on the environment. The last-mentioned question is perhaps the most fundamental and long-lived of the challenges within the Nordic *samhällsgeografi*.

The Nordic view on culture-nature is indelibly connected to the continuing reart-iculation of power relations emerging within the environmental discourses and written in the physical-symbolic landscapes under human agency. The emphasis of power rests in the historical sensitivity to shared decision-making and representa-tiveness in the Nordic societies and communal life. Collective responsibility among and between the families of the villages during the era of hunting economies (*erätalous*) and the ancient customary public access to lands and forests beyond the centers of settlement (*allemansrätten*) have become rooted in the modern Nordic practices of culture-nature, only to be surfaced when threatened by the external pressures of modernisation (Åström 1978, Olwig 1992, Bladh 1995, Sporrong 2002). Therefore, the questions of freedom, equality and justice are integral elements of the Nordic identification, and they have also informed the basic formu-lation of geography. The Nordic *samhällsgeografi* can in fact be seen as a programme launched against regional and environmental inequalities as well as class and gender-based discriminations faced during the post World War II period of speeded modernisation (Asheim 1979, Vartiainen 1979, Simonsen et al. 1982, Simonsen 1985).

The above-described emphasis on the layered existence of socio-environmental discrimination can be understood as a specific sensitivity to various forms of biopolitical repression and empowerment, if following the Continental, Foucault-inspired discourses of nature and power, whereas the trans-Atlantic interpretation would underline the connections to socio-environmental justice issues. The biopolitical view sheds light on the conditions of culture-nature control, articulated through such concepts as governmentality and environmentality but it reaches its full explanatory power when focused on the most nuanced versions of (self-)control infiltrated in and through the everyday life, both in bodily and environmental terms (Simonsen 1996: 508–509, 2000, Hänninen and Karjalainen 1997, Foucault 1998, Haila 2000a, Hänninen 2000, Sairinen 2000). On the other hand, the sensitivity to in/justice is derived from the growing awareness of the alarmingly unfair distribution of environmental 'goods' and 'bads' (Cutter 1995, Harvey 1996, Hornborg 1998, Sandberg and Sörlin 1998, Lehtinen 1999, 2001b). In the Nordic geography, this interfacing has resulted in approaches where the new challenges of local and individual governance are seen as rooted to translocalisation launched both by the new economy of shareholder interests and by the global reach of environmental organisations. Here, the Nordic forest-based networking of power regimes covers both the local-global and culture-nature dimensions and can therefore be used as an illustrative example of the practical societal challenges of Nordic *samhällsgeografi*.

The biopolitical view referred to here is based on the understanding of power as a web of dependencies between countless actors and positions in a continuously evolving setting of fluid relations. Power has hence thoroughly permeated our societal practices and it emerges both in macro and micro levels of our socio-spatial being. It is an immanent and unavoidable element of social co-existence, taking shape via continuous processes of re-negotiations (Rabinow 1989, Foucault 1998:

70–71). Power (*makt*) becomes activated both through submission *(vanmakt)* and counter-reactions *(motmakt)*. This triangularity forms multilayered regimes with networks of reciprocal ties and endless series of inclusions and exclusions. Biopower emerges in those situations where both our bodily existence and our intimate socio-spatial relations become eroded according to the dominating interests (of systematisation and control), more or less reproduced in our daily decisions by our willing selves or through our respective reactions and proactions. For example, the biopolitics of forests surface in the negotiations of the contested origins of the timber behind the newspapers we consume on a daily basis. Biopolitical studies highlight the modes and variations of local-global 'paper landscapes' in the era of intensive forest-industrial restructuring. Here the question is about uneven distribution of information related to decision-making power, including positional variation in the ability to encode and decode the signals of forest-based knowledge materialised in paper processing and consumption (Mathiesen 1982, Pehkonen 1999, Lloyd 2001).[3]

The comparative elaboration of biopolitical and justice approaches is especially linked to the gradual strengthening of the eco-social sensitivity of *samhällsgeografi*, informed both by continental and trans-Atlantic debates on geography and power. The question of justice was included in the process from the beginning in the form of criticism against the unevennes of economic development (Folke 1973, Harvey 1973, Buch-Hansen et al. 1976). Later this orientation was criticised as being economistic and it faced the demand of more nuanced and multilayered articulation of power relations (Olwig 1986, Simonsen 1988, Baerenholdt 1989, Lehtinen 1990a). The biopolitical vocabulary became gradually integrated in this reorientation – as a line of thought – but it also seemed to distance Nordic human geographers from societal involvements and activities. The cultural turn in general, while contrasted with the painful traps of recession of the 1990s in the environing world, was even seen as a return to conservative geographies and resulting in an aestheticisation of societal relations of domination (see e.g. Rose 1993, Lash 1995, Barnett 1998, Castree 1999, Heyman 2001, Massey 2001 and within the Nordic geography: Lehtinen 1993, Häkli 1994, 1997, Kotilainen 1996, 1997, Baerenholdt 1998, Hottola 1999: 179–221).

In the Finnish context, psychohistorian Juha Siltala (1996, 1999), while rooting his argument in the social criticism of the Frankfurt School (see Marcuse 1966, Horkheimer and Adorno 1981), has polemised in detail the fashionable turn of social scientists towards deconstructions, discourse analyses and biopolitical choreography. According to him, the 'discourse orientation' has become a methodological fetish which closes the connection to individual authenticity under the concrete conditions of societal change, therefore constraining our ability to renew ourselves as researchers in dialogue with the subjects in study focus. Moreover, Siltala argues, it limits our understanding of the human and social existence behind the symbolic representations, surfacing e.g. in the form of disconnections, overreactions and other

---

[3]   The biopolitical view applied here should not be confused with the conceptualisation of biopolitics as a synonym to green or environmental politics (see e.g. Goodman 1999, see also Koivusalo 2000:118).

discontinuities in the spheres of communication (Siltala 1999: 9–28, see also Häkli 1997: 340–341, and a slightly parallel intonation by Inger Birkeland 2002, inspired by Luce Irigaray and Julia Kristeva).

The biopolitical analysis is crucially dependent on the creativity of the scholars applying it: the limits we face are primarily the limits of our own. However, the Foucault-inspired cultural turn in human geography has undoubtedly faced difficulties in noticing the multilayered needs and motives of individuals anchored in the multilayered dynamics of societal projections, and this has become evident in connection to the more unarticulated spheres of human existence. Consequently, it has a tendency to distance us as professional geographers from the lay geographies of the everyday (see Kaisa Pennanen 1998 and her insightful interpretation of Eric Dardell's *L'homme et la terre. Nature de la réalité géographique*). It hence weakens the social constitution of our critical voice.

The stance promoted here is (a) broadly utilising the sensitivity of the biopolitical view within the field of articulated power but it is carefully (b) situated in a dialogue between the 'politics of academia' and the 'poetics of activism' and (c) linked to an aim to get closer to the community-based variations of coping with oppression and violations of the sense of justice. This interpretation has, as I see it, permeated the traditions of *samhällsgeografi* and it also enables us to critically assess the current challenges of culture-nature in the Nordic 'branches' of human geography.

To specify, this article leans on the Nordic traditions of *samhällsgeografi* by interpreting them in the broader framework of politicisation of nature, which refers both to general conceptual and paradigmatic renewal in disciplinary approaches as well as to socio-cultural changes within the society 'out there', behind the academic circles. The interpretation is inspired both by the political ecology literature highlighting the justice concerns in resource exploitation and environmentalism and by the (post)constructionist approaches broadly under the umbrella of biopolitics. This framework is further developed in the context of Nordic forest-industrial restructuring. The question is formulated in connection to the Nordic forest provinces with their own traditions of community-based decision-making, and with tensions impelled through ages by external demands of modernisation. As part of this gradual modernisation, the traditional local senses of self-sufficiency and justice have become eroded by the modern industrial and environmentalistic practices and, accordingly, challenged by the more translocal models of decision-making. In other words, the earlier sensitivity to local representativeness and mutual responsibility has faced the subsequent demands of intensifying resource extraction and nature conservation, both based on the high status of landownership and, consequently, become a confusing hybrid with remnants from all the eras of the past. Derived from these assumptions, the current uneven positioning of forest communities, both local and translocal, is discussed and related to the ongoing globalisation of the Nordic forest industry.

Throughout the centuries of forest-based modernisation, the local and regional forest communities have been modified by the 'export actors' of forest trade. The market interests, emerging beyond the conditions of negotiated decision-making, have been infiltrated into the local life worlds and they have gradually become part of the local lifemodes. Some have benefited from the new challenges, some others have suffered. Today, in the era of intensive forest-industrial internationalisation, the setting is still much the same. However, the more translocal the companies have grown the less dependent they have become on specific localities, or provinces, as their partners. Therefore, while making new contracts, the companies can more easily ignore those local interests that deviate from their strategies. Broadly, as seen from the viewpoint of individual actors or partners, the question is about loyalty to two confronting formulations of interests and, moreover, tensions between two forums of identification: the local and translocal (forest) communities. This is the argument of my article and the basis for further elaboration on the proceeding pages: during the current local-global transformation, our community basis is under intensive redefinition and this has an impact on our understanding of socio-ecological governance, sustainability and sense of justice.

Biopolitics and environmental justice

The more recent environmental debate has increasingly questioned the expansive societal modification of nature, including the modification of culture via the changes in nature. The animal liberation movement has been especially active in highlighting the ethical problems in animal testing, livestock husbandry and outdoor hunting, and from here we can find the most informative articulations of culture-natures as co-productive processes and collective associations (Dawson 1999, Goodman 1999, Anderson 2000). The contested reconfiguration of the positions of the various coalitions of culture-nature is by no means an exclusive characteristic of the animal liberation debate. On the contrary, it seems to take shape as one of the organising principles of the environmental debate.

Examples of this kind of new contestation are numerous and easily recognised. The widely-applied biodiversity programmes in environmental monitoring are tools for underlining the injustices in the exploitation of natural resources but they also function as universal(ising) matrices and claims for various community-based practices of culture-nature. The concept of biodiversity has *'progressed from a scientific community of North American conservation biologists to North Karelian lumberjacks'*, states Kotilainen (1996: 67) and polemices its discursive dominance in the Eastern Finnish context. The spread of concern for biodiversity is a good example of the biopolitical configuration of power. The question is primarily about the increasing domination of the (late) modern technological trajectories with eco-socially erosive and discriminatory outcomes. Hence, the apparent conflict between nature conservation and exploitation – dividing nature and culture into oppositional entities – turns into a more nuanced, interdiscursive and fragmented battle over particular hegemonic positions. The question is about the contingent emergence of organising power or, more precisely, about the macrogeometrics of globally uneven development which becomes articulated as time-space specific modifications of the environment, identifiable only within and through the microgeometrics of the everyday (see e.g. Dalby 1992, 1998, Peet and Watts 1996, Sandberg and Sörlin 1998, Massey 1995, 2001).

The criticism of the new manifestations of biopower has recently surfaced rather dramatically in the form of large-scale civic demonstrations in different parts of the world against the politics of the World Trade Organisation and International

Monetary Fund. The wave of actions started in Seattle on November 30th in 1999 and has thereafter seemed to become an integral part of global corporational and intergovernmental meetings (Fannin et al. 2000, Lähde 2001). The demonstrations have brought the environmental risks and injustices of current economic-technological globalisation into public attention. The media success of the actions has also forced the criticised ones to raise their voice against the activists, claiming that the new wave of demonstrations is based on a hierarchic networking which takes shape according to the impulses of the few centres of globalisation critique. Some ideological leaders of the global movement such as Walden Bello, Susan George and Lori Wallach have been brought to the limelight (Manninen 2000). The new movement is hence criticised for using methods of biopower similar to those used by the main forces of globalisation.

Environmental justice is a familiar concept and well-known viewpoint to researchers. Geographers especially have studied it carefully, both theoretically and as an empirical research challenge (see e.g. Cutter 1995, Harvey 1996, Proctor and Smith 1999). The questions of discrimination and justice in environmental research have mainly concentrated on the ethical basis and the social responsibility dimensions of societal practices. The mechanisms of uneven eco-social development have been examined, including ecosystems with their defenders and transformers, individual consumers and consumer groups, both non- and (inter)governmental bodies of regulation, as well as transnational companies with their suppliers and clients (Murdoch 1998, Hornborg 1998, McAfee 1999, Lovio 1999, Kortelainen 1999, Saether 1999, Murdoch et al. 2000). Thus, in research practices, the clear boundary between ecological and societal concerns has vanished and it is considered a rather outdated construction from the past. This is especially true in the European debate on nature-based discrimination. According to Wolfgang Sachs (1999: 28), the crisis of justice and the crisis of nature stand in an inverse relationship to each other. Thus, any attempt to ease the crisis of justice threatens to aggravate the crisis of nature, and vice versa: any attempt to ease the crisis of nature threatens to aggravate the crisis of justice. The changes in nature turn into changes in society turn into changes in nature. Nature and society became indivisible.

This unification has bred new questions and, also, new ways of formulating the old ones. First, the content of 'nature', as a central constituent of the Western world view (Glacken 1967, Williams 1979, Latour 1993), is, once again, under intensive redefinition. The motor of the current change is connected to the articulations of biodiversity concerns and animal rights. Poor living conditions of livestock concern both the animals and their defenders but, in addition, they have also emerged as questions of health for the consumers and, therefore, returned to the producers as new entrepreneurial risks (Buttimer 1996). Bovine Spongiform Encephalopathy (BSE), or, in popular language, mad cow disease, is a dramatic example of this kind of boomerang phenomenon within the interrelations of nature and culture, guiding consumers to demand safer food production and even transitions towards organic farming (see Adam 1998).

Second, during the era of dramatic global time-space compressions the interconnections between the self (e.g. as a Western consumer) and the other (e.g. as child labour in SE Asia) have surfaced as questions of moral reflection; continuous local-global scaling is part of our daily lifeworld while shopping in the nearby grocery. The certificates of sustainability, demanded by the critical consumers and focused both on the products and the processes behind them, are presently under contested definition. The reading of these certificates has consequently become a necessity for a careful consumer: both the price tags and green labels are today essential while making purchases. In addition, the lengthening of product chains has emphasised the eco-social costs of transporting. Therefore, regional preferences in production and consumption patterns, e.g. the 'local food' projects, are introduced as part of the sustainability criteria (Buttimer 1998, Murdoch et al. 2000, Silvasti and Mononen 2001).

Third, the companies embedded in the globalising economy have faced new risks based on the fluidity of their operational contexts. Today, the credibility problems caused by 'wrong moves' or bad images easily get reflected both to the final product markets and within the stock markets in the form of worsening options. This kind of new vulnerability has become an integral part of the competing markets, and especially the most expansive companies have become much more sensitive to external signals and changing value horizons (Saether 1999, Rytteri 2000, Donner-Amnell 2001, Lehtinen 2002a).

The geographically and biopolitically interesting debate on environmental justice is focused on how the use of nature is intertwined with power. This tradition concentrates on concrete societal situations and practices and on the analysis of the social and ecological impacts of environmental changes by examining the mechanisms that cause inequality and injustice in the routines of everyday life. Laura Pulido (1996) refers to environmental racism when environmentally harmful land use has a tendency to accumulate in the areas inhabited by people from ethnic minorities. Douglas J. Porteous (1988) used the concept of topocide while witnessing the dramatic weakening of local conditions of living caused by the development projects accepted and run by the municipal authorities. In a similar manner, Blaikie et al. (1994) analyse the progression of social and ecological vulnerability, following certain patterns which we often take for granted and consider natural. Perhaps, however, the most common dimension of the predicament of environmental justice has appeared along the debate on sustainable development: the worries about future generations is indeed a sign of sensitivity to the trajectories of biopower, now across the generations.

In regard to the forest-based development processes in northern Europe, fundamental questions of environmental discrimination readily emerge as issues related to the position of the northern periphery, including both nature and human communities, in the deepening integration of Europe. In addition, the impact of the globalising forest trade already has remarkably, often throughout, modified local and regional conditions (Eskelinen and Kautonen 1997). Furthermore, the questions of environmental discrimination cover a variety of social effects arising from the programmes of nature conservation. Local cultural values in the northern peripheries quite often seem to be undervalued, or even ignored, when appearing as if set against translocal conservation plans (Rannikko 1999a).

We should not, however, consider the question of environmental injustice merely as a tension between local and translocal interest, when it also permeates through the established ways of action of the localities and interest groups themselves. The question of representativeness, including age, gender and other social dimensions, is important both in the formation of local voices and governmental policy plans, as well as within transnational corporate strategies (Bladh 1995, Birkeland 1999, Hottola 1999, Koskela 1999). The identification of the critical moments of inclusion and exclusion is a complicated research challenge indeed, loaded with risks emerging from the side of the subject groups as well as from within the institutional academic world. Susan L. Cutter (1995) has called attention to the difficulty of verifying environmental discrimination. While debating the correlation between the definition of research topics and the results achieved, she elaborates on the problem of geographical scaling: environmental changes with locally worrying consequences might completely disappear while framing the question within a broader socio-spatial scale.

This question of perspectives is of key importance when studying biopower. The credibility of the research is easily questioned among the broader audience if proved that the results do vary according to perspective framing or the level of abstraction. In addition, researchers with a different background can easily nullify the work of their colleagues by showing remarkably deviating results. Accordingly, the interconnections between the researcher and her/his subject groups are often sensitive. Local experiences of injustice can be modified – exaggerated or underrated – to meet the explicit or implicit research premise by varying the basic focusing and framing. For a professional academic, covering these modifications with technical choices or ways of representation is easy. Therefore, as it seems evident, the research always and inevitably becomes interlinked with the mechanisms that strengthen or weaken the practices of discrimination.

The perspective problem can, at least partially, be overcome by comparative research settings, and e.g. by careful reflections upon the consequences of socio-spatial scaling. It is especially important to learn to recognise the context-specific conditions whence and within the sensitivity to certain forms of domination and the sense of justice grow. Giovanna Di Chiro (1996: 310) discusses the critical role of communities in (re)producing the notions of nature and the sense of justice. In her own words: *'Environmental justice groups, while strongly criticising mainstream conceptions of nature, also produce a distinct theoretical and material connection between human/nature, human/environment relations through notions of 'community'. Community becomes at once the idea, place, and the relations and practices that generate what these activists consider more socially just and ecologically sound human/environment configurations'.*

Hence the community, e.g. in the form of a locality or network, lays both the value basis and practical frames that condition the shaping of environmental preferences and the sensitivities to discrimination. The community produces the system of identification by which the ideas and practices of culture-nature are formulated. This system can only be understandable and meaningful in authentic situations, from inside, while set against the ideas, values and experiences shared by the members of the community (Ryden 1993, Beckley 1995, Lindén 1998, Lloyd 2001). This authenticity demand, based on socially negotiated experiences and interpretations of socio-spatial order – that is, conceived and lived spaces – can emerge as an insuperable barrier for the researcher but it can, nevertheless, function as basic research motivation and a challenge, too.

Communities, domination and the sense of justice

The need to identify the community-based variations in environmental preferences is by no means a new question in geographical research. However, the community-based dynamic behind the development of the sense of (environmental) domination and justice can help us, as researchers, to become more sensitive to the uneven distribution of risks, including fears of them, too, faced in the daily lives of communities. The questions thus are: How do major environmental changes, and the culturally varying responses to these changes, take shape in different contexts? How are the changes articulated and justified? What are the outcomes of these changes? These research questions contain at least three complementary formulations which are presented here as a brief introduction to Nordic forest communities.

First, in the Nordic forest provinces the traditional formulation of the culture-nature relationship was, of course, a local process. Today, local and regional communities are still important media for the development of the sense of justice. The Nordic academic activities within geography and regional studies have resulted in interesting and influential openings in community and identity research, e.g. in historical landscape research (Sörlin 1988, Jones 1991, Bladh 1995, Raivo 1996, Olwig 1996) and in connection to village studies (Hautamäki 1979, Rouhinen 1981, Oksa and Rannikko 1985, Knuuttila et al. 1996). These studies have remarkably strengthened the understanding of the historical spaces that are both socially inherited and societally produced, including the reciprocal dependencies between them, too. However, much still remains unexamined, e.g. in the fields of socio-spatial commemoration and collective regional inheritance (see Connerton 1989, Schama 1995, Graham and Ashworth 2000) as well as in connection to environmental questions with their current local-global configurations. For example the contested settings between local environmental preferences in the Nordic provinces and translocal regulations, introduced by the European Union or in the form of global intergovernmental agreements, would need more careful examination today.

Such a research emphasis would inform us about the background of the provincial criticism against the EU integration and against expanding nature conservation. Local expressions often seem to become labelled as provincial and outdated exaggerations in the dominating media even though the problem would, at least partly, rise from the experience of humiliation based on marginalisation (from the central information flows) and deep, heritage-like experiences of injustice (Lehtinen 1996, Rannikko 1999a). Environmental policy measures are confronted in the forest provinces in the context of the local sense of justice which is more or less internally shared, and this too often tends to differ from the external translocal principles of justice derived from the more universal standards.

For the people in the provinces, biodiversity programmes can appear strange means for promoting nature conservation, while the 'lived diversity of land' is based on inherited patterns of land use and topographic identifications, including e.g. the immediate experiences of seasonal changes – against which the viability of human existence is finally constructed. The multiple senses of snow (Hoeg 1992) hardly belong to the vocabularies of biodiversity programmes and might perhaps more easily be connected to notions of earthly sensitivity and geodiversity relations (Karjalainen 1986, Pennanen 1998). In a similar manner, to give a tangible and acute example, people in the backwood villages in Eastern Finland find it difficult to cope with the EU limitations on hunting bears that terrorise the forest farms and villages (Lehtinen 2002b).

Even though local or regional community voices in the Nordic forest peripheries have never been turned into oppressive patrimonial unison (Karlsson 1992, Sporrong 2002), uneven social positioning has been an unavoidable and common feature in northern Europe (Axelsson et al. 1980, Knuuttila 1980, 1985: 360–365, 1992: 71–77, Lehtinen 1991:125–135). The Nordic regional voices have traditionally taken shape through certain representative practices, by the so-called *'ting'* meetings (Koch and Ross 1949), but not without distress between pressures of conformity and socio-cultural diversification. The regional power relationships have later gone through intensive transformations towards broader representativeness but, also, towards external dependencies. During the centuries of forest industrial modernisation, the local and regional voices have become tied to interests of export orientation and this has turned into a new source of experiencing injustice. Tangibly, external demand challenged the specific structuring of land ownership, economic positions, gender settings and age distributions and, simultaneously, modified these internal relationships (Bladh 1995). In general, the development projections 'from above', including cultural variations in adaptation, have differentiated the local social groupings and, consequently, increased local heterogeneity and powerlessness against the external interests with their local representatives and branch organisations. In this respect, the region is perhaps a weaker actor today than ever before.

Second, the culture-nature relationship is also (re)produced within the translocal or nonlocal connections and networks that we are connected to through our daily practices. Today, it is argued, these posttraditional community relations even exceed the local community effects as conditioning factors of our life worlds (Giddens 1995). Within this translocal world, the basic formulation of environmental values takes place indirectly, without personal experience of the immediate strength of the environing nature (first nature). Nature becomes modified to second nature which becomes meaningful to us e.g. in the form of questions about pollution control and trade (Adam 1998: 29–39, see also Häkli 1996). Within the Nordic countries, and in connection to forest politics, the most central of these translocal 'network communities' are the big forest companies with their resource areas, suppliers and clients, as well as the (inter)governmental and nongovernmental organisations for environmental regulation.

The current intensive internationalisation of forest industrial activities of the Nordic companies (Saether 1998, 1999, Saastamoinen 1999, Donner-Amnell 2001, Moen and Lilja 2001, Lehtinen 2002a) puts a lot of pressure on the researchers to conduct studies on the regional eco-social consequences of this change, both within the Nordic forest peripheries and within the new target countries of the companies. Careful monitoring of these changes is, of course, important for the peripheral communities but it has become a necessity for the central international actors, too. The question is about vulnerability. Today, companies with transcontinetal strategies need to be sensitive to the voices of suppliers, consumers and shareholders. In addition, a more respectful attitude towards environmental pressure groups has become a necessity. Bad images easily turn to credibility traps and worsening economic options. In a similar manner, the networks of environmentalists need to be aware of the risks of becoming labelled as green imperialists or busy professionals for whom the planet earth is primarily a management object (Sachs 1999, Haila 1999a).

Third, the community-based culture-nature relationship emerges as a question of academic engagement, too (see e.g. Routledge 1996, Maxey 1999). The research projects normally, or at least in successful cases, bring up facts and viewpoints that are invisible in the everyday life world. In other words, research is supposed to add something analytical, interpretative or summary-like to the articulations and actual views produced by the subject actors of the case studies. Consequently, research might even become emancipatory while opening new views – latent options and risks – on the questions under investigation. The societal relevance of research depends on its capability to cope with the socio-ecological factors constraining and conditioning the action spaces of the subject groups. From this viewpoint, the acute environmental questions emerge as questions that are both shaping, as well as becoming shaped by, the shifting content of the actualised representations of environmental problems.

While focusing on biopolitics and environmental discrimination, my primary interest here has been to highlight those eco-social processes and projections that remarkably modify the most marginal(ised) of the lands and people of northern Europe. This task has directed our attention to those historical mechanisms of exclusion and inclusion that have been, and still are, dominating the practices and experiences of our lived spaces in the Nordic forest peripheries, including, if possible, the voiceless groups of the North. In the conclusive part of this chapter, the community approach is therefore discussed in the context of Nordic human geography facing the challenge of co-emerging exclusions/inclusions within the multilayered regimes of culture-nature.

Just geography?

This chapter has tried to collect the Nordic links of the biopolitically informed justice approach in human geography interested in environmental and forest questions. It was argued that the specific Nordic interpretation in human geography, which underlines the basic (hybrid-like) vestedness of societal and cultural as well as natural and cultural 'spheres' of human existence, has responded to and further developed the more recent trans-Atlantic and Continental debates of environmental discrimination and empowerment. The Nordic approach could also identify well the most critical questions of the Nordic forest-based development. Some methodological difficulties were, however, found and they demand a conclusive treatment here.

First, despite the decades-long re-thinking of the interrelations of culture-nature in human geography, the connections to physical geographies have however remained the most troubled ones. There have been only a few serious attempts to cover this gap (see Jones 1991, Vartiainen and Vesajoki 1991, Bladh 1995, Jones and Olwig 2002). Hansen and Buciek (2000:73) express the challenge most clearly (translated from Danish by AL): *'To see the cultural values and social, economic and political processes that emerge in our experience and representation of landscape is a central element of the new cultural geography. Therefore, it is not relevant to study the processes of nature in the landscape.'* The hybrid approach could, however, allow us to identify the substance and agency of nature as part of human geography, too, and hence demolish the analytical arrogance toward the material foundations of social life – in a similar manner as the new disciplines of environmental sociology and policy as well as environmental history have already done (Haila 1999b, 2000b, Myllyntaus and Saikku 2001). It seems that the disciplinary history of Nordic *samhällsgeografi* prevents us from seriously engaging in ecological matters and overcoming the distance between human and physical geography, both within disciplinary practices as well as in relation to the world 'out there'. The situation is strange, keeping in mind the institutional structure of the discipline, stretching across physical and human faculties.

Second, the specific view from Europe and especially from the European North should not be abandoned during the speeded-up Anglophonisation of *samhällsgeografi*. The Nordic countries are part of the northernmost circumpolar zone of the inhabited world and this needs continuous reflection. The spaces of culture-nature are different in the North and this difference has repercussions on geography practices. The urban life of the North has a dynamics of its own, as does the rural North and this needs repeated updating and re-conceptualisation in geography. We cannot stay indifferent to the difference of the North (see Jakobs 2000). The key words of geography which seem to lead into fruitful views on the megacities of the Continental and trans-Atlantic West cannot directly be translated into the urban-rural North. The sensitivity to the various forms of biopolitical annihilation of the North would also mean careful re-reading of our own papers: how often we have in fact ignored our own 'lands and lives' while joining the Anglophonic avantgarde, or used the North merely as 'an interesting case' for theory-testing (Heininen 1998, Lehtinen 2002c).

Geographers cannot exclude or distance themselves from the symbolic and geopolitical contestation between the regimes of the Nordic North. Human geography is an indelible part of the redefinition of the North, and today – as throughout the known history – this re-naming has taken place under conditions introduced and adopted from the South and the West (Tanner 1929, Lehtinen 2001a). Both the North and the geographers of the North currently face the same pressure of submissive adjustment under the ideological discourse on globalisation, emerging among the ranks of geographers and within the world 'out there'. The call of globalisation tends to sound attractive for those who feel willing to participate in it, and universities are by definition centrally located in this project. This has an inevitable impact on the geographical thinking but it can also grow into a painful reminder of our own dependence on the fluid networks of universalisation, often becoming concrete in the form of tightening pressures to adopt a common wor(l)d order and uniform language, English (King 1996). The uneasiness grows from the awareness that the Anglophonic North is different from the Scandinavian North which in turn is different from the Norths of the various Finno-Ugric peoples. Multiperspectivity is not alien to Nordic human geographers, as was briefly discussed in the introduction of this article, even though the approaches from within the North and from within the East have been primarily shadowed by the Continental and trans-Atlantic innovations. The balancing of perspectives would help us to free ourselves from the remnants of colonialism in geography, and it could also be taken as a natural outcome of Nordic *samhällsgeografi* during the cultural and environmental turns.

Third, the culturalisation of human geography has brought along nuances in the analyses of power and empowerment but it has also meant neglect of the studies of the societal power relations and dominations. Critical stances have turned into sophisticated analyses of the microcircuits of power, often readable only by the colleagues with shared academic background. Doubts have been also expressed whether the cultural turn is merely a turn towards academic neoconservatism aiming at instructing younger generations *'in what, for the state and business, are the desirable arts of clear thinking, problem solving, clear speaking, and coherent writing, and other core transferable skills'* (Castree 1999: 260, see also Barnett 1998, Heyman 2001).

Anne Buttimer, when receiving an honorary doctorate at the University of Joensuu in 1999, critically discussed the threat of geography becoming too sophisticated to be able to deal with the most central topics of our global and local worlds. Doreen Massey's (2001) thought-provoking discussion on the powerlessness of academic geography can be taken as a similar kind of warning: it is not only 'the society' that is to be blamed if nobody 'out there' is able to read us. The sensitivity to endlessly fragmented practices of biopower can be regarded – as I do here – a welcome step forward in the human geography of culture-nature but we should not be satisfied with that only. The most critical of our referees stay beyond the academic forums and it might be wise to listen to them, too. Massey (2001:10) argues that *'changing discourses is part of changing the world'*, and she looks forward to influential societal involvements. We could call this an invitation to move from the cartography of biopolitics toward more participatory studies of justice or, alternatively, a leap from intertextual choreogeographies to emancipatory practices. The question is: How much do we geographers identify ourselves as activists in the biopolitics of our daily lives? How do we define today the 'third-spaces' between action and research? Olli Tammilehto (1991: 212), a veteran activist and eco-philosopher from Finland, was once worried about the popularity of environmental research among the younger social scientists. He thought they had turned to environmental research due to personal conviction: they believed the environmental questions were important. *'But why don't they have anything more pressing to do with these questions then?'*, he continued.

Perhaps we should not be beset by such scepticism toward scientific enterprises as is apparent in Tammilehto's provocative remark. It is of course necessary to repeatedly question and examine our motives. But we can re-think our geo-profiles at a more practical level, too. Is it just geography we are engaged in? Let this be the final one of our conclusive thoughts here. We have to elaborate on it through the forest excursion completed earlier. The challenge of globalisation, which was illustrated here via the forest communities, primarily addressed the need for hybrid-like re-conceptualisations of the interrelations of society-culture-nature but it also demanded a more participatory method, i.e. a stance connecting the academic regimes to the biopolitical contestation taking place within the various spheres of society.

As was witnessed above, the multilayered translocalisation of the forest communities makes research more dependent on secondary sources. Therefore, the reliability of the actors is increasingly based on different kinds of performative profiles produced for varying purposes. Today, according to Lloyd (2001), the competition over the criteria which guarantee both the social and ecological sustainability of the wood-based products is becoming increasingly intensive. The current certification procedures regarding the forest sector concentrate mainly on forest management, searching for frames of sustainable forestry. Most of the societal elements conditioning the forestry practices discussed in this article are still excluded. The social justification of resource use and the creation of inequality are, as was argued, central threshold questions for the continuing globalisation of the forest-industry activities. A lot of work – in the form of 'academic activism' – is needed in the implementation of these elements into paper production and consumption. This process means integrating matters of environmental justice into the market evaluation, in other words, the sketching of criteria for an eco-socially just forest industry. Geographical research could e.g. be focused on the strengthening of the voices of those in the socio-spatial margins by opening new channels for participation and information dissemination. The Nordic model is perhaps not worth exporting as such but experiences from the forest past, including the various associations of folk, justice and forests, could be worth keeping in mind now, while entering the era of continuous local-global co-negotiations.

References

Adam, Barbara (1998). *Timescapes of modernity*. Routledge, London.
Anderson, Alice (2000). Environmental pressure groups and the 'risk society'. In Allan, Stuart, Barbara Adam and Cynthia Carter (eds.): *Environmental risks and the media*, 93–104. Routledge, London.
Åquist, Ann-Cathrine (1989). Om patriarkatteorin – en o-modern betraktelse. *Nordisk Samhällsgeografisk Tidskrift* 10, 37–48.
Åquist, Ann-Cathrine (1994). Idehistorisk översikt. In Öhman, Jan (ed.): *Traditioner i Nordisk kulturgeografi*, 1–14. Nordisk Samhällsgeografisk Tidskrift, Uppsala.
Asheim, Bjorn T. (1979). Social geography – welfare state ideology or critical social science? *Geoforum* 10:1, 5–18.
Asheim, Bjorn T. (1985a). The history of geographical thought in Scandinavia. *Meddelser fra Geografisk Institutt, Universitet i Oslo, Ny Kulturgeografisk Serie* 15. Olso.
Asheim, Bjorn T. (1985b). Uformell okonomi, småforetaksvekst og regional utvikling i Italia. *Nordisk Samhällsgeografisk Tidskrift* 2, 34–47.
Åström, Sven-Erik (1978). *Natur och byte. Ekologiska synpunkter på Finlands ekonomiska historia*. Söderströms, Ekenäs.
Axelsson, Björn, Sune Berger and Jon Hogdal (1980). *Vikmanshyttan: Lära för framtida bruk. En bok om studiearbete, frigörelser och Stora Kopparberg*. Prisma, Arlöv.
Bærenholdt, Jorgen Ole (1989). Livsformer og natursammenhaenge i kritisk geografi. *Nordisk Samhällsgeografisk Tidskrift* 9, 15–25.
Bærenholdt, Jorgen Ole, Kirsten Simonsen, Ole Beier Sorensen and Peter Vogelius (1990). Lifemodes and social practice. *Nordisk Samhällsgeografisk Tidskrift* 11, 72–86.
Bærenholdt, Jorgen Ole (1991). Bygdeliv. *Forskningsrapport 78, Institut for Geografi, Samfundsanalyse og Datalogi*. Roskilde Universitetscenter, Roskilde.
Bærenholdt, Jorgen Ole (1998). Regioner er politiske rum – også for geografer. *Nordisk Samhällsgeografisk Tidskrift* 26, 3–21.
Barnett, Clive (1998). Cultural twists and turns. *Society and Space* 16, 631–634.

Beckley, Thomas (1995). Pluralism by default: community power in a paper mill town. *Forest Science* 42:1, 35–45.

Berg, Lawrence D. (1999). Cultural politics and the local(e). *Nordisk Samhällsgeografisk Tidskrift* 28, 3–22.

Berger, Sune (1991). Samhällets geografi – en introduktion. In Berger, Sune (ed.): *Samhällets geografi*. Nordisk Samhällsgeografisk Tidskrift, Uppsala.

Berglund, Eeva (1997a). Lost in the woods? Competing knowledges in Finland's forest debates. *Discussion Papers*. College of Natural Resources, University of California, Berkeley. (http://www.cnr.berkeley.edu/csrd/dis.paper)

Berglund, Eeva (1997b). *Knowing nature, knowing science. An ethnography of local environmental Activism*. White Horse Press, Cambridge.

Birkeland, Inger (1994). The feminine hotel and the man-made cultural landscape. *Nordisk Samhällsgeografisk Tidskrift* 19, 64–74.

Birkeland, Inger (1998). Nature and the 'cultural turn' in human geography. *Norsk Geografisk Tidsskrift* 52: 229–240.

Birkeland, Inger (1999). The mytho-poetic in northern travel. In Crouch, David (ed.): *Leisure/tourism geographies. Practices and geographical knowledge*, 17–33. Routledge, London.

Birkeland, Inger (2002). *Stories from the North. Travel as place-making in the context of modern holiday-travel to North Cape, Norway*. Dissertation for the Dr. Polit. Degree in the Department of Sociology and Human Geography, University of Oslo.

Bladh, Gabriel (1995). Finnskogens landskap och människor under fyra sekler. *Högskolan i Karlstad, Forskningsrapport 95:11*. University of Karlstac, Karlstad.

Blaikie, Piers, Terry Cannon, Ian Davis and Ben Wisner (1994). *At risk. Natural hazards, people's vulnerability, and disasters*. Routledge, London.

Buch-Hansen, Mogens and Bue Nielsen (1977). Marxist Geography and the Concept of Territorial Structure. *Antipode* 9, 35–44.

Buch-Hansen, Mogens, Hans Folke, Steen Folke, Jette Gottlieb, Frank Hansen, Anna Marie Hellmers, Poul Kroijer and Bue Nielsen (1976). *Om geografi*. Hans Reitzel, Copenhagen.

Burgess, Jacquelin and Carolyn M. Harrison (1993). The circulation of claims in the cultural politics of environmental change. In Hansen, Anders (ed.): *The mass media and environmental issues*, 198–221. Leicester University Press, Leicester.

Buttimer, Anne (ed.1992). A special issue on cultural variations in concepts of nature. *Geojournal* 2, 99–172.

Buttimer, Anne (1993). *Geography and the human spirit*. The Johns Hopkins University Press, London.

Buttimer, Anne (1996). Circuits of calories: flows of food and energy in Germany, Ireland, the Netherlands and Sweden 1960–1990. *European Review* 4:3, 193–214.

Buttimer, Anne (1998). Landscape and life: appropriate scales for sustainable development. *Irish Geography* 31:1, 1–33.

Buttimer, Anne, Stefan Anderberg, Tom Andersson, Klas Sandell and Sverker Sörlin (1992). Woodland polyphony. In Svedin, Uno and Britt Hägerhäll Aniansson (eds.): *Society and the environment: A Swedish research perspective*, 177–198. Kluwer, Dordrecht.

Castree, Noel (1999). Situating cultural twists and turns. *Society and Space* 17, 257–260.

Di Chiro, Giovanna (1996). Nature as community. In Cronon, William (ed.): *Uncommon ground*, 298–320. Norton, New York.

Christiansen, Sofus, Peter Hagget and Perttu Vartiainen (1999). *Swedish research in human geography*. Brytpunkt/Swedish Council for Research in the Humanities and Social Sciences, Uppsala.

Connerton, Paul (1989). *How societies remember?* University Press, Cambridge.

Cutter, Susan (1995). Race, class and environmental justice. *Progress in Human Geography* 19:1, 111–122.

Dalby, Simon (1992). Ecopolitical discourse: 'environmental security' and political geography. *Progress in Human Geography* 16:4, 503–522.

Dalby, Simon (1998). Environmental geopolitics, introduction. In Ó. Tuathail, Gearóid, Simon Dalby and Paul Routledge (eds.): *The geopolitics reader*, 179–186. Routledge, London.

Dawson, Alice (1999). The problem of pigs. In Proctor, James and David M. Smith (eds.): *Geography and ethics*, 193–206. Routledge, London.

Demeritt, David (1994). The nature of metaphors in cultural geography and environmental history. *Progress in Human Geography* 18:2, 163–184.

Demeritt, David (2001). Scientific forest conservation and the statistical picturing of nature's limits in the Progressive-era United States. Society and Space 19.4, 431–459.

Donner-Amnell, Jakob (2001). To be or not to be Nordic? How internationalisation has affected the character of the Nordic forest industry and forest utilisation in the Nordic countries. *Nordisk Samhällsgeografisk Tidksrift* 33, 87–124.

Eden, Sally (2001). Environmental issues: nature versus the environment. *Progress in Human Geography* 25:1, 79–85.

Eskelinen, Heikki and Mika Kautonen (1997). In the shadow of the dominant cluster – the case of furniture industry in Finland. In Eskelinen, Heikki (ed.): Regional specialisation and local environment – learning and competitiveness. *NordREFO 1997:3*. Copenhagen.

Fannin, Maria, Sarah Fort, Jeanine Marley, Joe Miller and Sarah Wright (2000). The battle in Seattle: A response from local geographers in the midst of the WTO Ministerial Meetings. *Antipode* 32:3, 215–221.

Folke, Steen (1973). First thoughts on the geography of imperialism. *Antipode* 5:3, 16–20.

Folke, Steen (1985). The development of radical geography in Scandinavia. *Antipode* 17, 2–3.

Foucault, Michel (1998). *Seksuaalisuuden historia*. Gaudeamus, Helsinki.

Giddens, Anthony (1995). Elämää traditionaalisessa yhteiskunnassa. In Beck, Ulrich, Anthony Giddens and Scott Lash (eds.): *Nykyajan jäljillä*, 83–152. Vastapaino, Tampere.

Glacken, Clarence (1967). *Traces on the Rhodian shore*. University of California Press, Berkeley.

Goodman, David (1999). Agro-food studies in the 'age of ecology': Nature, corporeality, bio-politics. *Sociologia Ruralis* 39:1, 17–38.

Gosgrove, Denis (1984). *Social formation and symbolic landscape*. Croom Helm, London.

Graham, Brian and G.J.Ashworth (2000). *A geography of heritage*. Arnold, London.

Granfelt, TiiaRiitta (ed. 1999). *Managing the globalized environment*. Intermediate Technology Publications, London.

Granö, J.G. (1997, orig. 1929). *Pure geography* (edited by Olavi Granö and Anssi Paasi). The Johns Hopkins University Press, London. Published in 1929 under the title *Reine Geographie* and in 1930 in Finnish as *Puhdas maantiede*.

Gregory, Derek (1994). *Geographical imaginations*. Blackwell, Oxford.

Hägerstrand, Torsten (1985). Time geography: Focus on the corporeality of man, society and environment. *Science and Praxis*, 193–216. United Nations University, New York.

Haila, Yrjö (1999a). The north as/and the other: ecology, domination, solidarity. In Fischer, Frank and Maarten A. Hajer (eds.): *Living with nature*, 42–57. Oxford University Press.

Haila, Yrjö (1999b). Socioecologies. *Ecography* 22, 337–348.

Haila, Yrjö (2000a). Beyond the nature-culture dualism. *Biology & Philosophy* 15, 155–175.

Haila, Yrjö (2000b). Ekologiasta politiikkaan: kurinpitoa vai solidaarisuutta? *Tiede ja Edistys* 25:2, 81–96.

Haila, Yrjö and Richard Levins (1992). *Humanity and nature*. Pluto Press, London.

Haila, Yrjö and Lassi Heininen (1995). Ecology: A new discipline for disciplining? *Social Text* 42, 153–171.

Häkli, Jouni (1994). Territoriality and the rise of modern state. *Fennia* 172:1, pp. 1–82.

Häkli, Jouni (1996). Culture and politics of nature in the city. *Capitalism, Nature, Socialism* 7:2,125–138.

Häkli, Jouni (1997). Discourse in the production of political space: decolonising the symbolism of provinces in Finland. *Political Geography* 17, 331–363.

Häkli, Jouni (1999). *Meta hodos. Johdatus ihmismaantieteeseen*. Vastapaino, Tampere.

Hallin, Per Olof (1993). Miljökris och gröna handlingstilar. *Nordisk Samhällsgeografisk Tidskrift* 17, 14–22.

Hänninen, Sakari (ed. 2000). *Displacement of politics*. SoPhi, Jyväskylä.

Hänninen, Sakari and Jouko Karjalainen (eds. 1997). *Biovallan kysymyksiä*. Gaudeamus, Helsinki.

Hansen, Frank (1990). Nature in Geography. *Nordisk Samhällsgeografisk Tidskrift* 11, 87–97.

Hansen, Tina and Keld Buciek (2000). Landskabet som smafundsmaessig forestilling. *Nordisk Samhällsgeografisk Tidskrift* 31, 59–76.

Haraway, Donna (1991). *Simians, cyborgs, and women*. Free Association Books, London.

Harvey, David (1973). *Social justice and the city*. Edward Arnold, London.

Harvey, David (1996). *Justice, nature and the geography of difference*. Blackwell, Oxford.

Hautamäki, Lauri (1979). *Kylätoiminnan opas*. Gummerus, Jyväskylä.

Heininen, Lassi (1998). The international situation and cooperation. In Granberg, Leo (ed.): *The snowbelt*, 199–230. Kikimora Publications, Helsinki.

Heyman, Richard (2001). Guest editorial: Pedagogy and the 'cultural turn' in geography. *Society and Space* 19, 1–6.

Hjort af Ornäs, Anders (1996). *Approaching nature from local communities. Security perceived and achieved*. Environmental Policy and Society, Linköping University. Linköping.

Hjort af Ornäs, Anders and Sverre Lodgaard (eds. 1992). *The environment and international security*. Research Programmme on Environmental Policy and Society, University of Uppsala.

Hoeg, Peter (1992). *Froken Smillas fornämmelse for sne*. Munksgaard, Cobenhagen.

Horkheimer, Max and Theodor W. Adorno (1981). *Upplysningens dialektik*. Röda Bokförlaget, Gothenburg.

Hornborg, Alf (1998). Mi'kmak environmentalism: local incentives and global projections. In Sandberg, L. Anders and Sverker Sörlin (eds.) *Sustainability the challenge. People, power and the environment*, 202–211. Black Rose Books, Montréal.

Hottola, Petri (1999). *The intercultural body*. University of Joensuu, Department fo Geography Publications 7. Joensuu.

Hustich, Ilmari (ed. 1960). A special issue on man's influence on nature in Finland. *Fennia* 85.

Jakobs, Jane M. (2000). Editorial: Difference and its other. *Transactions of the Institute of British Geographers, New Series* 25, 403–407.

Jensen, John and Kirsten Simonsen (1981). The local state, planning and social movements. *Acta Sociologica* 24:4, 279–291.

Jones, Michael (1991). The elusive reality of landscape. *Norsk Geografisk Tidskrift* 45, 229–244.

Jones, Michael and Kenneth Olwig (eds. 2002). *Nordscapes. Thinking landscapes and regional identity on the northern edge of Europe*. University of Minnesota Press, Minneapolis. Forthcoming.

Karjalainen, Pauli Tapani (1986). Geodiversity as a lived world. *University of Joensuu, Publications in Social Sciences* 7. Joensuu.

Karjalainen, Pauli and PerttuVartiainen (1990). Dwelling in geography: Joensuu. *Nordisk Samhällsgeografisk Tidskrift* 11, 98–105.

Karlsson, Svenolof (ed. 1992). *Source of freedom*. Nordic Council, Stockholm.

Karvinen, Marko (1995). The interpretation of sea in urban planning in Helsinki. *Nordisk Samhällsgeografisk Tidskrift* 20, 131–139.

Katz, Cindy and Andrew Kirby (1991). In the nature of things: The environment and everyday life. *Transactions of the Institute of British Geographers, New Series* 3, 259–271.

King, A.D. (1996). Opening up the social sciences to the humanities: A response to Peter Taylor. *Environment and Planning A* 28, 1954–1959.

Knuuttila, Seppo (1980). Kansanomainen yhteisö ja avunanto. *Mielenterveys* 1, 7–11.

Knuuttila, Seppo (1985). Kansanomaisen maailmankuvan ihanteita. In Hakamäki, Toivo, Heikki Kirkinen and Arno Rautavaara (eds.): *Sukupolvien perintö 2, talonpoikaiskulttuurin kasvu*, 347–365. Suomalaisen Kirjallisuuden Seura, Helsinki.

Knuuttila, Seppo (1992). *Kansanhuumorin mieli.* Suomalaisen Kirjallisuuden Seura, Helsinki.

Knuuttila, Seppo, Ilkka Liikanen, Pertti Rannikko, Hannu Itkonen, Merja Koistinen, Jukka Oksa and Sinikka Vakimo (1996). Kyläläiset, kansalaiset. University of Joensuu, *Karelian Institute Publications* 114. Joensuu.

Koch, Hal and Alf Ross (1949). Nordisk demokrati. Westermanns Forlag, Copenhagen.

Koivusalo, Markku (2000). Biopolitical displacement and the antinomies of biopolitical reason. In Hänninen, Sakari and Jussi Vähämäki (eds.): *Displacement of Politics.* SoPhi, Jyväskylä.

Kortelainen, Jarmo (1999). The river as an actor-network and river systems. *Geoforum* 30, 235–247.

Kortelainen, Jarmo (2000). *Vihertyvä kaupunkiseutu. Suunnittelun ja hallinnan ekomoderni käänne.* SoPhi, Jyväskylä.

Koskela, Hille (1999). Fear, control and space. *Publicationes Instituti Geographici Universitatis Helsingiensis* A 137. University of Helsinki, Helsinki.

Kotilainen, Juha (1996). Between the global and the local in environmental politics. *Nordisk Samhällsgeografisk Tidskrift* 23, 61–68.

Kotilainen, Juha (1997). Globaali luonto – tarua vai totta? University of Joensuu, Department of Geography. Phil.lic. dissertation. Mimeo.

Kumpulainen, Mikko (1999). Maan ja talouden välissä.Viisi kertomusta suomalaisen luontosuhteen muutoksesta. University of Joensuu, *Department of Geography Publications* 5. Joensuu.

Lähde, Ville (2001). Viisi vuotta Muutoksen Kevättä. *Muutoksen Kevät* 20, 4.

Lash, Scott (1995). Refleksiivisyys ja sen vastinparit: rakenne, estetiikka, yhteisö. In Beck, Ulrich, Anthony Giddens and Scott Lash (1995): *Nykyajan jäljillä.* Vastapaino, Tampere.

Latour, Bruno (1987). *Science in action.* Harvard University Press, Cambridge, Massachusetts.

Latour, Bruno (1993). *We have never been modern.* Harvester Wheatsheaf, Hempstead.

Lehtinen, Ari (1987). Regionalismin ja ekokehityksen yhteys aluepoliittisessa murroksessa. Esimerkkinä Mikkelin ekolääni. *Suunnittelumaantieteen yhdistyksen julkaisuja* 28. Helsinki.

Lehtinen, Ari (1990a). Lokalsamhället och skogsgränskonflikten. *Nordisk Samhällsgeografisk Tidskrift* 11, 40–51.

Lehtinen, Ari (1990b). 'Oren geografi' och dess samhällspraxis. *Nordisk Samhällsgeografisk Tidskrift* 12, 73–74.

Lehtinen, Ari (1991). Northern natures. A study of the forest question emerging within the timber-line conflict in Finland. *Fennia* 169:1, 57–169.

Lehtinen, Ari (1993). Kulttuuristuminen yhteiskuntatutkimuksessa: ihmisläheisyyttä vai todellisuuspakoa? In Karjalainen, Pauli Tapani (ed.): Maantieteen maisemissa, 73–82. *Unversity of Joensuu, Human Geography and Planning, Occasional Papers* 25. Joensuu.

Lehtinen, Ari (1996). Tales from the Northern backwoods: Fairy tales and conspirators in Finnish forest politics. In Hjort af Ornäs, Anders (ed.): *Approaching nature from local communities.* Environmental Policy and Society, Linköping University.

Lehtinen, Ari (1999). Ympäristönkäytön oikeudenmukaisuus – haaste maantieteelliselle tutkimukselle. *Terra* 111:4, 209–212.

254   *Voices from the North*

Lehtinen, Ari (2000). Mires as mirrors. Peatlands – hybrid landscapes of the North. *Fennia* 178:1, 125–137.

Lehtinen, Ari (2001a). Modernization and the concept of nature: on the reproduction of environmental stereotypes. In Myllyntaus, Timo and Mikko Saikku (eds.): *Encountering the past in nature*, 29–48. Ohio University Press, Athens.

Lehtinen, Ari (2001b). Nordic forest communities, vulnerability and the question of environmental justice – a view from geography. In Hytönen, Marjatta (ed.): *Social sustainability of forestry in northern Europe*, 315–332. Nordic Council of Ministers, Copenhagen.

Lehtinen, Ari (2002a). Globalisation and the Finnish forest sector. In Westerholm, John and Pauliina Raento (eds.): Atlas of Finland. A special issue of *Fennia* 180:1. Forthcoming. (http://www.mediakeel.com/fennia/pages/lehtinen.htm)

Lehtinen, Ari (2002b). Landscapes of domination. In Jones, Michael and Kenneth Olwig (eds.): *Nordscapes*. University of Minnesota Press. Forthcoming.

Lehtinen, Ari (2002c). Mnemonic North. Multilayered geographies of the Barents Region. In Möller, Frank and Samu Pehkonen (eds.): *Encountering the North*. Ashgate, Aldershot. Forthcoming.

Lidskog, Rolf (1998). Teknologiska katastrofer i det senmoderna samhället. *Nordisk Samhällsgeografisk Tidskrift* 27, 29–50.

Lindén, Anna-Lisa (1998). Values of nature in every-day life. In Sandberg, Anders L. and Sverker Sörlin (eds.): *Sustainability the challenge. People, power and the environment*, 34–41. Black Rose Books, Montréal.

Lloyd, Sarah (2001). The emergent forest landscape in Sweden: A case study of relationships between socio-economic and ecological space in Jokkmokk. A master's thesis in the Swedish University of Agricultural Sciences, Department of Rural Development Studies. Mimeo.

Lovio, Raimo (1999). Yritykset, alueet ja ympäristöt – luonnolliset ja luodut ympäristökilpailutekijät. *Alue ja Ympäristö* 28:1, 44–53.

Lundqvist, Jan (1994). Trade and regulations of pesticide usage. Some observations regarding the Third World situation. In Hjort af Ornäs, Anders and Jan Lundqvist (eds.): *The environment and free trade*. Research Programme on Environmental Policy and Society/ EPOS, Uppsala University.

Lynch, Michael (1993). *Scientific practice and ordinary action. Ethnomethodology and social studies of science*. Cambridge University Press, New York.

Manninen, Mari (2000). Kansalaisliikkeiden mielipidevalta on hyvin pienellä ydinjoukolla. *Helsingin Sanomat* 1.4.2000, C1.

Marcuse, Herbert (1966). *Eros and civilization*. Beacon Press, Boston.

Massa, Ilmo (1984). Problem of the development of the north between the wars: some reflections of Väinö Tanner's human geography. *Fennia* 162:2, 201–215.

Massey, Doreen (1995). Imagining the world. In Allen, John and Doreen Massey (eds.): *Geographical worlds*, 5–51. Open University, London.

Massey, Doreen (2001). Geography on the agenda. *Progress in Human Geography* 25:1, 5–17.

Mathiesen, Thomas (1982). *Makt och motmakt*. Korpen, Gothenburg.

Maxey, Ian (1999). Beyond boundaries? Activism, academia, reflexivity and research. *Area* 31:3, 199–208.

McAfee, Kathleen (1999). Selling nature to save it? *Society and Space* 17, 133–154.

Miettinen, Otto and Tove Selin (1999). *Harkittu riski. UPM-Kymmene Indonesian sademetsissä*. Vihreä Sivistysliitto, Helsinki.

Moen, Eli and Kari Lilja (2001). Constructing global corporations: contrasting national legacies in the Nordic forest industry. In Morgan G., P.H. Kristensen and R. Whitley (eds.). *Organizing internationally: Restructuring firms and markets in the global economy*, 145–168. Oxford University Press, Oxford.

Möller, Frank and Samu Pehkonen (eds. 2002). *Encountering the north. Cultural geography, international relations and the northern landscape.* Ashgate, Aldershot. Forthcoming.

Murdoch, Jonathan (1998). The spaces of actor-network theory. *Geoforum* 29:4, 357–374.

Murdoch, Jonathan, Terry Marsden and Jo Banks (2000). Quality, nature, and embeddedness: Some considerations in the context of food sector. *Economic Geography* 79: 107–125.

Myllyntaus, Timo and Mikko Saikku (eds. 2001). *Encountering the past in nature. Essays in environmental history.* Ohio University Press, Athens.

Nevalainen, Jaana (1995). Ikuisesta kesästä talvikaupunkiin – vuodenajat suomalaisessa kaupunkiympäristössä. *Alue ja Ympäristö* 24:2, 6–14.

Nielsen, Bue (1976). Naturens betydning for territorialstrukturens udvikling. *Fagligt Forum – Kulturgeografiske Haefter* 9, 68–78.

Nynäs, Helena (1990). Hur är det möjligt att ha monopol på kritik? *Nordisk Sammhällsgeografisk Tidskrift* 12, 72–73.

Nynäs, Helena (1992). Ekokommuner som motkultur i Norge. Uppfattningar om naturen och lokalsamhället. Hovedoppgave i Samfunnsgeografi, Avdeling for Samfunnsgeografi, Universitetet i Oslo. Master's thesis in the Department of Human Geography, Oslo University. Mimeo.

Oksa, Jukka and Pertti Rannikko (1985): Kylä yhteiskunnassa. University of Joensuu, *Publications of the Karelian Institute* 11. Joensuu.

Olsson, Gunnar (1985). Om planeringens paradoxer. *Nordisk Samhällsgeografisk Tidskrift* 2, 3–9.

Olwig, Kenneth Robert (1980). Historical geography and the society/nature 'problematic': The perspective of J.F. Schouw, G.P. Marsh and E. Reclus. *Journal of Historical Geography* 6, 29–45.

Olwig, Kenneth Robert (1984). *Nature's ideological landscape.* George Allen & Unwin, London.

Olwig, Kenneth Robert (1986). The childhood 'deconstruction' of nature and the construction of 'natural' housing environments for children. *Scandinavian Housing and Planning Research* 3, 129–143.

Olwig, Kenneth Robert (1992). Eurooppalaisen kansakunnan pohjoinen luonne. In Karlsson, Svenolof (ed.): *Vapauden lähde. Pohjolan merkitys Euroopalle*, 158–182. Vapk Publishing, Helsinki.

Olwig, Kenneth Robert (1996). Recovering the substantive nature of landscape. *Annals of the Association of American Geographers* 86:4, 630–653.

Olwig, Kenneth Robert (2002). *Landscape, nature, and the body politic.* The University of Wisconsin Press, Madison.

Ossenbrügge, Jürgen (1993). *Umweltrisiko und Raumentwicklung.* Springer-Verlag, Berlin.

Paasi, Anssi (1982). Subjektiivisen elementin merkityksestä J.G. Granön maantieteellisessä ajattelussa. *Terra* 94:2, 140–156.

Paasi, Anssi (1984). Den regionala identiteten och det samhälleliga medvetandet. *Nordisk Samhällsgeografisk Tidskrift* 1, 47–53.

Paasi, Anssi (1986). The institutionalization of regions. Theory and comparative case studies. *Fennia* 164, 105–146.

Paasi, Anssi (1996). *Territories, boundaries and consciousness: The changing geographies of the Finnish-Russian border.* Wiley, Chichester.

Peet, Richard and Michael Watts (1996). Liberation ecology. In Peet, Richard and Watts, Michael (eds.): *Liberation ecologies. Environment, development, social movements, 1–45.* Routledge, London.

Pehkonen, Samu (1999). 'Tänne, muttei pidemmälle!' Alta-kamppailu ja Pohjois-Norjan monikulttuurinen maisema. *Tampere Peace Research Institute, Research Reports 88.* Tampere.

Pennanen, Kaisa (1998). Ihminen ja maa. Eric Dardellin maantieteestä. *University of Joensuu, Department of Geography Publications 2*.

Porteous, Douglas J. (1988). Topocide: the annihilation of place. In Eyles, John and David M. Smith (eds.): *Qualitative methods in human geography*, 75–93. Routledge, London.

Proctor, James and David M. Smith (eds. 1999). *Geography and ethics*. Routledge, London.

Pulido, Laura (1996). A critical review of the methodology of environmental racism research. *Antipode* 28:2,122–142.

Rabinow, Paul (1989). Kaupunkitilan säätely. In Foucault, Michel and Paul Rabinow (1989): Kaupunki, tila, valta. *Tampere University of Technology, Department of Community Planning Publications* 16, Tampere.

Raivo, Petri (1996). Maiseman kulttuurinen transformaatio. *Nordia* 25:1. Oulu.

Rannikko, Pertti (1997). From functional to symbolic local community: A case study of a forest village in eastern Finland. *Research in Community Sociology* 7, 223–246.

Rannikko, Pertti (1999a). Combining social and ecological sustainablity in the Nordic forest periphery. *Sociologia Ruralis* 39:3, 394–410.

Rannikko, Pertti (1999b). Forest work as the cause of settlement and depopulation in the remote parts Finland. In Reunala, Aarne and Ilpo Tikkanen (eds.): *The green kingdom. Finland's forest cluster*, 222–226. Metsämiesten Säätiö Foundation, Helsinki.

Raumolin, Jussi (1981). Global scene, natural resources and development problems in the periphery country Finland: Some reflections on Ilmari Hustich's world view. *Fennia* 159:1, 15–23.

Rose, Gillian (1993). *Feminism and geography: The limits of geographical knowledge*. Polity Press, Cambridge.

Rouhinen, Sauli (1981). A new social movement in search of new foundations for the development of the countryside: the Finnish action-oriented Village Study 76 and 1300 village committees. *Acta Sociologica* 24:4, 265–278.

Routledge, Paul (1996). The third space of critical engagement. *Antipode* 28:4,399–419.

Ryden, Kent C. (1993). *Mapping the invisible landscape*. University of Iowa Press, Iowa City.

Rytteri, Teijo (2000). Metsäteollisuuden yhteiskunnallinen vastuu. *Alue ja ympäristö* 29:1,5–17.

Rytteri, Teijo (2002). Metsäteollisuusyrityksen luonto. Tutkimus Enso-Gutzeitin ympäristö- ja yhteiskuntavastuun muotoutumisesta. University of Joensuu, *Department of Geography Publications 10*. Joensuu.

Saastamoinen, Olli (1999). The strategies of the Scandinavian forest industries. In Saastamoinen, O., A. Chubinsky and T. Torniainen (eds.): Economic problems of the forest complex of the Northwest Russia during a transition period. *Proceedings of the workshop held in St. Petersburg Forest Terchnical Academy* in February 11–13, 1999. St. Petersburg.

Sachs, Wolfgang (1999). Sustainable development and the crisis of nature: On the political anatomy of an oxymoron. In Fischer, Frank and Maarten A. Hajer (eds.): *Living with nature*, 23–41. Oxford University Press. Oxford.

Saether, Bjornår (1998). Environmental improvements in the Norwegian pulp and paper industry – from place and government to space and market. *Norsk Geografisk Tidskrift* 52, 181–194.

Saether, Bjornår (1999). *Regulering og innovasjon: miljoarbeid i norsk treforedlingsindustri 1974–1998*. Dr. Polit. Dissertation in the Department of Sociology and Human Geography, Oslo University, Oslo.

Sairinen, Rauno (2000). Regulatory reform of Finnish environmental policy. *Helsinki University of Technology, Centre for Urban and Regional Studies Publications* A 27. Espoo.

Sandberg, Anders L. and Sverker Sörlin (1998). Rearticulating the environment: Towards a pluralist vision of natural resource use. In Sandberg, L. Anders and Sverker Sörlin (eds.):

Sustainability the challenge. People, power and the environment, 1–18. Black Rose Books, Montréal.
Sandell, Klas (1991). Outdoor recreation – re-creation of recreation? *Nordisk Samhällsgeografisk Tidskrift* 14, 35–46.
Schama, Simon (1995). *Landscape and memory*. Fontana Press, London.
Setten, Gunhild (2000). Gendered landscapes: the relevance of a gendered nature-culture. Dualism in Norwegian farming practices. In Szczygiel, Bonj, Carubia, Josephine and Dowler, Lorraine (eds.): *Gendered landscapes*. The Center for Studies in Landscape History, Pennsylvania Sate University.
Short, John Rennie (1991). *Imagined Country. Environment, culture and society*. Routledge, London.
Siltala, Juha (1996). Yksilöllisyyden historialliset ja psykologiset ehdot. In Hautamäki, Antti, Eerik Lagerspetz, Juha Silvola, Juha Siltala and Jarmo Tarkki (eds.): *Yksilö modernin murroksessa*, 117–204. Gaudeamus, Helsinki.
Siltala, Juha (1999). *Valkoisen äidin pojat*. Otava, Helsinki.
Silvasti, Tiina and Tuija Mononen (2001). Ruoka liikkeessä. *Yhteiskuntapolitiikka* 66:1, 43–51.
Simonsen, Kirsten (1985). Konsumtion, reproduktion og den rumlige dimension – udfordringen fra kvindeforskningen. In Tonboe, Jens (ed.): *Farvel til byen?* Aalborg Universitetsforlag, Aalborg.
Simonsen, Kirsten (1988). 'Postmodernisme' og kritisk geografi. *Nordisk Samhällsgeografisk Tidskrift* 8, 7–13.
Simonsen, Kirsten (1991). 'Postmodernisme og kvindegeografi. *Nordisk Samhällsgeografisk Tidskrift* 13, 44–52.
Simonsen, Kirsten (1996). What kind of space in what kind of social theory? *Progress in Human Geography* 20:4, 494–512.
Simonsen, Kirsten (2000). The body as battlefield. *Transactions of the Institute of British Geographers, New Series* 25:1, 7–9.
Simonsen, Kirsten, Henrik Toft Jensen and Frank Hansen (1982). *Lokalsamfund og sociale bevegelser*. Kritisk samfundsgeografi II. Roskilde.
Sjöberg, Michael (1995). Writing the edge: revisiting the margins of spatial restructuring. *Nordisk Samhällsgeografisk Tidskrift* 20, 75–87.
Smith, Neil (1984). *Uneven Development*. Basil Blackwell, Oxford.
de Souza, Peter (1989). Territorial production complexes in the Soviet Union – with special focus on Siberia. *University of Gothenburg, Department of Geography Publications*, B 80.
Sörlin, Sverker (1988). *Framtidslandet. Debatten om Norrland och naturrersurserna under det industriella genombrottet*. Carlsson, Stockholm.
Sörlin, Sverker (1999). The articulation of territory: landscape and the constitution of regional and national identity. *Norsk Geografisk Tidskrift* 53, 103–112.
Sporrong, Ulf (2002). The province of Dalarna – Heartland or Anomaly? In Jones, Michael and Kenneth Olwig (eds.): *Nordscapes. Thinking landscapes and regional identity on the northern edge of Europe*. University of Minnesota Press. Forthcoming.
Susiluoto, Paulo (2000). Suomen ajan ihmismaantiedettä Petsamosta. In Susiluoto, Paulo (ed.): *Väinö Tanner. Ihmismaantieteellisiä tutkimuksia Petsamon seudulta*, 9–31. Suomalaisen Kirjallisuuden Seura, Helsinki.
Svanqvist, Berit K. (2000). Naturumänge ur ett individperspektiv. *Nordisk Samhällsgeografisk Tidskrift* 31, 37–57.
Tammilehto, Olli (1991). Tutkijankammio ympäristökriisin myllerryksessä. In Massa, Ilmo and Rauno Sairinen (eds.): *Ympäristökysymys*. Gaudeamus, Helsinki.
Tanner, Väinö (1929). Antropogeografiska studier inom Petsamo-området I. Skoltlapparna. *Fennia* 49, 1–518.

258 Voices from the North

Tanskanen, Minna (2000). Näkyvän takana. Tutkimus metsäojitetun suomaiseman kulttuurisuudesta. *University of Joensuu, Department of Geography Publications* 8. Joensuu.

Tuan, Yi-fu (1998). *Escapism*. The Johns Hopkins University Press, Baltimore.

Vartiainen, Perttu (1979). Maantieteilijän 'luonnosta' ja ns. luonnonmaantieteestä. *Terra* 91:4, 240–248.

Vartiainen, Perttu (1984). Maantieteen konstituoitumisesta ihmistieteenä. *Joensuun yliopison yhteiskuntatieteellisiä julkaisuja* 3. Joensuu.

Vartiainen, Perttu (1986a). Om 'det geografiska' i samhällsteorin. *Nordisk Samhällgeografisk Tidskrift* 3, 3–16.

Vartiainen, Perttu (1986b). Kritisk samhällsgeografi i Västtyskland – om Eisels och Becks kontext och produktion. In Vartiainen, Perttu, Bo Forsström and Seija Virkkala (eds.): Den senindustriella utvecklingen och den regionala problematiken i Norden. *Publikationer av föreningen för planeringsgeografi* 24, 13–22.

Vartiainen, Perttu (1987). The strategy of territorial integration in regional development: defining territoriality. *Geoforum* 18, 117–126.

Vartiainen, Perttu (1988). (Kritisk) Samhällsgeografi i Finland? *Nordisk Samhällsgeografisk Tidskrift* 7, 25–33.

Vartiainen, Perttu and Heikki Vesajoki (1991). Ekologisen maantieteen haasteista. In Hakamies, Pekka, Väinö Jääskeläinen and Ilkka Savijärvi (eds.): *Saimaalta Kolille. Karjalan tutkimuslaitos 1971–1991*. Karelian Institute, Joensuu University, Joensuu.

Vepsäläinen, Mia (2000). Environmental image of the industrial town – Image aspirations of town authorities and industrial companies in Varkaus during the 20th century. *Nordisk Sammhällsgeografisk Tidskrift* 30, 75–92.

Virtanen, Anne (2000). Tilasta paikkaan, estetiikasta ekologiaan. Maantieteellisiä tulkintoja eletystä kaupungista. *Annales Universitatis Turkuensis* C 155. Ph.D. Dissertation in geography at the Turku University, Turku.

Westholm, Erik (1992). Mark, människor och moderna skiftesreformer i Dalarna. *Geografiska Regionstudier 25*. Doctoral Dissertation at Uppsala University.

Williams, Raymond (1979). *Key words*. Fontana, Glasgow.

Zimmerer, Karl (1994). Human geography and the 'new ecology': The prospect and promise of integration. *Annals of the Association of American Geographers* 84:1, 108–125.

PART V
DIFFERENCE, DISTINCTION
AND POWER

Chapter 14

Racialization and migration in urban segregation processes
Key issues for critical geographers

Roger Andersson and Irene Molina

This chapter argues for a holistic understanding of residential segregation. By this we mean that contemporary social geography research, when trying to explain spatial distributions, not only has to engage in studying distributions as such, as it has been traditionally, but causes and effects as well; not only material (visible) but even immaterial and symbolic aspects; not only situations but also contexts and dynamic processes.

With the word segregation, one is usually alluding either to the general inner differentiation in the city, i.e., the geographical separation of different population groups, but sometimes also the spatially expressed division between housing areas and workplaces. The term is, however, most often used to refer to the disparate spatial distribution of neighbourhoods by diverse population groups; in other words, residential segregation. This common perceptions of segregation tend to neglect the most important components of the process: the people and the constant dynamism within and between these separate, segregated spaces in the form of e.g., daily travel, migration and transfers. Other neglected aspects are borders that are reinforced, crossed or eliminated; frictions in the space as indicators of the fact that this spatial separation occurs on everything but equitable terms. These disregarded dynamic aspects are not only a consequence of segregated settlement patterns, but are rather frequently replicating agents in themselves, therewith constituting part of the set of mechanisms for which there is found no explanation in current research. The concept is moreover vague, ignores prevailing and historic balances of power and contains a misleading element of neutrality. One can say that the definitions of residential segregation that have long dominated the research field look upon the phenomenon too statically and help neither towards understanding the causative mechanisms or the development of residential segregation, nor towards the everyday realities of the actors involved.

The traditional, almost mechanical concept of ethnic residential segregation must be examined, and it seems thus far that the redefinition of the phenomenon of segregation sought in this chapter requires a revision of old definitions and a reformulation of the concept and the processes it encompasses, in new terms. This may very well be regarded as some sort of deconstructivist exercise. In the next pages we are going to introduce two alternative and complementary models for the understanding of the processes of ethnic residential segregation in Swedish cities.

We are going to combine these two models, in order to offer a more holistic understanding of these processes than those that are dominated both within academia and politics in Sweden. The first model – the racialization model – starts from the idea that housing, i.e., various dimensions connected to the issues of how and where people live, may be regarded as a history of ideas, discourses, political measures and spatial praxis that are expressed in social geographical settlement patterns. To understand these patterns and their significance to people, the chosen perspectives, concepts and research methods are of pivotal importance. To change the perspective for analysis of the phenomenon traditionally called ethnic residential segregation and instead place it within the framework of the theory of racialization represents, as we shall see further on in the text, an attempt to deal with the inadequacies mentioned above. The second model – the migration model – is rather focusing on the process of segregation in terms of mobility and dynamics of individuals and groups in the city. This model too tries to integrate different actors and structures involved in the movements of in- and out-migration that generate segregated urban patterns. It furthermore acknowledges racialization processes as being part and parcel of the out-migration of 'native Swedes' from neighbourhoods experiencing increasing numbers of non-European and muslim immigrants. Aspects related to power relations are also involved in this model as for instance constraints for mobility for people's housing carriers. In both models a dynamic spatial analysis as well as the presence of time-space dimensions are central aspects for the analysis. Let us begin with the first model, which is based on the theoretical framework of racialization in society.

The racialization of the Swedish city: A history and a geography

The theory of racialization has had various areas of application, of which the foremost has probably been the British labour market and the status of the immigrant population within it. This explains why the theory was later used mainly in political-economic contexts, where it is now said to have two closely related implications. First, racialization is a process for the maintenance of borders that prevent certain population groups from selling their labour in determined parts of a particular society's labour market. Second, racialization is an allocation mechanism that places determined groups in determined positions in the production process (Satzewich 1988). However, fields of research other than the political-economic have employed the theory of racialization, such as for the study of European welfare states (Faist 1995), institutionalized racism and the impact of a national racist discourse that legitimizes racially discriminatory practices by social institutions (Wilkerson and Gresham 1989), historical studies of the global balance of power (Takaki 1992), internal critical review of academic language (Berg 1993, Jackson 1992, 190), and so on.

The racialization of the city can be said to be about *the processes that lead individuals, groups and institutions in a determined housing market to think, act and discriminate based upon a notion of 'race' in such a way that this housing market is differentiated spatially according to imagined racial differences and ascribed racial affiliations.* In light of that reasoning, it is conceivable that the missing link between structuralist and cultural reductionist studies of ethnic residential segregation is the global balance of power. The structuring (and socially constructed) categories that articulate these relationships of power are gender, class and, first and foremost, race. The *racialization of the city* can therewith be understood as a process which entails that certain ethnic groups, primarily but not solely non-European, stand for the most markedly segregated patterns among all groups of foreign background. An important message in the terminology of racialization is therewith that a racialized reality – ethnic residential segregation among else – does not simply happen by itself. It is rather a result of a set of intricate mechanisms of various nature that act on different levels in society.

There are several parallels between Swedish and international patterns of ethnic residential segregation. The similarities may be summed up by saying that certain immigrant groups occupy the lowest rungs on the housing and labour market ladders. What these positions entail for human living conditions in tangible terms and how these patterns look is, however, determined by each concrete historical-geographical context. Study of the racialization of the city shows how the history and geography of Swedish ethnic residential segregation are linked by ideas and notions about housing and about *The Other*. The ideological framework of contemporary ethnic segregation in Sweden can, when viewed in this way, be interpreted as the idea set that was the basis for Sweden's great social project of the 20th century: the modernization of society under the umbrella term the *people's home*. Swedish ethnic residential segregation has taken its concrete form in a continual conceptual and political course of events. How and by which mechanisms the processes of racialization of the Swedish city take place may be explained for analytical purposes using four fields, *the ideological, the political, the discursive and the spatial-material*. In reality, these four fields interact in every historical-geographical context and thus cannot be separated other than on an abstract plane.

The ideological field

Even though the housing issue is and has always been a tremendously important private and societal concern, housing research has long ignored several aspects of the issue. Underlying ideological structures concerning the design of housing policy are one of the aspects upon which far too little light has been shed. The housing issue was a central element in the construction of the people's home and the design of the Swedish welfare state. We believe that by illuminating underlying ideological aspects of the idea of the people's home, such as social hygiene, the concept of society and the city as an organism/a body, the view on worker housing, as well as notions about The Other, one can place the current question of ethnic residential segregation in a relevant historical light. Class relations and race relations are key aspects to understanding how the patterns of ethnic residential segregation found in Swedish cities have been shaped through the years.

Very little research has been done on possible relationships between ideological discourses such as eugenics, home hygiene, the concept of society and the city as an organism/a body and, for example, the view on worker housing at the turn of the last century and the housing policy and settlement patterns of the 1990s. These relationships may, however, be key aspects to understanding patterns of ethnic residential segregation in modern Swedish cities as historical products. The people's home, as part of the Swedish modernization project, has not only a political but also an ideological history that is relevant to the understanding of the housing issue in Sweden. The symbiosis established between the body, health, cleanliness and order debouched into the paradigm of social hygiene, which became the word of the day thereafter. In the same way that social hygiene stood as the ideological frame in the construction of early worker housing, one can say that this ideology can count the housing projects of the 1960s and 1970s among its last spatial footholds. The legacy of the doctrine of social hygiene, which gave rise to a housing policy and city planning methods that were partly intended to improve and socially adapt the living patterns of the working class and other deviant groups, lives on to a certain extent in the geography of the contemporary Swedish city. The role in Swedish society assumed by immigrants beginning in the 1960s, after the foundation of the people's home had been laid and the housing policy established, can in many ways be put on a par with the former position of the working class. In some cases, one can discern the remains of several decades of the past in the integration rhetoric now prevailing in modern public discourse on The Other. In the discourse of eugenics in the 1930s, tinkers, the Romany people, the mentally ill and even women were deviant elements in society. They were The Other and must be disciplined. The discursive equivalent today is the immigrants who must be integrated. Even if the differences between the two epochs are rather extensive, the notion of The Other has not ceased to be, but has only been shifted from certain groups to certain others. Present day Million Dwellings Programme neighbourhoods with high percentages of immigrant residents, which are pointed out as synonymous with residential segregation, correspond in several ways to the working class neighbourhoods of the early 20th century. Both the neighbourhoods and their populations are stamped as problems. The historical-geographical social order of the turn of the century is bound to today's through a continual ideological development and its associated discourses, where the *link* between the two epochs may be discerned in the formation of the people's home, with its ideological and sociopolitical development. Many were the groups who were difficult to discipline into the understanding of normality of the people's home. Among them were found the so-called tinkers, who far into the 1940s were often regarded as 'a hybrid race between Swedes and Gypsies.' (Broberg and Tydén 1991, 147). In other words, they did not submit to discipline. The undesirables of the people's home were thus not primarily genetically inferior members of society, but rather the 'negligent' and socially marginalized individuals, as well as deviant women (Broberg and Tydén 1991, 184–5). As Frykman and Löfgren point out, the picture of the Swedes who were to inhabit the people's home was constructed using opposing pictures. These opposing pictures consisted of the bourgeois view of the working class and others in relationship to the groups that deviated from the bourgeois way of life.

> Personal identity was built with the help of symbolic inversion: 'the others' are as black as we are white, as rough-hewn as we are slender-limbed, as coarse as we are courteous, as slovenly as we are proper…Little by little, the child became a participant in the thought pattern that was one of the pillars of the bourgeoisie's (usually unconscious) class analysis.

Here was developed the view of the people, of workers, of the lower class as a lesser sort of people: more primitive, less cultivated (see Frykman and Löfgren 1985, 28).

A reminder of these currents of ideas is relevant in the context wherein Sweden once again is dividing itself between the normal and the deviant, between We and They. The question is whether 'immigrants' as a socially constructed group do not have the same function today as the working class at the turn of the century, and which tinkers, the Romany people and other groups stamped as deviant once did, primarily during the 1930s. Normality could nowadays be rounded off with the word *Swedishness*. The search for a *Swedish identity* indicates that the division of the population today is not based upon racial differences in the biological sense, but rather that the rhetoric is now dominated by 'culture' (Molina 1997, Pred 2000).

Eugenics should in any case not be considered a wholly concluded epoch in Swedish history that disappeared along with the people's home. That would be far too simple an interpretation. In the sense that eugenics becomes what it is made into, one can say that there exists a Swedish character. In Swedish circumstances, eugenics became not an isolated scientific theory on genes, nor solely a method. Eugenics was a social phenomenon and was integrated in several areas beyond the medical and the scientific. It found its place in the art of social engineering that designed the people's home (Broberg and Tydén 1991, 178–90). Side by side with the population issue, the housing issue was one of the areas where eugenics – via home hygiene – gained its clearest application. The home in general, and the worker's home in particular, became an efficient instrument in the disciplining of citizens who deviated from the bourgeois family ideal (Karlsson 1993).

The political field

The most immediately decisive field in the formulation of processes of residential segregation in general and of ethnic segregation in particular is perhaps the political. The housing policy of the postwar era has left behind a lasting structure of forms of tenancy in Sweden. The categories of outright ownership, tenant-owned condominiums and rental housing demonstrate a relatively clear spatial separation, and people of foreign background are concentrated in the so-called Million Dwellings Programme areas where rental housing is the most common form. There are several ways in which the Swedish state as an institution has through the housing policy influenced the patterns of ethnic residential segregation. One example is heavy subsidization of single-family home construction and housing, even if the Home of One's Own project was not originally intended for the middle class, but rather for workers. *A home of one's own*, as the express objective of the postwar housing policy, has overall favoured the housing conditions of certain social groups ahead of others: those who could afford to take advantage of the state's various benefits in order to build or purchase single-family homes. However, the subsidy system has undeniably made it possible for many working class families to acquire homes of their own. The Swedish model for provision of housing has without doubt been characterized by considerations of fairness, even if the production process has been driven by private profit motives. The historically persistent housing shortage was eliminated for all practical purposes during the early 1970s (although recent reports show that it is growing to seriously high levels, at least in some regions of the country after the housing reforms of the beginning of the nineties), while high housing standards and state housing subsidies have made decent housing available to the absolute majority of Sweden's population. Through comprehensive regulation coupled to the subsidy system, the state has also been able to control much of housing construction with respect to *what* shall be built and *where*. Fundamental socioeconomic differences still determine, however, the form of tenancy available to households. Various forms of housing and forms of tenancy in particular are at the disposal of differing social groups. Despite everything, one of the paradoxes of Swedish housing policy is that it has experienced little success in living up to its objective of avoiding residential segregation, even as Swedish residential segregation, particularly during the past fifteen years, has undergone a change of character from a purely socioeconomic division to an ever-more racialized pattern.

Social groups other than those who live on the low-status side of the segregation fence have been illuminated – homeowners in neighbourhoods of single-family homes. Self-evidently, ethnically and socioeconomically based spatial separatism in Sweden's cities has not reached the degree of a military enclave with electronic surveillance as it has done in certain neighborhoods in Los Angeles and other cities around the world, in the so-called 'gated communities' and 'high-security neighborhoods,' etc. Nevertheless, there exists such a marked division between 'immigrant' and 'Swedish' sections in certain urban neighborhoods with heavy immigrant populations that people have begun talking of 'physical barriers,' 'ethnic walls' and the 'white reservation.' The step-by-step abandonment of housing subsidies (Turner and Whitehead, 2001), which had played a critical role in the housing policy aimed at achieving fairness as early as the 1940s has, combined with an unusually poor economy and consequently high unemployment, had an accelerating effect, paradoxically enough, upon increased residential segregation in most cities all over the country. That this tendency towards increased separation between native-born and (especially) non-European-born people persists also in the latter part of the 1990s is shown by Table 14.1.

Partial subsidizing of single-family home construction, with home ownership as the Swedish family's encouraged housing ideal, has also affected the process of racialization of the city. The state as an institution gave some social groups the motive and opportunity to strive to buy their own house. Households with relatively good economic situations have, with the help of the state, left rental apartment houses for single-family housing throughout most of the 20th century, which – due to the spatial separations of types of houses and tenure forms – has entailed the development of spatially separated neighbourhood categories.

The major property companies that own and manage the majority of rental housing in larger Swedish cities have in turn often actively welcomed new immigrants and others with little scope for action in the housing market to certain determined areas, often the same neighborhoods that 'Swedes' are moving away from. Households of foreign background are frequently actively directed to particular neighbourhoods. Some tenants have experienced this direction as force on the part of the authorities (Molina 1997). A piece of knowledge missing as a complementary picture is the role that private landlords can play in segregation processes. There have been some isolated and noticed cases where ethnic discrimination has conceivably occurred in connection with housing applications in the private rental market, but there has been no systematic study to cast light on this issue. Statistics show that foreign-born tenants, particularly those born in non-European countries, are markedly underrepresented within the private rental market, despite their palpable overrepresentation in the rental market as a whole (Table 14.2). This, of course, partly explains why the authorities responsible for refugee accomodation, find no alternative but to direct new immigrants to already 'immigrant-dense' neighbourhoods.

Table 14.1 Index of Dissimilarity* in 16 medium-sized Swedish cities 1995 and 1998

	1995		1998		Segr.
Municipality	Born in 6 countries**	Foreign-born	Born in 6 countries**	Foreign-born	tendency 6 countries
Trolhättan	0,67	0,39	0,69	0,38	increase
Luleå	0,60	0,27	0,56	0,25	decrease
Umeå	0,59	0,31	0,55	0,30	decrease
Borlänge	0,57	0,25	0,62	0,29	increase
Örebro	0,57	0,35	0,60	0,39	increase
Eskilstuna	0,57	0,30	0,62	0,30	increase
Jönköping	0,55	0,32	0,58	0,33	increase
Uppsala	0,55	0,36	0,56	0,35	increase
Gävle	0,54	0,29	0,56	0,30	increase
Karlstad	0,52	0,27	0,55	0,29	increase
Sundsvall	0,51	0,27	0,54	0,27	increase
Östersund	0,50	0,17	0,47	0,17	decrease
Västerås	0,47	0,23	0,48	0,24	increase
Norrköping	0,47	0,33	0,51	0,34	increase
Halmstad	0,46	0,34	0,51	0,35	increase
Skellefteå	0,37	0,21	0,40	0,20	increase

*   The index of Dissimilarity sums up the spatial residential differences between a particular population category and, in this case, the native-born population.
** People born in Ethiopia, Chile, Iraq, Iran, Lebanon, Turkey.

Source: Andersson 2000.

Table 14.2 Distribution of tenants between the municipal and private rental markets in Sweden, in percent, categorized according to country of birth, 1990

Country/region of birth	Municipal landlord	Private landlord	Other landlord	Total rental market
Sweden	15	7	7	29
Scandinavia	22	6	9	37
Former Yugoslavia	38	5	12	55
Greece	45	5	11	61
Poland	33	6	12	51
Europe outside Scandinavia	21	7	10	38
Africa	43	4	9	56
North America	19	8	9	36
South America	44	4	9	56
Turkey	66	2	9	77
Asia	47	3	9	59
Other	25	7	10	42
Total	16	7	8	30

Source: Total population and property registers, Statistics Sweden.

Residential segregation has never been expressed as a desirable situation in the context of Swedish housing policy. However, the prioritized objectives of the housing policy, despite having been an important instrument in guaranteeing all social groups access to decent housing (see, in particular, Kemeny 1995), have caused a systematic deepening of residential segregation processes. Residential segregation has not emerged arbitrarily, as the debate about 'what has gone wrong' usually implies.

Residential segregation is – despite political objectives to counteract it – a consequential result of a set of mechanisms that has acted so that while individuals and families with relatively greater resources have been able to realize 'the dream of a home of one's own' and have been concentrated in more attractive neighbourhoods, the less well-favoured in society have had severely limited choices. In this way, one could say that residential segregation is one of the paradoxes of the people's home. With respect to the ethnic variant, one can state that the concentration of people of foreign background in certain neighbourhoods is nevertheless a rather predictable result when many families arriving in Sweden from abroad are systematically directed to certain determined neighbourhoods. The role of social institutions in racialization processes has, naturally, not solely and not always been directly active, but their lack of long-term planning has had a significant impact in reinforcing racialized segregation patterns. The passive acceptance of the authorities of the terms and conditions in the housing market and the consequences for the status of various groups in this market have been at least equally decisive in these processes. The nation's Million Dwellings Program has produced neighbourhoods in the city where there have often been empty apartments that could be allocated to immigrant families. This has not been counteracted by a more proactive immigrant housing policy strategy that could have helped open 'Swedish' neighbourhoods to immigrants.

It may sound like a paradox that an important political objective in postwar housing policy, particularly beginning in the 1970s, has been to counteract residential segregation. Despite this, residential segregation has, albeit in various forms, characterized settlement patterns for the entire century. The relevant question is whether it is possible at all within the framework of a sectorial policy – the housing policy – to eliminate a phenomenon that essentially involves every structure in society, including that of ideas.

The discursive field

Notions about other people and about processes and relationships in society are reflected by and shaped in language. The vernacular reflects the balance of power in society, while at the same time, language can shape and reshape the balance of power. This makes discourses in society in general and the discourse on The Other in particular, critical to the social legitimization of the balance of power, not least of all in Sweden. As we have seen in earlier pages, the ideological field is maintained and reproduced by discourses, in this particular case by two kinds of discourses, firstly housing discourses and secondly, racialized discourses on the Other. The previous century's discourse of eugenics, and that of home hygiene related to it, identified the working class and its values and 'culture' as being responsible for the unacceptable way of life of workers, from a sanitary and moral point of view. One of the equivalents in today's Sweden is the opinion that immigrants create segregation by settling in the concrete block buildings of the Million Dwellings Programme because they want to retain 'their culture.' A new racist romanticism is creating images of The Other that are placed in opposition to traditional, nationalistic symbols. The Swedish identity must be defended and preserved against foreign deviations (Ålund and Schierup 1991, 12).

Furthermore, the social debate is increasingly tending to refer diverse evils in society to a question of culture. By culture, however, is seldom meant a mutable and borderless process that encompasses society as a whole, which is both the cause of changes and the effect of these changes. Culture is often considered in a narrow sense, as the values that immigrants bring in the form of baggage from the country of origin. The notion that immigrants strive to live near one another as a means of preserving their culture is spreading in commissions of inquiry, debates in the mass media and in the vernacular. Indirectly, this declares immigrant families from 'foreign cultures' guilty of creating segregation. The culturalist discourse on immigrants, The Other, thus legitimizes the prevailing order with respect to the housing issue, among else. More recent studies add nuance to this picture and show that these immigrant families have had very limited choices regarding housing. Their preferences with respect to housing are no different from those of other inhabitants in the community. In other words, had they been allowed to choose, they would probably have largely followed the same patterns demonstrated by 'ordinary' Swedes (Molina 1997).

However, the discourse of Swedish residential segregation is not only about the people. At least equally interesting from an ethnogeographic perspective is that neighbourhoods are objectified and stigmatized. Stigmatizing spatial representations are transmitted via mass media, but also by word of mouth, in the form of everyday discourses of individuals. In actuality, simplifications such as 'immigrant neighbourhood,' 'problem neighbourhood' and 'Million Dwellings Programme areas' conceal a multiplicity of realities that are constantly played out in the spatially visible and invisible neighbourhoods. From the inside out, various pictures of the neighbourhood reflect its inhabitants' diversity of experience, while pictures created from the outside usually constitute imagined geographies. As an unlimited multiplicity of individuals are clustered together and stigmatized in the category of immigrants, stereotypes are constructed of the neighbourhoods in which these immigrants are concentrated.

A hidden, often probably unconscious, discrimination that has been established in diverse representations – of both spatial and other nature – may play an important role in the maintenance and replication of racialization processes in the city. A neighbourhood and its inhabitants can through such discourses and imagined geographies be stigmatized into becoming a 'problem.' The consequences for the local population are negative. A more active symbolic element in the racialization of the city is the drawing of neighbourhood boundaries in the guise of 'Grannsamverkan mot brott,' the Swedish equivalent of 'Neighbourhood Watch.' Through activating and reinforcing a sense of We, which unites positive values like security and honesty within the neighbourhood, while crime is assumed to exist outside and be committed by The Other, a geographic border is drawn between We and They. The perpetrator is not found within the closed community within the neighbourhood. He or she is not a part of us, but rather the Other.

The interesting thing here is not the extent to which spatial barriers of this kind between We and They apply exclusively to immigrants. The point is rather that these and other imagined geographies seldom work in isolation from ideologies. The discourse on The Other is not only about immigrants. There are other groups in society who are also stigmatized as deviant and subjected to exclusion (Harrison 1995, 72). The inhabitants' discourses, the housing policy discourse, the mass-media discourse and various demarcations of borders contribute to the definition of the role that suburbs have been given in the racialized city. Imagined geographies in urban contexts encompass the people's own response to stigmatization. Expressions such as 'I don't live in Gottsunda, I live in Sunnersta,' the latter an upper middle class neighbourhood of single-family homes adjacent to the former so-called 'immigrant neighbourhood' are not unusual. Moreover, one may ask whether the many Swedish flags hanging from some balconies and terraces in the middle of or near these 'immigrant neighbourhoods' are not a silent cry that 'Swedes still live here'?

The spatial-material field

We will not be devoting any larger space to the last field here, since it is that which is most frequently dealt with in empirical studies of ethnic residential segregation. The concrete, spatial expression of segregation, that is, the concentration of certain groups and underrepresentation of others and the attendant consequences, are what is found in the spatial-material field. Certain less noticed aspects in this field, if any should be mentioned, are perhaps the various kinds of dynamics of social interaction generated in the neighbourhood. Social interaction is influenced both by the physical environment and the social composition of the local population. Immigrant households are concentrated mainly in neighbourhoods that were, before their arrival, already characterized by low socioeconomic status and a strong domination of apartment buildings. The neighbours that immigrant households encounter often include social outcasts with substantial abuse problems and, frequently, mentally ill individuals as well. These people have also been allocated to apartments in Million Programme areas. The immigrant families in these neighbourhoods often perceive this as a problem. Feelings of insecurity and threat are frequently expressed in diverse studies of local conditions in segregated neighbourhoods. They would like to have contact with 'ordinary Swedes' (Molina 1997).

Under these and other given circumstances, one may ask oneself, e.g., what forms of local citizenship and grassroots movements emerge in ethnically segregated neighbourhoods? Research has an important task in studying the prerequisites for the emergence of social interaction and local mobilization (see Blanc and Smith 1997). The social and ethnic heterogeneity found in virtually all areas in which immigrants are concentrated makes residential segregation in Swedish cities a scholarly interesting and politically relevant phenomenon to study.

The creation of 'immigrant-dense' neighbourhoods: A dynamic model

The second model that we want to present here starts from the observation that although urban sociologists and geographers have tried to grasp the segregation issue by focusing on the migration of households – using concepts like invasion and succession (Burgess 1925), filtering out/in (Hoyt 1939, Firey 1945), housing chains (White 1971), gentrification (Williams 1976) and 'blow-out' (Harvey 1973) – there is a need for further development of dynamic approaches. When segregation is to be addressed more dynamically we need to include also the long-term socio-cultural *effects* of the segregated city, not only basic economic and institutional factors and actors. Segregation processes could not be understood or explained if the social effects are left out of the analysis (see for instance Harvey and Chatterjee 1973, Scott 1986, Smith 1989a and 1989b, Friedrichs 1997).

Patterns of residential segregation are the result of migration. Almost every adult person resides in a particular house in a particular area because (s)he has moved there, either voluntarily or due to various degrees of force. Understanding migration, primarily intra-urban migration, is thereby a crucial condition for grasping segregation processes. And in order to better understand ethnic/racialized housing segregation we need to address not only the institutional and housing policy context but the question why individuals of a certain ethnic origin (for instance native Swedes) move out from some residential areas and why individuals of some other ethnic origin (a foreign-born category), non-voluntarily or voluntarily move into the same areas.

In Figure 14.1, a simple dynamic model is presented. The segregation process is viewed from the perspective of selective migrations. Although the model may be relevant for analysing similar processes in other countries, it has been developed in order to investigate the Swedish case and we will discuss it using Swedish examples.

1. The proto-segregation phase

Figure 14.1   A heuristic model for analysing ethnic/racial segregation dynamics

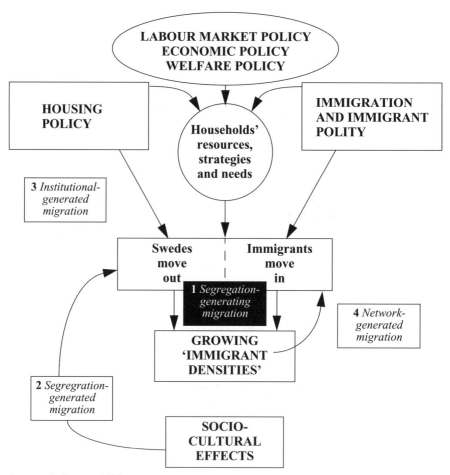

Source: Andersson 1998c.

It is a fact that all residential areas that have high immigrant concentrations today used to have much smaller concentrations some 10, 20 or 30 years ago. The most discussed Swedish example is Rinkeby, located in north-western Stockholm, where 12% were of non-Swedish origin in 1970 whereas c. 80% fall into that category in 2000. In the model, this kind of ethnic-selective migration is called *segregation-generating migration*. It could be said to start when a neighbourhood reaches a level of 'non-Swedes' higher than the city average. The reason for the initial phase – we might call it the proto-segregation phase – to emerge may vary over time and space. In Sweden, most research evidence points in the direction of two relevant explanations. Firstly, only residential areas having a rather high level of turnover and vacancies are exposed to these processes. Sudden changes in the population composition seem to cause instability and lack of cohesion. With a few exceptions, these characteristics are only found in the rental segment of the housing market and especially in the larger estates. Figure 14.2 gives a couple of examples of such neighbourhood trajectories in the city of Gothenburg. Secondly, as discussed above, new refugees as well as other population segments lacking economic and political resources, are actively directed to some particular residential areas. In the two Gothenburg housing estates identified in Figure 14.2, such a placement strategy has certainly affected the development towards increasing immigrant densities. But, and that is crucial to our understanding of racialization processes, this would not have been possible if more native-born people had stayed in the area.

Figure 14.2   The relative share of Swedish citizens in Gothenburg city and in two Gothenburg neighbourhoods 1975–1995

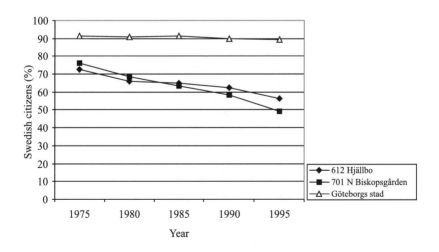

Source: Andersson & Bråmå 2001.

2. Segregation-generated migration

As soon as this type of migration starts at some scale there will be direct and indirect effects upon the rest of the residents. Some will move out because they don't feel at ease with the increasing numbers of foreigners in the area. Others, probably a larger number, will move out because of the secondary effects in the day nurseries and in the schools, or in other local social institutions (or perhaps simply because the area starts getting a bad reputation). As the number of non-native speaking children starts to grow, and some of them perhaps need more attention and support than could be allocated by the authorities to meet their needs, many parents feel uncertain about the quality of the school education and of socialization processes in general. In particular those families having economic resources tend to move out in this still early process of ethnic selective migration. It should be stressed, that 'the problem' should not be primarily defined as a problem of ethnicity or a problem of who lives in the area, but rather as a problem of institutional quality. In many cases teachers do not have the best quality or they have to handle too many pupils or have very limited resources.

These indirect migrations – caused by the initial sequence of segregation-generating migration – are called *segregation-generated migration.* Tentatively, there seem to exist thresholds in these processes. Many residential areas have had 'immigrant densities' ('first generation immigrants') well above the city average (normally 10–15%) without leading to segregation-generated migration at a larger scale. However, it seems like these migrations become common in areas where the immigrant density approaches or passes 20%, more so and at a lower level if these immigrants have a non-European, 'Third World' origin.

Another threshold might be found at 'immigrant densities' around 40–50%. In many of these latter areas – which were very few in Sweden only 10 years ago – segregation-generated migration has rapidly turned the areas into 'immigrant enclaves', where the remaining Swedish families are very few indeed. Newly arrived immigrants, like other migrants, are young and they have in some cases more children than Swedish families. It is therefore common to find that some classes in schools, and in some cases entire schools, located in such areas, almost totally comprise children with foreign-born parents. This is indicated by some further data for a dozen of the most immigrant-dense Swedish neighbourhoods, see Table 14.3. As can be seen, despite the fact that a clear majority of the children are born in Sweden about 90% of the 30–39 year age group are foreign-born in these neighbourhoods.

It is easy to realize that to learn the Swedish language in such a context raises severe problems, and these problems will to some extent exist also for children having Swedish-speaking parents. And they will probably be even more negatively perceived by the latter.

In 1995, 55 out of Sweden's 9400 neighbourhoods had a majority of residents being born abroad. Three years later, the number of neighbourhoods dominated by 'first generation immigrants' had increased to 100. We call these neighbourhoods 'Sparsely populated by Swedes' (SPS-areas) rather than 'Immigrant-dense areas'. In fact, all areas having more than 30% 'non-Swedish'-born residents have a majority of people being either born abroad or being children of immigrants. The total

Table 14.3   Immigrant-dense Swedish neighbourhoods

Neighbour-hood code	Municipality & Neighbourhood	Percentage foreign-born per age-group						
		0–19	20–29	30–39	40–49	50–64	Over 65	Total
12800274	Malmö: Rosengård/Herrgården	51	96	98	95	90	84	72
14800783	Gothenburg: Hjällbo	44	91	96	96	88	58	72
12800281	Malmö: Rosengård/Örtagården	34	84	95	91	78	64	61
12800273	Malmö: Rosengård/Törnrosen	40	86	94	88	78	67	66
14800781	Gothenburg: Hjällbo	36	89	93	94	84	72	65
1270011	Botkyrka: Fittja	29	79	92	88	77	70	64
1800148	Stockholm: Rinkeby	26	67	91	90	79	74	61
1800151	Stockholm: Tensta	26	71	89	83	61	54	58
12800280	Malmö: Rosengård/Örtagården	36	81	89	88	71	75	62
12800276	Malmö: Rosengård/Kryddgården	34	71	88	72	55	29	52
1270001	Botkyrka: Alby S	24	68	86	79	65	70	59
1800154	Stockholm: Husby	23	69	86	74	57	40	56

Source: Andersson 2000b.

number of SPS-areas defined in the latter way (+30% born abroad) increased from 281 to 424 in the 1995 to 1998 period and they comprised in 1998 22.8% of all foreign-born in Sweden (around 200 000 immigrants). In these areas we find only 3.7% of the native population (which includes the children of immigrants). The level of ethnic residential segregation thus increased not only in Stockholm, Gothenburg and Malmö but in 13 of 16 studied middle-sized cities as well (see Table 14.1). By and large ethnic selective migration drives this process, and especially the 'white flight'-phenomenon.

We argue that *segregation-generated migration has a ground in existing socio-material conditions.* But this does not imply that we could overlook the symbolic production that is intertwined with the development of these conditions. As we argue above, the symbolic production takes place both within and outside this particular residential area. When the residential area starts getting a 'doubtful reputation', a process that often takes place outside the area itself, people within the area will become affected. People with extensive social networks outside the area will probably be more affected than those who have more local, bounded social networks. Unemployed immigrants will probably more often be found within the latter category while a dual career Swedish-born family would be a candidate for a typical example of the former, and this family will probably also have the option to move. Although we still lack research evidence based on interviews with native Swedes leaving SPS areas, migration flows as such suggest that racialization processes cannot be overlooked when such ethnically selective migration patterns are to be explained.

3. Institutionally-generated migration

Thirdly, many political decisions constantly affect the dynamics of the housing market and intra-urban migration patterns. It is not possible within the format of this chapter to discuss the institutional setting and the housing policies in any detail, but except what has already been discussed above, a few further remarks should be made to point out the importance of these frameworks.

Almost without exception, all the 'problem areas' of today were constructed during the 'Million Dwellings Programme' era, a housing policy programme launched in the mid 1960s in order to find a fast solution of some major spatial and demographic changes that affected Sweden at that time. The demand for housing was enormous and there was money around for a great modernization of the housing stock. From 1965 to 1974, nearly one million new dwellings were constructed and the quantitative aim of the Million Programme was almost achieved. Great days for construction businesses and for the art of social engineering, but according to many critics close to a disaster in terms of architectural values and social development. Of course, similar estates were built in most countries, and with similar results.

Not only were the new areas on a larger scale than had been built before, they were often located on or beyond the existing urban fringe, which made them less attractive for the growing number of elderly people or for other groups not possessing a private car. Public communications were sometimes not adequate, and the social and commercial centres that were planned came often into existence much too late or in some cases not at all. Furthermore, as the programme approached its final years, demand for new housing started to fall and many of the new residential areas had problems with empty flats. Meanwhile, the State also subsidized the construction of owner-occupied housing and both working class and middle class families had economic motives for buying houses as the mortgage costs could be fully used for a tax reduction.

All in all, the housing policy led to social segregation, and the households in many cities were more than ever before allocated in the urban space in accordance with tenure forms and levels of incomes and wealth. The publicly owned multifamily houses needed to be filled if costs were to be kept at a reasonable level. One solution was to allocate these new dwellings to all sorts of newcomers in the local housing market: young families, migrants from the rest of Sweden, labour immigrants etc. These groups often lacked roots in the particular urban site and they were rather mobile. Those who could afford to move left the area within a year or two. This caused a high turnover which became a problem in itself. But worst of all, these areas became the housing solution and last resort for all sorts of people needing social assistance; alcoholics, other sorts of drug abusers, mentally ill people etc. As these groups had to rely upon social benefits and could not pay the rent by themselves, they were allocated to areas where demand was low and empty dwellings were available. As a consequence, many Million Programme areas gained a bad reputation and they became stigmatized. Although some of them have now recovered and could be expected to recover even further (especially in smaller cities), they still seem to function as regulators in the housing market. When demand is low they immediately face the problem of many vacancies. When demand for housing rises, they are the last areas to become fully occupied.

The Million Programme is but one out of many examples of how a political decision and the financial system that backs it up causes great changes in terms of settlement patterns and intraurban migration flows. Other important components in the institutional framework are the fiscal system, the general welfare schemes, immigration and immigrant policy (for example the 'Sweden-wide strategy for refugee reception'), just to mention a few but important regulatory mechanisms (Andersson 1998c.) Although most attention in the public debate is being paid to the local gatekeepers, for example civil servants within the public immigrant administration or the housing associations, such gatekeepers are part of a complex set of institutional actors and their room for manoeuvre is decided at the political levels (central state and local authorities). In the model, migration decisions influenced by these kind of frameworks and political decisions are called *institutionally-generated migration.*

4. The network-oriented migration

Finally we reach the 'cultural'/'ways of living'-domain. Although the *network-oriented migration* always has to be taken into consideration (it is of course a general, not an 'immigrant-specific', phenomenon) we are – as stated above – convinced that the argument that immigrants want to live near their fellow countrymen has been pushed far too hard in the Swedish case. It is normal in Sweden to find as many as fifty or sometimes even more than one hundred different nationalities in some residential areas; on average, the dozen neighbourhoods listed in Table 14.3 have about 100 nationalities represented in their populations. The residents in these areas often share the immigrant experience but not the ethnic origin. In some cases 'enemies' from the area of origin live closer together in Sweden than they did before they decided or were forced to emigrate (for example people from different parts of former Yugoslavia and from the Middle East). The segregation pattern that we have to understand is more than anything else a growing separation between the Swedish-born population and in particular the non-European post-1984 immigrant cohort (see Figures 14.3 and 14.4).

Conclusion

The patterns shown in Figures 14.3 and 14.4 have been observed in other contexts than the housing market, most clearly in studies of the Swedish labour market. The different positions occupied by national groups are systematically repeated in the way that the figures evidence, namely a descending scale that begins with the population born in North-European countries occupying the most privileged positions whatever the variable analysed, and ending with Non-European countries. This selective pattern is what we in several earlier works have called 'the ethnic/racial hierarchy'. This hierarchy can hardly be explained by reference to 'free choices' made by individuals and groups. On the contrary, it can only be understood as the result of a complex setting of mechanisms that act towards the unconscious or conscious discrimination and exclusion of particular ethnic/racial groups in Swedish

Figure 14.3   Segregation in the city of Malmö: Index of Dissimilarity according to country of birth, 1998

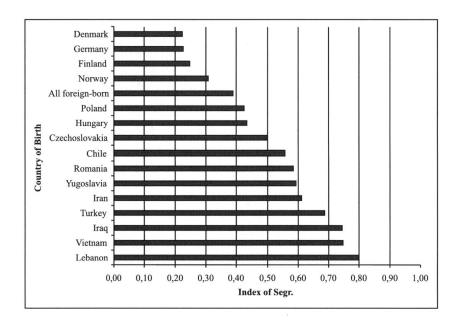

Source: Andersson 2000.

society. Our combining of the two presented models is an attempt to increase the understanding of those mechanisms.

It was not long ago that Swedish – and we guess all Nordic – people reacted strongly against apartheid in South Africa and were strongly critical also to American racism and, as part of that, ghetto formation in U.S. cities. In fact, we would like to argue that by identifying racism as something external to Nordic societies such perceptions made it possible to build a myth that 'we' were morally speaking better than other people. It is today not easy to uphold such a view in neither of the Nordic countries. For sure, quantitatively speaking (Sweden has far more immigrants) problems are worse in Sweden than in Finland, Norway, Denmark and Iceland. Qualitatively, it might be the other way around when it comes down to judging the level of xenophobia and racist sentiments that are present in public debates and important parts of some political party programmes in Scandinavian countries. We do not know that, but recent events in Denmark and Norway do not convince us that racial stereotypes, race-based discrimination and subordination of non-Europeans and Muslims would be less common in the other countries of the region than in Sweden. Moreover, at the institutional level, the Swedish state has taken a more progressive attitude towards the international refugee problem by

Figure 14.4   Segregation in the city of Gothenburg: Index of Dissimilarity according to country of birth, 1998

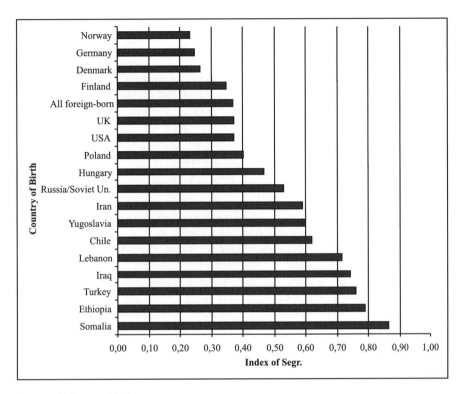

Source: Andersson 2000.

allowing far more people to enter since the last phase of political and war refugee migration commenced in the early 1970s. The country today has about one million first generation immigrants and if we include the children of these about 20% of the population has an immigrant experience. Furthermore, more than 40% of these are of a non-European, non-West origin. Nevertheless, this does not excuse the way these immigrants are received, the poor level of structural integration of ethnic and racial minorities that has been achieved, and the more and more frequent evidence of racial discrimination in many sectors of society, but we should bear it in mind when discussing immigration and integration policies in the Nordic context.

The situation in the 1990s and the early years of the new millennium suggests that Scandinavian cities and nations face great challenges if the trend towards deeper socioeconomic and racial segregation should be reversed. The people's home, as part of the Swedish modernization project, has not only a political but also an ideological history that is relevant to the understanding of the housing issue in Sweden. Geographers in Scandinavia have paid too little attention to segregation issues in general and in particular to 'race' relations. This situation is probably changing since the sharpening of social problems associated to the segregated city has become evident. There are now signs that geographers both in their undergraduate training and in scholarly research are beginning to pay more attention to such issues. Although this is indeed a broad field, which needs analytical attention from most social science and humanistic disciplines, geographers can hopefully make a difference. Understanding the nature of contemporary racialization and migration processes is a first step in trying to formulate a policy strategy that can reverse the present state of separation, subordination and exclusion of people born in other parts of the world.

References

Ålund, Aleksandra and Schierup, Carl-Ulrik (1991) *Paradoxes of Multiculturalism. Essays on Swedish Society*. Aldershot: Gower.

Andersson, Roger (1998a) Segregation Dynamics and Urban Policy Issues in Sweden. Metropolis Inter Conference: International Conference on Divided Cities and Strategies for Undivided Cities, Göteborg University, pp. 63–109.

Andersson, Roger (1998b) Segregering, segmentering och socio-ekonomisk polarizering. Stockholmsregionen och sysselsättningskrisen 1990–95. Partnership for Multi-ethnic inclusion, PfMI, Report 2/98.

Andersson, Roger (1998c) Socio-spatial dynamics: Ethnic divisions of mobility and housing in Post-Palme Sweden. *Urban Studies*, Vol. 35, No. 3 pp. 397–428.

Andersson, Roger (1999) "Divided cities" as a policy-based notion in Sweden. *Housing Studies,* Vol. 14, No, 5 pp. 601–624.

Andersson, Roger (2000a) Etnisk och socioekonomisk segregation i Sverige 1990–1998. SOU 2000:37, *Arbetsmarknad, Demografi och Segregation.* Stockholm: Fritzes Offentliga Publikationer, pp. 223–266.

Andersson, Roger (2000b) Rörligheten och de utsatta bostadsområdena. *Hemort Sverige*, Norrköping: Integrationsverket, pp. 197–225.

Andersson, Roger (2001) Skapandet av svenskglesa bostadsområden. I: Lena Magnusson (ed.) *Den delade staden*, pp. 115–153. Umeå: Boréa.

Andersson, Roger and Bråmå, Åsa (2001) Skapandet av svenskglesa bostadsområden: segregations- och nätverksgenererade flyttningar i det urbana Sverige. Forskningsansökan ställd till FORMAS, Institute for Housing and Urban Research, Uppsala university.

Andersson, Roger and Molina, Irene (1996) Etnisk boendesegregation i teori och praktik. SOU 1996:55, *Vägar in i Sverige*, pp. 155–204.

Andersson, Roger, Molina, Irene and Sandberg, Andreas (1992) *Social Geografi och etniska relationer*. Uppsala Universitet: Forskningsrapporter från Kulturgeografiska Institutionen No. 103.

Berg, Lawrence D. (1993) Racialization in Academic Discourse. *Urban Geography*, vol 14, No. 2, 1993, pp. 194–200.

Blanc, Maurice and Smith, David M. (1997) Grassroots, Democracy and Participation: A New Analytical and Practical Approach. In *Society and Space*, No. 2, 1997.

Broberg, Gunnar and Tydén, Mattias (1991) *Oönskade i folkhemmet. Rashygien och sterilisering i Sverige*. Stockholm: Gidlunds.

Burgess, E.W. (1925) The Growth of the city, in: R.J. Park (Ed.), *The city*. Chicago: University of Chicago Press.

Campbell, Beatrix (1993) *Goliath. Britain's Dangerous Places*. London: Methuen.

Carter, Bob, Green, Marci and Halpern, Rick (1996) Immigration policy and the racialization of migrant labour: the construction of national identities in the USA and Britain. In *Ethnic and Racial Studies*, vol 19, No. 1, pp. 135–157.

Dickens, Peter, Duncan, Simon Goodwin, Mark and Gray, Fred (1985) *Housing, States and Localities*. Methuen: London and New York.

Faist, Thomas (1995) Ethnicization and racialization of welfare-state politics in Germany and the USA. In *Ethnic and Racial Studies*, vol 18, No. 2, pp. 219–250.

Firey, W. (1945) Sentiment and symbolism as ecological variables. *American Sociological Review* 10, pp. 140–148.

Friedrichs, Jürgen (1997) Do Poor Neighborhoods make their residents poorer? Context effects of poverty neighborhoods on residents, forthcoming in: H-J. Andress (Ed.) *Empirical Poverty Research*. Aldershot: Avebury.

Frykman, Jonas and Löfgren, Orvar (eds) (1985) *Modärna tider. Vision och vardag i folkhemmet*. Malmö: Liber Förlag.

Harlow, Michael (1995) *The People's home? Social rented housing in Europe and America*. Oxford: Basil Blackwell.

Harrison, M.L. (1995) *Housing, 'Race', Social Policy and Empowerment*. Aldershot: Avebury.

Harvey, David and Chatterjee, Lata (1973) Absolute Rent and the Structuring of Space by Governmental and Financial Institutions. *Antipode* 6:1, pp. 22–36.

Harvey, David (1973) *Social justice and the city*. London: Edward Arnold.

Holm, Per (1985) Swedish Planning 1945–1985: ideology, methods and results. *Plan International* 1985.

Hoyt, H. (1939) *The structure and growth of residential neighbourhoods in American cities*. Washington D.C.: Federal Housing Administration.

Jackson, Peter (1992) The Racialization of Labour in Post-war Bradford. In *Journal of Historical Geography*, vol 18, No. 2, pp. 190–209.

Johnston, Ronald J., Gregory, Derek and Smith, David M. (ed.) (1986) [1981] *The Dictionary of Human Geography. Second Edition*. Oxford: Basil Blackwell.

Karlsson, Sten O. (1993) *Arbetarfamiljen och det nya hemmet. Om bostadshygienism och klasskultur i mellankrigstidens Göteborg*. Stockholm/Stehag: Symposion Graduale.

Kemeny, Jim (1987) Immigrant Housing Conditions in Sweden. *Research Report* SB:5. Gävle: The National Swedish Institute for Building Research.

Kemeny, Jim (1991) *Housing and Social Theory*. London: Routledge.

Kemeny, Jim (1995) *From Public Housing to the Social Market*. London: Routledge.

Lindberg, Göran and Lindén, Anna-Lisa (1989) *Social segmentation på den svenska bostadsmarknaden*. Rapport från forskargruppen Boende och bebyggelse. Sociologiska institutionen, Lunds universitet.

Miles, Robert (1989) *Racism*. London: Routledge.

Miles, Robert (1990) The Racialization of British Politics. I *Political Studies*, vol 38, No. 2, pp. 277–285.

Miles, Robert (1993) *Race after Race Relations*. London: Routledge.

Molina, Irene (1997) Stadens rasifiering. Etnisk boendesegregation i folkhemmet. Uppsala universitet, Kulturgeografiska institutionen, Geografiska regionstudier No. 32.

Molina, Irene (2001) Den rasifierade staden. I: Lena Magnusson (ed.) *Den delade staden*, pp. 49–81. Umeå: Boréa.

Paasi, Ansi (1986) The Institutionalization of Regions: a Theoretical Framework for Understanding the Emergence of Regions and the Constitution of Regional Identity. *Fennia*, No. 164, pp. 105–146.

Paasi, Ansi (1991) Deconstructing Regions: Notes on the Scale of Spatial Life. In *Environment & Planning A*, vol. 23, pp. 239–256.

Pred, Allan (2000) Even in Sweden. Racisms, Racialized Spaces, and the Popular Geographical Imagination. University California Press.

Satzewich, Vic (1988) The Canadian State and the Racialization of Caribbean Migrant Farm Labour 1947–1966. In *Ethnic and Racial Studies*, vol 11, No. 3, pp. 282–304.

Schulman, Mikaela (2000) Stadspolitik och urbanforskning i Norden. *Nordregio* WP 2000:4.

Scott, Allen J. (1986) *Metropolis. From the division of labor to urban form*. Berkeley: University of California Press.

Siksjö, Ola (1991) Bostadsvalet ur ett sociologiskt perspektiv. Statens institut för byggnadsforskning, forskningsrapport SB: 40.

Smith, Susan (Ed) (1992) Race and Housing in Britain, Review and Research Agenda, Annotated Bibliography, Commentary, Workshop Reports. Proceedings of a Conference Supported by the Joseph Rowntree Foundation. Department of Geography, University of Edinburgh.

Smith, Susan J. (1989a) *The Politics of 'Race' and Residence. Citizenship, Segregation and White Supremacy in Britain*. Cambridge: Polity Press.

Smith, Susan J. (1989b) Society, Space and Citizenship: A Human Geography for the "New Times". *Transactions of the Institute of British Geographers* 14, pp. 144–56.

SoS-1994:10, *Social rapport 1994*. Stockholm: Socialstyrelsen.

SOU 1975:51 *Bostadsförsörjning och bostadsbidrag. Slutbetänkande av boende- och bostadsfinansieringsutredningen*. Stockholm.

SOU 1990:20 *Välfärd och segregation i storstadsrregionerna*. Underlagsrapport från Storstadsutredningen.

Svanberg, Ingvar and Runblom, Harald (ed) (1988) *Det mångkulturella Sverige. En handbok om etniska grupper och minoriteter*. Stockholm: Gidlunds.

Takaki, Ronald (1992) The Tempest in the Wilderness: The Racialization of Savagery. In *The Journal of American History*, vol 79, No. 3, pp. 893–912.

Turner, Bengt and Whitehead, Christine (2001) Reducing Housing Subsidy – What happened to Swedish Social Housing Policy? [Draft; Institute for Housing and Urban Research, Uppsala University and London School of Economics].

White, H.C. (1971) Multipliers, vacancy chains and filtering in housing. *Journal of the American Institute of Planners* 37, pp. 88–94.

Wilkerson, Margaret B. and Gresham, Jewell Handy (1989) Sexual Politics of Welfare. The racialization of Poverty. In: *The Nation*, vol 249, No. 4, pp. 126–131.

Williams, P.R. (1976) The role of institutions in the inner London housing market, the case of Islington. *Transactions of the Institute of British Geographers*, New Series 1, pp. 72–82.

Chapter 15

'In visible city'

Insecurity, gender, and power relations in urban space

Hille Koskela

There is no need for arms, physical violence, material constraints. Just a gaze. An inspecting gaze, a gaze which each individual under its weight will end by interiorising to the point that he is his own overseer, each individual thus exercising this surveillance over, and against, himself. A superb formula: power exercised continuously and for what turns out to be a minimal cost. (Foucault 1980: 155)

Obsession with security

The geography of fear

Urban crime as a social problem has long been a field of interest, especially in Anglo-American countries. Research addressing crime from various viewpoints has been conducted within the fields of criminology, sociology, anthropology, and lately increasingly also within geography. Among geographers the special focus has been on the connections between crime and space. In this tradition fear of crime has been identified as a problem in its own right. Increasing research has shown that the relationship between fear and crime is more complicated than it seems to be at first sight: fear is partly unrelated to actual victimisation. Fear of crime can contribute to lowering the quality of people's lives as much as crime does, and thus, fear can be as great a problem as crime itself. Furthermore, as much as crime, fear of crime also has spatial dimensions.

In Scandinavian countries research on *the geography of fear* is relatively new. National crime surveys have reported experienced fear for a while but qualitative research has been carried out only more recently. Several masters theses and articles have been written on the geography of fear: in Sweden (Tiby 1991, Listerborn 1996, 2000), Norway (Auren 1996, 1999), Denmark (Djurhuus and Skovsgaard 2000) and also in Estonia (Sargma 1998). In Finland, fear of crime has gradually been perceived as an important object of study and safety is acknowledged to be among the aims of urban planning. The spatial dimensions of fear are also finally becoming a field of interest (e.g. Karisto and Tuominen 1993, Koskela 1996, 1999, Kejonen 2000, Laakkonen and Mustikkamäki 2000).

Also the question on how to improve urban security – how to plan safer cities – is a matter of growing concern. There are many views of how cities should be developed and who should be able to take part in this development. There has been both theoretical reasoning on the causes and structures of fear (e.g. Smith 1987,

Gordon and Riger 1989, Valentine 1989, Pain 1991) and attempts to create 'safe city initiatives' by applying this knowledge in urban policies and planning procedures (e.g. Trench et al. 1992, Wekerle and Whitzman 1995). When it comes to planning, it is important to understand that fear is not a personal problem of each individual, but has wide consequences to society and to urban design. As a collective phenomenon it is likely to change the nature of urban space.

In Scandinavia the point that safety on the streets could – and should – be improved has just emerged. In Finland, for example, there are planning regulations for environmental impact assessment and for disabled access, but not much for safety and security. It has just recently been recognised that safety on the whole should be among the aims of planning: the new land use and building act is for the first time declaring safety to be among the general aims of land use planning. A number of cities are currently taking steps to make urban space safer. Therefore, there is not only a need to acknowledge safety as a crucial challenge for contemporary planning but there should also be critical consideration of the measures used in attempting to increase it.

The postmodern sense of insecurity

How to improve security without producing insecurity simultaneously is perhaps the most crucial question here. The subject of urban planning as a means for increasing safety is itself controversial in many ways. It can be questioned whether the feeling of safety on the whole can be influenced by urban planning. Many proportions have proved to be ambiguous: either there is no positive evidence of increased safety or it is increased from a partial point of view. Much of the discussion of planning for safety has had a tendency to focus on physical environments and 'design' without acknowledging the social and symbolic connotations of space.

The *obsession with security* has been claimed to be 'the master narrative' of contemporary urban design. While the main theme in planning in the 1960s was efficiency, and in the 1980s ecology, the leading trend of urban planning in the 21st century is *fear*. The writings of Mike Davis, and other scholars interpreting the design of 'Los Angeles School' architects have enunciated polemic notions on 'the urban fortress model' where safety is guaranteed by exclusionary design and technological surveillance (Davis 1990, Flusty 1994, Ellin 1996, Soja 1996, Dear and Flusty 1998, among others). They show where the *defence mentality* in its extreme forms can lead: urban spaces have been divided and polarised. Some parts have been transformed into controlled, guarded fortresses, which are privately owned and maintained, whereas other places have become neglected and have been left to deteriorate. Social polarisation, inequality and segregation are clearly legible in urban form.

According to dystopian visions, increased fear causes social groups to flee from each other into isolated homogenous enclaves (Davis 1990). The massive expansion of protection is claimed to lead to a vicious circle of defence: while increasing security might make some feel safer, it also creates increasing fear, racism and distrust among people (Ellin 1996). The concept of risk itself is culturally constructed (Walklate 1997). What is perceived to be real, becomes real in its consequences. Various forms of surveillance are used to maintain the existing social and economic order. Design and urban policy are characterised by paranoia, protectionism, and a lack of common interest, behind this is a collective emotion – a kind of a 'moral panic' – what has been called 'the postmodern sense of insecurity' (Ellin 1997: 25). The development of protection mechanisms and defensible architecture has been rapid. 'Forms of fear' – forms that ostensibly aim to increase safety and security, but simultaneously create fear – are expanding (Ellin 1996). The patterns of exclusive architecture are manifold: walls, fences, gates, surveillance cameras, check points, hidden entrances, uncomfortable benches, absence of public toilets, etc. (Davis 1990, Flusty 1994). Exclusive forms and electronic means of surveillance are also increasingly *replacing* informal social control. A common response to insecurity is intensive and increasing control – the 'militarisation' of space and social practices. When reflecting upon the fortress type architecture in Los Angeles, it becomes clear that feelings of safety and confidence are not always achieved by the same means than maximal crime prevention. An area that is planned to detect crime with heavy measures easily becomes unpleasant to live in. In addition, trying to prevent crime in certain areas increases polarisation: some areas become walled communities characterised by paranoia, and others become deprived 'pocket ghettos' (Flusty 1994: 25).

Although it is clear that urban structure and design in Los Angeles is quite different from those in Scandinavian cities, similar questions on increasing safety have been addressed. Thus, the same dilemmas should be acknowledged. There has not yet been much idea about *operationalisation* of planning for safer cities in Finland. The choice between 'a fortress approach' and 'an increased tolerance approach' seems not to have been realised. In crime prevention policies it is pointed out at the same time how important such things as work against racism is, and measures suggested which rely on clear territorial functions (Rakennettu ympäristö, rikollisuus... 1995, Turvallisuustalkoot 1998). An increased feeling of territoriality and increased tolerance of difference are quite difficult to achieve simultaneously, unless territoriality is based on some new kind of urban sociability that includes acceptance of diversity. However, the very concept of territoriality includes exclusion and intolerance: 'we wish to exclude but not to be excluded' (Marcuse 1997). 'The utopia of urban village' (Cohen 1985) is unattainable. This choice is political: the politics of openness and closeness are difficult to exercise simultaneously.

Rise of the gated communities

Changes can be seen happening in public urban space but a parallel development is going on in housing areas. There are analogous development trends in various spaces: increasing surveillance of public spaces as well as growth in locked car and house doors, security systems, 'gated' or 'secure' communities, (Ellin 1997). It has been argued that 'the contemporary built environment contains increasingly less meaningful public space, and existing public space is increasingly controlled by various forms of surveillance and increasingly invested with private meanings' (Ellin 1997: 36). Gated communities are residential areas with restricted access such that normally public spaces – i.e. parks, squares and streets – have been privatised, spaces where 'the fear of crime and the outsiders is the foremost motivation for defensive fortifications' (Blakely and Snyder 1997: 85, 93).

Gated communities create physical barriers to access, and they privatise community space, not merely individual space. As Nan Ellin argues, 'strategies such as gating, policing and other surveillance systems, and defensive urbanism do provide certain people with a limited sense of security. But such settings do not, according to recent studies, always diminish actual danger.' (Ellin 1997: 42). Many of these communities also privatise civic responsibilities, such as police protection, and communal services, such as education, recreation, and entertainment (Blakely and Snyder 1997: 85).

Although the circumstances in Scandinavian cities are not as extreme as in the United States, where gated communities have become extremely common and popular, comparable development can be seen happening here, too. Many new housing areas are patrolled by sophisticated security systems. In Sweden, Malmö, there is an older housing area where the community has decided to build a fence around the area to restrict access of the unwanted public. In Finland, there is a plan for a heavily guarded new office area outside Helsinki, called 'The Security Valley'. In Helsinki there are also areas of public housing – for example in Maunula and Roihuvuori – where surveillance cameras have been installed to monitor the area, and residents can see from their home television who is walking in their yard (Koskela 2000). In wealthier areas – such as Kulosaari, Marjaniemi or Westend – many house owners have installed surveillance cameras and built fences and gates to protect their property. The new urban design seeks to acknowledge current needs and tastes and to take full advantage of new technologies for achieving these ends (Ellin 1997: 30).

The differences between Scandinavian and American cities are incontestable, especially when it comes to the amount of gated communities and the people living in them. Also the policies behind urban planning in general differ from each other. In Scandinavian cities the share of public space compared to private space has traditionally been – and still is – much higher than in the US, or even in Britain. Welfare state housing policies have aimed to develop mixed housing areas, where people from different backgrounds and income groups live in a same area, rather than 'isolated enclaves' which gated communities represent. Income differences have not been as extreme as in the US, which has meant that no really high-class housing areas have developed. Accordingly, wherever safety has been considered to be an issue, it has been a public issue rather than a private one. However, from these points of departure, the current development of gated areas in Scandinavian countries can be seen as even more worrying than elsewhere: it is a clear anti-statement against the planning traditions and values of the welfare state.

Exaggerated visibilities

The eyes upon the street

In publicly accessible urban spaces *video surveillance* has become an increasingly popular way to control crime and increase safety. Public and semi-public urban space is under constant scrutiny. An attentive walk around almost any city will make the point. Surveillance cameras are everywhere: in streets, squares and market places, shops and shopping malls, banks and autotellers, metro and train stations, cafeterias, libraries, hospitals, universities, schools, and even in churches. It has been suggested that the ever increasing surveillance has meant 'destruction of the street, or city centre, as an arena for the celebration of difference' (Fyfe et al. 1998: 26).

In Finland video surveillance, especially considering its frequency and rapid expansion, is one of the least regulated practices in urban space. On the streets of Helsinki permission is needed for public meetings, or selling handicrafts but not for video surveillance (Koskela 2000). Anybody can install a surveillance camera. There are innumerable cameras operated by private institutions as well as by the police. Nevertheless, there is no legislation regulating video surveillance in particular. A bill, which would regulate some aspects of surveillance by for example forbidding cameras in spaces of an intimate nature, is in preparation (Takala 1998). Currently, regulation is possible only by virtue of bills dealing with eavesdropping, indexes of persons, and domestic peace. At the moment very few countries within the European Union have legislation especially designed for surveillance. Only Belgium, Sweden and Denmark demand that those who wish to install a surveillance camera should have permits (Takala 1998). In most countries varying combination of laws considering privacy protection and data security are used to regulate surveillance. Legislation has obvious difficulties in keeping pace with evolving technology.

Video surveillance has recently been evaluated in relation to crime control, invasion to citizens' privacy as well as in relation to the design trends of urban space (e.g. Lyon 1994, Fyfe and Bannister 1996, 1998, Oc and Tiesdell 1997). A number of problems caused by expanding surveillance have been identified: concerns have been raised about invaded privacy, and the limits and regulations needed as surveillance technology becomes ever more effective, cheap, small, and accessible. The public has become worried about potential misuse of surveillance cameras and videotapes. Surveillance is feared to have a negative 'chilling effect' on urban life and culture. Further, it has also been questioned whether surveillance cameras are effective for the task they were to meet in the first place: to curb crime.

Despite all the policing with surveillance cameras, there is little agreement among researchers about whether the cameras actually reduce crime (Flusty 1994, Fyfe and Bannister 1998, Takala 1998). Studies on surveillance have produced contradictory results. There is evidence that surveillance causes 'displacement' of crime, since whereas the areas under surveillance become safer, the areas not covered by cameras become more dangerous (Tilley 1993, Fyfe and Bannister 1996). Sometimes, however, cameras can 'spread' their influence so that crime rates are reduced both in areas under surveillance and in the surrounding areas (Poyner 1992, Brown 1995). Studies suggest that the use of cameras has reduced property crime such as criminal damage, vehicle crime, theft, and burglary (Fyfe and Bannister 1996, Brown 1995). There is much less evidence showing that cameras can reduce *violent crime*, such as battery and sexual violence.

In Finland, a study conducted recently in the city of Joensuu showed that during the three year period after installation of surveillance cameras into the city centre, the crime figures in the monitored area had come up, not down (Koskela, 2001). Public opinion towards surveillance was, however, quite positive. The residents of Joensuu did not find surveillance of public places as invading their privacy.

Approximately half of the respondents said that surveillance had improved their personal feelings of safety.

What is at issue, however, is not just whether a particular space is monitored or not. There are numerous other questions to be considered: who maintains surveillance, where, why, how, and with what kinds of consequences? What kinds of power-relationships are embedded within surveillance? Who has the right to look and who will be looked at? What behaviour or appearance in a particular context is regarded as 'deviant'? How do increasing control and surveillance contribute to the production of urban space?

Doubts arise from multiple causes. First, it is not obvious who is watching and where, or how trustworthy the watchers can be expected to be. Surveillance is also directed to solving crime and gathering evidence rather than preventing it and so is not able enough to erase experiences of violence. Some aspects of the technical abilities of surveillance cameras, such as lack of an audio facility, make them too insensitive to detect incidents such as sexual harassment. Further, there are many ways in which surveillance can be misused and directed to invade privacy. Finally, there can be basic 'emotional resistance': it is simply unpleasant to be constantly observed by a camera.

Expansion of panoptic discipline

Deriving from Foucault's work on power and space (e.g. 1977, 1980) it is possible to increase understanding on the effects of surveillance in contemporary urban space. Some of the power-relationships embedded within surveillance change space, and produce complex relationships between power and space. The idea of video surveillance is very similar as the idea of a famous prison 'the Panopticon': to be seen but to never know when or by whom. According to Foucault Jeremy Bentham – the designer of the Panopticon – 'invented a technology of power designed to solve the promlems of surveillance' (1980: 148). It can be claimed that through surveillance cameras the panoptic technology of power has been electronically extended: our cities have become like enormous Panopticons (Davis 1990, Lyon 1994, Oc and Tiesdell 1997).

As a number of authors have pointed out, the panopticon-like nature of the surveillance of cities shows interesting and important parallels to Foucault's thought (Cohen 1985, Fyfe and Bannister 1996, Herbert 1996, Soja 1996). Heavily monitored cities, as the Panopticon, can be seen as a 'laboratory of power' (Foucault 1977: 204). In both cases surveillance 'links knowledge, power and space' (Herbert 1996: 49). The 'disciplinary power' of surveillance ties together 'the moments of observation, judgement and enforcement of normality' (Hannah 1997: 177). In cities, the routine of surveillance makes the use of power almost instinctive; people are controlled, categorised, disciplined and normalised without any particular reason. Public space can actually be seen as if it 'refers to places under public scrutiny' (Domosh 1998: 209). 'The public' is eroding.

In present urban space the obsession with visibility is persistent. By increasing surveillance '[a] dream of a transparent society' (Foucault 1980:152), a society where everything is subjugated to visual control, has almost been realised. Surveillance has become a mechanism that aims to guarantee purity and to exclude feared strangers: 'the Other' in a literal as well as metaphorical sense. The question is not about 'crime control' but rather about 'control' in a wider sense. What makes visibility so important is 'fear of darkened spaces' which are 'zones of disorder' (Foucault 1980: 153) and are not to be tolerated since they constitute a threat. Visibility is to ensure normalisation and control. It produces 'purity' (Douglas 1966). The exercise of power, in the context of surveillance, is 'disguised and difficult to identify because it is not localised, because its agents are rarely self-aware, because it is largely internalised, and because it therefore goes largely unnoticed' (Ellin 1997: 35).

Increased visibility is perhaps the most crucial factor in surveillance. However, it has been noted that the public is not necessarily aware that they are being watched (Hillier 1996, Lyon 1994, Koskela 2001). Sometimes the cameras are hidden, sometimes the public just does not notice them. However, even if the cameras are not seen, the public may still not be aware of the location of the monitoring rooms. The watchers themselves remain hidden. From the location of the camera it is impossible to infer the location of the persons behind the camera. There is hardly ever a direct contact between the security personnel and the public. Under a surveillance camera one does not know whether there is anybody looking, and if there is someone, who they are or how far away they are.

Hence, while everything and everybody under vigilance is becoming more visible, the forces behind this are becoming less so. To people under surveillance these forces are the potential helpers who should intervene if they are attacked. In the contemporary urban architecture forms are transparent from one side and opaque from the other, and have became what Steven Flusty (1994) calls 'stealthy' and 'jittery' space. Although the purpose of surveillance is to increase safety, this design produces uncertainty instead. This leaves the public passive and unable to be subjects of their own being.

It would be impossible for them to seek help from the persons behind the camera. They are 'under surveillance' but by invisible unknown persons in an unknown place. Locations and information about locations become loaded with meanings: they are an important way to reproduce the positions of subjects and objects and to sustain power. The possibility of personal contact is absent. Consequently, the camera leaves the monitored persons as potential victims. The camera places them as objects without a possibility to influence their own destiny. The camera is reduced – as per the idea of the Panopticon – to be 'just a gaze', a depersonalised and distant overseer (Foucault 1980).

Gendered field of vision

Among other forms of power, it is also essential to ask whether the practices and conceptual questions of surveillance are *gendered*, and, if so, how. This setting is not simple or straightforward. On one hand, since the purpose of surveillance is to increase urban safety and women are known to be the ones that are most often afraid, it might be especially beneficial for women. On the other hand, the validness of this reasoning should not be taken for granted. Surveillance includes multiple power-relationships that do not remain without gender aspects. In public space, even the ostensibly innocent practices of seeing and being seen are gendered (Rose 1993,

Gardner 1995). 'The field of vision' is deeply gendered (Nast and Kobayashi 1996). The complex relationships between security, surveillance technology and gender are worth exploring.

When examining the gender relations of surveillance at the simplest level we should ask who occupies the opposite side of a surveillance camera? If we look at the places and spaces under surveillance, and the maintenance of surveillance, can we see practices which could be gendered? In public and semi-public space, the places where surveillance most often is practised are the shopping malls and the shopping areas of city centres, and likewise public transport areas. Who usually negotiates and decides about surveillance is the management: managers of shopping malls, leading politicians, city mayors etc. Furthermore, people who take care of the maintenance of surveillance are the police and private guards. From this it is possible to draw some conclusions about the gender structure of surveillance. Women spend more of their time shopping than men. Everyday purchases for the family are mostly bought by women. Also the a majority of the users of public transport are women. Thus women are quite often found in the typical places under surveillance. In contrast, the occupations in charge of deciding on surveillance are male dominated. Even more importantly, the professions that maintain surveillance, police and guards, are also male dominated. Thus, *at this simplest level*, surveillance is, indeed, gendered.

However, there are also other more complicated features of gender structures. Beyond the positions that women and men occupy are *gendered social practices*. Women are constantly reminded that an invisible observer is a threat. In crime prevention advice, for example, women are recommended to shield themselves from a potential attacker or observer who is presented to be male (Gardner 1995). Hence, reliability of the potential observer is of crucial importance to women. The 'masculine culture' of those who are 'in control' is causing mistrust towards surveillance: women do not rely on those behind the camera because of the reproduction of patriarchal power by the guards and the police who are responsible for the daily routine of surveillance (e.g. Wajcman 1991, Fyfe 1995). Video surveillance is sometimes interpreted as a part of 'male policing in the broadest sense' (Brown 1998: 217).

Furthermore, surveillance in practice is insensitive to issues that would be of particular importance to women. A video is unable to identify situations where a sensitive interpretation of a social situation is needed. For example, the overseers responsible for surveillance easily remark on clearly seen but otherwise minor offences – such as someone smoking a cigarette in a metro station – while ignoring more serious situations which they regard as ambivalent – such as sexual harassment. Most cameras are unable to interpret threatening situations, which are not visually recognisable, and cases of harassment are therefore left without notice. By using a surveillance camera, sexual harassment is more difficult to identify, and to interrupt, than by the police or guards patrolling by foot. Alcohol related disturbances are also often not considered to be serious enough to be interrupted by the overseers. Consequently, Sheila Brown (1998: 218) has argued that video surveillance '*cannot change the general intimidation, verbal harassment, staring, and drunken rowdiness amongst groups of men which constrains women's movement most strongly*'.

The insensitivity of surveillance cameras is not all that there is in question. This insensitivity can be understood as a 'passive' relation between surveillance and harassment. However, there is also a concept, which could be understood as an 'active' relation between surveillance and harassment. It has been shown that there is public concern about the 'potential "Peeping Tom" element' of surveillance cameras (Honess and Charman 1992), that women are worried about possible 'voyeurism' (Trench 1997, Brown 1998), and that cameras placed in spaces of any intimate nature irritate women (Koskela 1999).

Indeed, it is possible *to use surveillance cameras as an actual means of harassment.* Scrutiny is a common and effective form of harassment (Gardner 1995). There is some voyeuristic fascination in looking, in being able to see. In urban space women are likely to be the ones who are looked at, the objects of the gaze (Massey 1994). Arguably, the female body is still an object of a gaze in different way than the male body. Women's appearance is public information addressed 'to whom it may concern' (Gardner 1995: 23). Women are placed to be constantly objects of a gaze.

This also applies to their being viewed through a surveillance camera. An anecdote, which illustrates this well, is an advertisement of a major Finnish department store Stockmann that lately announced above some pictures of latest women's fashion: *'You perform for the surveillance cameras every day. Are you dressed for it?'* (see Koskela 2000). The phrase was placed to sell classy women's dresses. It well describes how women are the objects of the gaze. Women are used to constantly police their appearance in public space and to search for an outfit which is suitable for each particular situation (Gardner 1995). However, rhetoric such as the one presented above indicates that women are not only gazed by people on the street but also by the hidden gazes behind the camera.

However, the gender relations within surveillance are far from straightforward. There is evidence based on a research project conducted in Joensuu, showing that women are less critical towards surveillance than men, and find it increasing their safety in public urban space more than men do (Koskela 2001). On the other hand, according to this study, women are also more worried about possible harassment and invasions to privacy, especially when surveillance covers spaces of intimate nature.

One of the very reasons for women's insecurity is their 'exaggerated visibility' (Brown 1998). Paradoxically, women are marginalised by being at the centre (of the looks) (cf. Rose 1993). Used by an abuser, a 'look' can be a weapon. Surveillance can be a way of reproducing and reinforcing male power. It is 'opening up new possibilities for harassment and stalking' (Ainley 1998: 92). Since the gender structure of the persons positioned on each side of the camera is as described above, there is a temptation to (mis)use surveillance for voyeuristic purposes.

Gradually, incidents come up which reveal exactly the kind of abuse by the cameras that women are most worried about. Leisure centres with male control operators have been observed to have cameras placed in women's changing rooms. Operators have been caught using surveillance cameras to spy on women and then making obscene phone calls to them from the control room. Police officers have been reprimanded for improper voyeuristic use of surveillance cameras. Real and manipulated images from the surveillance system – including sex acts and other intimate contacts – have been edited onto tapes for commercial purposes, as was the case in the UK in 1996. An abusive incident was documented also in Australia where the security camera operators in a casino had videotaped women in toilets and artists' changing rooms, zooming on their exposed body parts, and edited the individual video sequences onto one tape which was shown at local house parties (Hillier 1996: 99). In Scandinavia, a piece of news circulated in 1997, which shocked and irritated women (e.g. *Helsingin Sanomat* 17 December 1997). It had been discovered that Swedish conscript solders had been 'entertaining' themselves in summer 1997 by monitoring women on a beach near their navy base. They had videotaped topless women, printed pictures of them, and hung these pictures on the walls of their barracks. Since the cameras used were meant for military purposes, they were of extremely high quality and, therefore, the pictures were quite explicit. These cases show glaring examples of gendered abuse of surveillance cameras.

Clearly, a debate on surveillance – its legal and moral aspects as well as on the blurring boundaries between public and private space and activities – is needed. It has been shown that there is a possibility of gendering of surveillance and control, and that surveillance can be used as an active instrument for harassment. Because of this possible 'active' role in harassment, surveillance reproduces the embodiment and sexualisation of women, and contributes to the process of masculinisation of space.

'The production of space' revisited

Towards gender sensitive planning?

Lately, there has been quite a lot of discussion on planning 'for women' and implementing urban policies that would take women's special needs into account. It has been argued that in the mainstream discussions of urban politics and planning the gender dimension is lacking or undervalued, and that women have not gained equal recognition in urban design (e.g. Little et al. 1988, Simonsen 1990, Greed, 1994). Feminist planners and researchers have claimed that the gender difference is apparent from the built forms of the city: that women are forced to live in 'the man-made environment' (Matrix 1984), that 'our cities are patriarchy written in stone, brick, glass and concrete' (Darke 1996: 88), and that there is a 'fundamental gender bias in the philosophy and practice of town planning' (Greed 1994: 9). A common presupposition has been that the sole presence of women in the planning process would make planning 'less masculine': that the male dominance has produced 'hegemonic assumptions within the planning profession' (Darke 1996: 95), and that female planners would reject these points of departure. The differences between women and men as planners – and the special qualities of women – are inaccurately taken for granted. This notion should be critically evaluated (see Boys 1990, Björk 1991). It is important to challenge the notion that female planners – automatically and inevitably – would advocate a more humane environment. Rather than just the presence of women in planning process, increased understanding of issues related to gender relations, power and space, would be of crucial importance.

Within the established conceptualisation of gender, it is obvious that there is no single monolithic 'womanhood', whose interests planning could meet. Since the late 1980s feminist discourses have acknowledged differences amongst women.

Consequently, this has been echoed in feminist geography, which has also contributed to the conceptualisation of gender in relation to space (McDowell 1993, Rose 1993, Massey 1994, to name but a few). The critique of essential femininity has produced a notion of multiple womanhood embodied with differences. However, within planning studies there seems to be confusion on this matter. On one hand, it has been argued that the differences among women have nothing whatsoever to do with the aims of women-friendly planning, and that instead of developing 'abstract' and 'elitistic' theories women researchers should turn back to 'good old practical women and planning' (Greed 1996: 17). On the other hand, it has been claimed that the relationship between the physical environment and the social relations and values behind it is extremely complicated, and that there is a need for a new theory in gender and design which would be more sensitive to the issues of class, culture and identity as well as gender (Boys 1990: 253–255).

However, despite all the critics, it is clear that there are elements of urban life that cannot be understood without gender relations. The disruption of monolithic womanhood has not meant that there are no longer any women's issues. For example, fear-evoking experiences – such as sexual harassment, threat of violence, and actual violence – can be experienced by all women despite their differences. This is not to deny the notion of multiple womanhood. However, it could be claimed that in relation to sexual violence – and to fear of it – femaleness as an unifying quality is more crucial than the differences among women.

Since women are the ones that are most afraid and, thus, most restrict their use of space, it is clear that 'a gender sensitive planning' should take the challenge of safety seriously. Despite this, safety has not always been among the most significant aims of a planning that takes better account of women's needs. This is apparent especially in the Scandinavian countries. Such planning has been considered to be about ecological housing, healthy building materials, more democratic planning process, lower housing costs, better transport facilities, better income opportunities for rural women, etc. (*NordRefo* 1989, Friberg 1990, Björk 1991, Kyttä 1993). Until the late 1990s safety was hardly discussed.

However, it is crucial not only to develop gender sensitive practices but to challenge the very notion of planning. If planning is understood to be *physical design* solely, it undisputedly 'remains severely restricted in the extent to which it can intervene in safety issues' (Morrell 1996: 107). Technical solutions, such as surveillance cameras – or 'the urban fortress model' more generally – show this clearly. The root causes of fear are social and, thus, physical interventions or technical solutions will not help. In order to achieve improvements in safety, the role of the built environment in reducing fear should be understood within a wider context of social and economic measures (Pain 1991). The concept of planning needs to be re-evaluated. It should be seen as a comprehensive process aiming to develop not only physical but also *socially produced space*. In addition, it should aim to understand and take into account the symbolic connotations embedded in space and, perhaps of most importance, the social relations that contribute to the production of space. What it comes to planning for safety, gender relations are particularly crucial. In this matter, it is also important to develop understanding on space.

In practice this could mean that instead of developing separate strategies for different fields – i.e. urban architecture, policing, or women's issues – it would be of great importance to head for cooperation. Consequently, physical design could be filled with social understanding. A concrete example of this is crime prevention policy: when maximal crime reduction is the aim, it is easy to use simple design strategies, such as 'target hardening' and increased control. However, when the importance of the social production of space is understood, it becomes more important to develop crime prevention strategies which aim for cutting racism or chauvinism. In the latter case, cooperation and schooling become very important, and at the end of the day, 'opening spaces' and increasing accessibility may be of more importance than 'hardening' the urban environment.

Emotions, power relations and space

The development of the concept of space has been the focus of theoretical geographical research, and the basis for empirical work for quite a long time. Geography is understood to be a socially and theoretically informed science, which is interested in human spatiality and aims to develop understanding of space. Space is no longer taken for granted. It is no longer regarded as the innocent materiality of physical reality, but recognised as being important aspect of social processes and structures. An increasing number of geographers have accepted the Lefebvre's challenge, shifting attention 'from things in space to the actual production of space' (1991: 37). Space is considered to be, and further conceptualised as both the medium and the outcome of social practices (Gregory and Urry 1985, Rose 1993, Massey 1994, Liggett and Perry 1995, among others). It is constituted, (re)produced and changed by various social, political and cultural processes. Furthermore, space has an important role in exercising power.

However, from the notion that space is not merely physical it does not follow that the existence of physical (spatial) reality is entirely denied. As the work of Foucault shows, physical material space also has its social aspects. Physical space is interesting in the context in which it enables, reproduces, denies, or constrains certain social practices. On the other hand, space is not just a macro-structure completely separate from human reality, but has an experienced dimension. Space is interpreted and confronted in the 'micropolitics' of everyday life (Domosh 1998). It is experienced here and now. Fear of violence above all demonstrates this: space is experienced with strong emotion, associated with roughness and dread, including bodily feelings. However, the point here is that this personally experienced space is also socially produced to the last degree, and not purely subjective. 'The experience' is not free from power relations.

In geographical thought the idea of space being produced in social practices has usually been conceptualised in relation to political or macro-economic social structures. More and more, however, space is understood to be constructed out of the multiplicity of social relations (e.g. Rose 1993, Massey 1994). It is produced not only in political, economic and cultural processes, but in the practices and power relations of everyday life. However, emotions and feelings or the micropolitics of the everyday life have rarely been the centre of geographical observation. It is essential to ask why this has been the case; why have emotions not be seen as contributing to the production of space? One possible explanation of this can be found within the geographical discourse. Emotions and feelings have traditionally been considered to be the field of humanistic geography and other fields of geography have often rejected them as an object of study. This tradition has generally regarded emotions as strictly subjective, not intersubjective. From this point of departure, the role of emotions in the social process of production of space seems almost impossible.

Yet, there is another possible point of departure: emotions are conceptualised as being produced, to the last degree, by social power relations. This, of course, does not apply to all emotions, but to some, especially such as fear of violence, distrust, or racism – or fear of 'the Other'. With respect to such emotions, there is no conceptual contradiction: it becomes plausible that emotions contribute to the intersubjective power-related production of space.

It must be acknowledged that in geographical research the role of emotions – and the different points of view they can be looked at – has, indeed, strengthened lately. A deeper understanding on the relations between such issues as emotions, identity, subjectivity, and bodily practices has also been developed (see e.g. Simonsen in this book). 'The embodied city' or the city of emotions are no longer curiosities but taken seriously, innovative and important objects of study. The traditional understanding of space remains a restricted external viewpoint, as it sees space 'from above', distanced from everyday practices. From the point of emotions the city should be seen as a space 'below the threshold at which visibility begins' (de Certeau 1984: 93). By examining the issues of fear and surveillance – the contemporary 'vicious circle of defence' – we can increase understanding of the interacting emotional and power-related processes that play a role in producing space. Space is produced, among other things, by fear of violence and its consequences. Space is produced in social practices and reproduced ever more with 'the architecture of fear'.

References

Ainley, R., 1998, Watching the detectors: Control and the panopticon. In R. Ainley, ed., *New Frontiers of Space, Bodies and Gender.* London: Routledge, 88–100.

Auren, T.H.,1996, Et Kjönnet Byrom? Om kvinners bruk av det offentlige byrom i Oslo med focus på frykt. Hovedoppgave i samfundsgeografi. Institutt for sosiologi og samfundsgeografi. Universitetet i Oslo. Unpublished thesis.

Auren, T.B., 1999, Fryktens steder – kvinnens opplevelse av Oslos offentliga byrom. *Sosiologi i dag* 4/1999: 91–110.

Björk, M., 1991, Women as planners – a difference in visions: A conference on building and planning on women's terms. *Scandinavian Housing and Planning Research,* Vol. 8, 45–49.

Blakely, E.J. and Snyder, M.G., 1997, Divided we fall: Gated and walled communities in the United States. In N. Ellin, ed., *The Architecture of Fear.* New York: Princeton Architectural Press, 85–99.

Boys, J., 1990, Women and the designed environment: dealing with difference. *Built Environment* 16, 249–256.

Brown, B., 1995, CCTV in town centres: Three case studies. *Crime Detection and Prevention Series,* paper 68. London: Home Office Police Research Group.

Brown, S., 1998, What's the problem girls? CCTV and the gendering of public safety. In C. Norris, J. Moran and G. Armstrong, eds., *Surveillance, Closed Circuit Television and Social Control.* Aldershot: Ashgate, 207–220.

de Certeau, M., 1984, *The practice of everyday life*. University of California Press, Berkeley.

Cohen, S., 1985, *Visions of social control. Crime, punishment and classification*. Polity Press, Cambridge.

Darke, J., 1996, The man-shaped city. In C. Booth, J. Darke and S. Yeandle (eds.), *Changing places. Women's lives in the city*. Paul Chapman, London.

Davis, M., 1990, *The City of Quartz. Excavating the Future in Los Angeles*. New York: Vintage.

Dear, M. and Flusty, S., 1998, Postmodern urbanism. *Annals of the Association of American Geographers*, Vol. 88, 50–72.

Djurhuus, M. and Skovsgaard, A.M., 2000, Kvinders oplevelse af frygt og tryghed i brugen af byens rum. Geografisk Institut, Köbenhavns Universitet. Unpublished thesis.

Domosh, M., 1998, Those 'Gorgeous incongruities': polite politics and public space on the streets of nineteenth-century New York City. *Annals of the Association of American Geographers*, Vol. 88, 209–226.

Douglas, M., 1966, *Purity and danger: an analysis of concepts of pollution and taboo*. Harmondsworth: Penguin Books.

Ellin, N., 1996, *Postmodern Urbanism*. Oxford: Blackwell.

Ellin, N., 1997, Shelter from the storm or form follows fear and vice versa. In N. Ellin, ed., *The Architecture of Fear*. New York: Princeton Architectural Press, 13–45.

Flusty, S., 1994, *Building Paranoia: The Proliferation of Interdictory Space and the Erosion of Spatial Justice*. Los Angeles Forum for Architecture and Urban Design.

Foucault, M., 1977, *Discipline and Punish: The Birth of a Prison*. London: Penguin Books.

Foucault, M., 1980, The eye of power. In C., Gordon ed., *Power/Knowledge. Selected interviews and other writings 1972–1977 by Michel Foucault*. Sussex: Harvester Press, 146–165.

Friberg, T., 1990, *Kvinnors vardag – om kvinnors arbete och liv. Anpassningsstrategier i tid och rum*. Lund University Press.

Fyfe, N.R., 1995, Policing the city. *Urban Studies*, Vol. 32, 759–778.

Fyfe, N.R. and Bannister, J., 1996, City watching: Closed circuit television surveillance in public spaces. *Area*, Vol. 28, 37–46.

Fyfe, N.R. and Bannister, J., 1998, The 'eyes upon the street': Closed circuit television surveillance and the city. In N.R. Fyfe, ed., *Images of the Street: Representation, Experience and Control in Public Space*. London: Routledge, 254–267.

Fyfe, N.R., Bannister, J. and Kearns, A., 1998, Closed circuit television and the city. In C. Norris, J. Moran and G. Armstrong, eds., *Surveillance, Closed Circuit Television and Social Control*. Aldershot: Ashgate, 21–39.

Gardner, C.B., 1995, *Passing By. Gender and Public Harassment*. Berkeley: University of California Press.

Gordon, M.T. and Riger, S., 1989, *The Female Fear: The Social Cost of Rape*. Urbana: University of Illinois Press.

Greed, C.H., 1994, *Women and Planning. Creating Gendered Realities*. London: Routledge.

Greed, C., 1996, Promise or progress: women and planning. *Built Environment* 22, 9–21.

Gregory, D. and Urry, R., eds.,1985, *Social relations and spatial structures*. Macmillan.

Hannah, M., 1997, Space and the structuring of disciplinary power: An interpretive review. *Geografiska Annaler*, Vol. 79B, 171–180.

Helsingin Sanomat, 17 December 1997, 'Ruotsin varusmiehet videoivat rannikolla sukellusveneiden sijasta nakutyttöjä'.

Herbert, S., 1996, The geopolitics of the police: Foucault, disciplinary power and the tactics of the Los Angeles Police Department. *Political Geography*, Vol. 15, 47–45.

Hillier, J., 1996, The gaze in the city: Video surveillance in Perth. *Australian Geographical Studies*, Vol. 34, 95–105.

'In visible city' 297

Honess, T. and Charman E., 1992, Closed circuit television in public places. *Crime Prevention Unit Series*, paper 35. London: Home Office Police Research Group.

Karisto, A. and Tuominen M., 1993, *Kirjoituksia kaupunkipeloista.* Helsingin kaupungin tietokeskus, tutkimuksia 1993:8.

Kejonen, P., 2000, Nainen, pelko ja tilan käyttö Turun kampusalueella. Maantieteen tutkielma. Turun yliopiston maantieteen laitos. Unpublished thesis.

Koskela, H., 1996, Rädsla och kontroll i ett könsbundet stadsrum. *Nordisk Samhällsgeografisk Tidskrift*, 22, 71–80.

Koskela, H., 1999, *Fear, control and space. Geographies of gender, fear of violence and video surveillance.* Helsinki: Publications of the Department of Geography at the University of Helsinki, A 137.

Koskela, H., 2000, Turva-kamera-kontrolli: kadun näkymättömät katseet, In Stadipiiri, eds., *URBS. Kirja Helsingin Kaupunkikulttuurista.* Helsinki: The City of Helsinki Information Management Centre and Edita, 167–181.

Koskela, H., 2001, *Joensuun torialueen kameravalvonnan vaikutus kaupunkilaisten turvallisuuteen.* Joensuun kihlakunnan poliisilaitos, Joensuun keskustakehittämisyhdistys.

Kyttä, M., ed., 1993, Naiset suunnittelussa. Ympäristöministeriö, kaavoitus- ja rakennusosasto, muistio 1/1993.

Laakkonen, K. and Mustikkamäki, N., 2000, *Kaupunkitila, -pelko ja -suunnittelu.* Tampereen yliopisto, Aluetieteen ja ympäristöpolitiikan laitos. Tutkimuksia, sarja B 72/2000.

Lefebvre, H., 1991, *The production of space.* Blackwell, Oxford.

Liggett, H. and Perry D.C. eds., 1995, *Spatial practices. Critical explorations in social/ spatial theory.* SAGE, Thousand Oaks.

Listerborn, C., 1996, *Att äga rum. Om rädslans geografi -- rädslans arkitektur.* Göteborgs universitet, Institutionet för kulturvård, 14/1996.

Listerborn, C., 2000, *Om rätten att slippa skyddas. En studie av trygghetsskapande och brottsförebyggande projekt och kvinnors rädsla för att röra sig i stadens rum.* Chalmers Tekniska Högskola, Arkitektursektionen, SACTH 2000:3 (A).

Little, J., Peake, L. and Richardson P., eds., 1988, *Women in Cities. Gender and the Urban Environment.* Macmillan.

Lyon, D., 1994, *The Electronic Eye. The Rise of Surveillance Society.* Cambridge: Polity Press.

Marcuse, P., 1997, Walls of fear and walls of support. In N. Ellin, ed., *The Architecture of Fear.* New York: Princeton Architectural Press, 101–114.

Massey, D., 1994, *Space, Place and Gender.* Cambridge: Polity Press.

Matrix, 1984, *Making Space. Women and the Man-Made Environment.* London: Pluto Press.

McDowell, L., 1993, Space, place and gender relations: Part II. Identity, difference, feminist geometries and geographies. *Progress in Human Geography*, Vol. 17, 305–318.

Morrell, H., 1996, Women's safety. In C. Booth, J. Darke and S. Yeandle, eds., Changing places. Women's lives in the city. Paul Chapman, London.

Nast, H.J. and Kobayashi, A., 1996, Re-corporealizing vision. In N. Duncan, ed., *BodySpace: Destabilizing Geographies of Gender and Sexuality.* London: Routledge, 75–93.

NordRefo, 1989, Kvinnor och Regional Utveckling. Vol. 19, No. 1.

Oc, T. and Tiesdell, S., 1997, Safer city centres: The role of closed circuit television. In T. Oc and S. Tiesdell, eds., *Safer City Centres. Reviving the Public Realm.* London: Paul Chapman, 130–142.

Pain, R., 1991, Space, sexual violence and social control: integrating geographical and feminist analyses of women's fear of crime. *Progress in Human Geography* 15, 415–431.

Poyner, B., 1992, Situational crime prevention in two parking facilities. In R.V. Clarke, ed., *Situational Crime Prevention: Successful Case Studies.* New York: Harrow and Heston.

Rakennettu ympäristö, rikollisuus ja turvattomuus. Ympäristöministeriö, Yhdyskunta ja rakennustutkimuksen neuvottelukunta, Rikoksentorjunnan neuvottelukunta, julkaisuja 1/ 1995.

Rose, G., 1993, *Feminism and Geography. The Limits of Geographical Knowledge.* Minneapolis: University of Minnesota Press.

Sargma, M., 1998, Naiste vägivallakarutus ja ruumikasutusgeograafia. Bakalaureusetöö inimigeograafias. Tartu ylikool, Bioloogia-geograafia teaduskond, Geograafia Instituut. Unpublished thesis.

Simonsen, K., 1990, Urban division of space: A gender category! The Danish case. *Scandinavian Housing and Planning Research,* Vol. 7, 143–153.

Smith, S.J., 1987, Fear of crime: Beyond a geography of deviance. *Progress in Human Geography*, Vol. 11, 1–23.

Soja, E.W., 1996, *Thirdspace. Journeys to Los Angeles and Other Real-and-Imagined Places.* Cambridge, Massachusetts: Blackwell.

Takala, H., 1998, Videovalvonta ja rikollisuuden ehkäisy. Helsinki: *National Research Institute of Legal Policy, Research Communications*, 41.

Tiby, E., 1991, Kvinna och rädd? In G. Wiklund, ed., Rädslan för brott. BRÅ-rapport 1991:2, Swedish National Council for Crime Prevention, Stockholm.

Tilley, N., 1993, Understanding car parks, crime and CCTV: Evaluation lessons from safer cities. *Crime Prevention Unit Series*, paper 42. London: Home Office Police Research Group.

Trench, S., 1997, Safer transport and parking. In T. Oc and S. Tiesdell, eds., *Safer City Centres. Reviving the Public Realm.* London: Paul Chapman, 143–155.

Trench, S., Oc, T. and Tiesdell, S., 1992, Safer cities for women: Perceived risks and planning measures. *Town Planning Review*, Vol. 63, 279–296.

Turvallisuustalkoot. Ehdotus kansalliseksi rikoksentorjuntaohjelmaksi. Rikoksentorjunnan neuvottelukunta, 1998.

Valentine, G., 1989, The geography of women's fear, *Area*, Vol. 21, 385–390.

Wajcman, J., 1991, *Feminism Confronts Technology*. Cambridge: Polity Press.

Walklate, S., 1997, Risk and criminal victimisation: a modernist dilemma? *British Journal of Criminology* 37, 35–45.

Wekerle, G.R. and Whitzman, C., 1995, *Safe Cities: Guidelines for Planning, Design and Management.* New York: Van Nostrand Reinhold.

Chapter 16

Landscape of landscapes

Gunnar Olsson

Ανδρα μοι εννεπε, Μουσα, πολυτροπον, σζ μαλα πολλα
πλαγχθη, επει Τροιηζ ιερον πτολιεθρον επερσε
πολλῶν δ' ανθρωπων ιδεν αστεα και νοον εγνω,
πολλα δ' ο γ' εν ποντω παθεν αλγεα ον κατα θυμοῶ
αρνυμενοζ ην τε ψυχην και νοστον εταιρων.
αλλ ουε ῶζ εταρονζ ερρυσατο, ιεμενοζ περ

L'uomo ricco d'astuzie raccontami, o Musa che a lungo
errò dopo ch'ebbe distrutto la rocca sacra di Troia;
di molti uomini le città vide e conobbe la mente,
molti dolori patí in cuore sul mare,
lottando per la sua vita e pel ritono dei suoi.
Ma non li salvò, benché tanto volesse,

Sing in me, Muse, and through me tell the story
of that man skilled in all ways of contending,
the wanderer, harried for years on end,
after he plundered the stronghold
on the proud height of Troy.
　　　　　He saw the townlands
and learned the minds of many distant men,
and weathered many bitter nights and days
in his deep heart at sea, while he fought only
to save his life, to bring his shipmates home.
But not by will nor valor could he save them,

Sångmö, sjung om den man, som länge i skiftande öden
irrade kring, när han Troja förstört, den heliga staden.
Många människors städer han såg och lärde dem känna,
många de lidanden voro på hav, som hans hjärta fick utstå
under hans kamp för sitt liv och för kämparnas lyckliga hemkomst.
Dock sina män han ej frälste ändå, hur än han försökte,

* * *

In the sense just illustrated by these quotations from the first lines of *The Odyssey*,
every understanding is an exercise in translation, every translation a journey back

and forth between the completely alien and the vaguely familiar. Such is also my own approach to the concept of landscape: an encounter with an original composed in a language I do not comprehend. And therein lies not only the attraction but also the challenge, for like everything else from the taboo-ridden interface between ontological categories, so also the subject of the present essay refuses to be captured, refuses to be named.

The reason is that a landscape is not as simple as it might first appear, not limited to what meets the eye but equally present in the mind. Put differently, landscapes are in neither body nor mind, but in the conjunction of the two. It follows that any understanding of a landscape must consider not only trees and waters, stones and birds, but also hopes and fears, joys and griefs; not only smell and taste but pride and hate; not only light and shadow but power and submission. Understood in that manner there are close parallels between my own conception of landscape, and Karl Marx's conception of the commodity, for in both cases there is a braiding of reification and deification, fetishism and alienation. To be precise (Marx 1967: 71–72),

> a commodity appears, at first sight, a very trivial thing, and easily understood. Its analysis shows that it is, in reality, a very queer thing, abounding in metaphysical subtleties and theological niceties. So far as it is a value in use, there is nothing mysterious about it ...... [b]ut as soon as it steps forth as a commodity, it changes into something transcendent.... To find an analogy, we must have recourse to the mist-enveloped regions of the religious world.

The Marxian conception of commodities can readily be extended to signs in general, hence also to the analysis of landscapes. Thus, just as the commodity melts into one the two realities of use-value and exchange-value, so the sign does the same with the concepts of Signifier and signified. In the landscape, the corresponding transformations are in the conjunction of the five senses of the body and the sixth sense of culture, in the relation between the *perspectiva naturalis* of the optical eye and the *perspectiva artificialis* of social imagination.

* *

The text to which I venture for an analogy is *Genesis* 25–36, those crucial chapters of the Old Testament that tell the story of Jacob, one of the worst crooks ever to be born. Yet one of the most richly rewarded.

Everyone remembers how Jacob repeatedly and most intentionally had betrayed both his twin brother and their father. First he had forced the starving Esau to sell his birthright for a slice of bread and a bowl of lentil soup, then he had come before the blind Isaac dressed in the smelly clothes of his hairy brother, pretending to be what he was not. And the ailing Isaac blessed Jacob, thinking he was the first-born, the legitimate heir, who the father loved because he was a skilful hunter and because he liked the taste of his game. In its sadness the story is unique (*Genesis* 27: 30–38):

> As soon as Isaac had finished blessing Jacob, when Jacob had scarcely gone out from the presence of Isaac his father, Esau his brother, came in from his hunting. He also prepared savory food, and brought it to his father. And he said to his father, 'Let my father arise, and eat of his son's game, that you may bless me.' His father Isaac said to him, 'Who are you?'

He answered, 'I am your son, your first-born, Esau.' Then Isaac trembled violently, and said, 'Who was it then that hunted game and brought to me, and I ate it all before you came and I have blessed him? – Yes, and he shall be blessed.' When Esau heard the words of his father he cried out with an exceedingly bitter cry, and said to his father, 'Bless me, even me also, O my father!' But he said, 'Your brother came with guile, and he has taken away your blessing.' Esau said, 'Is he not rightly called Jacob? For he has supplanted me these two times. He took away my birthright; and behold, now he has taken away my blessing.' Then he said, 'Have you not reserved a blessing for me?' Isaac answered Esau, 'Behold, I have made him your lord, and all his brothers I have given to him for servants, and with grain and wine I have sustained him. What can I do for you, my son?' Esau said to his father, 'Have you but one blessing, my father? Bless me, even me also, O my father.' And Esau lifted up his voice and cried.

Isaac's point is that even though he knows that he has made a mistake, he insists that a blessing is a blessing, that a word is a word, a promise a promise, a patriarch a patriarch. And therein lies the crucial difference between Isaac and his LORD, for whereas the former is obliged never to revoke a blessing, the latter is free to change his commands as he pleases. No doubt Isaac remembers how long ago he himself had been tied to the altar, the boy set to be sacrificed as proof of his father's obedience, the sharp knife on his throat. But in his ears also ring the cries of the angel, 'Stop, stop! For heaven's sake. The LORD has changed his mind, no need to execute your son, you have already killed yourself.' And in the same moment that the God-sent messenger saves the boy's life, the Almighty institutionalizes the rule by terror, shows by his reversal that his words are not to be trusted, that he is free to knock on any door at any time, that he alone sets the rules of the game, that no power will be permitted to stand above or next to him. Dictator of dictators, the Absolute of the absolute.

Esau has learned his family history and therefore he is the first to realize that he might be in for the same treatment as his father and grandfather before him. But unlike them he will not accept whatever comes his way. And from the beginning he knows his enemy. For already in their mother's womb Jacob, his twin, had tried to hold his brother fast, struggling to get out first, determined to claim the rights of the first-born. And that is exactly why Jacob was called 'Jacob', a name which literally means 'he who takes by the heel' or 'he who supplants'.

No wonder that Esau came to hate his brother. And he vowed to kill him. Jacob, warned by Rebekah, their scheming mother, had no choice but to escape. He left Beer-sheba and went to Haran, as frightened as he deserved to be.

*

Such is the power-filled context in which the first landscape was created. As told in *Genesis* 28: 11–22 (emphases added):

And he came to a certain place, and stayed there that night, because the sun had set. Taking one of the stones of the place, he put it under his head and lay down in that place to sleep. And he dreamed that there was a ladder set up on the earth, and the top of it reached to heaven; and behold, the angels of God were ascending and descending on it! And behold, the LORD stood above it, and said, 'I am the LORD, the God of Abraham your father and the God of Isaac; *the land on which you lie will I give to you and to your descendants*; and your descendants shall be like the dust of the earth, and you shall spread abroad to the west and to the east and to the north and to the south; and by you and your descendants shall all the families of the earth bless themselves. Behold I am with you and will keep you wherever you go, and will bring you back to this land; for I will not leave you until I have done that of which I have spoken to you.' Then Jacob awoke from his sleep and said,'[6] Surely the LORD is in this place! This is none other than the house of God, and this is the gate of heaven.' So Jacob rose early in the morning, and he took the stone which he had put under his head and set it up for a pillar and poured oil on top of it. He called the name of the place Bethel (a name which in a footnote is explained to mean 'the house of God'). Then Jacob made a vow, saying, '*If* God will be with me, and [*if he*] will keep me in this way that I go, and [*if he*] will give me bread to eat and clothing to wear, so that I come again to my father's house in peace, *then* the LORD shall be *my* God, and this stone, which I have set up for a pillar, shall be God's house; and of all that thou givest me I will give the tenth to thee.'

What a remarkable text from the mist-enveloped realities of ontological transformations. What a fantastic story of how a landscape is born from a rock. The secret reveals itself in the fact that the two terms 'Bethel' and 'Landscape' are different designations of the same place – that certain place at which the Mindscape of pure spirituality and the Stonescape of pure materiality came together and merged into one. Any fugitive resting on a mattress of gravel and a pillow of stone is prone to dream strange dreams, to hear voices from afar, to imagine pictures of the surreal. And to stay sane, Jacob did what every therapist after Freud would recommend him to do: he held his mind in place by ontologically transforming anxiety into fear, by thingifying the social, naming the unnameable. Comforting sigh of relief, Søren Kierkegaard in advance of himself.

But relief is no cure and the only thing that remains to hang on to is the hard fact of the stone, the pillow on which Jacob puts his head, when he lies down in the evening – a piece of rock detectable by the five senses of the body, but essentially outside the sixth sense of culture. In contrast, the top of the ladder reaches into heaven, the epitome of those mist-enveloped regions where everything is invisible and unmentionable, where there is nothing to sense, yet everything to imagine. Connecting the two extremes is the ladder, *La Scala*, the cartographical translation function through which material matter and spiritual spirit are transformed into mutually meaningful statements. Busily trying to tie the two worlds together is a host of angels ascending and descending the scale, a corps of ambassadors charged with the impossible mission of negotiating a lasting peace between heaven and earth, visible and invisible, inner and outer.

If the two rulers of Stonescape and Mindscape can be said to speak at all, they do so in mutually incompatible languages. Just as you and I cannot grasp what they are saying, they too are unable to understand the tongue of the other. Their respective statements are equally non-translatable – literally on the other side of Wittgenstein's limit – for ruler of Stonescape is a Matter so utterly material that it emits no meaning whatsoever, ruler of Mindscape a Meaning so meaningfully meaningful that no matter is rich enough to express it. It follows that both absolutes share the characteristic of being beyond the senses, beyond rephrasing, beyond the limits of representation.

And yet it is only through the trick of renaming that the two potentates can be approached, only through acts of labelling that they can be tied down and held in captivity. It hurts to officiate at the ceremony, but in the present case rape is the only alternative, for understanding is by definition a deed of reformulation, reformulation always an issue of force. Therefore – albeit unwillingly – I hereby baptize the ruler of Stonescape as **a,** a thing-like phenomenon which simply is. In the same mood I name the ruler of Mindscape **a=a,** a misty noumenon defined as that which is what it is: a tautology. Let there be! And there is.

Awakening from his dream, Jacob realizes that he himself is one of the ambassadors who travels back and forth between the two realms, carrying secret messages from one end of the ontological scale to the other. He is a good negotiator and he manages to bring the two rulers **a** and **a=a** together in the smoke-filled Landscape of **a=b,** another and more informative synonym for the proper name 'Bethel' and the definite description 'God's House'. As a seal of the peace treaty, the horizontal pillow is turned on high and changed into a vertical pillar, the right angle invented in the process. It is in the origo of the thus constructed coordinate net that that the godly house Bethel is erected – a social invention of the highest order.

But this so called 'House of God' is in reality not a house at all but an abstract place, the only point at which its is possible to cross the otherwise closed border between Stonescape and Mindscape. It is exactly out of this small hole in the wall – the perpendicular intersection of the silent lines of the vertical and the horizontal – that the landscape of landscapes springs forth, new gods and new goods flooding out with the embryotic fluid. The ecological debates, the Sierra Clubs, the Nature walkers, the American Indians, the whale protectors, the forest companies, the road builders, the farmers, all bear testimony to the fact that in the disputes about what can and cannot be done to the landscape, the forces of deification and reification are as intimately interwoven today as ever before. And just as the principle of mutual distrust ruled at Bethel, so it permeates the current struggles as well. But which ruler exercises more power over the **a=b** affairs of the social landscape, the shadowy **a** from the material Stonescape or the tautological **a=a** from the spiritual Mindscape?

To those questions of master and slave, Jacob and Marx offer closely related answers. For instance, it is only under certain, clearly defined conditions, that Jacob is willing to call the LORD *his own God.* Only *if,* only *if,* only *if, then* he will pay the ten percent tax. From personal experience he knows that lying and cheating often pays off and he is not to be fooled. Therefore he trusts no one, not even the God of his forefathers, that self-made and self-named entity called **a=a**; the usurper is determined not to give in and that is regardless of whoever the adversary may be. And in this sense the authors of *Genesis* and of *Das Kapital* are alike: even though the landscape of **a=b** is partly for contemplation, it must yield a profit as well.

In that context of ontologial transformations, there are striking similarities also between Jacob's ladder and the divided line of Plato's *Republic.* Both devices in fact serve as a kind of epistemological-ontological translation function in which degrees of truth and degrees of being are made to correspond to one another. While in the *Republic* the measuring thread hangs suspended from the Good of the Sun (as the Sun is in the world of the visible, so the Good is in the realm of the intelligible), in Jacob's dream the same hook is named 'God'; in my own vocabulary both fix-points are labelled **a=a.** Dangling at the other end of the scale is the pure materiality, the realm of things where the ruler bears the non-translatable name of **a.** Somewhere in between lies the thin line of **a=b,** the Saussurean Bar where not a member is sober, where invisible ideology is turned to touchable stone, meaningless stone to meaningful spirit, JHWH to Christ, *pistis* to *dianoia, eide* to *zoa*. And yet, even though this transition-point corresponds to the zero-mark on Celsius' thermometer – the point at which water freezes to ice and ice melts to water – the absolute zero of human thought-and-action is in the **a=a**, by definition always true but never informative. Here – and nowhere else – is the ultimate limit of Jacob's power. In Plato's universe the counterpart to the tautology is in the proposition that without the light of the Sun nothing can be seen, without the idea of the Good nothing can be understood.

And so it is that both the monotheistic Jew and the polytheistic Greek are condemned to hitting their heads against the ceiling of language. But which really *are* the relations between original and copy, the invisible and godly forms up there and the visible and graven images down here, the ideas and the shadows? Every ambassador knows the answer, every angel and every muse as well. For they have all learned from experience that unless both forms and images are distorted, peace will never come. And thus it is that the messengers play such pivotal roles not because they are what they are but because the do what they do, not for their providence but for their function, not for the sakes of their ontological Being but for the relations of their epistemological Becoming.

*

The demonstrated richness notwithstanding, the power-filled story has hardly begun. More analogies to be drawn, more insights to be gained.

Once again Jacob is on the move, flying Dutchman, wandering Jew, incarnated evil. A haunted man obsessed with the idea of trapping his brother in a net of poisonous gifts and generous bribes. What happens is this (*Genesis 32: 22–32*, emphasis added):

> The same night he arose and took his two wives, his two maids, and his eleven children, and crossed the ford of the Jabbok. He took them and sent them across the stream, and likewise everything that he had. And Jacob was left alone; and a man wrestles with him until the breaking of the day. When the man saw that he did not prevail against Jacob, he touched the hollow of his thigh; and Jacob's thigh was put out of joint as he wrestled with him. Then he said, 'Let me go, for the day is breaking.' But Jacob said, 'I will not let you go, unless you bless me.' And he said to him, 'What is your name?' And he said, 'Jacob.' Then he said, 'Your name shall no longer be Jacob, but Israel, for you have striven with God *and* with man, and have prevailed.' Then Jacob asked him, 'Tell me, I pray, your name.' But he said, 'Why is it that you ask my name?' And there he blessed him. So Jacob called the name of the place Peniel, saying 'For I have seen God face to face, and yet my life has been preserved.' The sun rose upon him as he passed Penuel (*sic*), limping because of his thigh.

For the cartographer of power it is especially noteworthy that the self-proclaimed victor spreads the news by naming a place, not by telling a story. And by choosing the word 'Peniel' as the name of the meeting-place, the second-born shows that in his lust for power everything is permitted. Not even his relations to the Almighty are sacred enough to be left alone.

The key to the hidden meaning is in a footnote to verse 30, in which it is explained that the term 'Peniel' literally means 'the face of God', at the same time a proper name and a definite description. But in its audacity this descriptive name is completely outrageous, for if there is anything the LORD has made perfectly clear, it is that his face must never – under any circumstances – be seen. As he later reminded Moses (*Exodus* 33: 19–20):

> I will make all my goodness pass before you, and I will proclaim before you my name 'The LORD'; and I will be gracious to whom I shall be gracious, and will show mercy on whom I will show mercy. But,' he said, 'you cannot see my face; for man shall not see me and live.'

And yet, in his remarkable dispatch from the front, this is exactly what Jacob claims to have done: seen God's face and survived. In the eyes of the Almighty the blasphemy of blasphemies, in the propaganda of the usurper merely a way of legitimating his own behavior. For with whom did the run-away actually wrestle? With his bad conscience or with his twin-brother? The Biblical narrator refuses to distinguish, flatly stating that Jacob had striven with God *and* man. The fact nevertheless remains: in the abstractness of Mindscape ambiguity rules, in the concreteness of Stonescape certainty matters.

And thus it is that if Bethel is the name of the border station between the ontological realms of Stonescape and Mindscape – a primordial Checkpoint Charlie – then Peniel is the torture chamber in which all travellers have their papers checked and their bodies marked. In that context of enforced socialization, it is telling that in the English version of the Christian confession, the sinners beg the LORD to forgive their trespasses. But the word 'trespass' is unusually rich, noun and verb in one, hence a crucial term in the vocabulary of cartographical reason; according to the OED, the term means both 'to unlawfully enter on the land of another', and 'to pass beyond this life; to die.' As my old favorite Kris Kristofferson once put it,

> When you're headin' for the border lord,
> you're bound to cross the line.

Not surprisingly, it is when Jacob assumes the role of immigration officer that he runs into greater difficulties than ever before. For it turns out that the asylum seekers he encounters in the office of Peniel are citizens of two different countries – either they come from the land of Stonescape which is ruled by the shadowy **a,** or from the realm of Mindscape which is governed by the evasive **a=a,** better known as JHWH. What ties these absolutes together is that once their respective name is rephrased its bearer dies; thus, while **a** whispers in a voice that cannot be heard, the **a=a** keeps chanting that 'I am I', 'I am who I am'. The name of the former denotes the silence of silence, that of the latter the tautology of tautologies. Together these expressions form the outer limit of every translation, the beginning and end of all understanding, the border that no one can trespass and live.

And in that insight lies the pivotal point not only of Jacob's story but of power itself. For in his report from the battle-field, Jacob does nothing less than violate the Second Commandment, that God-given decree which states that the Almighty ruler of Mindscape must be neither seen nor named. No graven image, no definite description, merely the obligation to keep the sabbath day holy and to honor your father and your mother. Pushed to this ultimate limit, the LORD has no alternative but to demonstrate that the double privilege of categorizing and naming rests with him and with him alone. With great dispatch and fitting cruelty he kills the offender by moving him from one category to another; after a touch of the divine wand, the solid man Jacob melts into the airy people of Israel, no longer an independent human being but an obedient member of a social class. Balls cut with the knife of self-reference, not a drop of blood spilled in the process. And when God calls out 'There you are!', then Jacob replies with the same words as once his harassed forefathers: 'Here I am'.

It was this response that made Søren Kierkegaard fear and tremble (Kierkegaard 1954). In contrast, the cartographer of power interprets the same exchange as an outstanding example of how the ontological war between Stonescape and Mindscape is actually waged: through a strategic deployment of personal pronouns, adverbs and prepositions. The landscape of landscape is indeed contested territory, its constitution chiselled onto Moses' first stone tablet, *the* blueprint of absolute power.

*

Thus far Jacob comes. Thus far and no farther. As a way out, Marxists often argue that real power is not lodged in the magic of ontological transformations, but in the factual solidity of the material. Tied to that reductionist suggestion are nevertheless a host of problems, mainly connected with the Kantian tendency to treat others *as if they were* dead things rather than human beings. But that fetishist temptation must surely be resisted, for it is well established – not the least by Karl Marx himself – that material relations in reality are social relations, just as social relations are material relations. Thus, when commodities converse with each other, they constantly wonder why people believe them to be reified use-values, while within themselves they know that they are nothing but deified exchange-values.

Ironies abound. But when the Owl of Minerva takes off in the evening, then Swedish cats are said to be grey and English cows to be black, a distinction that illustrates how the exact coupling between metaphor and metonymy depends on the particular language in which it is performed. Queer things, these political subtleties and psychological niceties. Fog-horns sounding through the mist. And the sun rose upon him as he passed the shoal, the prow shearing the waves.

Giambattista Vico knew what he did, when he preached the gospel of *Factum verum* – the true is the made. But the professor of rhetoric also realized that to share the world is to play a game of *topoi*, to allow metonymic associations to move from one metaphorical *topos* to another. The art of convincing is by definition a journey back and forth between the here and the there, the there and the here. Odysseus himself spent a lifetime demonstrating that the point of travelling is not to reach a destination but to return to an origin, not to rest content in the arms of Nausikaa but to slaughter the suitors who are occupying his house and making passes at his wife. As told already at the outset, the cunning trickster fought only to save his life, to bring his shipmates home. But not by will nor valor could he save them, for their own recklessness destroyed them all.

*

Perhaps it is by rereading the past that we prewrite the future, for now as then it is the double metaphysics of origin and presence that prevails. The truth is that even though power never sits still, its strategies and techniques remain essentially unaltered: turning the horizontal into the vertical; transforming a silent thing into a speaking symbol, a stone into a pillar; naming the unnameable. In the game of power the only predictable is the unpredictable. For just as the Almighty *says* that he will be gracious to whom he will be gracious and show mercy to whom he will show mercy, through his acts he *shows* that he will destroy whom he will destroy. As a counterdote to the arbitrary capriciousness, every discourse contains a dash of nostalgia.

And that is why this tour through the landscape of landscapes now moves on from the fearfilled memories of Beer-sheba and checkpoint Charlie to the alienated poetry of Verner von Heidenstam. More than a century ago that fellow-Swede created his own reality in exile, much as I have spent three decades doing for myself (*Ensamhetens tankar*, fourth stanza):

> Jag längtar hem sen åtta långa år.
> I själva sömnen har jag längtan känt.
> Jag längtar hem. Jag längtar var jag går
> - men ej till människor. Jag längtar marken,
> jag längtar stenarna där barn jag lekt.

For most readers as non-understandable as the Greek quotation from which this excursion took off. In rough translation, more for the meaning of the words, less for the rhythm of the music:

> I yearn for home. Since eight long years.
> In the deepest sleep I felt the longing.
> I yearn for home. I yearn wherever I go
> – but not people. I yearn the ground,
> I yearn the stones where once I played.

*   *

As the LORD proclaimed, the land on which you lie will be given to you and to your descendants. And therefore, sang William Shakespeare in one of his *Sonnets* (CXXVIII):

> I lie with her, and she with me,
> And in our faults by lies we flatter'd be.

Heidegger called it 'Home', Jacob named it 'Bethel'. Regardless of when and where, there is a stony ground in every culture, a cultural meaning in every stone. Power is a game of ontological transformations, now as well as then, here as well as there.

The various authors of the Bible knew it well. Homer too. Plato, Kant and Nietzsche followed the lead. Should the giants be left to rest in peace? Or are we condemned to a ceaseless chasing of their ghosts, our thoughts-and-actions harnessed in the principles of cartographical reason?

* * *

Referencees

Damisch, Hubert: *The Origin of Perspective.* Cambridge, MA: MIT Press, 1994.

Farinelli, Franco: 'Did Anaximander Ever Say (or Write) Any Words? The Nature of Cartographical Reason,' *Ethics, Place and Environment,* Vol 1, 1998.

Farinelli, Franco, Gunnar Olsson and Dagmar Reichert (eds.): *Limits of Representation.* München: Accedo, 1993.

Fauconnier, Gilles: *Mappings in Thought and Language.* Cambridge: Cambridge University Press, 1997.

Frye, Northrop: *Words of Power. Being a Second Study of 'The Bible and Literature'.* New York: Harcout Brace Jovanovich, 1990.

von Heidenstam, Verner: *Vallfart och vandringsår.* Stockholm: Bonniers, 1888.

Holy Bible. Revised standard version. Dallas: Melton, 1952.

Homer: *The Odyssey.* Translated by Robert Fitzgerald. New York: Doubleday, 1963.

Homeros: *Odysséen.* Translated by Erland Lagerlöf. Lund: Gleerups, 1957.

Jensson, Gunnael (alias Ole Michael Jensen and Gunnar Olsson): *Mappa Mundi Universalis.* Uppsala: Eventa 5, 2000.

Kierkegaard, Søren: *Fear and Trembling.* Translated by Walter Lowrie. Princeton: Princeton University Press, 1954.

Kristofferson, Kris: *Border Lord.* New York: Monument Record Corporation, 1972.

Kronholm, Tryggve: *De tio orden.* Stockholm: Verbum, 1992.

Marx, Karl: *Kapital.* Translated by Samuel Moore and Edward Aveling. New York: International Publishers, 1967.

Miles, Jack: *God: A Biography.* New York: Simon and Schuster, 1995.

Olsson, Gunnar: *Birds in Egg/Eggs in Bird.* London: Pion, 1980.

Olsson, Gunnar: *Lines of Power/Limits of Language.* Minneapolis: University of Minnesota Press, 1991.

Olsson, Gunnar: 'Heretic Cartography,' *Ecumene,* Vol. 1, 1994.

Olsson, Gunnar: 'Towards a Critique of Cartographical Reason,' *Ethics, Place and Environment,* Vol. 1, 1998.

Olsson, Gunnar: 'From a=b to a=a,' *Environment and Planning A,* Vol. 32, 2000.

Olsson, Gunnar: 'Detta är detta,' *Nordisk Estetisk Tidskrift,* Vol. 19, 2000.

Omero: *Odissea.* 'Testo a fronte'. Translated by Rosa Calzecchi Onesti. Torino: Einaudi, 1963.

Oxford English Dictionary. The Compact Edition. Oxford: Oxford University Press, 1971.

Plato: *Collected Dialogues.* Edited by Edith Hamilton and Huntington Cairns. Princeton: Princeton University Press, 1969.

Reichert, Dagmar (Hrsg.): *Räumliches Denken.* Zürich: Verlag der Fachvereine, 1996.

Reichert, Dagmar: 'Obituary,' *Ethics, Place and Environment,* Vol 1, 1998.

Serres, Michel: *Les origines de la géométrie.* Paris: Flammarion, 1993.

Revised version of 'Landscape – Border Station Between Stonescape and Mindscape,' previously published in Girolamo Cusimano (cura di): *La construzione del paesaggio siciliano: geografi e scrittori a confronto.* Palermo: Alloro, 1999.

Index

CL

304.
209
48
VOI

60005693443